TOO YOUNG TO DIE

Dennis M. Kessel

TOO YOUNG TO DIE

*Boy Soldiers
of the
Union Army*

1861-1865

DENNIS M. KEESEE

BLUE ACORN PRESS
Huntington, West Virginia

Published by

Blue Acorn Press
P.O. Box 2684
Huntington, West Virginia 25726

ISBN 1-885033-28-1

Keesee, Dennis M., 1959—

TOO YOUNG TO DIE: BOY SOLDIERS OF THE UNION ARMY 1861-1865

Illustrated.
Includes bibliographical references and index.

History — American Civil War

First Edition: May 2001

Manufactured in the United States of America

Design & typography by Richard A. Baumgartner

Jacket graphics by Mike Stretch, Pine Creek Design, Cincinnati

CONTENTS

ACKNOWLEDGMENTS

As a young boy I was blessed to move with my three siblings and parents, Thomas and Marjorie Keesee, into a house recently built on a portion of my grandparents' farm outside New Albany, Ohio. Near the whitewashed brick homestead where my grandparents Chester and Gladys Doran lived stood a massive barn with a 35-star American flag fronting Bevelhymer Road. Painted on the clapboards as if floating in the breeze, the banner glorified the contributions of five family members who left the surrounding fields to fight for the Union cause. Alexander Doran added the patriotic symbol to the structure in the 1890s. Inspired by living under the flag, I became fascinated with the Civil War at an early age.

In April 1983 I attended an estate sale where I purchased a small box of photographs, including several of John McClay, who I learned was a 13-year-old musician in the 43rd Ohio Infantry Regiment. That single event laid the foundation for this work. Not only did the treasures spark an interest in the young boys who participated in the war, because of the purchase I became friends with photo historian Larry M. Strayer, a fellow Ohioan, who seven years later introduced me to Richard A. "Rick" Baumgartner.

By 1991 I had accumulated a substantial collection of photographs and information related to young Union boys, and mentioned to Rick that I was entertaining thoughts of writing a book about this little-covered aspect of the war. A former journalist and author of several highly acclaimed Civil War books, he energetically encouraged and prodded me through the next nine years of research and writing. We made numerous trips together to the National Archives and other institutions as I searched for project material. Rick photographed 90 percent of the images found on the following pages, and I am greatly indebted to him for editing the manuscript and creating the book's design. With his help my long-standing dream of showcasing these boy soldiers became reality. Thank you, Rick, my friend.

Quite a few Civil War photography collectors and curators unselfishly shared their images. Some photograph contributors were mere acquaintances met at Civil War memorabilia shows, but they eagerly made available prized images even though I was a virtual stranger. Other collectors I have known for years and they, sensing my enthusiasm, offered their best for inclusion. I will contend that no larger collection of quality boy-soldier images has ever been compiled, and to all who graciously contributed I owe genuine appreciation.

I especially wish to thank the National Archives' staff in Washington, as well as those who assisted me at the U.S. Army Military History Institute at Carlisle Barracks, Pennsylvania, for their courtesy and professionalism. Sincere gratitude also is extended to the book, paper and photograph dealers I've met over the years, and to collectors and friends who took time to steer valuable material my way. There are dozens of people due thanks, and I apologize to anyone inadvertently omitted.

In California: John Halliday, Benicia.

In Connecticut: Mike Brackin, Manchester.

In Georgia: George S. Whiteley IV, Atlanta; Nancy Griffith, Augusta; Brad L. Pruden, Marietta.

In Illinois: Richard K. Tibbals, Berwyn; George Loss, Elmhurst; Allen Cebula, Naperville; Karl Sundstrom, North Riverside; Jeffrey J. Kowalis, Orland Park; Mary Michals, audio-visual curator, Illinois State Historical Library, Springfield; Franklin Brandt, Stewardson.

In Indiana: Mick Kissick, Albany.

In Kentucky: David Yunt, Louisville; Jerry Raisor, Owenton.

In Maryland: Gil Barrett, Laurel; Roger D. Hunt, Rockville.

In Massachusetts: Henry Deeks, Acton.

In Michigan: George Wilkinson, Dexter; Brian Boeve, Holland; David D. Finney Jr., Howell; Jerry B. Everts, Lambertville; Dale R. Niesen, South Rockwood; Michael Waskul, Ypsilanti.

In Missouri: Jon Miller, Rolla.

In New Jersey: Bob and Pat Bartosz, Wenonah.

In New York: Scott Hilts, Arcade; Fred Wilkens, Farmingdale; Benedict R. Maryniak, Lancaster.

In North Carolina: Krista Eldridge, Charlotte.

In Ohio: Georgia Hicks, Alexandria; Thomas and Crystal Molocea, Boardman; Teresa Ross, Chesapeake; Mike Stretch, Rick Riggs, Alan E. Hoeweler, Peg McFarland, Cincinnati; Stephen Altic, Ed Hoffman, Mike McClung, James M. Merkel, Mark Reese, Gary Saum, Philip W. Stichter, Columbus; James C.

Frasca, Croton; Richard F. Carlile, Gary Delscamp, Larry M. Strayer, Dayton; Christopher Jarvis, Dublin; Nan Card, manuscripts curator, Rutherford B. Hayes Presidential Center, Fremont; B. Kevin Bennett, Granville; Ellsworth (Ed) and Jessica Rees, John Varnado, Hebron; Vickie Piper, Raejeanne Powers, Elaine Roberts, Maria Rogers, Dennis Scott, Johnstown; James Featherston, Madison; Donald Lingafelter, Mentor; Douglas L. Auld, New Albany; Larry Stevens, Nancy Winkler, Newark; Jeffrey S. Creamer, Monclova; Rudy Sever, Westerville; Steven L. Davis, Xenia.

In Pennsylvania: Michael J. Winey and Randy Hackenburg, U.S. Army Military History Institute, Carlisle Barracks; Wes Small, The Horse Soldier, Gettysburg; Ronn Palm, Kittanning; John Seyfert, Lancaster; Paul M. Smith, McKnightstown; Michael G. Kraus, Pittsburgh.

In Tennessee: Paul Gibson, Blountville; the Lotz House Museum, Franklin; Herb Peck Jr., Nashville; William Acree, Pigeon Forge.

In Texas: L.B. "Mike" Paul, Pleasanton.

In Virginia: Chris Nelson, Annandale; Don Farlow, Virginia Beach; Thomas P. and Beverly Lowry, Woodbridge.

In West Virginia: the late Timothy Landacre, Bridgeport; John F. Walters, East Lynn; Chris Jordan, Harpers Ferry.

In Wisconsin: State Historical Society of Wisconsin, Madison; Racine Heritage Museum, Racine.

Dennis M. Keesee
New Albany, Ohio
March 2001

For my nine-year-old son
Corey Michael Keesee.
May God bless his generation with peace.

INTRODUCTION

They marched away
with the naïve innocence of youth

As night's welcome coolness enveloped the seemingly endless miles of earthworks and trenches outside Petersburg, Virginia, on July 29, 1864, the troopers of the 13th Ohio Volunteer Cavalry were in especially high spirits. Serving dismounted as part of the Ninth Corps, the regiment had been in the forward trenches for 11 days facing Elliott's Salient less than 200 yards away. Two of the Ohioans already had been killed in front of the foreboding earthen fort, but as a blanket of stars replaced the searing sunlight word was passed that the troopers were to be relieved from the exposed position and sent to the rear for rest and a well needed cleansing. To add to the joy the regiment had received a large mail from home. Canned fruit, herring, tobacco and, ironically, bandages from the United States Christian Commission appeared a little later.[1]

About two o'clock the next morning the regiment's relief was heard approaching from the rear. To the cavalrymen's surprise the arriving column's muskets glistened with fixed bayonets. Questions at once were hurled at the replacements. "What's up?" Back

came the reply, "Don't know, but guess we're going to make a charge."[2] As the relieving troops plodded forward, the order was given for the 13th to march to the rear. After going a short way the command was turned to the left and marched some 300 yards. Here it was halted for the purpose of letting more troops pass. Moving on, the happy troopers turned left again and were spread out through a depression in a bluff overlooking the salient. They were placed in line of battle facing the outer works they had just vacated. It suddenly became apparent they were not going to the rear after all.

Occasional Confederate rifle fire buzzed through the lines and a number of missiles found their marks. One cavalryman, making light of events at hand, suddenly clasped his hand to his hip and exclaimed, "Jiminy, I'm hit!"[3] Most of those in line were not joking, however; many were rereading the letters just delivered and reminiscing of home for possibly the last time. Others contemplated what morning's light might bring.

For weeks the men had heard of a mine being dug underneath the salient by soldiers of Colonel Henry Pleasants' 48th Pennsylvania. This indeed was true, and Pleasants' mine was to be exploded below the Confederate works by means of 8,000 pounds of gunpowder. Then, according to the Union plan, the Ninth Corps would smash through the resulting breach in the Confederate line and open the way to Petersburg. As the Ohioans hugged the reddish-brown clay of their reserve trench, word spread that today had been chosen for the mine's detonation.

At 4:40 a.m. on July 30, the ground trembled with a jarring roar. Looking to the front the Union soldiers witnessed a huge geyser of dirt, dust, smoke and flame rise 200 feet high, curl over and cascade to earth with a dull thud. "I could see in the column of fire and smoke, the bodies of men, arms and legs, pieces of timber, and a gun carriage," recalled one of the Ohio cavalrymen. "I felt very weak and pale, and the faces of my comrades never looked more blanched." [4]

Nearby, crouching with the other troopers on that fateful morning was a member of Company H about to experience the defining moment of his life. Nathaniel McLean Gwynne was a blue-eyed boy of 15 standing barely five feet six inches tall. [5] His light skin had been baked by the Virginia sun to a dark bronze matching the prized bugle he clutched in his hand. Lying there in his colorful musician's jacket, he was approached by his commanding officer who warned, "Young man, remember you are not mustered in. You had better stay behind. That's an order." [6] Incredibly, here at the front was a young American boy clothed and fed by the United States government, yet was not recognized as a soldier by the same entity he was fighting for. He shared the same privations and wretched conditions — heat and filth, hunger and thirst, fear and death — as any soldier in the field. To his many comrades he was looked upon as a soldier in every sense of the word, but in the government's eyes he was unknown.

Nathaniel Gwynne was born July 5, 1849, at Urbana, Ohio. [7] At age 11 he watched the country dive headlong into civil war and, like thousands of others not quite of age, envisioned himself marching off to glory. "Nat," as he was called by family and friends, could stand it no longer and in early 1864 decided to run away and join the Army. This was done without the consent of his parents or their knowledge. [8]

Like many youngsters he was enthralled by the glamor of the cavalry and tried to enlist in that branch of service. After repeated rebuffs he finally was given permission to tag along with the newly formed 13th Ohio Cavalry. This was the last cavalry regiment raised by Ohio and luckily for Nat, he was accepted. The 13th was recruited from the state at large but was mustered at Camp Chase in Columbus, where Nat

signed up on May 3, 1864. Due to the age restriction of 18, however, and not having parental consent to bypass this formality, he did not pass muster. Instead, like hundreds of others in the Army, he was allowed to become a mascot of sorts. Soon he was issued a bugle and made bugler of Company H. [9]

Now, after less than three months of active service, he was lying with his comrades watching one of the most horrible events of the war unfold before his eyes. His commanding officer was giving him a direct order not to advance. With the same indignance bestowed upon his parents when leaving home without their permission, he rebuked the officer by stating, "But that's not what I'm here for. I came to fight and fight I will." [10] Before the words were silenced with the wind, bugles blared and Nat and his comrades headed for the mine's yawning crater.

Thirty minutes had elapsed since the explosion when the 13th started. Advancing on foot in columns of fours, the troopers were relieved to lie down when about half way to the crater. Artillery solid shot and canister swept their position. The 10-minute break seemed like an hour. Again came the command "Forward!" and the troopers reached the huge hole in short order. [11]

To the division already stuffed in the crater, the cavalrymen's arrival must have looked like a flock of monarchs had descended on the scene. Their yellow-trimmed jackets seemed out of place in the remorseless struggle of life and death. As the carnage continued throughout the morning, the Union attack dissolved into a full retreat with survival the only prize obtainable. Slowly the firing slackened, more by exhaustion than design.

It was during the fighting's height that Nathaniel's military career came to an abrupt end. At a crucial moment in the struggle the regimental colors went down, and young Gwynne rushed to save them. Unfortunately his heroic decision proved costly. On his way back with the flag, Confederate lead struck his left arm three inches below the shoulder. Gripping the flagstaff firmer with his one good arm he continued his journey. Again he was hit, this time through a knee. The 15-year-old bugler had proved his pluck and brought the colors back, but for him the war was over. [12]

Considering the proximity of the combatants and the battle's intensity, an extremity wound was not all that bad. One of the cavalrymen recalled thinking at the beginning of the fight, "I would be a happy boy if I could get off with but the loss of a leg or arm."[13] In fact, 10 percent of Gwynne's comrades were killed outright on July 30 or died from wounds.

Within two hours of reaching safety in the Union works, Nat was lying on an operating table having chloroform administered in a field hospital. Surgeon Alphonso White of the 8th Maryland Infantry then amputated his left arm just below the shoulder by the flap method. Nat's knee wound also was examined and judged not severe enough to warrant another amputation.[14] Four days later he arrived at Douglas General Hospital in Washington, D.C. Already the dead skin was sloughing off to some degree, as his new doctor noted. On August 13 he was transferred again and spent the next few months at the Second Corps Hospital in Alexandria. Nat's brother arrived from Cincinnati during this period to help care for him. In early December someone in the War Department realized that Nat never had been mustered, and arranged to correct the oversight. On December 19, 1864, he officially became a United States soldier — his muster roll backdated to May 10, 1864 — thus enabling the young hero to receive pay for the entire time he had been with the Army. With Nathaniel's steady improvement his brother started a campaign to have him moved to a Cincinnati hospital. The transfer was approved within two weeks, and on December 30 the Gwynnes left for the Buckeye State.[15]

Soon after Nat arrived in the Queen City and his exploits became known to those at hand, the boy bugler was recommended for the country's highest honor, the Medal of Honor. The application was submitted January 3, 1865.[16] Just three weeks later, on January 27, the coveted medal was issued to Gwynne with the following citation: "When about entering upon the charge, this soldier, then but 15 years old, was cautioned not to go in, as he had not been mustered. He indignantly protested and participated in the charge, his left arm being crushed by a shell and amputated soon afterward."[17] After receiving the honor Nat spent another month in the Cincinnati hospital before leaving the Army with a disability discharge on March 21, 1865. On that day he started his journey home.[18]

Undaunted by his disability, Nat finished his education and became a lawyer in Kansas City, Missouri.

In 1873 he wed Nira Carter. The two were well known in that part of the state, being called upon at every function of the Grand Army of the Republic and other veteran organizations. Nat also started a militia group known as the McPherson Guards and acted as captain. Throughout the years, however, his arm stump and knee never quite healed completely and caused him intense pain. The arm discharged fluid periodically the whole while. Finally, toxins in his body prevailed and Gwynne died on January 6, 1883, at the age of 33. Befitting a soldier, his funeral procession was a military affair. Following the hearse was a gray horse that he, the gallant cavalryman, had ridden in many parades at the head of the McPherson Guards. The animal bore its master's empty saddle, his boots and spurs reversed in the stirrups.

Three years later Gwynne's young wife applied for a widow's pension. It was approved, stating that the death of her husband was a direct result of the wounds he received at the battle of the Crater 18 years earlier. The beardless boy bugler of the 13th Ohio Cavalry joined his slain comrades on the other side. He had paid for his youthful yearnings to become a soldier with the ultimate price, his life.[19]

The saga of Nathaniel Gwynne, though tragic, was not unique. Stories like his actually were quite common during the four long years of the American Civil War. Throughout that struggle countless young boys by any means attainable found their way into the two opposing armies. Once they gained approval to participate in the epic drama of their generation, they performed a wide variety of duties. A large number of the youngest recruits served as musicians and orderlies. Thousands of others carried muskets in the ranks. Young boys participated in practically every engagement of the war. Some served honorably, some did not. Many soon were home by the fireside in quick time, but for every one who shirked duty or responsibility there were those who stood tall and served like men. Many were wounded, some fell ill, and others were captured and became prisoners of war. To the chagrin of some boy soldiers their parents followed and herded them home. Others went off to war with fathers and brothers. Classmates and neighbors joined together, friends enlisting side by side. They marched away with the naïve innocence of youth. For many it became the greatest adventure of a lifetime. Even youngsters who stayed at home were touched by the burdens of the struggle, many stepping into the shoes of their soldier-fathers on the farm or in the shop. Boys as well as girls, who normally would have been pursuing their homework, filled thousands of jobs. The immense conflict strangling the country embraced nearly every child North and South from 1861 to 1865. Of the boys who did join the ranks, like Nathaniel Gwynne, many died.

The following pages provide a glimpse into the lives of part of the youthful generation that found itself immersed in the Civil War. For those who were moved to wear the blue and follow a soldier's fate, this is their story. Whether they were eight, 12 or 16 years old, the youngest boys in the Union armies willfully went forth during those perilous years and put themselves in harm's way. They truly were too young to die.

CHAPTER 1

'There were plenty of boys crazy to go to the tented field'

Boy

Noun, 1. A male child from birth to the age of physical maturity; lad; youth.[1]

The United States military had a long tradition of recruiting young boys by the time hostilities began in April 1861. The first published references to the enlistment of underage recruits in the U.S. Army appeared shortly after the War Department was established in 1789. The 1802 Army regulations stated that no person below the age of 21 should be enlisted without the consent of a parent, guardian or master, but no minimum age was defined. It only stands to reason that references are found so early, considering thousands of young boys joined the Continental Army and fought during the American Revolution. By 1813 the regulations specified that healthy, active boys between the ages of 14 and 18 could be enlisted as musicians with parental consent. After the War of 1812 the Secretary of War issued orders discharging all minors who were enlisted without proper consent in an attempt to rid the Army of many youngsters in the ranks.[2] However, the 1821 regulations set parameters for enlistment again without specifically stating a minimum age allowed. Recruiting Article 74, Section 13, contained the following instructions for recruiting officers: "All free white male persons, above eighteen and under thirty five years, who are able bodied, ac-tive, and free from disease, may be enlisted; and whenever a recruit, who is under age, shall have a parent, guardian, or master, his consent shall be obtained, in writing, and accompany the enlistment which is sent to the Adjutant General. Any loss accruing from the non-observance of this rule, will be borne by the recruiting officer."[3] The article was vague as to the minimum age the recruiter could accept under 18, and it never clearly defined what was considered "under age."

In 1825 the regulations were revised in a number of ways and a new edition printed. Recruiting Article 74 was amended to stipulate a minimum height of five feet six inches for the infantry and five feet eight inches for the artillery. Age requirements were kept the same as in the 1821 edition. In this printing age and size requirements were not applicable to musicians.[4] The reference clearly shows that drummer boys were well established in the Army by 1825. Once again, however, no minimum age for the young musicians was stated.

Underage soldiers became a topic of debate for the 22nd Congress in 1832. Legislation was enacted that year containing the following four points:

1. Of enlisting into the Army minors, from the ages of sixteen to seventeen, by and with the consent of their parents or guardians, to serve for the period of four years.

2. Of establishing schools at such military posts garrisoned exclusively by the troops so enlisted, for

A military school cadet of the early 1860s. Dozens of such institutions were established in Northern states in the decade prior to the war.

Author's Collection

the purpose of teaching such branches of education as will fit and prepare the soldiers for situations of usefulness in life, and of reducing their monthly pay in the ratio of two dollars for every five dollars now paid.

3. Of retaining the whiskey portion of the ration, to be paid either in money, military equipments, or in some suitable badge of honor.

4. Of exempting all such non-commissioned officers and privates, who shall have served for the period of four years, from militia duty, except in case of war, invasion, or other public emergency; and that the committee inquire how far such enlistments and provisions may tend to destroy or lessen the evil of frequent desertion.

Soon after the House of Representatives' resolution was passed, Major General Alexander Macomb, commanding the Army, addressed the lawmakers. It was his opinion that any parents permitting their sons to enlist at the prescribed ages of 16 and 17 probably were not doing so for altruistic reasons. Arguing that "none but idle, prolifigate, and incorrigible lads, who could not be controlled by their parents or guardians, would be permitted to be enlisted," General Macomb contended that a younger age would be more likely to produce good soldiers. "I would prefer that the ages of the boys should be much younger, and would propose not less than twelve or more than thirteen years, and the term of enlistment to be twelve years, or until they should, respectively, have attained the age of twenty-five years. At such a tender age, the boys might be instructed in the art of reading and writing the English language correctly; and as they advanced, they should be taught the principles of mathematics." He further suggested how these "cadets" should act and dress, and that a trial school be started at Fort Monroe, Virginia — necessities required, he believed, as the Army was having a difficult time obtaining recruits of good character and intelligence. Macomb presented his plan

to Congress in the form of a bill in December 1832.[5] Fortunately for the young boys who might hastily have joined under this plan and found themselves soldiers until age 25, the bill was never passed. No records can be found regarding actual establishment of instructional schools for young recruits as decreed in the original resolution. The actions taken on the recruiting of minors aged 16 and 17 were not mentioned in the next edition of the Army regulations.

The 1834 edition spelled out a recruiting officer's duties in greater detail, perhaps due to the congressional debate two years earlier. It stipulated that if "very young men present themselves, they are to be treated with great candor; the names and residences of their parents or guardian, if they have any, must be ascertained, and their friends must be informed of their wishes to enlist, that they may make their objections or give their consent." The officer also was instructed to have the recruit wait at least 24 hours before signing enlistment papers. In selecting recruits the height requirement was set at five feet six inches for all branches of the service. Age requirements were kept the same, at 18 to 35; however, those under 21 were to obtain written consent of a parent, guardian or master. Again it was stated that age and size requirements did not apply when recruiting musicians, and no minimum age was set for them.[6]

By 1841 the height requirement was lowered to five feet five inches. The issue of enlisting young boys as musicians finally was addressed that year, too. "The general superintendent will cause such of the recruits as are found to possess a natural talent for music to be instructed (besides in the drill of the soldier), on fife, bugle, and drum, and other military instruments; and boys of ten years of age, and upwards, may, under his direction, be enlisted for this purpose." Even though the recruiting officer now had a guideline for the very minimum age of enlistees, he was instructed to be wary in his selections. "Recruiting officers must be very particular in ascertaining the true age of a recruit. They are not always to take the word of a recruit, but are to rely on their own judgment for the ascertainment of his probable, if not actual, age."[7] The practice of lying about one's age to gain admittance to the military apparently was becoming widespread by that time. Recruiting officers during the Civil War frequently encountered the phenomenon. More importantly, the 1841 regulations clearly set the minimum age at 10 for musicians.

During the Mexican War in 1847 the Army issued another edition which differed little from the previous one as far as minors were concerned. The only alteration was that a recruit's height requirement was lowered once again, this time to five feet three inches. The basic age requirement of 18 to 35 remained in effect, as well as the stipulation that those under age 21 were to have written parental consent.[8]

A decade later the age requirement was retained, but minimum height was juggled to five feet four and a half inches. Again it was noted these requirements were not appicable to musicians, although they were to be scrutinized more closely. "... recruits under eighteen years of age and under size must be dis-

charged, if they are not capable of learning music [and] care should be taken to enlist those only who have a natural talent for music, and, if practical, they should be taken on a trial for some time before being enlisted."[9] The Army finally had established parameters that it expected recruiting officers to abide by. It would accept young boys for the sole purpose of being musicians. None could serve in any other capacity if under the age of 18.

Accepting youths on a trial basis before being mustered also was important. Apparently the option was regularly employed at recruiting stands a few years later when the Civil War began. Many children like Nathaniel Gwynne of the 13th Ohio Cavalry joined under trial conditions without officially being mustered.[10]

When Fort Sumter was bombarded on April 12, 1861, the 1857 regulations were in use by the Army. Its main guidelines for recruiting officers stated:

1. Minimum age of a recruit for the ranks, *eighteen.*

2. Minimum age of a recruit accepted without parental consent, *twenty-one.*

3. Minimum age of a recruit accepted as a musician, *twelve.*

4. Minimum height of a recruit for the ranks, *five feet four and a half inches.*

5. Minimum height of a recruit as a musician, *not applicable.*

6. Musicians could be enlisted on a *trial basis* [author's italics].

The 1857 edition further commented that if one "who has no parent or guardian offer[s] to enlist, a guardian (who must not be any one connected with the recruiting party) may be appointed by the proper legal authority." A parental consent form for the purpose of enlisting those under 21 was included in the 1857 regulations:

I _____, do certify that I am the (father, only surviving parent, legal master, or guardian, as the case may be) of _____; that the said _____ is ____ years of age; and I do hereby freely give my consent to his enlisting as a soldier in the Army of the United States for a period of five years.
Witness _____ _____ [11]

By 1861 the consent form was an integral part of enlistment papers. A Declaration of Recruit was printed on the reverse side. The declaration asked the recruit his age by year and month. If he was underage or the recruiting officer believed he was, requirements stipulated the recruit should have the consent form filled out. The regulations further stated, "The forms of declaration, and consent in case of a minor, having been signed and witnessed, the recruit will then be duly examined by the recruiting officer, and surgeon if one be present, and, if accepted the 20th and 78th Articles of War will be read to him; after which he will be allowed time to consider the subject until his mind appears to be fully made up before the oath is administered to him."[12]

The 20th and 78th articles of war were intended to impress upon a prospective recruit the seriousness of his enlistment. The 20th Article stated that all "officers and soldiers who have received pay, or have been duly enlisted in the service of the United States, and shall be convicted of having deserted the same, shall suffer death, or such other punishment as, by sentence of a court-martial, shall be inflicted." In 1830 the 20th Article was amended to read that no soldier should suffer the death penalty during peacetime. Once hostilities broke out in 1861, anyone who deserted was in danger of receiving the death penalty. The 78th Article stated that "non-commissioned officers and soldiers, charged with crimes, shall be confined until tried by a court-martial, or released by proper authority."[13] Both articles clearly outlined harsh punishment the military could inflict on recruits once they were mustered into service.

According to regulations the recruit was to be examined and passed by a surgeon before the articles of war were read to him and he was mustered. The surgeon's main objective in the recruitment process was to ascertain that recruits brought before him were "effective, able bodied" individuals, as determined by War Department guidelines.[14] Most thorough surgeons used methods listed in the 1858 *Manual of the Medical Officer of the Army of the United States.*

On the subject of recruiting minors the manual's author, Dr. Charles S. Tripler, warned of potential problems enlisting youthful recruits and questioned whether they possessed the vigor and physical development necessary for performance of a soldier's duties. Dr. Tripler noted:

When young men of this age are well made and have a true aptitude for the profession of arms, they are capable of making excellent soldiers. But it must not be lost sight of, that there are few at this age fit for this profession. The body has not yet attained the necessary strength, the organs have not yet arrived at that stage of vigor, which will permit them to pass rapidly without a careful transition, from a state of repose to one of violent exercise; and it must be borne in mind that by the term "organs" we do not mean only those of locomotion; as the expressions repose and exercise, we have just employed, might suggest; but at this age the gastrointestinal mucous membrane is too readily over-excitable. The lungs are too susceptible of morbid impressions. This is the epoch of pulmonary congestions, of haemoptysis, of obstinate bronchitis, the frequent recurrence of which leads almost inevitably to phthisis [tuberculosis]. At this age, likewise, the nervous system is far from having arrived at its maximum of functional development, its play is still most irregular. How then under so many disadvantages, is it possible to encounter successfully the fatigues and accidents of war? How, with an irritable stomach, accommodate oneself to food the most diverse and frequently the most indigestible? How with lungs so pre-disposed to disease, support such severe changes of temperature, heat, cold, moisture? How bivouac, how sleep in mud, in snow, without shelter, without fire? How with a nervous system still immature, at least in its functional relations, find in oneself sufficient moral energy to contend successfully against the soldier in campaign?

If we were then called upon to give our opinion upon this point, it would be an unfavorable one, and if we did not go so far as to reject it entirely, we should restrain its exercise within the narrowest limits, and reserve it for very rare contingencies, to be determined by special rules.

We can not but assent entirely to the physiological objections so forcibly urged against the enlistment of minors; and, considering the annoyances and losses to which the service is so constantly exposed from this class of recruits, the perjuries, falsehoods and forgeries they induce in the young and dissolute, the inconsiderable accession of force they bring to the ranks, we think they might profitably be forbidden altogether. But so long as these enlistments are authorized, the Medical Officer can not summarily refuse to recognize them. He must confine himself to the investigation of the physical qualifications of the individual recruit.

Let him then institute a closer scrutiny into the condition of the thoracic and abdominal viscera of the recruit under age. Learn if possible if he have any hereditary tendency to pulmonary or scrofulous [glandular] disease. Observe the degree of development of his muscular system, and be satisfied that his osseous [skeletal] system is so well developed as to preclude all danger of distortion and the like from the severe fatigues the young soldier is sure to be called upon to encounter.[15]

The Army had every intention of inspecting recruits that were to be inducted by the system designed. Most recruits were put through rigorous inspections and many young aspirants were turned homeward with the disdainful look of a surgeon seeing them off. With rapidity needed to fill up the vast armies going to the field, especially during the war's first two years, a sizeable number of recruits was only casually examined.

Delavan S. Miller recalled how easy it was at age 13 to join the 2nd New York Heavy Artillery in March 1862. "This was in the early days of the war and there was not much system about anything. Probably if it had been a year later and the boy had had to pass a regular examination and muster he would have been sent home. But he, with the rest of the recruits, was merged into the company without any formalities."[16] Harry M. Kieffer was a 16-year-old recruit who later wrote of his examination when enlisting in the 150th Pennsylvania. "Before we were mustered into the service, every man was thoroughly examined by a medical officer, who had us presented to him one by one, in *purus naturalibus*, in a large tent, where he sharply questioned us — 'Teeth sound? Eyes good? Ever had this, that, and the other disease?' — and pitiable was the case of that unfortunate man who, because of bad hearing, or defective eyesight, or some other physical blemish, was compelled to don his citizen's clothes again and take the next train home."[17]

For quite a few hopeful youngsters the medical exam was a make-or-break situation, completely dependent upon a surgeon's whims.

Throughout the Civil War the Army continued addressing the complex issue of minors in the ranks. New regulations were printed in 1861. This edition was the same as that of 1857, except in a few areas. The only change affecting young recruits was the lowering of the minimum height requirement from five feet four and a half inches to five feet three inches.[18] This afforded a few more youngsters the opportunity of passing muster. The Army lowered the height requirement that it might better be able to fill the ranks when so many troops were needed. The same height of five feet three inches was used during the Mexican War when the Army also demanded a large number of men.[19] It was only during those two conflicts that the Army set the height requirement so low.

Author's Collection

Unidentified.

To supplement the regulations, the War Department during the war issued 11 general orders to rectify problems in the Adjutant General's office caused by enlistment of minors.[20] Issued August 3, 1861, General Order 51 focused on the large number of young enlistees being discharged after serving only a short time. "Minors, who may be discharged either by the civil authority or upon the personal application of parents or friends, will be discharged without pay or allowance."[21] The order addressed monetary obligations in such cases, but did not correct the problem. Before the end of the month, on August 26, General Order 66 decreed: "Hereafter no minors will be mustered into the service of the United States or Volunteers without the consent of their parents or guardians."[22] This was not anything new — the regulations already included that provision — but due to the fact that so many youngsters were entering the service in the war's early days, the Adjutant General thought it best to restate the order with the inclusion of volunteer forces.

By September the War Department was getting tired of the revolving-door enlistments of minors. General Order 73 proclaimed, "Hereafter, no discharges will be granted to volunteers in the service of the United States on the grounds of minority."[23] Despite this order, many youngsters continued to be released from military obligation through legal and political channels. To stress the importance of following regulations, and to curtail loopholes in the system, General Order 104 was issued next. "As to minors, every precaution should be taken to prevent their enlistment, except as provided by the regulations. A true record of age is of great value. In a majority of the cases the recruiting officer may be justified in recording the age as stated by the person offering to enlist; yet many cases occur in which he should rely more upon his own judgment, if not his actual age."[24] Using one's judgment was nothing new to recruiting officers, but owing to scores of underage enlistees being discharged upon proof of actual age shown by a competent party, it was deemed necessary to reiterate the order.

On June 9, 1863, the Secretary of War modified the recruitment section of the 1861 regulations to read: "No person under the age of eighteen years is to be enlisted or re-enlisted without the written consent of his parent, guardian, or master. Recruiting officers must be very particular in ascertaining the true age of the recruit."[25] Before this change recruiters were to have the written consent forms filled out for any soldier under age 21; however, that was rarely done for those over 18 in the first place. This new recruiting change legalized a practice that had been commonly used since the war's beginning. Yet many by-the-book recruiters never veered from the true regulations. For youthful enlistees under their scrutiny, this was the opportunity they had long awaited. For those underage, it was easy to persuade a recruiter of being 18 if a lad was of good size. Smaller boys aged 14 through 17 still were being accepted as musicians if they could obtain parental consent. For those who could not, there was always the option of running away from home to act the orphan for some unwary recruiter.

By 1864 the battlefield's horrors were becoming well known to the general population. The Union's loss in men had been staggering. With 10,162 casual-ties at Shiloh, 19,739 in the Seven Days battles, 11,657 at Antietam, Chickamauga's 11,413, and 17,684 at Gettysburg, the manpower drain was deeply felt.[26] With the adoption of the draft in 1863, every able-bodied man eligible for military duty was being sought. For underage boys who continued trying to make their way into the Army, 1864 saw countless opportunities and a host of unscrupulous methods employed to gain admittance. Many youngsters were used as pawns by others to gain financially from local, state and federal bounties being offered. Andrew Richards was one of them.

During a court-martial hearing in regard to a desertion charge filed against him, Andrew's unusual case came to light. He was a member of Company K, 10th Vermont, when he left a hospital while recuperating from a fever to enlist in the 5th New Hampshire. After a few months in his new regiment he was located by his original command and charged with the offense. In his defense First Sergeant William H. Blake of Company K testified: "All I know about his age is that men who came from the same town and knew him told me the prisoner was only about fourteen years old. The man who told me is dead. He died last summer. The prisoner is not very bright. He is rather stupid. I think he cannot read or write."

Private Nathaniel Piper of the same company stated, "Have known [Richards] about three years. All I know about his age is that when I first saw him 3 years ago he was a small boy. About a year ago last December I was at home and I know that the man the prisoner lived with took him to the selectmen of the town to have him enlisted and they would not take him because he was not old enough. I was with the Company during the time he was with it. The prisoner is rather dull and has no learning."

Finally, Andrew was asked to add to the testimony where his misguidance was proved. He told the court: "I stayed at the hospital at Burlington, Vermont, till some time in Sept. last. I had the fever. I went down to the town one day on a pass from the hospital and a man gave me something to drink and I suppose I got drunk. The next thing I know I was on the cars west to Concord, N.H. with this man. I asked the man what it meant and he said I was enlisted. He took me to Concord and put me in a barracks and kept me there about a week and then they sent me with others to City Point, Va. There were about three hundred when we left Concord and only about 100 when we got to City Point. The rest ran away. I don't know the man's name who took me to Concord. I did not see him after I got to Concord. I did not go to a Provost Marshal's at Concord. Just before we got to Concord the man gave me fifty dollars. That is all I ever got. I have never received any pay since. I was paid once while in the 10th Vt. up to the 29th of February 1864. I think I got to the 5th N.H. about the 1st of October 1864 and remained with it till I was arrested and put in the guardhouse. That was about a week ago. When I first enlisted in the 10th Vt. the man I lived with got $300 bounty. I have no parents." As it was obvious Andrew had been game to others using him to obtain bounties being offered, the court ordered him to forfeit four months' pay and return to the 10th. It was a very light sentence considering the demand at that time to punish bounty jumpers who were prolific in 1864.[27]

To combat these problems, General Order 75, Section 20, stated: "The Secretary of War may order the discharge of all persons in the military service who are under the age of eighteen years at the time of the application for their discharge, when it shall appear upon due proof that such persons are in the service without the consent, either expressed or implied, of their parents or guardians; and provided further, that such persons, their parents or guardians, shall first repay to the government and to the State and local authorities all bounties and advance pay which may have been paid to them, anything in the act to which this is an amendment to the contrary notwithstanding."[28]

Money aside, the Army finally realized that boys *were* perhaps too young to die, and on July 6, 1864, issued General Order 224. This order not only revamped the Army's acceptable age, but also imposed stiff penalties to enforce the change. "... if any officer of the United States shall knowingly enlist or muster into the military service any person under the age of sixteen years, with or without the consent of his parent or guardian, such person so enlisted or recruited shall be immediately discharged upon repayment of all bounties received; and such recruiting or mustering officer who shall knowingly enlist any person under sixteen years of age, shall be dismissed from the service, with forfeiture of all pay and allowances, and shall be subject to such further punishment as a court martial may direct."[29]

From that day on the legal age requirement under any circumstance was 16. Yet, even as the order took effect, hundreds, and perhaps thousands, of youngsters below the new legal age were retained in the service, and despite warnings to officers many underage recruits were accepted through war's end. The question of just how many boys served, and who was the youngest, has perplexed students of the war even before the gunfire ended.

The U.S. Sanitary Commission, a civilian relief organization founded primarily to aid sick and wounded soldiers, initiated a statistical look at ages in the Union Army by August 1864. E.B. Elliott, the accomplished statistician and fellow of the American Society of Arts and Science, first suggested and then commenced collecting data on soldier ages while director of the commission's statistical department some time earlier. Clerks were employed for the tedious work of searching muster rolls for information needed in the study. One clerk, a Mr. Stockwell, was instrumental in the data recovery and almost single-handedly carried out the greater part of the work.

The research digested in the study included recruits from 27 states, territories and geographical regions, exhibiting the number of men at each year of age in the volunteer organizations at the time of their muster into national service. Officers were tabulated as a distinct class, and the Army's three branches — infantry, cavalry and artillery — likewise were treated separately. Recruits who joined regiments on a date after the original organization was federalized were not included. The investigation also excluded all drafted men and substitutes. Moreover, other regiments were omitted because they were organized after data was collected for the states to which they belonged. But that number was comparatively small to exert any discernible effect upon the results.

The total number of volunteers whose records were used was 1,049,457, of whom 1,012,273 were enlisted men and 37,184 were commissioned officers. According to the results, all except 1.5 percent of the men, and 3.3 percent of the officers, were between the ages of 18 and 45 at the time of their enlistment or commission. Of the numbers investigated, only 15,626 were found to be under age 18 or over age 45 combined. Dr. Benjamin Gould, president of the

James F. Ward

Lucien F. Thorp

Author's Collection

In addition to boys there were thousands above the prescribed age of 45 in the Union armies as well. An Ohio officer characterized the older men's soldiering abilities: "With a few exceptions, it was the young men who fought the rebellion to its death. Those above the age of forty did not lack in zeal or courage, but they could not endure the toil, hardship and exposure, and within a year fully three-fourths of them had disappeared from our ranks — died from disease or discharged for disability. It was the same in all regiments through the army."

James F. Ward, serving as a drummer in Company B, 76th Ohio, was, at 60, three years younger than his company's wagoner, George Devilbliss. Both enlisted in October 1861 and were gone inside of a year. Lucien F. Thorp, a musician in Company G, 67th Ohio, was 54 when he died at Hilton Head, South Carolina, after serving 34 months, part of that time as a nurse attached to the Veteran Reserve Corps.

American Association for the Advancement of Science, as acting actuary to the commission, reflected at the study's completion, "These represent two classes, viz. the boys, chiefly drummers, musicians, etc., and the men who, although past the legal age, were so sturdy or earnest that the enrolling officers did not, at that time of great national peril, feel justified in insisting on an absolute compliance with the legal qualifications."[30]

Breaking down the calculations further, the study showed that 1 percent was under age 18 (roughly 10,000), and .5 percent was over 45. Of the number of enlisted men there were 127 aged 13, 330 aged 14, 773 aged 15, 2,758 aged 16, 6,425 aged 17 and 133,475 aged 18. Applying these calculations to the total enrollment of the Union Army, approximately 460,000 recruits were 18 or younger. Nowhere in the study was a number given for boys who enlisted under age 13, even though the regulations allowed 12-year-olds to enlist while others, still younger, are listed as such on the rolls. Presumably, soldiers under age 13 were included in the number 127.[31]

The Sanitary Commission's report was by far the most in-depth age analysis of Union soldiers using muster rolls and enlistment forms. It has been cited and used many times by historians and writers through the years. But the exhaustive study does contain faults — chiefly, that all data used were as written when a soldier enlisted. There was no mention or inclusion of the fact that a serious problem existed of incorrect ages being given by those trying to gain admission to the service. The military recognized this as early as 1841, when the abuse first was addressed in Army regulations. Each subsequent edition contained cautions for recruiters in the matter as well.

Another examination of soldier ages, conducted nearly four decades after the war by George L. Kilmer, was published in *The Century* in June 1905. Kilmer's article, "Boys in the Union Army," was the first serious analysis to show there were many incorrect or overstated ages given by recruits during the war. "There are ample data to prove that the average age of Union soldiers upon enlistment was not beyond the period commonly called boyhood," Kilmer postulated. "A young man of twenty-two or twenty-five, doing man's work — and soldiering is man's work — is, by courtesy spoken of as a boy. The compliment tends to ennoble his deeds. Trustworthy tables of averages show that the mean age of the soldiers of the Union army upon enlistment was twenty-five. This figure may be too high by half a year. In fixing the average at twenty-five the ages of those recorded as eighteen and twenty-one upon enlistment were assumed to be correct, yet it is evident that tens of thousands, perhaps during the whole war over one hundred thousand recruits, gave their ages as eighteen when they were not seventeen, many not even sixteen."[32]

Kilmer also commented on Gould's earlier study. "The matter of false ages stated by boys under eighteen seems to have escaped the attention of the statistician, although he noticed and explained the unusual proportion of ages set down at twenty-one. Boys of twenty and strapping lads of nineteen were desirous of being classed as men, and so in all rolls and in all aggregations of ages from various sources those put down at twenty-one greatly outnumber those at twenty and twenty-two. This is significant when the tables of ages from eighteen upward to twenty-five and thirty are considered. The numbers at twenty and twenty-two are about equal; those at twenty-one stand a third higher than either. Probably 200,000 recruits overstated their ages a year or more."[33]

Neither Dr. Gould nor Kilmer took into consideration Army regulations when analyzing the proportion of soldiers claiming to be 21. The requirement for recruits without written permission of parents or guardian was 21 until July 1864. Many not having consent were induced to declare their age as 21 to circumvent the legality, thereby creating the study's uneven ratios. Kilmer incorrectly believed the legal age was 18, and did not fully understand the regulations as far as the age of 21 was concerned.

Gould's tabulations placed the percentage of soldiers 18 and under at just over 14 percent. Kilmer, in scrutinizing muster rolls of 11 randomly selected infantry regiments and one of cavalry, came up with 16 percent for the same age group. Calculations by both, however, were limited to ages recorded on enlistment forms.[34]

In recent years many new research avenues have been opened to substantiate soldier ages during the war. Accessibility and indexing of the 1860 census provide the most important data to ascertain ages. During collection of the census there was no reason to supply false ages. Submitted ages thereby can be accepted as unbiased, and in most cases correct. The second most important records available are pension files. Whenever a soldier submitted a pension claim he was required to fill out a questionnaire which asked his age. This information can be compared to ages submitted at muster for inconsistencies.

The post-war years yielded an abundance of published regimental histories and soldier narratives. Many of these works contain corrected rosters or other insights to aid the contemporary researcher. Most older soldiers were particularly fond of their commands' youngest members, and employed regimental histories as vehicles to show appreciation to boy comrades.

A soldier's "boyish" looks occasionally can be misleading with reference to actual age. Musician William A. Underwood of Company G, 6th Massachusetts, was listed as 18 in August 1862 when this portrait was made at Lowell, Massachusetts. Nineteen months later, however, his age upon enlistment in the U.S. Navy was given as 21. Underwood served aboard the receiving ship *Ohio* and the U.S.S. *Iosco,* from which he was discharged in March 1865 as nurse.

Richard F. Carlile Collection

Some writers used their books to tout their boy as being the fiercest and youngest in the Army. For decades after the war newspaper and magazine articles nominated different youthful veterans as the new heir to the title of "youngest" soldier. The pages of *The National Tribune,* a popular post-war publication targeting Civil War veterans, are filled with such letters or short stories. Many of these writings can and have shed light on minors whose military records otherwise show them of age.

By studying the photographic legacy that remains, clues to determining a soldier's age sometimes are found in period notations written on an image or in its protective case. A soldier's physical appearance can be scrutinized to see if his features corroborate an age listed in the records. If the age seems too old judging by photographic evidence, records are then viewed to

resolve the discrepancy. Since the war lasted four years there were many beardless boys who matured while in the service. Dating a photograph to a certain year can be of great importance when determining a soldier's age at the time of the sitting or his enlistment.

Unfortunately, even research methods employed today fall short in obtaining completely accurate numbers and ages for youthful soldiers. The census, although assumed correct, is full of inconsistencies when comparing ages listed in 1860 and 1870. Where birthdays fell in relation to when the census taker came around could create a discrepancy of as much as two years.

Pension files also can contain conflicting information when comparing ages listed during different application submissions. Frustration wrought while researching soldier files can best be understood by the case of Ovid P. Webster. In the post-war years Ovid applied for an invalid pension for a disability sustained as a member of the 45th Pennsylvania. On five different occasions he submitted applications with his age recorded to his nearest birthday. In November 1883 he listed his age as 37, indicating he was born in 1846. Three years later, on August 30, 1886, he gave his age as 46, placing his birthday around 1840. In May 1890, age 45 was recorded. That would make his birth year 1845, creating a five-year discrepancy between the 1886 and 1890 applications.[35] When Ovid enlisted on October 18, 1861, he marked his age as 18 for the recruiting officer, thereby having him born in 1843 and matching none of the pension ages. Complicating the issue further, on January 1, 1864, the five foot five inch soldier reenlisted, filling his declaration of recruit form with a stated age of 18 years and four months — again setting his birthday in 1846.[36]

In the 45th Pennsylvania's published history, Webster's best friend Ira Odell furnished a story of their enlistment and recalled they were "two boys, both somewhat under 16 years of age, who had not the consent of their parents to go to the war." [37] This revelation indicates Ovid was indeed a lad of no more than 16 summers when he marched off in 1861. Unfortunately, his pension records do not reveal his actual birthday. Although many files do contain birthdates, cases like Ovid Webster's require information from varied sources to establish any conclusion. The pre-

dominating evidence of his age at enlistment points to 16, possibly 15.

Photographs at times can be just as misleading. When first viewing the wartime portrait of Henry A. Bull of Company A, 9th New York Heavy Artillery, the five foot three inch soldier appears to be only 14 or 15. His muster roll records his age as 18 when he enlisted January 4, 1864. To the doubtful eye there seems to be a discrepancy pointing to further study. His father, Aaron, signed the consent form as required and further endorsed his son's age as 18. By obtaining the father's name Henry's supposed age was cross-referenced with census records. These were recorded by head of household with occupants and family sublisted below. In the 1860 New York census Aaron Bull of Huron was listed as head of household with a son named Henry. The given age was 14, fully solidifying Henry being 18 in 1864. Whenever viewing photographs it is best to realize they are just a starting point, and cannot always stand on their own merit.[38]

Utilizing a variety of different research tools, it is the author's contention that a much larger number of minors served in the Union Army than either Dr. Gould or Kilmer believed. Both of their reports included all soldiers below age 18, but because my research dealt only with the youngest who served the maximum age of 16 was chosen. For example, Ohio furnished some 313,180 soldiers to the Army, this total being the third largest number credited to any Northern state during the war.[39] Using muster rolls prepared in book form by the state of Ohio in the 1880s, the ages of more than 300,000 names were inspected.[40] These rolls represent 230 regiments, 26 independent artillery batteries, five independent companies of cavalry, several companies of sharpshooters and a few other organizations credited to West Virginia and Kentucky.[41] A listing of soldiers aged 16 and

Although he looks younger, farmer Henry A. Bull actually was 18 at the time of his January 1864 enlistment in Company A, 9th New York Heavy Artillery. Image by photographer C.H. Ravell, Wolcott, New York.

Author's Collection

A mere 10 weeks after mustering into Company C, 32nd Maine, Private Henry C. Houston's field service ended at Cold Harbor, Virginia. On June 3, 1864, he was shot in the right thigh and discharged for disability nine months later.

The Thirty-Second Maine Regiment of Infantry Volunteers

lower was tabulated from the 300,000-plus entries. The number of soldiers listed at age 16 was 1,023; at 15 – 207; at 14 – 79; at 13 – 41; at 12 – 11; at 11 – one; and at age 10, six. No one nine years old or below was recorded. The combined number of all under 16 officially recorded represents a tiny fraction of Ohio's manpower contribution. The percentage, although small, still contains 1,368 soldiers two years or more under age that served from the Buckeye State alone. The rosters mention none below age 10, even though there *were* some younger, and list hundreds as 18 that are known to be under age. An example is Albert C. White of Company D, 64th Ohio. Listed in his company descriptive book as being 18, he actually was nine years and one month old when he enlisted December 14, 1861. In Company G of the 32nd Ohio, not one soldier in the roster is listed as being under 18, yet William T. Dollison is quoted in the regiment's history as stating "there were but ten or twelve who were old enough to raise even the slightest beard; many of them were boys from fourteen to sixteen years of age — plucky, manly boys." The same can be said of Company K's official roster, in spite of which regimental historian Ebenezer Z. Hays wrote: "Samuel Crawford was the youngest soldier of the company, being less than fifteen years old when mustered. Quite a number who appear on the rolls as being eighteen were in fact from one to two years younger." [42] After examining hundreds of records and scanning scores of regimentals, it can be deduced that most every regiment, from every Northern state, possessed underage soldiers who were listed erroneously as being of age. Veterans were well aware of the fact and discussed the matter freely.

Henry Houston was one of a sizeable number of boy soldiers that wrote regimental histories after the war. Henry was born July 26, 1847. His age legally

would have kept him out of the service for the war's duration, but from the first day of conflict he desired to be a soldier. After twice being rejected he finally was accepted at age 16 for muster in the 32nd Maine in March 1864. Many late-war regimental rosters are filled with young soldiers who enlisted as the strain on manpower escalated. Henry wrote of the phenomenon:

One characteristic which presented itself to the attention at first glance was the great preponderance in the ranks [of the 32nd Maine] of very young men — boys in their teens, as many of them were. The legal military age was between eighteen and forty-five, and as a matter of course, upon enlistment papers and muster rolls, none were represented as being less than the minimum age, except in the case of one or two of the musicians — drummers, about whom there was not so particular inquiry as to age and physical capacity. But it is at once curious and suggestive to glance over the rolls, and observe how many of the enlisted men had just reached, according to their own statements, the exact age at which the Government would accept their services.

when he and his father, Benjamin F. Milliken, entered the service together. And there were many others in our ranks, who while somewhat older than Comrade Milliken, would yet have never served their country as soldiers if they had waited till they were actually eighteen before enlisting. The collapse of the rebellion, and the end of the necessity for soldiers in the field would have come before they had arrived at that age.[43]

Wilbur F. Hinman of the 65th Ohio also wrote of the preponderance of young soldiers in the closing stages of the conflict:

Under the regulations, which were then more or less adhered to, no person could be received in the military service under the age of eighteen. But there were plenty of boys, whose span of life had not reached the limit of youth, who were crazy to go to the tented field, and many of them managed to slip through the meshes of the net and get in. True, they had to follow the example of Ananias and tell fibs to the recruiting officers, satisfying their consciences with the argument that in such a cause deception was justifiable.

It was the same in the infantry. In the ranks of the Sixty-fourth and Sixty-fifth [Ohio] there were many a fresh, sturdy, rosy lad, the record of whose birth in the big family bible at home was greatly at variance with the figures on the muster roll. When one of these lads wanted to enlist the recruiting officer "sized him up" and if the inspection was satisfactory he winked slyly as the boy gave his age as "Eighteen, sir!" and signed his name to the list. Most of these boys made prime soldiers. They grew and developed rapidly under the fructifying influence of army life. They endured the hardships of the service much better than the average of men above the age of forty. Animated by the fiery enthusiasm and ambition of youth, their courage in battle fairly challenged that of their older comrades.

Later in the war, when the wave of excitement that during the first year swept hundreds of thousands into the

At least one third of the entire number of enlisted men are recorded as being eighteen years of age, while only a very small proportion are shown as being above thirty. Some considerable number range from twenty to twenty-five and thirty, but about every third man is exactly eighteen. This does not apply, however, with so much force to non-commissioned officers as to privates, the former being, as has been said, in many instances men who had already seen some service in other regiments. But among the privates there were unquestionably a considerable number who in claiming to have arrived at the legal age for enlistment, had anticipated the course of events, and "borrowed time" to some extent.

The writer is willing to confess now that he was himself guilty of having "borrowed" something near a year and a half to add enough to actual age to enable him to "pass muster." And he is sure he was by no means the youngest man, or boy, in the regiment, but that there were many who had seen fewer years than himself. Indeed the honor of having been the youngest soldier from the state of Maine who carried a musket, and did duty in the ranks, has for some time past been generally conceded to Edwin C. Milliken of Co. H, who was but a few days more than fourteen

army had spent its force, and enlistments were a little slow, the recruiting officers stretched the regulations and received thousands of these youngsters. We all remember the division of the Twenty-third corps, during the Atlanta campaign, commanded by General [Alvin P.] Hovey. It was composed mostly of new troops from Ohio and Indiana, and contained so many below the age of eighteen that the division was known as Hovey's babies.[44]

In mid-June 1864 General Hovey was transferred to command the Department of Indiana and given the task of overseeing recruitment of 10,000 soldiers. He succeeded in this assignment by seeking only unmarried men. It was this group of recruits that was referred to as "Hovey's babies," many of them being underage.[45]

Not only did new regiments full of youngsters go to the field in 1864 like the 32nd Maine, a considerable number of older ones upon returning home for veteran furlough replenished their ranks with minors as well. John Arbuckle related how the furloughs helped in his decision to join the Army:

The immediate effect of the presence of these men from the field of war among the people at home, relating their experiences of campaigns and battles, was to fire the spirit of the boys, who in the meantime had come to the years of 16 to 18; thus they were instrumental in bringing to the colors large contingents of new recruits; which were specially needed at this time as the quotas of a 500,000 call were being made up, soon to be followed by another

500,000 call in July, and again a 300,000 call in December, making a total of 1,300,000 men called to the colors in less than 8 months of 1864.

In order to make up these quotas of this first 500,000 call of 1864, with a view to avoiding conscription, about anything that would fill a rank by way of enlistment was being accepted. The recruits received on this call, while the veterans were home on furlough, were designated as Veteran Recruits.

Like many other lads of only 16 or 17 years, I was taken with the fever to enlist. Others of my chums were enlisting. Not deeming it wise to take the matter up with my parents, one blustery March morning, after the farm chores were all done, I mounted my good saddle horse, and set across the prairies a distance of 14 miles to Clarinda, our country town, and on arrival made a bee line for the recruiting office; was promptly accepted and sworn in as a soldier in the United States Army, Company K, Fourth Iowa Veteran Volunteer Infantry, March 26, 1864.[46]

Throughout the war underage recruits were accepted and at times eagerly sought. The list will never be complete of all who served for the various reasons already stated. Whenever new exploration of records begins a true answer to just how many underage soldiers really fought seems farther away. Despite regulations, general orders, surgeons' standards and whims, and the objections of parents, there was an abundance of youth that went forward into the ranks of blue. They all wanted to join the Army.

CHAPTER 2

'My mind was made up,
and I was bound to enlist'

Few single events in history galvanized a nation as did the April 1861 firing upon Fort Sumter. Every newspaper and voice in the land heralded the action. Like wild fire, battle reports swept through cities, towns and villages within days. The offense of their Southern countrymen ignited disdain in the North that led to a searing desire for vengeance. Calls to arms and patriotic speeches kindled hateful fervor in the populace that was unquenchable. Within three days of the Sumter bombardment President Abraham Lincoln issued a proclamation calling out 75,000 militiamen for three months. A stampede of volunteers soon swamped recruitment stands to the extent that thousands were turned away. In May, Lincoln appealed for another 42,000 three-year troops as well. Again volunteers appeared in droves, many fearing they would miss the war if not prompt in going. All the while martial music rent the air, orators aroused spirited action, clergymen pronounced blessings, parades filled the streets and people prepared for war. Times were exciting and anxiety-filled for young boys who witnessed the clamor. Few would ever forget where they were or what they were doing when news came.[1]

"I remember clearly the morning of this memorable 12th of April," recalled Elbridge J. Copp of Nashua, New Hampshire, who soldiered at 16. "I was standing at one of the counters of my brother's store folding the morning papers when the telegraph wires flashed over the country and over the world the news of the firing upon Fort Sumter, the opening guns of the war. My brother Charles was standing behind the opposite counter, my uncle Elbridge P. Brown was sitting near the old coal stove reading the paper. Several customers, too, I think, were in the store and all as by a flash of lightning were stirred to the highest pitch of excitement, my Uncle Brown remarking, 'We are going to have a terrible war.' I was scarcely able to continue my work, and with a feeling incident to youth I inwardly rejoiced, and was at once filled with a determination to have a part in it."[2]

War's proposition had many different effects on youngsters. At first, George T. Ulmer saw opportunity in the fast-moving events. "When Fort Sumter was bombarded I was a midget of a boy, a barefooted, ragged newsboy in the city of New York. The bombardment was threatened for several weeks before it actually occurred; and many nights I would have been bankrupted, but that everyone was on the *qui vive* for the event, and I got myself into lots of trouble by shouting occasionally, 'Fort Sumter Bombarded!' I needed money; it sold my papers and I forgave myself. When the authentic news did come, I think it stirred up within me as big a piece of fighting desire as it did in larger and older people. I mourned the fact that I was then too small to fight, but lived in hopes that the war would last until I should grow. If I could have gone south, I felt that I could have conquered the rebellious faction alone, so confident was I of my fighting abilities." [3]

"When Sumter was fired on April 12, 1861, I was excited," wrote Charles W. Bardeen of Fitchburg, Massachusetts, who enlisted at 14. "I remember walking up and down the sitting room, puffing out my breast as though the responsibility rested on my poor little shoulders, shaking my fist at the South, and threatening her with dire calamities which I thought some of inflicting on her myself." Charles began to ready for the fight, yet was unsure how to proceed as events swirled around him. "I joined the Orange County grammar school and took fencing lessons. As men began to enlist I wished I were older. I don't know why I did not happen to think of getting in as a drummer boy; perhaps because I didn't know how to drum or have any means of learning, though as I afterward discovered, that was no obstacle.

A Little Fifer's War Diary

Charles Bardeen sent this photograph to his mother after mustering as a drummer. Describing himself as "conceited, boastful, self willed and disobedient," he was nearly sent to a reform school before joining the Army.

"At last there came a possible chance. Captain John F. Appleton, of the 12th Maine in the brigade Gen. Butler was recruiting to the distress of Gov. Andrew, was a cousin of my mother's second husband and promised to try to enlist me in his company. So on Dec. 3, 1861 I went to Lowell, and was taken by the captain to Gen. Butler's tent. 'This boy is rather young,' the captain said, 'but he is healthy and strong and intelligent, and I should like to have him in my company.' Gen. Butler was writing at a table and did not look up till just as the captain finished. One squinting glance was enough. 'Take the damn little snipe away,' he said; 'we've got babies enough in this brigade already.'

"But six months later I had better luck. A second cousin of mine was sent home from the front as a recruiting sergeant, and I went down to Boston to see him. He arranged the matter for me at once, and said I could learn to drum after I was enlisted. He even tried to enter me as a private to be detailed as a drummer, so that I could draw thirteen dollars a month instead of twelve. I had to undergo a medical inspection which I thought rather severe, taking off all my clothes and having among other tests to jump, to be sure I was sound in wind and limb; but I passed it, and on July 21, 1862, I became a Massachusetts soldier, assigned as musician to Co. D of the 1st Massachusetts Infantry." [4]

Commodore Perry Byam immediately thought of drumming to gain admission as a soldier. He had been drumming for a few years before the war and actually

Leaving home for Army service could be an emotionally trying experience, as depicted in the December 19, 1863, issue of *Harper's Weekly*.

Author's Collection

was quite cocky about his aptitude. Perry explained: "The sound of the drum entranced me. ... In about the year 1859, while we were living in Mt. Vernon, Iowa, I was given a drum; and guided by the instructions of a drummer of the neighborhood soon became very proficient, and in the troubled days just preceding the war, was in great demand as a drummer at all public gatherings; greatly to my own personal vanity, and the undisguised envy of all my boy associates. But when later, in my first uniform cap and short waterproof cape I marched with my drum at the head of a column of torchbearing 'Wideawakes,' I felt myself indeed to be the 'whole show' beyond the question of a doubt.

"From the first news of the firing on Fort Sumter, my ambition centered itself in the desire to become a soldier. No war governor of that period was troubled with more anxiety, or employed more actively at this time than myself. This indeed was my busy season; early and late I could be found where I was most in the way; volunteering much advice and 'drumming' upon the slightest provocation. Finally my tenacious persistency was rewarded, and I was permitted to enlist. Then followed a season of most harrowing doubt. Would I pass muster? The day arrived; I stood expectantly in the ranks, receiving in great seriousness the jocular advice of my older comrades. One counseled me to stand out of sight immediately behind the drum, and thus get passed; another advised that I stand on a sheet of paper, and by that means increase my height; with many other suggestions of a like nature. My turn came at last, my name was called, and answered to by myself with an outward assumption of great confidence, but with many secret misgivings. The mustering officer without seeming to notice me checked off my name and passing on, left me to my unbounded joy, a real sol-

Garbed in military attire, the lad below showed his patriotic zeal with an American flag.

Author's Collection

dier. This occurred on August 22, 1862, when I was exactly nine years and ten months old." Perry indeed was mustered without much difficulty into Company D, 24th Iowa. He declined to point out that his father, Eber C. Byam, was colonel of the regiment. [5]

Throughout the war's first months newly-formed regiments were quickly organized and sent to the front. As each group hastened off, sorrowful farewell scenes were acted out by family members and loved ones. Drummer boys who considered themselves lucky enough to be a part of the adventure were indelibly impressed. "The happiest day of my life, I think,

Schoolboys like these photographed in 1862 at the New London, Connecticut, Hill Street Public School were easily recruited by trusted teachers turned soldiers as they aged sufficiently.

Author's Collection

was when I donned my blue uniform and received my new drum," wrote William Bircher, who enlisted in Company K of the 2nd Minnesota at age 15. He elaborated:

Now, at last, after so many efforts, I was really a full-fledged drummer, and going south to do and die for my country if need be. October 14 [1861] we embarked on steamboats and proceeded down the [Mississippi] river to St. Paul, where we disembarked at the upper landing and marched through the city. Here we found the streets crowded with people waving their handkerchiefs; the band played, the flags waved, and the boys cheered back, and the young men brought their sweethearts in their carriages and fell in line with the dusty procession. Even the old people became much excited. As we passed they gave three cheers for the Union forever, and stood waving their hats after us

until we were hid from sight. We found the city ablaze with bunting, and so wrought up with excitement that all thought of work had been given up for that day. As we formed in line and marched down the main street towards the river, the sidewalks were everywhere crowded with people, with boys who wore red, white and blue neckties, and boys who wore fatigue hats; with girls who carried flags, and girls who carried flowers; with women who waved their handkerchiefs, and old men who waved their walking sticks, while here and there, as we passed along, at windows and door-ways were faces red with long weeping, for Johnny was off to the war, and maybe mother, sisters and sweethearts would never see him again. Drawn up in line on the lower levee, awaiting the steamboat from the upper landing, there was scarcely a man, woman or child in that great crowd around us but had to pass up for a last shake of hands, a last goodbye, and a last "God bless you, boys!" And so, amid cheering and hand-shaking and flag-waving, the steamboat came floating down the stream and we were off, with the band playing the "Star Spangled Banner." [6]

During those early days it was relatively easy for underage hopefuls to gain admission to the ranks. Many young boys already were established as musicians in dozens of Zouave and militia companies popular throughout the North. When groups enlisted together as a unit, young drummers scooted along on their shirttails. War's horrors had not yet been experienced, so numerous parents did not object as their little ones stepped off leading parades while smartly beating their drums.

Among the first youngsters enlisted during the conflict was William O'Meara, who had belonged to a pre-war Zouave organization. William enlisted as a drummer April 13, 1861, at 11 years and eight months old, in the 5th Battalion District of Columbia Volunteers. His enlistment papers state he was 12 and stood four foot four. In an interview years later he declared: "I was not quite twelve years old but when the muster officer came around the captain told [me] to say I was twelve years old. When I went up to enlist the officer told me to go home, but I wouldn't go. On the next day I was made drillmaster of the company. I had belonged to a Zouave company of boys raised when [Elmer] Ellsworth went through the country, and I knew something about it." When asked if he saw any service, William responded, "Some; I was the first United States soldier — that is, volunteer soldier — who put his foot on Virginia soil. Our company was organized for the defense of the District. We were on duty at the Long Bridge [spanning the Potomac River]. Word came to guard the Virginia end of the bridge, as the report was that the 'rebs' were going to burn the bridge. Our company volunteered to go over, and we went. Boy-like, I ran ahead of them, and was first to reach the other side." He further described his time upriver near Seneca, Maryland, where two Germans of the battalion were killed. He believed they were the first volunteers to die in the war. Asked if he reenlisted after his three-month term was completed, William said, "No, no; my mother collared me and sent me away to school." [7]

Companies and regiments formed at that time often were recruited from small localities. Officers generally were well-known businessmen, politicians or schoolteachers. In such positions they already had earned trust and respect which helped them spur enlistments. Commissions were issued on condition the officer could recruit and enlist a company. At first this was a relatively easy task, but as time passed enlistments lagged and the job became unenviable. Teachers and clergymen possessed an advantage obtaining recruits, having had contact with many young men in

Karl Sundstrom Collection

Colonel Alexander D. Adams, 27th New York.

their professions. As principal of Lyons Academy in Lyons, New York, Alexander D. Adams recruited a company comprised mostly of students from his school for the 27th New York. The muster rolls for Captain Adams' Company B show 39 percent under age 20. Adams was only 28 when he became colonel of the regiment in 1862.

Reverend James H. Perry, who left the pulpit to take up the sword, organized the 48th New York. At the outbreak of war he was the highly respected pastor of Pacific Street Methodist Evangelical Church in Brooklyn. Many of the regiment's officers were ministers, and it was said the boys from their congregations gained parental consent to enlist because their captains were Christian gentlemen. It was well known to all who applied for enlistment that the regiment was seeking only "high-toned," moral young men. To obtain such a class of soldiers, recruiters not only visited area churches, they also placed advertisements in the *New York Christian Advocate.* Many who came forward were even asked to bring letters of recommendation from their churches. Company D was recruited by Captain Daniel C. Knowles, a language instructor and clergyman at a Pennington, New Jersey, seminary. Many of the recruits were pulled from the school when Captain Knowles stated his intention of serving under Colonel Perry. Company D's personnel soon were called the "Die-No-Mores" because of a Christian song containing those words they constantly sang. In the regiment's ranks was quite a number of underage soldiers, the "baby" being Abraham J. Pal-

U.S. Army Military History Institute

Colonel James H. Perry, 48th New York

mer of Company D, who wrote the 48th's history. Due to the regiment's religious affiliations the nickname "Perry's Saints" clung to the 48th through the war.[9]

Oscar L. Jackson had just finished teaching at Side Hill Academy #5 in Hocking County, Ohio, and returned home to Pennsylvania when the Fort Sumter bombardment took place. After unsuccessfully seeking a commission in his native state he went back to Ohio and obtained a recruiting permit. In Hocking County Jackson used his influence as a teacher to sign up 85 individuals for his company. Only 20 years of age, he relied heavily on his former students enlisting and recalled, "The schools in which I had been teaching the preceding years had more than the usual number of large boys and they furnished quite a large squad of recruits of the very best material for good soldiers to start the proposed company. They were also helpful in securing other recruits. By this time the first excitement of enlisting had passed and it was slow, difficult work to enlist men for three years' service." Through diligence, Jackson completed organization of his company and was elected captain of Company H, 63rd Ohio.[10]

Corporal Isaac Jarvis, right, was one of five siblings that served in the Union Army. He and younger brother Simon were recruited by their former teacher, Captain Oscar L. Jackson, for Company H, 63rd Ohio. On October 4, 1862, in the battle of Corinth, Mississippi, Isaac received two gunshot wounds — one below an eye and the other in the neck. He was killed instantly, buried on the field and later interred in Corinth's national cemetery, Section B, Grave 30. The same day Jackson, while in charge of a skirmish line, also suffered two wounds — including a gunshot to the face. The ball entered near his right eye and lodged in the frontal bone, remaining there for the rest of his life.

Author's Collection

Civil War recruiting officers constantly faced pressure from superiors to find more soldiers. They were sent into cities, villages and the countryside to glean the best possible crop. Recruiting parties usually consisted of one lieutenant, one non-commissioned officer, two privates, and a drummer and fifer. All supplies were distributed through the Adjutant General's office, which oversaw recruitment. The task of keeping accurate records for each recruit was monumental. Thirty-one different forms were inventoried to help overburdened recruiting staff; however, responsibility for rejecting or accepting recruits was left solely to the officer. They repeatedly were cautioned not to accept underage recruits giving false information. But many officers' commissions were riding on the number of enlistments obtained, and it is easy to understand their inducement to accept youthful recruits in spite of the warnings.[11]

On August 8, 1862, 16-year-old William H. Albee enlisted in the 18th Connecticut. Hiding his true age he wrote 18 when signing the declaration of recruit form on his enlistment paper. To complete his enrollment he needed the parental consent form filled out. Because neither of William's parents were present recruiting officer Samuel R. Knapp signed it as guardian. The five foot three inch teenager had fooled no one, but he was needed. To bypass regulations, Knapp finished the rest of the form but declined to state the recruit's age. By leaving it blank the lieutenant added a name to the rolls without jeopardizing his commission if William's real age became an issue. For Albee, who also used the alias William Webb, it never did and he was mustered the same day.[12]

Musicians were especially important to recruiting details, having the responsibility of invoking patriotic fervor by playing. Good recruiting officers made grand appearances as they entered towns accompanied

On June 5, 1864, near Piedmont, Virginia, William H. Albee of Company I, 18th Connecticut, was severely wounded by a minié ball above the left ear. Following nearly a year of hospitalization he returned to the ranks, but was forever plagued with memory loss and numbness to the side of his head.

Brian Boeve Collection

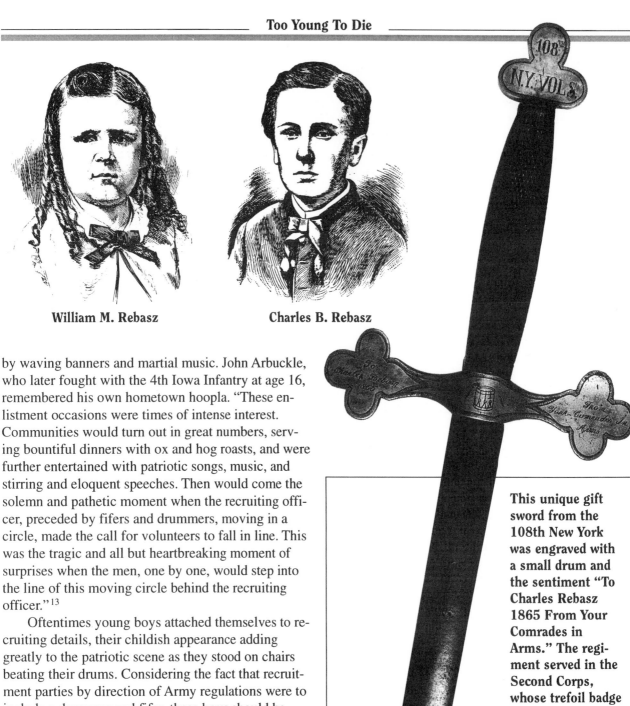

William M. Rebasz   Charles B. Rebasz

by waving banners and martial music. John Arbuckle, who later fought with the 4th Iowa Infantry at age 16, remembered his own hometown hoopla. "These enlistment occasions were times of intense interest. Communities would turn out in great numbers, serving bountiful dinners with ox and hog roasts, and were further entertained with patriotic songs, music, and stirring and eloquent speeches. Then would come the solemn and pathetic moment when the recruiting officer, preceded by fifers and drummers, moving in a circle, made the call for volunteers to fall in line. This was the tragic and all but heartbreaking moment of surprises when the men, one by one, would step into the line of this moving circle behind the recruiting officer."[13]

Oftentimes young boys attached themselves to recruiting details, their childish appearance adding greatly to the patriotic scene as they stood on chairs beating their drums. Considering the fact that recruitment parties by direction of Army regulations were to include a drummer and fifer, these boys should be credited with serving their country as well as those who went to the front. Recruitment Form #11, enumerating a recruitment party's monthly strength, provided a space pre-printed "Boys learning music."[14] With that in mind, the youngest known boy who served the Union during the war was William M. Rebasz of Rochester, New York.

In 1861 William and his older brother Charles decided to learn to play snare drums in order to aid recruiting efforts. When President Lincoln issued his

This unique gift sword from the 108th New York was engraved with a small drum and the sentiment "To Charles Rebasz 1865 From Your Comrades in Arms." The regiment served in the Second Corps, whose trefoil badge was incorporated into the hilt's design.

Author's Collection

call for more volunteers in 1862 they were both very good drummers. At that time they offered their services to recruiting officers of the 108th New York — Charles being 10 years old and William just five. Although very young the boys eagerly were sought as musicians at recruiting tents pitched in front of the courthouse and at war meetings held in Monroe County. William's father was opposed to his going, but soon was persuaded by the little chaps to give his consent. During the regiment's recruitment the boys, with drums almost as big as themselves, were placed on wooden chairs or in church pulpits to play the instruments as an inducement for men to enlist.[15] After the 108th New York returned home in 1865, its veterans showed their appreciation to the boys by presenting them with engraved swords.

Ten-year-old Gilbert Vanzant also began his military career drumming at enlistment rallies. His transition from schoolboy to soldier was recorded years later by a Chicago newspaperman:

In the summer of 1862 a certain Lieutenant [Cyrus] Ellwood[16] came with a six-mule team and three or four soldiers, recruiting for the army, into the little country town of Port William in Clinton County, Ohio. A bright little fellow by the name of Gilbert Van Zandt [sic], a native of this place, volunteered to drum for him at the soldiers' meeting held in the old brick school-house, and at its close the lieutenant tossed him a fifty cent piece, the first money the boy ever earned. He then was taken over the country by Captain [George B.] Hicks to drum for recruits, and, imagining that a soldier's life was a continuous succession of such pleasant duties, he enlisted Aug. 6, 1862, with Company D, 79th Ohio Volunteer Infantry, as its drummer. At that time he was 10 years, 7 months and 16 days old, the date of his birth being December 20, 1851. The enlistment of the little fellow was, after all, not such a cruel thing as might be supposed. His recruiting service had served as an easy transition to army life. His schoolteacher enlisted at the same time and was soon promoted to the captaincy of Company H. In addition with "Little Gib," as he was called, marched away twenty young men of the neighborhood, true friends, his ideals of manhood, whose departure, if he had been left behind in the little depopulated Ohio village, would have rendered him more genuinely homesick than he ever was among familiar faces in the army. Then too he was engaged in the most delightful task in the world, and one at which he was adept — drumming. He drummed in the regimental band as well as in the field, and so became the pet and pride of the entire regiment.... Young as he was there was no better or more faithful soldier in Sherman's Army.

Gilbert afterward recalled the schoolhouse scene when his teacher announced to the class his intention of entering the Army. "Previous to my enlistment I was going to school, my teacher being A.H. Botkin.

He also enlisted, being made first lieutenant of our company. Later he was promoted to the captaincy of Company H of the regiment. After his enlistment he was telling the scholars he was going to war and perhaps would never see them again. He had them all crying. Turning in my seat and looking at a little girl sitting behind me who also was in tears, I said to her, 'If my father goes to war I am going with him.' In an angry voice she said, 'I don't care if you do.'"

Gilbert's father, John Vanzant, enlisted in Company D, and as the boy proclaimed to his classmate he joined, too. Gilbert's mother never intended her 10-year-old son to go off to war. She and her husband thought it harmless fun for him to run around with the recruiters, beating his drum to everyone's amazement, and most insisted he was doing good by provoking enlistments. Mrs. Vanzant even made a uniform for him to wear. When he began talking of going with the men to camp both parents assumed his yearnings soon would fade. Still, he was allowed to enlist at the beginning of August with the others and embark for Camp Dennison near Cincinnati, where the regiment was being formed. Even then the officers thought it best not to have him mustered in case he decided he wanted to return home. Finally, after a number of weeks had passed, all, including his father, were in agreement that he intended to stay. He was mustered on October 31, 1862. His mother, reflecting on the occurrence, was recorded as saying, "War times make folks do funny things, and they stole him from me, really, his father and the rest, and took him to Camp Dennison, and then, first thing I knew he was enlisted." Gilbert proved he was equal to the task, serving through the war and earning a reputation as a fine young man and soldier. He ranks as one of the youngest to complete a three-year enlistment term.[17]

Stanton P. Allen, who later served with the 1st Massachusetts Cavalry, recalled a situation at school that nearly led to confrontation. In April 1861 Stanton was a 12-year-old student living on his family's farm near Berlin, New York. He was immediately afflicted with war fever and constantly thought of becoming a soldier. Then, his chum and hired farmhand Nathaniel Bass decided to enlist. Stanton wished to go but was persuaded to stay home by his friend. During the spring of 1862 Bass was discharged as the cavalry unit to which he belonged was disbanded. As a token of friendship Bass presented his jacket and cap to Stanton, who wore them to school the following term. He remembered:

I was the proudest boy in the Brimmer district at the opening of school the next winter. I fairly "paralyzed" the teacher, George Powell, and all the scholars, when I marched in wearing Nat's cavalry jacket and forage cap. I was the lion of the day. The jacket fitted me like a sentry box, but the girls voted the rig "perfectly lovely." Half a dozen big boys threatened to punch my eyes out if I did not "leave that ugly old jacket at home." I enjoyed the notoriety, and continued to wear the jacket. But one day Jim Duffy ... came into the school with an artillery jacket on. It was of the same pattern as the jacket I wore, but had red trimmings in place of yellow. The girls decided that Jim's jacket was the prettier. I made up my mind to challenge Jim at the afternoon recess, but my anger moderated as I heard one of the small girls remark:

"But Jim ain't got no sojer cap, so he ain't no real sojer — he's only a make-b-lief."

"Sure enough!" chorused the girls.

Then I expected Duffy to challenge me, but he did not, and there was no fight.[18]

A primary concern for parents was that their boys would be well taken care of by those who shouldered that responsibility. Joseph B. Parsons was given such a task while captain of Company C, 10th Massachusetts. During the spring of 1861 he encountered a small lad at Northampton, where Parsons was recruiting his company. The boy desired to fill a drummer's vacancy and let his wishes be known to the captain, who quickly remarked, "What can you do? You could not take a twenty-eight-inch step to save your life, and besides, your parents will not let you go to war."

"But I can drum," replied the hopeful lad. He finally was told to come back the next day, which he did, bringing his mother with him. The boy then was asked to play his drum and step off. Parsons was surprised that he hit 30 inches every step. Passing the test and with his mother's consent, 14-year-old Myron P. Walker was made drummer of Company C. His mother approached the captain and said, "We give him into your charge."

The years slipped by and the 10th Massachusetts returned home at the close of its three-year enlistment. Captain Parsons had risen to lieutenant colonel, but never once forgot his promise to care for the boy. As the regiment enjoyed a welcoming party, the colonel made his way through the crowd to the side of Walker's mother, now a widow, who was at that moment embracing Myron for the first time, and said, "I re-

In 1888 Myron P. Walker, shown at left in 1861, was elected commander of the Massachusetts Department, Grand Army of the Republic, and appointed Colonel Joseph B. Parsons, his first wartime captain, to his staff. "Can't you hear him kicking when he did not like his orders?" Myron asked at a regimental reunion. "But I simply reminded him that for three years I was obliged to obey him, and assured him that for one year I proposed to make it as pleasant for him as he made it for me."

The Tenth Regiment Massachusetts Volunteer Infantry, 1861-1864

member your charge; he has been a good boy and we have brought him safely back to you."[19]

Loren S. Tyler wrote of a similar promise made by William W. Belknap, who finished the war a brevet major general. "When Major Belknap was home recruiting for the [15th Iowa] Regiment in the summer of 1862, he enlisted a boy in Keokuk named Darby Graley, who entered Company F; afterwards became his orderly, and with Private Clements [Finley D. Clemmons] of the 11th Iowa, as another orderly, followed his fortunes and clung to him faithfully to the end of the war. They were both daring boys, full of adventure, splendid foragers and thoroughly fearless. When Darby was marching in the street at Keokuk to the boat which was to carry him south, his mother, a respectable old Irish lady, rushed from the sidewalk, seized him, objected to his going, said that he was not eighteen years of age, and that he could not and should not go. Major Belknap remonstrated; told her that Darby had sworn that he was eighteen, and that the oath he had taken was, under the law, conclusive as to his age. But she was inexorable, and demanded her boy.

"Major Belknap, rather than take Darby by force, told her of the honorable character of a soldier's service, of the applause that would greet her son when he returned from the war, and of her patriotic duty in the matter, and said that he would personally see that her son was cared for. This last promise caused her to relent. Raising her hands and blessing both the major and the boy, she said: 'God bless you Darby and good bye. Stay by the major Darby! Stay by the major, and you will never get hurted.'

"Darby did stay by the major. He braved countless dangers and lived through the war, but lost his life in Colorado — killed by the Indians."[20]

In June 1865 General William W. Belknap posed with orderlies Finley D. Clemmons, 11th Iowa, and Darby Graley, 15th Iowa. After the war Belknap became Secretary of War in the Grant administration.

U.S. Army Military History Institute

James Martin was another boy who earlier accompanied Belknap to Tennessee. Although not mustered, he went along privately employed to help with the major's needs. At the battle of Shiloh on April 6, 1862, "Jim" became excited and, grabbing a musket, rushed to the ranks and fought with the men all day.[21]

Such careful attention bestowed upon youngsters by officers and others was repeated throughout the war. To older men the sight of a lad marching alongside swelled memories of home and those left behind. These thoughts invoked courage and a sense of duty during trying times by reminding them of what they were fighting for. Between assaults during the 1864 battle of Peachtree Creek in Georgia, Captain John Speed of the U.S. Regulars observed General John Newton sitting on a log with musician Gilbert Vanzant perched on his knee.[22] Many of the younger boys like 10-year-old Gilbert were called "pets" by the men. On numerous occasions they were given special treatment; they reciprocated by being "bright spots" in a tumultuous world.

Determined to become a soldier, store clerk Elbridge Copp bargained with both recruiting officer and his father to obtain admission. Eventually an understanding was reached between the two men about how the boy was to be treated. Copp recalled: "In Nashua, New Hampshire, James F. Randlett was commissioned to raise a company for the 3rd regiment, and had set up a recruiting office in the old armory, the attic of the City Hall building, and to Captain Randlett I made known my purpose to enlist in his company, if I could get the consent of my father. He thought I was rather young and small for a soldier, not quite up to the standard in age, nor feet and inches. I was fully determined to go, and was not long in persuading Captain Randlett that I could be of service to him in the capacity of clerk, if not in the ranks. I was then in a position to approach my father to secure his consent to the enlistment. At first it was a flat refusal. To him it was absurd, that a boy of my age should go into the army. He finally gave his consent, however, upon the condition that I should go as a clerk to the captain of the company, and with the understanding that I was not to be in the ranks in the event of a battle. I do not know what pledges were made, but I remember well the promise of the captain to my father that he would be my friend and protector."[23]

Colonel J.L. Kirby Smith of the 43rd Ohio made a like promise to Michael Kelly when enlisting his 16-year-old son Matthias at Mount Vernon, Ohio, late in 1861. After Matthias became ill the following summer and was sent to numerous hospitals to recover, his father began losing hope and wrote to Colonel Smith, reminding him of their bargain.

Mt. Vernon, Ohio Aug. 12, 1862

Dear Sir & Col.

I hope you will excuse the liberty I take to write to you but when you must know my feelings in regard to my son's afflictions who is now in the hospital you can no doubt give these lines proper attention, and I then have no fears but that you will do your best to comply.

You will please remember that when you were about to leave Mt. Vernon you assured me that if my boy (Matthias) was disabled or any thing happened to him you would send him home.

Now Dear Colonel will you make good your promise and send him at once if it can be done and if it cannot be at the expense of the government I will remit it myself.

Yours truly, Michael Kelly

Colonel Smith was not able to keep his promise, being mortally wounded in the battle of Corinth. Matthias spent three months recuperating before returning to duty. Tragically, on May 31, 1864, near Dallas, Georgia, he was wounded in camp by a musket's accidental discharge. The costly error claimed his life two weeks later.[24]

After John Dearborn Walker's half-brother enlisted in the 22nd Wisconsin, John traipsed to camp almost daily to watch the soldiers. He was born January 3, 1851, and was only 11 years old in the late summer of 1862. Standing four feet three inches, he was not considered an ideal recruit. But as he visited camp he became acquainted with many of the men, which fostered his thoughts of becoming a soldier himself. At home one night he tried to convince his parents to let him enlist, but his mother was adamant her boy should stay home. After a few days of his begging Mrs. Walker went to the 22nd's camp with hopes of persuading Colonel William L. Utley to discourage his intentions. Instead of agreeing with her cause, Utley stated that John was determined to go with the regiment and advised her to consent, rather than have the boy run away and enlist with strangers. He added that he felt John would tire of soldiering and become homesick before the regiment reached Chicago, and would want to return to Racine. Convinced by Utley's logic, she signed the consent form and John was mustered into the 22nd Wisconsin on September 1, 1862. In spite of the colonel's prognostication, he became even more content as time passed.[25]

The flow of excited volunteers eventually subsid-

David Wood, Company A, 6th Missouri Cavalry, wore unauthorized shoulder straps for this tintype portrait. In June 1862 he displayed budding business acumen: "I secured a cask of fresh water and some lemon extract and started making lemonade and selling it to the soldiers. The venture was so profitable that I made enough to buy some real lemons for a second batch. From this beginning I developed a sutler's outfit that made me in the neighborhood of $2,000 while I was in the army. Finding there was a great demand for small delicacies, I loaded up with everything I could think of that the men would buy. One of the generals from the main army loaned me an ambulance for the outfit, and soon I was handling quite a business. Among other things, I changed bills for the men, who allowed me twenty-five cents for changing a five- or ten-dollar bill. This was robbery, of course, but was allowed throughout the army until Lincoln printed small bills, called 'shin plasters,' for change."

Courtesy of James C. Frasca

ed as the conflict's terrible sting began touching Northern homes. Defeat at Bull Run in July 1861 eradicated all thoughts of a short and glorious war. Three-month regiments returned home, but with fewer numbers. Grief replaced cheers. Newspapers detailing great battles with casualty lists attached sobered the populace by bringing unwanted news to every door. The war had become personal for those left behind. Although enlistments continued, recruiting details were increased as the need for more soldiers was realized through late 1861 and early 1862. While the Army clamored for more men, many parents not wanting their loved ones to perish refused permission. Some families were strained in the pull between "duty to the cause" and duty to themselves. For others there was no question. "The Union must be preserved!" resounded as fathers and sons alike joined new regiments. Many lads with fathers wearing shoulder straps went along as company or regimental mascots, playing the part of orderlies. Others stood in the ranks side by side with their fathers. A few were even elevated to officer's rank themselves — some on their own merit, others because of family ties.

David Wood was 10 years old when the war broke out. His father Samuel had moved the family from Ohio to Kansas in 1854 to help "Free Staters" keep slavery out of the territory. The elder Wood forged a reputation as the "Fighting Quaker." Growing up surrounded by hostility it was natural for David to feel ready to march off with the troops when his father became lieutenant colonel of the 6th Missouri Cavalry in 1861. Wood's battalion was stationed at Rolla, from where it operated against Confederates in southern Missouri and Arkansas. At Rolla, David repeatedly begged his father to let him go along, but always was denied permission. One day while Colonel Wood was leading his men on a long march miles from headquarters, he noticed a commotion at the column's rear. Turning his white stallion he rode through the ranks, all the while ignoring distractions his men contrived to divert his attention elsewhere. At last he made his way to the rear where David was found riding on a pony, surrounded by a group of admiring soldiers who were using their mounts to conceal the lad. David continued the story:

"He didn't say much to me. I guess he realized he might as well yield to the inevitable. From then on he kept me with him, and on January 1, 1862, at Rolla, I

33

was regularly enlisted. My duties were principally that of an orderly, carrying dispatches here and there and sometimes going where grown men could not go." [26]

Finding one's son on the march or in camp happened more than once to bewildered fathers. Sixteen-year-old Ira Odell broached the subject of becoming a soldier with his father, Henry, in the training camp of the 45th Pennsylvania at Harrisburg. Ira and his best friend shared the adventure by heading to camp together, as described by Odell in this account written in the third person:

One day they learned that on a certain day Captain [Edward G.] Scheiffelin [commanding Company H] would leave Tioga for Camp Curtin with some recruits. So the boys worked until noon and got their dinners and then the problem was how to get to the train. The nearest and best road to take was blocked by both parents living near it. Consequently they started over the old log road and other by-ways for Lawrenceville some six miles away. It was a rush journey for they had only two and a half hours to make the run in. They were some distance from the station when the train pulled in but they managed to get aboard all right and the first man to greet them was the captain himself, who was glad to have the boys along for it would help to fill up his company. It then lacked a number of men of being full. But here something seemed to worry him. The father of one of the boys had already joined the company and was now in camp. But this boy was so anxious to go that the good captain said he would take him along and if the father did not want him to enlist he would send him back home again.

Those were two happy boys who were taken on that afternoon train from Lawrenceville for the capital city of the State as would-be soldiers. The train reached Harrisburg about noon the following day and the order was given, "Fall in!" What did they know about that command? It was soon explained to them and away they marched for Camp Curtin.

The boy whose father was at that very instant on duty near the entrance gate was not thinking that he would so soon see his son come marching into camp, and when he did he was dumbfounded but did not seem angry but urged the boy to go back. But the action of the father made the son braver; so he told his father that he would stay and that he should go home and take care of his mother and the little ones. This settled it and father and son both remained and the next day the two boys were examined and pronounced fit to be shot at, and father and son were soon drilling side by side and learning what soldiering was likely to be. [27]

Years later, Delavan Miller wrote of his own journey and his father's into the Army:

One bright morning in the fall of 1861 a motherless lad of less than thirteen saw his father go away with a company of men that had been recruited for the Morgan Flying Horse Artillery, then being organized at Staten Island in New York harbor. He wanted to go with his father, but the suggestion was not listened to. After the regiment was sent to Virginia, Capt. [Charles H.] Smith of the Carthage Company [H, 2nd New York Heavy Artillery] returned home after more men. He brought a letter to the little lad from his father and, patting the boy on his head, asked him in a joking way how he would like to be a soldier. This gave the boy an opportunity he was wanting, and he pleaded with the officer to take him back with him. The mother was dead, the home broken up; the little fellow argued that he would be better off with his father.

The tender hearted captain sympathized with the boy, but said he did not know what he could do with such a little fellow. The boy would not be put off, however. He had inherited persistency from his Scottish ancestors, and after much importuning the captain said that he did not know how it could be managed, but he would try to take the boy back with him.

In March 1862, when two months past thirteen years old, the one of whom I write started for the war with a squad of recruits in charge of Sergt. Wesley Powell. On that day the boy got up bright and early and went all around among his neighboring playmates and bade them goodbye. Didn't he feel important, though?

Miller and the new recruits boarded a train for New York and the trip south to the regiment. While passing through New Jersey a group of boys from a military school also boarded and took its place in the car near Sergeant Powell. They were clothed in new military-style uniforms and evidently were quite proud of their attire. Powell was dressed in the artillery's regulation uniform with red trim, brass epaulets and a black felt hat. In short time the sergeant motioned the cadets to his side and remarked, "I want to have you meet a little boy who, although he is not in uniform, is going to be a real soldier" — much to Delavan's delight and the awe of the boys.

The following day the squad disembarked and marched the last three miles to a fort outside Washington, where the 2nd New York Heavy Artillery was stationed and engaged in target practice. Delavan recalled that the earth shook and cold chills crept up his back as the party drew near the fort. His father, Loten Miller, had not been notified his son was coming to join him, and consequently was more than surprised

School drill units and other quasi-military organizations flourished in the North for those unable to enlist. The "school of the soldier" as well as drumming techniques were taught. Once trained, cadets like those above marched and entertained during recruitment drives, sanitary fairs and military funerals.

when he saw an officer leading by the hand a lad who he supposed was so far away.

Loten was not a man of many words. "What couldn't be cured must be endured," he sighed as he wiped away a tear and returned to command of his gun. Delavan then sat down on a pile of cannon balls, smelled the burning powder, heard the roar of the guns and wondered if he would not prefer being back in New York.[28]

Not all parents were as easy to convince as Loten Miller, Henry Odell or Colonel Samuel Wood. Many youngsters were kept at home for the duration of hostilities or until they reached the age of majority. Some parents thought they could wait out their sons' enthusiasm until it waned. One lad who shocked his parents

in the end displayed unusual persistency and fortitude until his goal was achieved.

His mother and father were certain George Ulmer, only five feet tall and childish in appearance, would never pass muster. With confidence in their belief they allowed him to try repeatedly to enlist, all the while expecting failure. At war's outbreak George was the New York newsboy slighting customers about the Fort Sumter bombardment. Nine months later he was living on a farm in upstate Maine. "The war grew more and more serious," he explained. "Newspapers were eagerly sought, and every word about the struggle was read over and over again. A new call for troops was made, another and still another, and I was all the time fretting and chaffing in the corn or potato field, be-

35

cause I was so young. I could not work; the fire of patriotism was burning me up. My elder brother had arrived at the age and required size to fit him for service; he enlisted and went to the front. This added new fuel to the flame already within me, and one day I threw down my hoe and declared that I would go to the war! I would join my brother at all hazards. My folks laughed at me and tried to dissuade me from so unwise a step, but my mind was made up, and I was bound to enlist. Enlist I did, when I was only fourteen years of age and extremely small for my years, but I thought I would answer for a drummer boy if nothing else. It was easy enough to enlist, but to get mustered into the service was a different thing. I tried for eight long weeks. I enlisted in my own town, but was rejected. I enlisted in an adjoining town — rejected, and so on for weeks and weeks. But I did not give up."

After being denied locally, George decided to try a new recruiting officer in a town farther away. His parents were unwilling to help in his quest, so he resolved to earn money and buy a horse to make the journey. During free moments he cut "hoop poles" from the local marshes — small birch or alder trees used for hoops on lime casks and worth a halfpenny each. Finally he had a good quantity to sell and piled the poles by the road. A man came along and bought 6,000 for $30, but rejected 9,000 due to their size. " 'Too small?' I exclaimed, 'why there is hardly any difference in them!' But he was buying and I was selling, and under the influence of a boy's anxiety he paid me thirty dollars, which I counted over and over again, and at every count the dollars seemed to murmur, 'A horse, a horse! War! War! To the front! Be a soldier!' I could picture nothing but a soldier's life; I could almost hear the sound of the drums, and almost see the long rows of blue-coated soldiers marching in glorious array with steady step to the music of the band. 'Thirty! Thirty!' I would repeat to myself, but finally concluded thirty dollars wouldn't buy much of a horse, but my heart was set upon it, and there was nothing for me to do but cut more poles."

In time young Ulmer harvested another 4,000 poles, and with the $30 bartered with a farmer for an aged, one-eyed mare, harness and cart. At last he was ready to find a recruiting officer who would take him.

 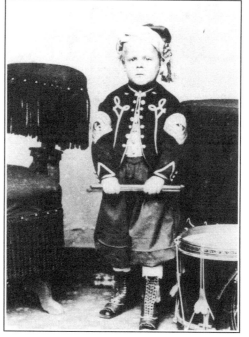

During the war P.T. Barnum's famed New York City museum employed exceptionally talented drummers, and the younger the better. Billed as "the Infant Drummers," Wisconsin native "Major" Willie Bagley, left, and "Master" Allie Turner, both four years old, amused crowds onstage at Barnum's while playing drums half their size.

Author's Collection

It became a customary daily routine for me to harness this poor old animal, start at sundown and drive all night. Where? Why to Augusta to try and get mustered in, but I would always ride back broken hearted and disappointed, my ardor, however, not dampened a bit. I became a guy to my brothers and neighbors. My father and stepsister indulged me in my fancy, helping me all they could, father by furnishing money and my stepsister by putting up little lunches for my pilgrimages during the night. They thought me partially insane, and judged it would soon wear off. But it didn't. I would not give up. The Yankee yearning for a fight had possession of me, and I could neither eat, sleep nor work. I was bound to be a soldier. I prayed for it, and I sometimes thought my prayers were answered, that the war should last till I was big enough to be one and it did.

I had enlisted four times in different towns, and each time I went before a mustering officer I was rejected. 'Too small' I was every time pronounced, but I was not discouraged or dismayed. After several attempts to be mustered into the service at Augusta, which was twenty-five miles from our little farm, I thought I would enlist from the town of Freedom and thereby get before a different mustering officer who was located in Belfast. I had grown, I thought, in the past six weeks, and before a new officer I thought my chances of being accepted would improve; so on a bright morning in September [1863] I mounted my 'gig' behind my little old gray horse, who seemed to say as he turned his head to look at me when I jumped onto the seat, 'What a fool you are, making me haul you all that distance, when you know they won't have you!' But kissing my little stepsister good-bye, with a wave of my hand to father and mother and brothers who stood in the yard and door of the dear old home, I drove away, and as I did so I could see the expressions of ridicule and doubt on their faces, while underneath it all there was a tinge of sadness and fear.

Well, I arrived in Belfast. Instead of driving direct to the stable and hotel, and putting my horse up, I drove direct to the office of the mustering officer. I entered that office like a young Napoleon. I had made up my mind to walk in before the officer very erect and dignified, even to raising myself up on tiptoes. On telling the clerk my errand, he ushered me into an inner office, and imagine my surprise — my consternation — when, swinging around in his chair, I found myself in the presence of the very officer who had rejected me in Augusta so many times.

"Damn it," said he, "will you never let up? Go home to your mother, boy, don't pester me any more. I will not accept you, and let that end it."

I tremblingly told him I had grown since he saw me last, and by the time I was mustered in I would grow some more, and that I would drum and fight if it should prove actually necessary.

Thus I pleaded with him for one full hour. Finally he said, "Well, damned if I don't muster you in just to get rid of you. Sergeant, make out this young devil's papers and let him go and get killed." My heart leaped into my mouth. I tried to thank him, but he would not have it. He hurried me through, and at 5:30 p.m., September 15, 1863, I was a United States soldier.[29] And when I donned that uniform, what a looking soldier! The smallest clothes they issued

> ## My family didn't believe our government would have such a little, ill-dressed soldier. Father said, looking me all over, 'Well, if they have mustered you in, after they see you in that uniform they will muster you out, my boy.'
>
> — George Ulmer

looked on me as if they would make a suit for my entire family, but in spite of the misfit I took them and put them on, with the pants legs rolled up to the knees, and the overcoat dragging on the ground.

Instead of giving the family a surprise, they had heard of my enlisting from the stage driver and I found them all in tears. But when I made my appearance tears changed to laughter, for the sight of me I think was enough to give them hope. They didn't believe our government would have such a little, ill-dressed soldier. Father said, looking me all over, "Well, if they have mustered you in, after they see you in that uniform they will muster you out, my boy."

In about ten days I received orders to report in Augusta. Then the family realized there was more in it than they had first thought, but consoled themselves with the belief that when I reached headquarters I would be found useless, and sent home. I went away, leaving them with that feeling of hope struggling behind their copious tears.

Well, I arrived in Portland, was sent to the barracks with three or four thousand others, was allotted a hard bunk, and then for the first time did I realize what I was doing, what I had committed myself to, and I think if I could have caught that mustering officer I should have appealed to him just as hard to muster me out.[30]

John C. Weber was another who refused to forsake his desire to join the Army. In 1897, while attending a reunion of the Ohio Sherman Brigade, he

narrated his enlistment story to Wilbur Hinman, who was preparing the brigade history.

When Lieutenant [Aaron] Baldwin was recruiting in Akron for the [6th Ohio] battery I wasn't quite seventeen, but I took the war fever and had it bad. I was a runt of a boy, but I made up my mind I was going in that battery. I couldn't see just how I was going to make the riffle, for my father, who kept a hotel in Akron, was dead against it. He wouldn't listen to it for a single minute. But I kept getting warmer and warmer till finally I couldn't stand it any longer. On the 21st of October [1861] I walked into the recruiting office and told Baldwin I wanted to 'list. He asked me how old I was and I said "eighteen last August." I guess Baldwin thought I was lying, but he went through all the red tape, told me to sign my name, and swore me in as a recruit. Of course I never let on at home, and nobody there knew anything about it till the lieutenant started with his men for Mansfield. This was two or three weeks after I enlisted. I thought if I could only give father the slip and get to camp it would be all right. At the time for the company to start I sneaked away from home and joined it at the depot. Before I could get aboard the train I felt somebody take hold of my ear. It was father, and he didn't let go till he

During 1864's Georgia campaign, Private John C. Weber of Huron County, Ohio, served as orderly on the artillery chief's staff for the 3rd Division, Fourth Corps, Army of the Cumberland.

Reunion of the Sherman Brigade, 1919

had got me home.

I lay low and kept quiet for a week, and father thought I had given it up. Lieutenant [Wilbur] Sanders had raised a squad of men for the Sixty-fourth [Ohio]. When he started for Camp Buckingham I stole away from home, got on the train and went with him. I joined the battery and then I thought everything was lovely. But after I had been in camp about a week I got a telegram from a friend in Akron, telling that father was going to start next day to take me home. This made me sick. I went to Lieutenant Baldwin and we both went to Captain [Cullen] Bradley to talk it over. I told them that I would go and stay in the woods while they coaxed father to let up. They advised me not to run away from him, but to go down and meet him at the depot, and I did. I wanted him to go right out to camp, but he made me go with him to a hotel and stay all night.

The next day we went out to camp and had a big talk. The officers tried to have him consent to my going but he still refused, and Captain Bradley told me I had better go home with him. I don't believe I ever felt so bad in my life, but of course I couldn't help myself. So I went back and stayed about ten days. In some way or other I managed to raise twenty-five dollars and one night I jumped on a train and returned to camp. Father saw that I was bound to go, and he wrote me that he would not oppose me any longer if I would come home and say good-bye. I would have gone but didn't get the chance, for the next day we got orders to start for Louisville. That's the way I got into the battery.

Weber faithfully served his entire three-year term, mustering out October 21, 1864.[31]

Despite John's youth, Asbury S. Fowler claimed to be the youngest member of the 6th Ohio Battery, joining the command during 1863 when only 13. He signed the rolls as being 19. In fact, the Sherman Brigade contained quite a number of young soldiers, including musician Albert C. White, who enlisted when nine. Samuel Dewees of Company I, 64th Ohio, had the distinction of being the youngest musket-toting soldier in the brigade, enlisting when only 14 years and nine months old. The list of those 16 or younger would fill a page.[32]

Navies have accepted boys since before the United States existed. Cabin boys and powder monkeys, as lads who carried charges for the cannons during a battle were known, were favored due to their diminutive size — a benefit in cramped quarters of early vessels. When the Civil War erupted the U.S. Navy also experienced a need for manpower. Already accustomed to young boys in their midst, it was not difficult to persuade Navy recruiters of one's usefulness.

James A. Dickinson detailed a fruitless attempt to join the Army in his 1863 diary. Like George Ulmer, he had trouble with Army recruiting officers due to his age, but was not resigned to return home. He visited a Navy recruiter instead.

May 14th 1863

Found a handbill in a farmer's wagon. It said recruits were wanted for the 113th O.V.I. The recruiting office is in Cleveland, Ohio. I spoke to Will Deal and Leo Bruner and they promised to run away and enlist. We will go tomorrow night if we can raise the spondulics [money].

May 15th 1863

Sold a lot of old iron and some lead and some copper to

A Department of the Cumberland army photographer caught this riverine Navy tar's jaunty pose in a Cincinnati studio.

Charley Thompson. Sold some rags to Mr. J.D. Botefur. Raised two dollars and eighty-five cents all told. Bought ten cents worth of peanuts and Leo Bruner, Will Deal and myself eat them up. Leo bought cigars ... and we smoked and talked about going to war. Leo and Will Deal will start early tomorrow morning and walk to Clyde [Ohio] where I will meet them on the cars.

May 16th 1863

Left home on the twelve o'clock train, arrived at Cleveland at half past three in the afternoon. (Did not find Will or Leo at Clyde or anywhere else. I guess they backed out). Went to Uncle Marshall's office and got directed to 4 1/2

Bank Street. Tried to enlist in the 113th Ohio Infantry. Officer wouldn't take me. I am not big enough for a soldier, they have all [the] drummers they want and my lips are too thick to play the bugle. I went and enlisted in the Navy anyhow, as a first-class boy and we are going to Vicksburg to take the place.

May 17th 1863

Today is Sunday and it is awful lonely. I have been loafing around all day watching the girls. Did not even look at a church and got tight in the bargain. Bought a plug of tobacco which I am going to chew because all sailors chew tobacco. There is about twenty other fellows enlisted. We get our grub at the City Hotel. I slept there last night.

May 18th 1863

I and another fellow named Douglass Cannon, who came from Erie and enlisted, went to a store and had our measurements taken for a suit of Navy clothes. I enlisted under Lieutenant Cottle as powder monkey for the term of service of one year. One of the boys who enlisted a few days ago is a girl. Lt. Cottle sent her home when I told him she was a woman.

May 19th 1863

They had a Union mass convention here yesterday and I saw Mr. Jack Harris, Mr. Downs, Flavel Downs and a lot of others from Fremont. There is about forty of us now. We paraded the streets yesterday and I met Uncle Marshall. I tried to dodge but he saw me.

May 20th 1863

We went up to the doctor's to-day to get examined and we were all pronounced sound after a careful examination. I sent some papers home to John and wrote a long letter to Mother. Saw Uncle Marshall and told him Mother gave her consent to my enlisting providing I went in the Navy. He told Lt. Cottle that I was not fourteen years old yet. I enlisted as sixteen years old.

May 21st 1863

I received my Navy clothes to-day. They fit me tip top. I sold my old clothes to a jew and got $1.50 for them and I spent it right off. I went up to Aunt Ellen's house to-day and saw her and Nellie and Marshy. Went down to the Lake-

Fourteen-year-old Valentine Brandt enlisted in 1863 "to learn music" in the U.S. Marine Corps. He served aboard the U.S.R.R. *Cugler,* U.S.S. *Savannah* and at the Marine barracks in Brooklyn, New York.

Author's Collection

shore this afternoon and had the rules and regulations of the Navy read to us. They are pretty tough.

May 22nd 1863

My birth-day. I am fourteen years old to-day. Got Lt. Cottle to give me a furlough for three days. Started home at four o'clock this afternoon; reached there at half past seven, found the folks all right.

Apparently James' mother Marguerite accepted his enlistment, and when his furlough expired she took him to the train depot where they said their farewells and he departed. James spent most of his year enlistment aboard the gunboat *Tawah* on the Tennessee and Mississippi rivers. Gunboat crews often skirmished with bushwhackers and on occasion were sent ashore, acting as infantrymen, to drive troublesome Rebels away from the river. James came near being added to the permanent casualty list more than once during his service. A ball once struck the Enfield rifle in his hand and glanced against an arm. Another day a bullet shattered an oar he was using while heading to shore. During October 1863 a wood splinter from the rowboat, chipped by a musket ball or canister shot, pierced his cheek, loosened some teeth and lacerated his tongue. The large piece of wood had to be cut off and pulled through, and the surgeon removed a tooth. Yet another time, as he stood deck watch on the *Tawah*, a Confederate rode down to the riverbank and blazed away at the boat, emptying his revolver. One of the shots struck James in the leg, but it was so spent that it barely broke the skin.

On May 6, 1864, as his service term neared completion, James inscribed in his diary that he might enlist in the Army. "Sailors do not get any bounty, nor any allowance for clothing and the pay is much smaller than that of the soldiers. Soldiers are getting big bounty[s] now, so I believe I will be a soldier." After a change of heart James returned to Fremont, Ohio, and finished his schooling.[33]

Overall, parents were not as lax on the enlistment subject as Marguerite Dickinson. For hopeful youngsters like William Walton, whose mother and father were determined to keep him home, there was no other option than to run away. Through tenacity and ingenuity hundreds of boys made their way to the ranks. Some played the part of the orphan after traveling great distances from home. In such cases they sometimes enlisted under false names or from fictitious towns. Andrew Brackett of Addison, Maine, was one such persistent boy who, following several disappointing attempts to join a regiment in Maine, ran off to New Hampshire. Born January 13, 1848, he finally passed muster at age 13 as an infantryman in the 12th New Hampshire. Shouldering a musket, Brackett served in the field until September 1864, when he fell sick. Considering his age, his record is indicative of the same remarkable courage and energy manifested by determined efforts to serve his country.[34]

James Henry Coughlin, whose independence of authority already had taken shape at an early age, was another lad among the ranks of runaways. During the winter of his first year of school at age six, he decided to play on the creek behind the schoolhouse, in spite of his father's admonitions. "It being a pleasant day and the pond frozen over, I was soon enjoying a slide on the ice," Coughlin recalled. "It was only a few minutes before all the school was enjoying the sliding. All at once two were seen to disappear through the ice — a boy and a girl, fourteen and fifteen years of age. The boy managed to save himself, but the girl was drowned; my back to-day shows traces of that event."

In 1857 his father died, and in his mind James became the man of the house. That year he hired himself out as a farm laborer for $7 a month to help his family, and was still at that work when the war began. While the 104th New York was being formed during the winter of 1861-1862, Coughlin, then 16, enrolled in Company B under the fictitious name of Jacob Stull, but was rejected by the recruiting officer on account of his age and not having his mother's consent. "I came back rather blue from this set back. Went back to my farm work for Mr. Colt, and gave up trying to become a soldier. In my work with the other hands, they rather ridiculed me as a coward. This I stood for a time, but finally became tired of it, and not being large enough to whip my tormentor, I took the only course open to me, and dared the cowardly six-footer to go to West Rush with me that night to the mass meeting of Company B, 108th Regiment. He went to the meeting but his courage failed him. I signed my name that night, with the understanding when the mustering officer asked my age the lieutenant was to answer for me. I was mustered in and sent to camp."

Coughlin was present for duty throughout the conflict, except after being wounded in May 1864 at Clover Hill near Spotsylvania, Virginia, where he more than proved himself worthy of wearing the blue. "Color bearer [Thomas] Crouch was wounded in the charge at Clover Hill," he stated. "I carried the colors off the field, and was carrying them when wounded by a spent bullet in the breast. Sergeant [Lyman] Wolcott helped me off the field." Coughlin's wound was only slight and he soon was back in the ranks, serving until the end of the war.[35]

Entering the Army under an assumed name led to many problems. In later years, when a soldier tried to obtain a pension for ailments or injuries incurred in the service, proving his true identity was not an easy task. Boy soldiers turned old sometimes found it quite difficult persuading comrades who they really were. One youthful soldier 30 years after the war called on his company's first captain at his home, taking along his former lieutenant. Entering the house under the pretext of asking about the neighbors, he soon had the captain reminiscing about the war years. At length the gray-haired boy tired of the ruse and told the captain who he was, but the captain would not believe him until the lieutenant entered and they all had a good laugh and visit. [36]

For those who needed affidavits signed to authenticate claims of service, lack of comrades remembering them put a virtual end to all hopes of obtaining a pension. For the youngest boys it was difficult to prove they had been soldiers. Lucious Harris encountered a trying time convincing the pension board he was a veteran because of his late birthday of November 30, 1852. In May 1864 Lucious, at the age of 11 years and five months, enlisted as a drummer in Company F, 133rd Ohio. Having no medical problems he was unable to apply for a pension until reaching age 62 in 1914, which qualified him under the Pension Act of 1912. Unfortunately, his claim was denied until he could prove his age and prior service. The pension agent, after securing family bible records and other documents, finally accepted his claim, writing on February 27, 1915: "I am willing to accept claimant's uniform and consistent statements of age together with the bible record to offset the adverse record of age at discharge. I believe he has given correct date of birth and waited until he reached the legal age before filing the claim. You may accept November 30, 1852 as date of birth." Another agent reviewing the claim was not convinced, and he suggested the 1860 census be used to verify Harris' age. The result was not recorded, but Lucious received his pension which was paid until his death in 1924 at Westerville, Ohio. [37]

It was a tragic fact that many boys fell in battle or died in hospitals known only by the false identities they had assumed when entering the service. Not only was it hard on the poor lad who quickly and unexpectedly sickened without time to notify loved ones, it also was a tremendous blow to parents who knew their son had run off but never learned what happened to him. Such was the case of Thomas A. Strahorn, who enlisted in January 1862 under the fake name of Thomas Craft in Company K, 103rd Pennsylvania. Thomas enrolled with an assumed identity to keep his mother from finding and returning him home because of his youth. After some time in the service, during which he was promoted to corporal, he acknowledged to Captain James Adams his true identity and reasons for the deception. Adams wrote to his mother a number of letters, complimenting young Thomas on his soldierly conduct with hope she would let her son

Corporal John A. Kelly was the youngest member of Company I, 103rd Pennsylvania. According to his company commander he "never asked any favors, never asked to be relieved of any duties and never missed a battle in which the company or Regiment was engaged."

History of the 103d Regiment Pennsylvania Volunteer Infantry

James W. Conger had this photograph taken
while home on veteran furlough
with the 43rd Ohio in January 1864.

Author's Collection

stay, which she did. Then, in the fall of 1863, Thomas
was stricken with fever. Still on the rolls under his
assumed name he was sent to a hospital at New Bern,
North Carolina, to convalesce. While there his entire
company was captured at Plymouth and sent to Southern prisons. With his comrades went the knowledge of
his true identity. The last word heard from Thomas
was a letter received by his mother, in which he informed her he was in the hospital, that he intended to
reenlist and then return home on furlough.

Although much effort was expended trying to find
Thomas after the war, his fate remains a mystery. As
late as 1910 his grieving mother was in contact with
103rd veterans, hoping they could shed some light on
his whereabouts. Whether he died in the hospital under the assumed name, or reenlisted and fell in battle,
may never be known. According to Army records he
was discharged at the end of his three-year term, but
authorities in Washington do not know what became
of Thomas Strahorn, alias Thomas Craft.[38]

Fourteen-year-old John A. Kelly was another runaway who served in the 103rd Pennsylvania, rising in
rank to corporal in Company I. He was wounded at
the battle of Fair Oaks, Virginia, and captured with
most of the regiment at Plymouth. For 10 months he
was held prisoner, part of that time at notorious Andersonville. When Kelly returned home in 1865 he
was saddened to find that his mother and father had
died in his absence.[39]

Death during the 1860s shadowed the young as
well as the elderly. The 1860 census enumerated
deaths by age group and established that 7.09 percent
of Americans aged 30 to 50 died. That was greater
than the 5.17 percent recorded for those between the
ages of 50 and 70.[40] Many soldiers received word of
loved ones' deaths at home. Especially heart-wrench-
ing for young soldiers was news of a parent's passing.
With 7 percent of those within their parenting years
dying, there were many boy soldiers who experienced

such a loss. Unfortunately, runaways like Corporal
Kelly knew little of affairs at the homes they were trying to avoid. Not only were parents unaware of the
deaths of their runaway sons, many of the runaways
were ignorant of a parent's death as well.

High mortality rates in America during the mid-
1800s plagued the country with thousands of orphans.
In rural areas, orphans readily were accepted to join
relatives' households. Such was the case of James W.
Conger, who lost his mother at 15 months and his father at six. Soon after his father's death he moved to
his grandparents' farm in Morrow County, Ohio,
where other relatives had settled. When the war commenced, 16-year-old James enlisted with three of his
cousins in Company B, 43rd Ohio.[41] By May 1865 he
had been promoted to regimental quartermaster sergeant.

Soldiers eagerly welcomed newsboys who often visited their camps with papers from home. For those on their own the job provided a small income.

Author's Collection

In large cities, where children often were considered less of an asset, landlords put thousands of orphans on the street for non-payment of rent after their parents died. Left to their own devices in a sea of people, they either fended for themselves or perished. New York had an exceptionally high number of orphans and unwanted or abandoned youths due to an influx of immigrants entering the country there. Many families fresh from Europe found the fabled city possessed insufficient housing and not enough jobs. Some desperate parents were forced to leave their babies on doorsteps or allowed their children loose to make their own way. Wandering the streets, some resorted to crime while others begged to survive. As early as the late 1840s the problem of unwanted children was noted by New York police chief George W. Matsell, who wrote, "There are nearly 10,000 children in the City not reached by any institution, who never attend the public schools, who but live upon the streets, many of them having no other home, night or day. They are not criminals in the eyes of the law, for their thefts, if they are guilty of stealing, are of very small amounts, and are entirely food or fuel to keep them from perishing." The waifs usually were found filthy with torn and ragged clothing in a half-starved state. To survive, many swept street crossings, gathered rags, boxes or refuse paper. They sold matches, toothpicks, apples, oranges and other small items. "A large class were newsboys," concluded Chief Matsell.[42]

In 1853 Charles Loring Bruce, a New York minister, recognized the problem and founded the Children's Aid Society to help those in the city. At first the society gathered children from the streets and provided a shelter where they were clothed and fed. The boys were put to work in a shoe shop they established, and girls were taught sewing and other light trades. Within a year it was realized the society could not handle the number of children gleaned from the streets and back alleys. In 1854 the society's board instituted

a placement program by sending 47 boys, ages seven to 15, on a train to Dowagiac, Michigan. There the boys were placed with farmers who were in need of unskilled labor. Those who accepted the youths agreed to treat them as part of their families, helping to educate and care for them. In essence, they were adopted.[43]

By the late 1850s the Emigration Department, or "Orphan Trains" as they were commonly called, was in full gear. In 1857 more than 1,000 children were dispatched from New York to towns west. The aid society sent agents to an area near a train station and advertised the train's arrival and need for foster homes. If enough interest was manifested the train would arrive a few weeks later bearing the youngsters. On that occasion the children were lined up at the station or treated to a meal as prospective foster parents looked them over and mingled for a while. Then, at a given time the children were placed in homes after selec-

For youngsters in need of clothing, military uniforms were tempting inducements to enlist.

Author's Collection

tions were made. Orphan Trains continued through the Civil War into the 1920s.[44]

Sometimes a choice did not work out. In 1862 an Ohio farmer returned a lad to the society, claiming he was "the worst tempered boy I ever had anything to do with," and further stated that all he would do at school was "kick the little boys and call the girls bad names." Likewise, there were many children who complained to agents of being treated as slaves or worse. But overall the trains helped a great many children and families.[45]

During the war years the society's work steadily increased as the number of youths orphaned or abandoned ballooned at a greater rate. For many young boys living in the streets of larger Northern cities the Army became a new alternative offering food and clothing. Joseph Revelle provided a sad story about enlisting during court-martial proceedings after he

was charged with desertion. At the age of 14 Joseph enlisted in Company H, 123rd Indiana. Three months later, in May 1864, he decided he had enough soldiering and started home. On June 24 he was arrested and brought back to the Army. "When I left the regiment," Joseph testified, "it was with the intention of going home to stay until I got tired, and then return to the regiment. I knew it was a crime to desert. Sometimes I was well treated in the Company and sometimes I was not. I was arrested before I got home. I was fourteen years old last February; when I enlisted I told them I was eighteen. I was born at Clarksville, Indiana. I do not know what year; my father died when I was two years old; my mother is living. I was bound out to a farmer when I was three years old, and lived with him about eleven years. He did not treat me well and I did not like to stay there; I was abused in every way and that was the reason I enlisted." Joseph's story did not fall on deaf ears and he was returned to his regiment with only a monetary penalty for his indiscretion. He served until discharged in August 1865.[46]

On November 4, 1862, Captain John A. Chase was recruiting members for Company F, 14th Ohio, when he was approached by a teenager standing a little over five feet tall. The boy stated his name was James Barrington, and mentioned he would like to enlist as a drummer. In the course of Chase's questioning, Barrington answered he had just turned 16 and had been on his own for more than a year since his parents died. Ascertaining the facts were correct, Chase filled out the "Consent in Case of Minor" form on the back of the boy's enlistment paper. "I, John Chase do certify, that the said James Barrington has no parents; that the said James Barrington is sixteen years of age; and I do hereby freely give my consent to his volunteering as a soldier in the Army of the United States for the period of three years."

Barrington was mustered November 24 as acting company musician. Within two years of his enlistment the orphan drummer was killed in action September 1,

1864, at the battle of Jonesboro, Georgia. He was just one of perhaps hundreds of young orphans who gave their lives without the shedding of a single tear by loved ones at home. Their comrades were all they had to sustain them during their last few minutes of life. Their company was their family and within it their single circle of friends. Only through these fellow soldiers could their memories and deeds be preserved.[47]

Whether they were orphans, runaways, members of patriotic families or sons of officers, getting into the Army seemed like a dream come true. Many quickly realized, however, that war produced little martial glory. Hardships they never envisioned now surrounded them as they donned the blue uniform so longingly coveted. Like it or not, they had fulfilled their desires and were at last soldiers in the United States' service.

CHAPTER 3

'The hardships and dangers and exposure of the soldier's life'

At the officer's request the men were called to attention and asked to raise their right hands. Looking around, Harry Kieffer witnessed every hand simultaneously shoot up with confidence. Then, as a chorus, each man commenced reciting the oath and he joined in. "I, Harry M. Kieffer, do solemnly swear that I will bear true allegiance to the United States of America, and that I will serve them honestly and faithfully against all their enemies or opposers whatsoever, and observe and obey the orders of the President of the United States, and the orders of the officers appointed over me, according to the rules and articles for the Government of the armies of the United States." [1]

The oath of allegiance was the last hurdle in the youthful recruit's quest of becoming a soldier. Before it was read he already had been through the surgeon's and recruiting officer's inspections, and completed all necessary paperwork. From the moment he mouthed the oath's concluding words there was no turning back or change of heart allowed.

Someone with any knowledge of what the word "soldier" means could hardly describe the Army's newest acquisitions as such. Known as citizen-soldiers, they were much more citizen than soldier at this point. Young boys were no better or worse off than their older compatriots during those first few days. Even a majority of officers was learning basics along the way.

The first order of business was securing quarters.

Nationwide, great camps of muster and instruction sprang up almost overnight to begin and sustain the process of turning citizens into soldiers. Once recruits were accepted they were sent to these sprawling tent cities to learn the basics of soldiering the best as time allowed.[2] In camp the men were issued uniforms and accouterments as they became available. Drummer Kieffer of the 150th Pennsylvania described the ordeal at Harrisburg's Camp Curtin:

As we now belonged to Uncle Sam, it was to be expected that he would next proceed to clothe us. This he punctually did a few days after the muster. We had no little merriment when we were called out and formed in line and marched up to the quartermaster's department at one side of the camp to draw our uniforms. There were so many men to be uniformed, and so little time in which to do it, that the blue clothes were passed out to us almost regardless of the size and weight of the prospective wearer. Each man received a pair of pantaloons, a coat, cap, overcoat, shoes, blanket, and underwear, of which later the shirt was — well, a revelation to most of us, both as to size and shape and material. It was so rough that no living mortal, probably, could wear it, except perhaps one who wished to do penance by wearing a hair shirt. Mine was promptly sent home with my citizen's clothes, with the request that it be kept as a sort of heirloom in the family for future generations to wonder at.

With our clothes on our arms we marched back to our tents, and there proceeded to get on the inside of our new uniforms. The result was in most cases astonishing. For, as might have been expected, scarcely one man in ten was fit-

I remember hearing about one poor fellow, in another company, a great, strapping six-footer, who could not be suited. The largest shoe furnished by the government was quite too small. The giant tried his best to force his foot in, but in vain. His comrades gathered about him and laughed and chaffed him unmercifully, whereupon he exclaimed, "Why, you don't think they are all boys that come to the army, do you? A man like me needs a man's shoe, not a baby's."[3]

For boys in the service, being properly clothed was especially difficult. The Army's smallest uniforms were too large for many and had to be altered before they could be worn. Others decided to have new outfits made entirely. George Ulmer of the 8th Maine tired of his first set of clothes that were "dragging on the ground," and the laughter they provoked. On his way to camp he purchased a new uniform made in Portland. Wearing a non-regulation uniform drew approving looks and stares as he made the trip to his regiment, but became a hindrance his first night in camp, as Ulmer recalled:

I had a tailor make me a very handsome suit of military clothes. He was as ignorant of the regulation style as I was. He only knew the colors and knew that I wanted it nice and handsome. He made it and so covered it over with gold braid and ornaments, that you could not tell whether I was a drum major or a brigadier general.

The first night I was tired out and started for Alexandria, [Virginia], arrived at headquarters about midnight, and told the sentry I must see the colonel. He thought that I had important messages, or was some officer, and escorted me to the colonel's quarters. I woke him up; told him I had reported and wanted a bed. The colonel said, "Is that all you want? Corporal, put this man in the guardhouse."

The next morning I was given a broom and put to work sweeping around camp with about twenty tough-looking customers. The broom did not look well with my uniform,

ted. The tall men had invariably received the short pantaloons, and presented an appearance, when they emerged from their tents, which was equalled only by that of the short men who had, of course, received the long pantaloons. One man's cap was perched away up on the top of his head, while another's rested on his ears.

And the shoes! Coarse, broad-soled, low-heeled "gunboats," as we afterwards learned to call them — what a time there was getting into them. Here came one fellow down the street with shoes so big that they could scarcely be kept on his feet, while over yonder another tugged and pulled and kicked himself red in the face over a pair that would not go on. But by trading off, the large men gradually got the large garments and the little men the small, so that in a few days we were all pretty well suited.

and as soon as an officer noticed me I was summoned before the colonel in command. He asked what I was. I told him I did not know yet — would not know till I reached my regiment. He had a hearty laugh at my appearance; said I ought to be sent to some fair instead of the front. However, he detailed me as his orderly. [4]

Throughout the war the problem of clothing diminutive soldiers continued. C. Perry Byam of the 24th Iowa wrote that the only suffering worth mentioning during his service was caused by ill-fitting or lack of clothing. "The smallest military cap was the only article that fitted me perfectly. I wore a size 13 shoe (in children's size), and any garment issued by the government contained material sufficient for several of me. All foraging parties I strictly enjoined to 'look out' for wearing apparel for me, especially shoes. For a considerable time I was forced to go barefooted, rarely possessed a shirt, and my clothing for a long period was reduced to a single pair of trousers and short jacket that buttoned up to the neck, and I was withal picturously lousy." [5]

Charles A. Willison of the 76th Ohio recalled how decrepit his garments had become after the 1863 Vicksburg campaign. "Personally, I was down to hardpan in the way of clothing. Our knapsacks were still back at Vicksburg. The shirt I had on was gone, all but the front and one sleeve. Before we reached [Big] Black River I was shirtless, my pants were in an indescribable condition, my blouse all rags, and my only fairly respectable covering a forage cap. Had put in a requisition before leaving Vicksburg for two shirts and a blouse, but there was a good prospect of going naked before they could be got to us and 'W' was reached in issuing them. Supplies were issued to the company in alphabetical order of its members' names and in case of shortage, which was not infrequent, we fellows at the tail end of the alphabet were 'minus.'" A few weeks later the 76th's baggage was transported to the regiment. Willison continued: "The arrival of our knapsacks was

Clothing usually was issued in order of the company line, formed right to left, tallest to shortest. Small-statured boys received discarded, ill-fitting garments of those ahead. This unidentified soldier is amply covered by an infantry overcoat. Carte de visite image by B.F. Baltzly of Wooster, Ohio.

Author's Collection

timely. My pants had lost all covering qualities and I had thrown them away, compelled for a day or two to serve my country garbed in underwear only. With my knapsack at hand my first move was down to the creek nearby, where I took a thorough scrubbing. Washed

Note absence of coat buttons except for the non-military one fastened at the top of this unidentified boy's blouse.

Courtesy of The Horse Soldier

my boots inside and out; then, after putting on clean shirt, drawers and socks, felt like a new being and in more comfortable condition to wait for the other clothing and equipment needed to complete my outfit we had been assured would be along soon." [6]

John McClay, 13, stood two inches shy of five feet tall when he enlisted in the 43rd Ohio. He continuously had trouble securing proper fitting clothing until Colonel Wager Swayne solved the problem. George M. Ziegler included the story in a newspaper series published after the war detailing McClay's service:

As was customary on long marches the soldiers lightened their knapsacks whenever opportunity offered. On this occasion Col. Swayne sent to the 43rd Regiment for an orderly. Johnny McClay was duly detailed for duty at headquarters. Casting off the old worn garments, he donned new ones drawn at Decatur, Alabama. The pants were four inches too long; but that trouble was soon overcome by tucking them under nicely. The blouse hung on him like a full-grown garment on a rose bush, the sleeves being six inches too long. That difficulty was overcome by the tucking up process.

Just as he entered the Colonel's headquarters, much to Johnny's discomfiture, the sleeves came down, and to hide this misfit, he ran his hands down deep into his pants' pockets, presenting a very unsoldierly appearance. The Colonel looked for a moment in astonishment and asked him if he knew whom he was addressing. Johnny replied, "You are Colonel Swayne commanding the 43rd Regiment O.V.I."

"Do you not know it is very unbecoming to appear before an officer with your hands in your pockets?"

"Yes, sir, I do," and Johnny drew himself up to attention, slowly pulling his hands out of his pockets, making a comical picture. The Colonel said laughingly, "You go and give Captain [Albert H.] Howe my compliments and tell him to report to me at once." And when the captain reported, the Colonel remarked to him, "If we have to raise this boy, we will have to clothe him differently. In the future have your company tailor remodel his clothes." And ever after Johnny appeared in a neat fitting suit. [7]

Being uniformed was only an introduction to soldier life. Shocking recruits further was the food. For most, the journey to camp was one continuous feast as townspeople supplied ample treats along the way. Once in camp many recruits still received a steady stream of eatables from family and friends, but some found themselves at the mercy of the commissary department or money-hungry sutlers to supply their needs. As time passed and fewer food parcels were received from home, all would find themselves confined to Army fare or included on a sutler's debt list. [8]

The Army distributed food in the form of rations. Each ration was supposed to represent enough food for an entire day, and usually was issued every three to five days. Specified rations included 12 ounces of pork or bacon, 12 ounces of hard bread (one pound in the field), 1.6 ounces of rice or beans, one ounce of coffee, two ounces of sugar, plus a touch of salt and vinegar. [9] Potatoes regularly were issued as a substitute for beans or rice, and fresh beef was exchanged for salt pork whenever possible. Soft bread was issued in permanent camps as well. The amounts were never sufficient, but the quality was usually worse. Beef or salt pork were sometimes so rancid they could not be eaten, and hardtack — thick, square, rock-hard and often wormy crackers — became legendary before war's end.

William Bircher wrote extensively about Army food in his narrative *A Drummer-Boy's Diary:*

Of provisions Uncle Sam usually gave us ... the table had little variety and fewer delicacies. On first entering the service the drawing of rations was not a small undertaking, for there were nearly a hundred of us in the company, and it took considerable weight of bread and pork to feed a hundred hungry stomachs. But after we had been in the field a year or two the call "Fall in for your hardtack!" was leisurely responded to by only about a dozen men — lean, sinewy, hungry-looking fellows, each with his haversack in hand. They would squat around a gum blanket, spread on the ground, on which was a small heap of sugar, another of coffee, another of rice, maybe, which the corporal was dealing out by successive spoonfuls. They held open their little black bags to receive their portion, while nearby lay a small piece of pork or beef, or possibly a small amount of dessicated vegetables.

Our hardtack were very hard. We could scarcely break them with our teeth. Some we could scarcely fracture with our fist.... It required some experience and no little hunger to enable one to appreciate hardtack rightly, and it demanded no small amount of inventive genius to understand how to cook hardtack as it ought to be cooked. If I remember correctly, in our section of the army we had fifteen different ways of preparing them. In other parts, I understand, they discovered one or two ways more, but with us fifteen was the limit of the culinary art. When this article of diet was on board, on the march they were usually not cooked at all, but eaten in the raw state. In order, however, to make them somewhat more palatable, a thin slice of nice fat pork was cut down and laid on the cracker, and a spoonful of good brown sugar put on top of the pork, and we had a dish fit for a soldier. Of course, the pork was raw and had just come out of the pickle. When we halted for coffee we sometimes fricasseed hardtack, prepared by toasting them before the hot coals, thus making them soft and spongy.

If there was time for frying, we either dropped them into the fat in the dry state and did them brown to turn, or soaked them in cool water and then fried them, or pounded them to a powder, mixed this with boiled rice, and made griddle cakes and honey, minus the honey.

When, as was generally the case on a march, our hardtack was broken into small pieces in our haversacks. We soaked these in water and fried them in fat pork, stirring well and seasoning with salt and pepper, thus making what was commonly called a "hell-fired stew." But the great tri-umph of the culinary art in camp, to my mind, was "hardtack pudding." This was made by placing the biscuit in a stout canvas bag and pounding it, bag and contents, with a club on a log until the biscuits were reduced to a fine powder; then we added a little wheat flour, if we had it — the more the better — and made a stiff dough, which we next rolled out on a cracker box lid, like a pie crust; then we covered this all over with a preparation of stewed dried apples, dropping in here and there a raisin or two just for "Auld Lang Syne's" sake, rolled and wrapped it in a cloth, boiled it for an hour or so, and ate it with wine sauce. The wine was usually omitted and hunger inserted in its stead. Thus we saw what truly vast and unsuspected possibilities resided in this innocent-looking, three and a half-inch square hardtack. Three made a meal and nine were a ration, and this was what fought the battles for the Union.

The army hardtack had but one rival. And that was the army bean — a small, white, round-ish soup bean. It was quite innocent looking, as was its inseparable companion, the hardtack, and like it, was possessed of possibilities which the uninitiated would never suspect.

It was not so plastic an edible as the hardtack; nor susceptible of so wide a range of use, but the one great dish which might be made of it was so pre-eminently excellent that it threw "hell-fired stew" and "hardtack pudding" quite into the shade. This was baked beans. I had heard of the dish before, but never remotely imagined what toothsome delights lurked in the recesses of a camp kettle of beans, baked after the orthodox, backwoods fashion, until one day Bill Hunter, of K company, whose home was in the lumber regions where the dish had no doubt been first invented, said to me, "Come around to our tent tomorrow morning; we're going to have baked beans for breakfast. If you will walk around to the lower end of our company street with me I will show you how we bake beans up in the country I came from."

It was about three o'clock in the afternoon, and the boys were already busy. They had an enormous camp-kettle about two-thirds full of parboiled beans. Nearby they had dug a hole in the ground about three feet square and two deep, in and on top of which a great fire was to be made about dusk, so as to get the hole thoroughly heated and full of red-hot coals by the time tattoo sounded. Into this hole the camp-kettle was then set, with several pounds of fat pork on top of the beans, and securely covered with an inverted mess pan. It was sunk into the red-hot coals, by which it was completely concealed, and was left there all night to bake, one of the camp guards throwing a log on the fire from time to time to keep matters going.

Early the next morning someone shook me roughly as I lay sleeping soundly in my tent: "Get up, Billy! Breakfast is ready. Come to our tent. If you never ate baked beans before, you never ate anything worth eating." I found three or four of the boys seated around the camp-kettle, each with a tin plate on his knee and a spoon in his hand, doing their very best to establish the truth of the old adage, "The proof of the pudding is in the eating." Now, it is a far more difficult matter to describe the experience of the palate than of either the eye or the ear, and therefore I shall not attempt to tell how very good baked beans are. The only trouble with a camp-kettle full of the delicious food was that it was gone too soon.[10]

Rations were to consist of amounts previously listed, but on many occasions men received whatever was on hand. At times there was not much and as William Bircher opined, "it was gone too soon."

Worse yet was when cooking went awry. Fourteen-year-old Charles Bardeen wrote about his company's unfulfilling dilemma of a burned batch of beans during October 1862. "It was this feast we had been anticipating as we shivered in our wet beds; we had longed for morning and beans. Morning came, but no beans; the hole had been too hot. Unhappily the company rations had been drawn in pork and beans so that we had nothing else to eat save our coffee and what hard tack happened to be left over in our haversacks. It was a doleful time."[11]

After enlisting in the 76th Ohio, 16-year-old Charles Willison was sent with other recruits to his regiment's camp near Helena, Arkansas. In Cincinnati they were obliged to stay a few days waiting for transportation. Due to the delay Willison and his comrades were sent to barracks on the north side of town. While there he was indoctrinated to Army food for the first time, which he never forgot. "Here I had my first taste of army fare and learned something of the sensations a decent, self-respecting, sensitive fellow feels or suffers when first compelled to herd with all sorts of characters and seemingly lose his individuality. This came to me in such experiences as the rush and struggle to get a place at a long rough board table, only to get a slice of plain bread and cup of black coffee. Just like a drove of pigs trying to get at a trough. These meals were served with tin plates and cups, with knives, forks and spoons to match." Later in life Willison reflected on the meal as "necessary to comb down whatever self-conceit any of us may have brought from home and prepare us for the almost loss of our identity in the trying practice of warfare into which we were about entering."[12]

It is understandable that Dr. Tripler warned against accepting underage recruits in his medical manual. "How, with an irritable stomach, can one accommodate oneself to food the most diverse and frequently the most indigestible?"[13] He was correct in his assessment, as today it is well established how important a role nutrition plays, especially during the adolescent years. Boys, some not yet having reached puberty, did not obtain sufficient calories or vitamins from issued rations for proper bone and organ growth. Combined with high levels of energy expended through drill or exhausting marches, youngsters were nearly always hungry and at times during the war, half starved. Famished soldiers were plentiful, and everywhere there were soldiers there were sutlers eager to supply delicacies the government could not provide.

Sutlers were entrepreneurs who accompanied troops or set up stands near the camps to sell anything they could think of to separate soldiers from their money. The number one item at these stands was food. A majority were honest businessmen who believed they were doing the service a favor by being present. Others who were corrupt charged exhorbitant prices to line their pockets with more than ample returns for the dollars invested. Naturally, soldiers disliked greedy sutlers, and felt it their duty to even the score whenever possible.

On one occasion, as the 108th New York was marching from Bolivar Heights to Belle Plain, it halted near Perryville, Virginia. While the men were resting a sutler drove up with two wagons full of soft bread. The New Yorkers had been dining exclusively on hardtack for some time, and at the sight of mounds of delightful bread their mouths began to water. At first the peddler was charging five cents a loaf, but as the crowd grew he raised his price to 10 cents. When he learned the troops were from New York he raised it further to 15. Insulted, the men devised a plan. While the sutler was doing business at the head of his first wagon the Company D men at the rear picked up one of their boys by the seat of his pants. Weighing just over 100 pounds, he was easily tossed high over the second wagon's wall on to the mound of bread.[14] Dutifully following instructions, he threw armloads of loaves to his comrades below. When the greedy seller noticed what was happening, he at first tried to gather himself and stop the pilfering. But he soon realized his plight, leaving his wagons to the plunderers and head-

ed off to regimental headquarters to file a complaint. There, some privates and Sergeant Alfred Ellwood of Company D were ordered to look into the matter. By the time the squad reached the wagons they were overturned and empty. The disconsolate peddler yelled, "They have stolen my bread and also my money-box." Ellwood did not place any stock in his story, but hoped he would not be forgotten by his comrades when reaching camp in the evening. Sure enough, later that night he found a pile of bread inside his tent. The sutler, meanwhile, righted his wagons and drove away a sadder if not wiser man, thanks to one of the boys.[15]

It did not take long for soldiers to forget morals and proper upbringings when confronted with situations like the bread riot. Foraging took on a new meaning during the war, generally being a polite way of admitting theft. Through the first two years punishment was relatively strict for hungry soldiers tempted

Hardtack and coffee — dietary staples of Union enlisted men, including the three boys seated in the foreground of an Army of the Potomac camp. One veteran observed: "As a general thing, coffee was issued roasted, but unground. It was sent down in the berry, by the hundred thousand pounds, and the bayonet and tin-cup served for crushing purposes." After his first encounter with Army crackers, a new enlistee "could understand why the doctor examined his teeth so carefully. ... He had been told that it was necessary to have good teeth in order to bite 'cartridges' successfully, but now he knew it was with reference to his ability to eat hardtack."

Courtesy of Thomas and Crystal Molocea

by the sight of such things as fine, fat pigs or chickens grazing near camp. As the war progressed and Union forces marched farther south, foraging became the rule rather than the exception. Charles Willison of the 76th Ohio started foraging soon after leaving Cincinnati on a boat trip down the Ohio River. "There were two or three stoppages along shore as we passed down the river which offered first rate opportunity to become initiated into the practice of foraging, and I took advantage of it to get a supply of melons, roasting ears, etc. As my captain not only winked at the proceedings, but smiled amiably, made no protest, and helped partake of the forage, I cannot recall that my conscience troubled me in the least at this radical departure from my home life principles." [16]

James Dickinson, 14, on his way south 12 days after joining the riverine Navy, also left his conscience back in Ohio. "We had our supper in Centralia tonight where we once more changed cars," he wrote in his diary. "I hooked two big pies and a piece of ham and my chum hooked all his pockets full of apples. One of the men saw us, but the boys said they would break his arms and legs, so he was scared and kept his mouth shut." [17]

Whether appetites were satisfied by rations or supplemented by foraging and purchases from sutlers, compared to home-cooked food Army victuals left much to be desired. Yet all three were integral parts of soldiering. Complaining about Army food and dreaming of home cooking have been universal features of military life for centuries. During the Civil War a lack of refrigerants and unsanitary packaging hampered the commissary's best intentions of storing quality food for the troops. But as the war progressed soldiers accepted less with more delight. Recruits who complained about being served "plain bread," like Charles Willison, later discovered it a treasure worth stealing.

Second Minnesota drummer William Bircher noted the change in attitude after a long night marching in drenching rain with the prospect of receiving rations nonexistent. "While living at Fort Snelling [Minnesota] we grumbled a great deal about the provisions furnished us, when we had quite a lengthy bill of fare, containing not only all the necessaries of life but many that might be counted luxuries. On arriving in Kentucky, and having some of the latter articles cut off, we grumbled again, and thought that we were making our stomachs suffer martyrdom for the good

of the cause, but amid all these afflictions we looked forward with dread and dismay to the time when we should begin our march and have nothing but hardtack, pork, and coffee to eat and drink. This, we thought, was the worst we could endure; but now we would have received our rations of hardtack and pork thankfully; indeed, we would have taken a deal of trouble upon ourselves to have procured them in any form." [18]

C. Perry Byam believed in procuring food in any fashion. "Being very resourceful, I rarely suffered the want of good fare. I was perfectly familiar with all the public entrances to the commissary department, and privately knew of several secret but safe exits. In this department I once entered, bodily, a barrel containing a few inches in depth of sauerkraut (being our regiment's portion of a supply sent the troops by a society of northern ladies), and perfectly screened therein from view, ate my fill of the 'raw material.' When hard pressed, or under suspicion, I had recourse to an old colored man who had long been an officer's cook and who received me in great good fellowship; and with a 'Is you hongry honey?' would at once proceed to 'dig up' something nice for me to eat." [19]

Army clothing and food were undoubtedly hard adjustments for new recruits, affecting them physically. To become soldiers they had to be trained as well. Mental and physical tuning were initiated as soon as their allegiance oaths were recited. For many, even the language and equipage of a soldier were unfamiliar. Terms such as roll call, guard duty, reveille, tattoo, flank, right-shoulder-shift, adjutant, epaulet, brevet, lanyard and breastwork had to be learned.

Stanton Allen, released from the 21st New York Cavalry on August 31, 1863, by *habeus corpus,* did not relinquish his dream of becoming a soldier despite threats by family and police. Within four months the 14-year-old ran away to the Bay State, where he enlisted in the 1st Massachusetts Cavalry. Once mustered, Stanton recalled he was clueless how to handle all the accouterments issued to him as a cavalryman. When he was handed his clothing he also received his horse equipment, which was piled on the floor. Asking if he could make two trips to his barracks or obtain some help, the fiery sergeant in charge said, "Tie up your clothing and arms in your bed blanket. You can put your horse furniture in your saddle blanket." In describing his confusion, Stanton borrowed from

Army regulations to help paint his picture:

Section 1,620 of the Revised United States Army Regulations of 1861, with an Appendix Containing the Changes and Laws Affecting Army Regulations and Articles of War to June 25, 1863, reads as follows:

"A complete set of horse equipments for mounted troops consists of 1 bridle, 1 watering bridle, 1 halter, 1 saddle, 1 pair saddle bags, 1 saddle blanket, 1 surcingle, 1 pair spurs, 1 curry comb, 1 horse brush, 1 picket pin and 1 lariat; 1 link and 1 nose bag when specially required."

The section reads smoothly enough. There is nothing formidable about it to the civilian. But, ah me! Surviving troopers of the great conflict will bear me out when I say that Section 1,620 aforesaid stands for a great deal more than it would be possible for the uninitiated to comprehend at one sitting. The bridle, for instance, is composed of one headstall, one bit, one pair of reins. And the headstall is composed of "1 crown piece, the ends split, forming 1 cheek strap and 1 throat lash billet on one side, and on the other 1 cheek strap and 1 throat lash, with 1 buckle, .625 inch, 2 chapes and 2 buckles, .75 inch, sewed to the ends of cheek piece to attach the bit; 1 brow band, the ends doubled and sewed from two loops on each end through which the cheek straps and throat lash and throat lash billet pass."

So much for the headstall. It would take three times the space given to the headstall to describe the bit, and then comes the reins. The watering bridle "is composed of 1 bit and 1 pair of reins." The halter's description uses up one third of a page. "The saddle is composed of 1 tree, 2 saddle skirts, 2 stirrups, 1 girth and girth strap, 1 surcingle, 1 crupper." Two pages of the regulations are required to describe the different pieces that go to make up the saddle complete, and which include six coat straps, one carbine socket, saddle skirts, saddle bags, saddle blanket, etc. The horse brush, curry comb, picket pin, lariat, link and nosebag all come in for detailed descriptions, each with its separate pieces.

Let it be borne in mind that all these articles were thrown into a heap on the floor, and that every strap, buckle, ring and other separate piece not riveted or sewed together was handed out by itself, the sergeant rattling on like a parrot all the time. Perhaps a faint idea of the situation may be obtained. But the real significance of the event can only be understood by the troopers who "were there."

As I emerged from the quartermaster's office I was a

Musicians Newton Peters, 15 (below flag's right star), and Samuel E. Scott, 16 (to Peters' left), belonged to the 93rd New York drum corps, photographed in August 1863 at Bealton, Virginia, where the regiment was part of the Army of the Potomac headquarters guard. A drum corps' full complement consisted of a fife major, bugler, bass drummer, 10 drummers and 10 fifers (one from each company), all commanded by the drum major or principal musician. When not in battle, stated Fife Major Bradford J. Wakeman, 33rd Illinois, the drum corps "awoke the boys in the morning with reveille and sent them to bed at night with taps. On the march their place was near the head of the regiment, just in front of the colors. In camp a detail of two musicians was made each day for duty at headquarters to play calls."

U.S. Army Military History Institute

Unidentified Massachusetts militia drummer.

Early in 1862 George B. Bruce, a member of the 7th New York State Militia and former chief instructor at Governors Island School of Practice, observed that standards of drum and fife playing were "rapidly deteriorating. The mere beating of a Quick-step in the street, however well it may be done, is by no means the whole of Drum-playing. The present war has revealed the fact that our militia drummers and fifers are but very imperfectly acquainted with camp and garrison duties, and, when at last there is a need of their services, they are incompetent to properly respond to their country's call."

Carte de visite image by J.W. Black, Boston.

Author's Collection

OPPOSITE: A pensive pose in front of a painted backdrop was struck by this young drummer, possibly a member of the 51st New York.

Courtesy of Fred Wilkens

sight to behold. Before I had fairly left the building my bundles broke loose and my military effects were scattered all around. By using the loose straps and surcingle I managed to pack my outfit in one bundle. But it was a large one, just about all I could lift.

When I got into the barracks I was very much discouraged. What to do with the things was a puzzle to me. I distributed them in the bunk, and began to speculate on how I could ever put all those little straps and buckles together. The more I studied over it the more complicated it seemed. I would begin with the headstall of the bridle. Having been raised on a farm I had some knowledge of double and single harness to some extent, but the bridles and halters that I had seen were not of the cavalry pattern. After I had buckled the straps together I would have several pieces left with no buckles to correspond.

As I was manipulating the straps [Giles] Taylor arrived with his outfit. He threw the bundle down in the lower bunk and exclaimed: "I wish I'd staid home."[20]

Orders during the first few weeks had to be explained at times, but the one recruits learned quickly

and heard most often was drill. For Civil War soldiers the word "drill" encompassed everything in the art of war. It virtually meant practice. If they were infantrymen they practiced with guns and accouterments; if cavalry, with horses and equipment; if artillery, with cannons and caissons; and if musicians, with their instruments. Officers nightly studied their manuals and in turn taught maneuvers and tactics to the recruits during the day. First they learned individual moves contained in the "School of the Soldier." Then they drilled in squads. When proficient enough they drilled by company, battalion, regiment and finally, on occasion, by brigade. For all soldiers the words "drill" and "Army" became synonymous.

A typical day for an infantry regiment began with reveille at sunrise. Roll call was at 7 a.m., breakfast 7:30, guard-mounting 8:30, squad drill 9 to 10, company drill 11 to noon, dinner 12:30 p.m., company drill 1:30 to 2:30, battalion drill 3:30 to 4:30, dress parade 5, supper 5:30, roll call 8:30, tattoo 9, and taps

Unidentified.

A drummer of the "Tenth Legion," 56th New York, wearing the regiment's distinctive, early-war cloth shield insignia on his chest.

Unidentified.

Flams and ferrididdles

Achieving competency with an instrument was not a simple task for many young musicians, whose initial efforts performing in unison often left much to be desired. John Folsom, an 11th New Hampshire musician, remembered his regimental drum corps' first public appearance "was not particularly hopeful. The fifers could play together only 'Yankee Doodle' and 'The girl I left behind me,' while the drummers beat their drums in the old-fashioned 'slam-bang style.' Nearly three years, however, of constant drill and practice made a wonderful difference."

The 12th New Hampshire's drum corps experienced an equally inauspicious debut in 1862 at Camp Belknap in Concord. Asa W. Bartlett of Company F recalled: "When the twenty knights of the drum and fife — two from each company — first came together ... they were quite as verdant in the practice of music as in the science of war. With one or two exceptions they had enlisted *as* musicians, not so much because they *were,* as because they *wanted* to be such; thinking, perhaps, if allowed to make their own music they would not be obliged to face the music of the enemy. It is doubtful if there were half of the drummers that knew a *'flam'* from a *'ferri-diddle,'* or two-four time from six-eight; and the fifers were but little better, although two or three of them could play quite well. But think not there was any lack of native talent or ambition in this crude score of ear distractors, for the development of both was soon apparent."

Once drums and fifes were mastered, a teenaged Pennsylvania drummer believed they "have more to do with the discipline of an army than an inexperienced person would imagine. The drum is the tongue of the camp."

Unidentified.

Mick Kissick Collection

at 10 p.m.[21] For boys accustomed to a normal day in school, the rigorous schedule was exhausting.

Because of lower age restrictions placed on musicians a majority of youngsters was mustered in that capacity. As earlier stated, Army regulations pointedly spelled out that those unable to fulfill their musical duties were to be discharged. With the threat of being sent home, boys were kept busy learning the proper calls and beats as fast as possible — and there was a lot to comprehend. The drummer soon heard and learned what was meant by a tap, flam, drag and roll, to name several beats. These patterns, combined with different speeds like common and quick time, comprised the different calls of the Army. Fifteen different beats of the drum for infantry, independent of mere police calls, were used as well as another 20 for skirmishers when bugles were not available. General calls on the bugle numbered 23, with an additional 23 needed for the skirmish line. Near camp the noisome sound of young boys beating drums and blowing bugles shrilly permeated the air. Usually, it was not the martial music their comrades expected to hear.

Stanton Allen long remembered "the babel of bugle blasts kept up by the recruit 'musicians' from the sounding of the first call for reveille till taps. A majority of the boys enlisted as buglers could not at first make a noise, not even a little toot on their instruments, but when, under the instruction of a veteran bugler, they had mastered the art of filling their horns and producing sound they made up for lost time with a vengeance. And what a chorus! Reveille, stable call, breakfast call, sick call, drill call, retreat, tattoo, taps — all the calls, or what the little fellows could do at them, were sounded at one time with agonizing effect."

Because Allen was 14 he was approached soon after mustering and assigned to the musicians. He did not stay long, however, being returned to the ranks on account of ineptitude.[22]

Not only did musicians have to learn to play an instrument, they also had to know how to maneuver it and themselves. The drum major or principal musician communicated what actions were necessary. These could entail unslinging drums, putting up drumsticks, grounding drums, etc. The boys also had to learn how to march and maneuver in the field as well as on parade or during drill. This led to another batch of commands necessary for them to learn. During or after a battle musicians were employed as stretcher bearers and hospital attendants. Not only did they have to master music but additionally were taught the rudiments of first aid. Many lives were saved by small boys who watched the surgeons at work, carrying some of the knowledge gained to the wounded at the front and administering aid in a timely manner. With all these combined duties it is no wonder some youngsters were unable to perform to expected standards, and were sent home.

As if the military day was not full enough learning the basics of their assignments, soldiers were plagued constantly by another word that, in time, was more despised than drill. "Detail" was the ever-present order of someone in authority to get something done by someone of a lesser stature. Colonel Henry L. Scott effectively explained the chain of command when he defined "detail" in his *Military Dictionary*. "A detail for duty was a roster, or table, for the regular performance of duty either in camp or garrison. The general detail is regulated by the adjutant-general, according to the strength of the several corps. The adjutant of each regiment superintends the detail of the officers and non-commissioned officers for duty, and orderly [first] sergeants detail the privates." [23]

As time passed drill was held less frequently. Details, on the other hand, seemed to increase. As the struggle escalated there was more to be done. Chores included unloading wagons, cleaning camp, guarding knapsacks, digging sinks [latrines], fetching water and filling canteens, retrieving wood and provisions, foraging, building bridges, tearing up railroad track, and burying the dead.

The most common detail endured by new recruits was guard or picket duty. Guards were placed at the entrances of military camps to inspect all those coming or going. They primarily checked for proper identification and paperwork; however, at the front they had to keep a close lookout for the enemy in case they slipped by the pickets. Pickets were detailed from the troops to stand outpost duty. Their job was to stay alert and warn the camp of any approaching enemy. Standing picket was lonely and dangerous. It was also very important that those entrusted with such duties as guard and picket did so efficiently.

At 16, Joseph Benson Foraker was among the first to enlist in the 89th Ohio. The regiment was filled and mustered into Federal service on August 26, 1862. De-

State Archives of Michigan

Dearborn Historical Museum

Wolverine musicians George H. Wheelock, 12, left, and Emory C. Fox, 14, may have been taught "Ashworth's system," deemed by top Army instructors to be the best method adapted for duty drumming. Wheelock, a member of Company D, 6th Michigan Infantry, posed with proper placement of drum and sticks. Fox, considered "a superior drummer" by his mustering officer, belonged to Companies B and H, 27th Michigan.

spite his youth, Joseph was appointed second sergeant of Company A. Within a few days of muster the 89th was ordered to the Kentucky side of the Ohio River to impede a threatened attack by General Edmund Kirby Smith, whose Confederate troops were reported raiding in the Bluegrass State. With virtually no training Joseph was detailed as sergeant of the camp guard his first night out. The Rebels did not make an appearance, but the night still was fraught with difficulty, as Foraker explained:

Shortly after I was assigned to duty, Company A was detailed for picket duty, and spent the night a quarter of a mile in advance of our camp in that kind of service. In this way I was deprived of the opportunity of conferring with the officers of my company in regard to the first serious experience and trouble I had as a soldier. I had never before been on such duty. Hardly anybody else in the regiment had ever had any such experience. It was our first night "at the front."

Sometime during the night, when it became my duty to put on a relief guard, I found one of the soldiers intoxicated; so much so that he was utterly unfit for duty. I put another man in his place and a guard over him, and in the morning, immediately after roll call, reported him to the officer of the day. Someone told the Colonel. He was very much incensed to think that on the very first day of service, in what he was pleased to call the "enemy's country," one

61

Charcoal drawing of Joseph B. Foraker as he appeared shortly after enlisting in the 89th Ohio.

Notes of a Busy Life

of the men should be guilty of such an offense. With a loud voice he called upon me as Sergeant of the guard to bring the offending soldier to his headquarters. This order made me nervous, for I had never been very near the Colonel. I had never before spoken to him nor had he ever spoken to me. To be unexpectedly called before him in such a way filled me with apprehension. At that time he was a very august person. It was, therefore, with fear and trembling that I brought the guilty offender forward, and stood by while the Colonel interrogated first the soldier and then myself as to what had happened.

After he became thus informed, and after almost the entire regiment had gathered about to see what was going on, he proceeded to make a speech in which he told of the serious character of the offense that had been committed; that nothing could be worse than that a soldier appointed to guard his sleeping comrades should be guilty of drinking to excess and making himself incapable of discharging that duty, thus putting the lives of all the regiment in jeopardy, for all this had happened not only in the enemy's country, but also in the very presence, as it were, of the enemy, who was expected to attack us almost any hour. He finally ended his discourse by sentencing him without court martial or any other proceeding, to have his head shaved, and directed me, as Sergeant in charge, to execute the sentence.

From the first my embarrassment had been increasing. This capped the climax. I did not know what to do, but I had to do something and do it at once. Never having shaved anybody's head, I timidly asked what I should shave his head with. The Colonel answered in a stern voice, which indicated impatience with my ignorance as to how to proceed, that I should shave his head with a razor, of course. I told him I had no razor; where could I get one? He then suggested that I might substitute a pair of scissors. I told him I had no scissors, and did not know where I could get a pair. With this he became very impatient and gave me a severe lecture for having neither razor nor scissors, but told me to cut his hair with my knife. I had a knife, but by this time I was so thoroughly confused that I had great difficulty to get my hand under my belted blouse and into my pocket. Finally, however, I got it out and opened it, but not knowing how to proceed to use it, I stood a moment hesitating what to do, when the Colonel, greatly to my relief, snatched it out of

my hand, grabbed the man by the hair and commenced to saw off one lock after another, the man groaning and the Colonel all the while commenting on the gravity of the offense and the propriety of the punishment he was administering as an object lesson to all others.

He cut away until the poor man's head was quite spotted. At last, satisfied with what he had accomplished, he directed me to remove the prisoner, but to set him to work digging a ditch as a further punishment for this very grave offense. What kind of a ditch and where it should be located he did not specify, and I profitting by experience, did not make any inquiries, but marched him down into a ravine near the edge of camp and set him to work with a spade. He continued at this work until guard mount came and I was relieved. Just when the soldier was relieved I do not recall.[24]

Foraker's ordeal, although disturbing, was not life threatening. Some pickets met untimely deaths or were wounded at their posts. One casualty was 16-year-old Private James D. Sellers of Troy, Iowa. He was a replacement mustered into Company E, 15th Iowa, on February 29, 1864. With virtually no experience soldiering he was thrown into the hard-fought summer Georgia campaign. On July 1 the musketry and artillery fire did not cease until midnight in front of the 15th Iowa's position at Kennesaw Mountain. During the day, while serving at the extreme front, James lost his life on picket.[25] His death illustrated how true were the lines written about picket duty in the war's popular poem *All Quiet Along the Potomac:*

'Tis nothing — a private or two, now and then,
Will not count in the news of the battle;
Not an officer lost — only one of the men,
Moaning out, all alone the death rattle.[26]

Even with such dangers many young boys serving as musicians volunteered for picket to break up camp's monotony. A little more than a year after enlisting, musician Harry Kieffer of the 150th Pennsylvania borrowed a gun and voluntarily accompanied a friend on picket. That night, while stationed along the Rappahannock River opposite the enemy, both boys felt their blood pressure rise when the discharge of a rifle sent a round zipping over their heads through the bushes. Grabbing their rifles and sliding behind a tree, they intensely scanned the opposite shore for the trigger-happy culprit. After a short time the "Johnny" on the other bank started a conversation, claiming that his gun had gone off accidentally and that he would not shoot if they did not. It was a tense night, yet both sides kept the bargain.[27]

Picket detail was dangerous whenever near the enemy, but other details were equally so. Many young boys experienced fright acting as orderlies and messengers. In these capacities they often were called upon to deliver orders to other camps near the enemy at night, or during daylight hours when they could not easily hide. Even mundane details like bridge building could become dangerous if the Rebels suddenly appeared in superior numbers. Despite the hardships and dangers presented to the boys, once enlisted a majority enjoyed and embraced the whole adventure.

John Mackey was about 13 and one of numerous unmustered youngsters who served in the Army. In 1862, when his father James closed his Clarion, Pennsylvania, carriage shop to become captain of Company H, 103rd Pennsylvania, John tagged along as servant and companion.[28] Two months later he wrote his mother detailing his experiences thus far: "Last night as I was going to bed I received your letter. We are now about 6 or 8 miles from Yorktown, and we have a very pleasant camp. One of the boys captured a mule the other day, and we were going to keep it, but he sold it."

John described the nearly sleepless two-day journey by train from western Pennsylvania to Harrisburg, Baltimore and Washington. Destined for Virginia's peninsula, his father's regiment travelled alternately on foot or by boat. On April 2 "our steamer ran into a schooner having five men on board, sinking it; one man was drowned, but the other four got safely aboard our boat." This death was the first ever witnessed by the boy. Two weeks later the regiment camped in an open field without shelter of any kind, but young Mackey's spirits soared so high he did not register a single complaint in his letter home.[29]

After a year's service Gilbert Vanzant of the 79th Ohio summarized his thoughts on being a soldier in correspondence to *The Clinton Republican* published in Wilmington, Ohio. Like John Mackey, he had few complaints.

Lavergne, Tenn.
August 1st, 1863

Mr. Editor,

Dear Sir — Thinking a few lines from me, perhaps, would interest you a little, I send these to you. Well, a little past ten years old, I, with my father and friends, on the 9th of last August entered Camp Dennison; and how proud I felt with my little drum on my back a-going in the army as a drummer boy, and be with the brave soldiers who had started out to defend our country. I was willing to leave my dear mother and my little brother and sister, and my little soft bed, and my mother's table, and my little friends and school mates, and pleasant home, to go in the army as a drummer boy, to share all of the hardships and dangers and exposure of the soldier's life; which I have done thus far with pleasure. I have been in the army almost one year now, and have spent the time and enjoyed myself bravely. I like to be a soldier, although we have seen some hard times; but I did not get home sick. I have not been home sick since I first came in the army; but I went home after being away about nine months. I was glad to see my dear mother and brother and sister once more; and after a visit of two weeks I again returned to the Regiment, and was glad to see my father and the rest of the soldiers, and my much esteemed friend Col. Doan [Lt. Col. Azariah W. Doan], and the rest of the officers, who are good and kind to me.

I have many kind friends in the Regiment, whom I never shall forget, long after the war is over and we are separated; and, won't never forget Colonel [Henry G.] Kennett for the kindness he has shown to me, and the little sword that he presented to me as a token of his love and respect. And this little sword I will take home with me when the war is over, and look at it and think of the giver with love and respect, and remember where I was when I received it, away down in Tennessee, about four hundred miles from my home, a little drummer boy in the great army of the Union. And how often I have looked at our beautiful flag, as it was borne along on some of our long marches in the sturdy hands of some of its defenders. I say how often I have looked at it, and asked God to bless it, and forbid that it should ever be destroyed. And oh how nice it flutters in the air when we are on battalion drill, and dress parade. It is a nice sight to see our Regiment on dress parade, when all of the soldiers are fixed up with their "rig" all bright and clean and their white gloves on.

I have seen a great many things, and been in a great many towns, and seen some rebs, and didn't like the looks of them. I have had good health all the time, better than I ever had at home; and sometimes had nothing to eat but hard crackers and fat meat, and black coffee, but I thought if the rest could live on it I could, so it was all right with me. And we have slept out on the ground in the rain and mud, and in the cold and warm, wet and dry. I expect some of my little friends would think that such usage would kill

them, and you may think it too hard for a little boy like me; but it hain't hurt me yet and I hope to keep in good health until I can beat the death-knell of the Southern Confederacy on my little drum. It was bright and new when I first came out, but now it looks quite old from the service in the army; but it sounds as well as ever yet.

Our Regiment is in good health and fine spirits, but we have had a good many to die; and oh how sad I felt beating the dead march going to their graves; and the mournful tune of the fife and the doleful sound of our drums created feelings that none but the soldier knows, following a comrade to his grave. These things I can never forget, but will ever remember them, that I, with the rest of the drummers, beat the dead march as we marched to their last resting place. But we think that it won't be long now until the war will be over, then I will throw my drum over my shoulder and return with my father and friends to my home in Port William. But I don't expect to go home anymore until the war is over, for I am too far from home now. We are down in Dixey and I can play the tune of Dixey on my drum pretty well, and I shall remember Dixey's land whenever I play the tune on my drum. But I like to be a soldier and will see the end of the war if I live, before I come home and leave the army.[30]

As "Little Gib" hinted, death was more likely to claim a soldier through sickness than enemy bullets. All the training in the world was powerless against deadly outbreaks of disease that often ravaged the ranks. It was a sad lesson quickly learned.

CHAPTER 4

'With the most profound feelings of sorrow'

Having completed his work the stone cutter laid aside the heavy mallet and chisel. Reaching into his pocket he withdrew a small memorandum book and carefully compared the spelling of words with those just carved on the grave marker.

Alonzo Roush

Died Oct. 3, 1862

Aged 16 years 1 month & 18 days

Private in Co. A 91 O.V.I.

Sleep brother dear

and take your rest.

God called you home

he thought it best.

Twas hard indeed

to part with thee.

But Christ's strong arm

supported me.

Assured that everything was correct he returned the well-worn black book to his pocket. Before 1862 ended it was used five more times to record orders for gravestones of Gallia County, Ohio, soldiers.[1]

Throughout the country stone carvers, casket makers and undertakers were kept busy by the war's human toll. On death lists compiled early in the conflict were a number of youngsters who recently thought they alone could win the war. Instead, they were all but memories to loved ones left behind by the time hostilities ended in 1865.

Alonzo Roush was a small, blue-eyed boy who enlisted to help his country, but never even saw the enemy. In August 1862 the teenager inflated his age to 18 and signed the rolls of Company A, 91st Ohio. Before he could leave the state he was stricken with typhoid fever, sent home to recuperate and died early in October. His patriotic and glory-seeking adventure had lasted less than two months.[2]

Dr. Charles Tripler warned that underage recruits were not physically able to withstand the rigorous life of soldiering.[3] During the war's early days it became painfully apparent he was correct. As troops gathered from all quarters of the Union they were exposed to germs and diseases as diverse as the citizen-soldiers themselves. For some the exposure was more than their immune systems could handle, and they soon sickened. Boys attacked by disease had youth on their side to aid in the struggle, but their small bodies were a handicap when debilitating fevers or fluid-depleting dysentery overcame them. Illnesses such as measles, typhoid, diarrhea, smallpox and influenza wreaked havoc in the ranks. There were many youngsters who, after taking extreme measures to enter the Army, found themselves sick far away from a mother's loving care. Others like Alonzo Roush sickened so quickly they were able to return home.

Private Charles C. Henderson of West Jefferson, Ohio, was armed and ready for the march after his September 5, 1861, enlistment in Company A, 40th Ohio. Despite his resolute stare he succumbed to disease in a Kentucky hospital the following February.

Author's Collection

After Company D of the 55th Ohio left the Buckeye State accompanied by its two young drummers, Guel M. Wood, 14, and William Waldron, about the same age, disease began cutting down the Ohioans while encamped at Grafton in western Virginia. "Sickness came to our regiment," wrote Private Sumner A. Wing, "and some twenty-two died there. Company D lost their little drummer [Waldron], a fair-faced boy of less than sixteen, a mother's darling. He died for his country as much as if he had fallen in battle."[4]

Edward P. Rettig was drummer boy of the 8th Ohio Infantry's Company H. Along with 55 other recruits he was mustered June 6, 1861, at Camp Dennison, Ohio.[5] Located north of Cincinnati, this facility was the rendezvous and training camp where completion of the 8th's organization took place. On July 8 the regiment received orders to break camp for the seat of war. That evening the men merrily boarded a train which carried them east. For young Edward the trip must have been thrilling. When daylight arrived the tracks literally were lined with people. At Zanesville the citizens prepared a splendid feast. The whole town was decorated with bunting, and throngs of people sang patriotic airs and shouted cheers for the 8th Ohio, president, flag and country. As the train crossed the Ohio River at Bellaire, nothing could be heard but the song "Dixie" parodied in the most uncomplimentary terms.[6]

The 8th's destination of Grafton was reached by morning after numerous delays were overcome. The men built fires among the trees and bedded down for sleep after the long journey. Before the first day ended Edward, with the rest of the drummers, was ordered to beat the long roll, rousing the regiment to form in line of battle. A contingent was sent to the surrounding hills as pickets, while Edward and the boys continued the long roll, advancing with the regiment. Desperate work was expected. One officer was said to have sallied forth with a Navy revolver in each hand and his sword clenched in his teeth. To Edward's chagrin and all present, one of the sentinels had fired at a cow, causing the excitement. Soon all were back in camp trying to catch up on well-needed rest. During its first month in the field the 8th, along with other regiments in the vicinity, marched, deployed and in general worried about the elusive enemy. Throughout their escapades the men were entertained by the area's grand scenery of wooded peaks and crystal-clear streams.[7]

On August 18 the regiment was ordered to report to Fort Pendleton at Potomac Bridge. This fort guarded a road over the mountains leading from western Virginia to Romney. Upon arrival the 8th was instructed to erect camp in a "deep, damp gorge in the mountain." The camp was so disagreeable that within a few days about 300 were sick in the hospital. The illness was a low-grade fever, and the men called it the disease of "Camp Maggoty Hollow." One of those who fell sick was Edward Rettig. His condition worsened so quickly that he was sent home to Medina, Ohio, to recuperate. A little more than a month had passed since he faithfully sounded the long roll calling out his regiment to battle the cow. None of his comrades foresaw his short tenure as he beat his drum with the fullness of youth's energy.[8] Edward did not recover, succumbing to the fever September 6 at his home. Hopefully, his parents' presence helped ease his suffering. For Company H, its drummer boy never returned.[9]

Young boys' deaths were common early in the war. Sixteen-year-old Horace H. Gebhart died at Munfordville, Kentucky, after serving four months with the 1st Ohio Infantry. Arthur T. Strong died in February 1862 at age 16 after two months' service with the 42nd Ohio, and James Buchanan of the 63rd Ohio lasted only 63 days before dying at Cincinnati. These were just a few early Buckeye fatalities.[10]

When a youngster died everyone noticed and numerous comrades took it extremely hard. At the first battle of Bull Run many members of the 2nd New York State Militia witnessed the death of drummer James Maxwell during a fierce Confederate cannonade as they waited to advance in a wooded portion of the field. Two comrades told the grim tale of his death in letters home. One named Norman wrote July 28, 1861, to his brother about the battle:

I tell you John though we were not in any active fight, we were in about as warm a place as I want to be in and in a worse place than if we had been in the open battle field. Where we was placed was in a thick pine woods where we could not see ten feet ahead of us and the enemy pouring the grape and canister into us like the devil, wounding and killing at every shot and we not able to return a shot at them. After that we were drawn up in line of battle alongside of a road and the enemy pegging away and killing at almost every shot. Within about four feet of where I was two men were killed with a cannon shot. It took the top right off one man's head so that when they picked him up to carry him away the whole brain dropped out on the ground without being broken, and completely mashed the other one's head into a jelly. I might tell of a number of such sights but I do not think they would be interesting to you and as the papers will tell you all about it. I was quite close to the little Drummer boy Maxwell when he was killed. Our little 1st sergeant, the German, perhaps you remember him, he was wounded in the shoulder and sent to a hospital in the rear...."[11]

John B. Wilson of Company C furnished a more detailed description of Maxwell's death:

Sixteen-year-old Andrew J. Ward was buried in a Nashville cemetery after his life was claimed by chronic diarrhea in July 1863. He had enlisted the previous November in Company E, 113th Ohio. Personal effects sent home included a "portfolio, pen knife, pocket book and spy glass." Carte de visite image by M.L. Albright, Urbana, Ohio.

Author's Collection

With lips fiercely pursed, Private Thomas Emmonson of Company C, 15th Wisconsin, brandishes a cocked M1851 Colt Navy revolver. The Norwegian native was living in Racine County, Wisconsin, when he enlisted in October 1861. He died of disease at Stevenson, Alabama, on October 20, 1863.

State Historical Society of Wisconsin

We started for Centreville [Virginia] about two o'clock in the morning of Sunday the 21st of July. We marched in stillness and darkness about three miles when we halted in a wood, for we knew we were near the enemy. Our regiment had orders that if any man had anything to do for himself now was the time. In about fifteen minutes afterwards we had orders to form in line of battle. We did so. The 1st Conn[ecticut], the 1st and 2nd Ohio and our regiment was all in one line two deep. The 1st Conn. to the right, the Ohio regiments in the center and our regiment on the left of the line and next the enemy. When formed we had orders to lie down flat on our grub cubbourds [sic] which we did. Then one of our batteries threw a couple of shells at the enemy who were a great distance from where we lay. We could not see them nor did they take any notice of the shot we sent. So in about an hour after our side tried it on again, but with the same effect and we lay still. In about two hours afterwards our guns opened again, this time touching him in a sore spot and for the first time they took notice of us and returned the fire with great spirit. While the firing was going on we were ordered to advance and try to take the battery by storm. But when we came to the edge of the woods we found ourselves within fifteen or twenty yards of the mouths of the rebel cannon which they were not slow in firing at us. We retreated back into the woods again and lay down for shelter amongst a perfect shower of grape and canister. At the third discharge a large shot came amongst our men killing two and wounding one. The wounded man was Lieutenant Dempsey. The ball first passed through the body of one of our drummer boys named Maxwell. He gave but one sigh, and I am sure those who heard it will never forget it. The other killed by the same ball was sitting behind a tree with his back against it. The ball struck the tree splitting it and passed through the man's head.[12]

One demoralizing death to occur early on was that of John Boulton Young. Boltie, as he was known to his comrades, was an eager volunteer from Sunbury, Pennsylvania, who enlisted in the 47th Pennsylvania.

The regiment was organized during the months of August and September 1861. After mustering it left Camp Curtin for Washington on September 21. A drummer boy of Company C, Boltie was four days shy of his 13th birthday. He gaily marched off with the others carrying a downsized, 13-inch red-rimmed drum. Stepping off, he was careful to keep the circular, red-tack design emblazoning the shell to the front as he stretched his four-foot frame at every stride. His new, bright-red pants ballooned from his leather leggings and rubbed against the drum suspended by a strap around his neck. The pants contrasted dramatically with his dark blue, non-regulation Zouave-style jacket, also trimmed in red. He was such a patriotic sight and so well liked by the men that they called him their "Pet Boltie." [13]

Unfortunately, the blond-haired boy gazing proudly with gray eyes at his comrades as they offered him praise that morning was, six weeks later, their first casualty. On October 17, 1861, a deep silence fell over the men as news spread of the young boy's death. They had known for a few days that he was sick and not do-

ing well, having been transferred to the eruptive fever ward at a hospital outside Washington. Despite the attention of attending Surgeon Robert I. Thomas and his staff, smallpox claimed the adolescent.[14] Captain John P.S. Gobin was burdened with the sad duty of writing a condolence letter to Boltie's parents:

It is with the most profound feelings of sorrow I have ever experienced that I am compelled to announce to you the death of our "Pet" and your son Boulton. When I received the word I immediately started for the Kalorama Hospital in Georgetown, hoping this message was unfounded and would prove untrue. When I arrived there I found that little form that I had so loved, prepared for the grave. Until a short time before he died the symptoms were very favorable, and every hope was entertained for his recovery. He was the life and light of our company, and his death caused a blight and a sadness to prevail, that only rude wheels of time can efface. Every attention was paid to him by the doctors and nurses, all being anxious to show their devotion to one so young. I have had him buried, and ordered a stone for his grave. I would have sent the body home but the nature of his disease prevented it. When we return, however, if we are so fortunate, the body will ac-

company us. Everything connected with Boltie shall be attended to, no matter what the cost. His effects that can safely be sent home, together with his pay, will be forwarded to you.[15]

Captain Gobin informed a friend back home:

I had him buried in the cemetery, had everything attended to regardless of the cost. The doctors at Kalorama Hospital told me it was the worst case they ever saw. It was a regular black confluent small pox. I had him vaccinated in Harrisburg, but it would not take, and he must have been exposed to the disease from one of the old Rebel camps we visited, as their army is full of it.[16]

A week later Sergeant William Hendricks of Company C wrote to his wife concerning Young's death:

What do the folks think of the company getting a monument for Boltie? Today Bob McNeal wrote to Miss Dix to save Boltie's suit until after the war was over, then he is going to get them and keep them, the poor fellow thinks of nothing but Bolt. The other day he was packing up some of the little fellow's clothes, and among them he found a small testament. "This," he said with a tear in his eye, "shall be mine and there is not a hundred dollars in the Army that could buy it from me." He carries it in his pocket all the time. Boltie's little drum we are going to send home as quick as we get a chance.[17]

After the threat of spreading the contagious disease dissipated, Boltie's body was disinterred and shipped back to Sunbury, arriving on January 28, 1862. A military funeral was held in Sunbury Cemetery three days later. A unit of three-month volunteers served as escort while throngs of local citizens turned out. Company C donated more than $100 for a stone adorned with a drum and sticks that was placed at the head of the grave. The words "He has beaten his last retreat, and will sleep peacefully until reveille on resurrection day" were etched below his name.[18]

**Drummer Albert L. Busiel,
Company I, 12th New Hampshire.**

History of the Twelfth Regiment New Hampshire Volunteers

The 47th Pennsylvania suffered many more losses during its service, but the death of its first casualty in drummer John Boulton Young was perhaps the hardest to accept. Richard Eddy, chaplain of the 60th New York, touched on this subject when writing about his regiment's loss, also a musician. "On the 19th of November [1861], the first death occurred in the regiment. Early in the morning Henry W. Powers, drummer of Company C, died of inflammation of the bowels. He had been very sick for several days, and his condition required that he should be buried immediately. Just at sunset, all things in readiness, we bore his remains to the Methodist burying-ground at Elkridge Landing, a mile from camp, and laid him to rest. The attendance at this funeral was uncommonly large, Company C coming up in a body from their camp, and all the officers and men who were off duty at headquarters, being present. It was a new and strange thing then. Alas! We little thought how common it would yet be to us."[19]

As difficult as it was for regiments as a whole to accept the death of one of the lads, it was even more of a blow to the remaining boys. Delavan Miller wrote of the 1862 demise of one of his fellow drummers in the 2nd New York Heavy Artillery: "Jimmie ... sickened and died. He had been a slender little fellow, and the [Second] Bull Run campaign was too much for him. He lingered along for weeks in the hospital and when he realized that he must answer the last roll call he wished the surgeon to send for his comrades of the drum corps. It was his wish that we should stand at parade rest in the aisle between the cots. From under his pillow he took a little bible and opening it at the 23rd Psalm, handed it to Harry Marshall, our drum major, and motioned for him to read the beautiful words. Need I say that there were no dry eyes? And I think from that moment life to most of the boys present had a more serious meaning. The next Sabbath afternoon with muffled drums and slow measured tread, we escorted his re-mains to a little knoll beneath a clump of pines near Arlington. A volley was fired over the grave, our drums unmuffled and back to camp we went, beating a lively quickstep."[20]

Disease continued to claim victims throughout the war. Its different forms killed nearly 200,000 Union soldiers, twice as many than died in combat.[21] Of this number some were mere boys like Franklin Bragg, drummer boy of Company D, 66th Illinois (Birge's Western Sharpshooters), who enlisted at 15 in 1861, and was dead at 16.[22] Thomas Parkinson also enlisted as a drummer at the age of 15. As a member of the 19th Ohio he died an agonizing death by lockjaw before his 17th birthday.[23] If every account of youngsters succumbing to disease was told, the total would fill volumes.

When Harrison M. Busiel discovered his oldest child Albert had joined Company I, 12th New Hampshire, on August 15, 1862, he enlisted the same day in Company E. He reasoned that if they served together he could help care for his boy if needed. Albert, born in October 1846, was 15 when he and his 37-year-old father were mustered into service. Tragically, before the regiment left the state Albert was dead. On September 25, 1862, he traipsed to a Concord gun shop to purchase a revolver. While looking over the piece, which was loaded, it discharged and killed the boy. Harrison accepted the death of Albert, described as a "bright, promising boy, full of life and energy," extremely hard. Being in his late 30s he probably would not have enlisted had his son been less of a motivating factor. Once mustered he was obliged to stay like everyone else, in spite of Albert's loss. Harrison served with the 12th New Hampshire until discharged for disability in 1864.[24]

Albert Busiel, like Boltie Young of the 47th Pennsylvania, was the first in his regiment to die. With so many untrained soldiers handling weapons in close proximity to one another it was a matter of short odds that terrible accidents sometimes occurred. In the cases of both the shock of their deaths was deeper because they were so young.

One of the saddest accounts of a boy being struck down in a gun mishap is the story of Clarence D. McKenzie. He was one of thousands of children growing up poor in Brooklyn's tenement houses during the 1850s. Born February 18, 1849, Clarence was the second oldest of five siblings. His early years were spent like those of most children, schoolwork and play competing with each other for his time. At age six he and his younger brother and sisters were introduced to a mission Sunday school, which they consistently attended. These schools were founded in the city's poor districts to assist destitute youths who otherwise roamed the streets. Clarence loved the mission and continued to attend, even though his family moved three times prior to the war.[25]

At age 11 Clarence joined the 13th Regiment of New York State Militia, the "National Grays," on July 9, 1860. Three months later he participated in his first military parade as a drummer boy for a reception of the Prince of Wales. When war came he was one of many youngsters who easily entered the Army due to his established position in a military organization. On April 30, 1861, the 13th Regiment was ordered out "for the seat of war," taking a steamer to Annapolis, Maryland.[26] On the trip Clarence was so fatigued by the excitement that Lieutenant Colonel Robert B. Clark found him asleep on deck.[27]

Once at Annapolis the regiment resumed training when not guarding railroads it was sent there to protect. On May 10 Clarence wrote to his parents, "I have plenty of fun all the time, sauntering around." He also mentioned he was anxiously awaiting the arrival of older brother William, who recently joined as a drummer. William turned up two days later. In a May 14 letter home he described how happy his little brother seemed. "It would be impossible for me to tell you how truly glad Clarence and myself were in meeting each other. He stood for some time on the dock ready to receive me. He felt so glad to see me that he would scarcely wait for the steamboat to touch the dock, before he was flying towards me. Clarence and myself sleep together and have good accommodations and are as happy as the day is long."[28]

The happiness shared by the boys was short-lived. On June 11 Clarence was sitting on a bench in his quarters, composing a letter to his parents. As he wrote, one of his friends, William L. McCormick, was practicing the manual of arms near him when the gun suddenly fired, shooting Clarence through the abdomen. A report detailing the incident was issued the following day.

Headquarters 13th Regiment, N.Y.S.M.
Annapolis, June 12th, 1861

I am sorry to have to record another death in our regiment by the accidental discharge of a gun. One of the members of Company B, being short a musket, borrowed one that belonged to one of the other members who was acting as cook, and which was loaded, though unknown to him at that time. A few moments previous to drill he was practicing the manual in the drummers' quarters, and in coming to a charge bayonet his hand struck the hammer of his piece, forcing it down — although he says it was half-cocked[29] — and discharging it, the ball striking Clarence McKenzie in the back, passing through and out at the stomach, and finally striking against a brick wall with such force as to break out part of the brick. He lived some two hours and was sensible, though part of the time unable to speak. The news flew through the camp — as all bad news does — like wildfire, and soon a crowd collected around the quarters of Company B, where he was lying, anxious to get the particulars, and when his death was announced they wended their ways to their rooms with saddened hearts. His body was on view during the evening, and through the kindness of some of the ladies of Annapolis, who supplied us with flowers, was very prettily laid out and looked quite natural, his countenance having changed but little. During the night it was packed in an ice box, and this morning sent on to Brooklyn with an escort of four men under the command of Captain [Henry] Balsdon, in whose company the drummer was enlisted. As the coffin was taken from the drummers' quarters, preceded by the balance of the drum corps and a fifer playing the slow and solemn tune of the dead march, the other companies of the regiment fell into line and followed it to the cars. The music was beautiful, yet sad, and many a man, who would not flinch on the field of battle, shed tears over the remains of poor Clarence. He was the smallest in the corps and liked by everyone who knew him, being well behaved, always in good spirits, and ready and willing to do whatever was asked of him; his comrade drummers and the drum-major were very much affected; they could not have felt worse had he been their own brother. A brother (William) of his went on with the body, and probably will remain in Brooklyn, as I understand this is the second boy his parents have lost within a short time, and they prefer to keep the remaining one home. His drum, knapsack, &c. have been tastily hung with crepe and wreaths of flowers out of respect of his comrades.[30]

First Lieutenant Oliver Cotter of Company F wrote how manfully Clarence had beat his drum during an expedition just a few days before. The boy was a favorite of the whole garrison, Cotter affirmed, and described the camp's doleful atmosphere. "The men were moved to tears this morning when the funeral cortege moved towards the cars for transportation to New York, his companions beating the dead march, at the same time moved to tears; it was a melancholy sight. All the drummer boys are well; there cannot be a better set of boys found in the state of New York."[31]

After learning details of the boy's last hours from Captain Balsdon, a member of Company G wrote to

the mission school Clarence attended:

He was conscious until he died. He did not shed a tear, but was perfectly calm and collected through it all. He was apparently free from pain until a short time before he died, when his bowels pained him. He said, "My dear doctor, what can you do for this pain in my stomach?" He called for some of his friends when he knew he was going to die, and bade them "good bye." He forgave the boy who shot him, and did not wish him to think he had any hard feelings against him, knowing it to have been purely accidental.[32]

In an account by Balsdon it was said the first words Clarence uttered after being shot were, "Shoot McCormick, shoot McCormick, for he has shot me!" But within a few minutes he realized it was an accident and forgave the boy.[33]

The captain asked a few moments before he died if he wished to send any message to his parents. He replied, "Tell them I am near dying; that is all." Balsdon prayed with Clarence, who asked God to help him recover but the captain told him there was no use in it. Clarence then became quiet. Noting the silence Balsdon covered the pallid face with his hands. The boy rolled to his left and expired.[34]

Not many weeks before, Clarence had been home persuading his reluctant mother to let him go. She was against it from the start and never fully agreed that he should. When she expressed fear that he would be killed, Clarence argued, "Oh, no! No! Mother, I am only a little boy — they will not want to shoot me." His father was very pleased and proud that his son was to be a drummer in Brooklyn's favorite regiment. The city's finest men commanded it and he thought it the post of honor for Clarence to be at its head.[35]

Time had passed quickly and now Clarence was dead. From Annapolis the terrible tidings flashed like a thunderbolt via telegraph to his parents. A military escort followed conveying the body, which had been handsomely arranged in the ice box for the trip. An express wagon pulled up in front of the two-story McKenzie house on Liberty Street. The family was gathered in the same parlor where Clarence earlier appealed to his mother to let him go. The small box was brought in and placed on two chairs under a front window. His father stood by stupefied, and the distraught mother had to be carried from the room in a state of frantic despair. Her worst fears had been realized.[36]

Among the many mourners that morning was Mr. Plummer, the mission school's superintendent who was accompanied by his daughter, one of Clarence's teachers. Plummer had a son of his own in the same regiment. After entering the McKenzie house they asked if they could see the drummer of the 13th Regiment, but the father retorted he had strict orders from the undertaker not to open the container or show Clar-

The Little Drummer Boy

Clarence D. McKenzie, Company D, 13th New York State Militia.

ence until he was removed to his coffin. However, he invited them into the parlor. There reposed the box covered with a national flag, upon which lay his cap, jacket and drumsticks. A floral wreath presented by Colonel Clark's wife sat at one end.[37]

Plummer stated he had seen the boy just a few days before in Baltimore while visiting his son. At that news the father asked William to retrieve his mother in

case she had any questions for them. As she entered the room she threw herself into a chair and sobbed uncontrollably. "Oh, my poor boy, my poor boy. He said to me when he went away, Mother, do not cry for me. No one will shoot me. I am only a little drummer boy." The conversation continued for some time when Mr. McKenzie suddenly insisted the box be opened and they see the boy. His wife was not prepared for such a sight and excused herself to the kitchen as the father and others gazed at Clarence's lifeless body for the first time. Together they reminisced of his childhood and discussed his wonderful disposition while his mother continued weeping in the adjoining room.[38]

At 4 p.m. on June 14, 1861, the funeral for Clarence David McKenzie was held in Brooklyn's St. John's Church. The body had been removed from the house and brought to St. John's under military escort earlier in the day in anticipation of a large crowd. The church was filled to capacity and an estimated 3,000 additional mourners gathered in the yard and surrounding streets. When the eulogies concluded the crowd, led by school children, passed the flag-draped coffin. Prior to the procession the lid was opened, exposing the drummer boy's remains to the onlookers who filed past for more than 30 minutes. The coffin then was loaded into a hearse and conveyed to Evergreen Cemetery. The sidewalks were filled with spectators as the military escort and carriages passed. At the gravesite three rounds of musketry were fired, concluding the solemnities but not the sorrow.[39]

If there was one person who felt the occasion's grief as deeply as the dead boy's parents, it was William McCormick. He had been one of Clarence's best friends even before they joined the Army. He was well known by the entire McKenzie family, and as the one responsible for the fatal accident wrote them a moving letter on June 19 from Baltimore, here excerpted.

"Dear Mr. and Mrs. McKenzie: With an aching

heart I sit down to indite to you what I trust to be a few lines of consolation. Too well I know, however, the futility of any attempt on my part to fill the vast void occasioned in your hearts by the loss of one so dear, so beloved by all, as was your Clarence. But was I not to express to you by thus writing, my sincere and heartfelt sympathy, which I entertain for you in your great bereavement, I should consider myself as unworthy of your forgiveness, and should only feel too miserable for existence....

"This I would say, that no one can feel worse next to yourselves than I do. You can have but little conception of the great agony of feeling that I have suffered during the last few days, and I can scarcely write this from heaviness of heart. None loved Clarence, dear Clarence, more than I, and oh, God knows that could I but bring him back to life again, I would give, did I possess it, the whole world and all its contents...."[40]

One more element of the funeral worth telling is the story of Jack — a small white terrier that belonged to Clarence, and was as a dog should be, a boy's true companion. In idle days before the war Clarence had taught Jack many impressive tricks, which he seemed to relish performing for his young master. When Clarence was leaving for the war he playfully positioned Jack on his hind legs and lectured the animal to be good until he returned. On the day the boy's body was placed in the parlor, Jack pawed and sniffed at the lid of the ice box in earnest. He howled and whimpered. That night he slept by the side of the box as if his master was in his bed.[41]

During the funeral procession the family thought it only fitting to have Jack along. He sat graveside through the orations and did not wander off until the musket volleys scared him away. After the crowd dispersed and silence prevailed, Jack came back to the spot and laid down on the freshly turned soil. For days afterward the dog made a silent pilgrimage to the site, lying there until dark when he returned home.[42] The story of Jack, if nothing else, illustrates how wasteful were the deaths of scores of young soldiers in the Civil War. Boys like Clarence McKenzie should have shared many more youthful, happy days playing with their dogs.

Death also reached youngsters who recently had been playing war at home with wooden swords or small cardboard soldiers arrayed to battle imaginary foes. Through fulfilled desires to participate in the war they now found themselves surrounded with real soldiers facing real foes. Unlike toys that were easily righted after being knocked over by wooden cannonballs, real soldiers who were struck down lay immobilized on the bloody, shot-torn ground. For boy soldiers who participated in their first battle, reality was nothing like they imagined. They quickly observed it was anything but play.

Andrew J. Smith's views of his introduction to combat were typical of many youngsters' experiences. At age 16 he was accepted in December 1861 as a drummer in Company B, 104th Pennsylvania. Repeated attempts were necessary to receive his father's coveted signature that allowed him to enlist. Andrew's first taste of battle was May 31, 1862, at Fair Oaks, Virginia. His experiences that day were recorded a decade later, but visions of the struggle still were etched clearly in his memory.[43]

The engagement was begun by the enemy, and our regiment, from the first, was in the thickest of the fight. The shells came fearfully close to us, and I was in momentary expectation of being killed. The noise of the artillery and musketry was deafening, while our forces for a time were driven back and through our camp, which was occupied by the enemy. All was confusion, as can well be imagined; and I began to desire a place of safety. My work was not exciting enough to inspire courage [as a musician, Andrew was detailed to help care for the injured]. Wounded men were being carried hurriedly to the rear, mangled, groaning and dying. The spectacle was horrifying. I did not join our regiment again until sundown. Great as was their danger, I felt somewhat secure in their company. But how changed their appearance! From six hundred strong in the morning, now only about a hundred and twenty-five answered roll call. Darkness had brought the battle to a close. Our men were ordered into the rifle pits, and directed to hold them until re-enforcements could arrive. Re-enforcements did come to their relief during the night, but not until late. I spent much of the night in assisting the wounded men. In the morning the enemy was driven back and our camp recovered.

My visit to the camp and battlefield was blood curdling indeed. The wounded had nearly all been removed, mostly by the enemy, but the dead remained for us to bury. The sight was horrible, and the stench already sickening. Men and horses were piled everywhere in confusion, and mangled in the most shocking manner. Some were pierced only by bullets, and looked peaceful and human in death, while others were torn almost to atoms. On many parts of the field the blue and the gray were mingled together, sleeping side by side in death like friends, though bitterest foes in life. On one spot about fifteen feet square, I counted twenty dead men; and these masses of dead were common. They had gone down under the fire of grape, and winnows had been made in their ranks. In many instances a group of men would be lying dead under the shade and protection of a tree, whither as wounded men they had crowded, and where at last in agony and without attention they had died. For those whom we could recognize we dug single graves, and marked their places of slumber. For the unrecognized we dug trenches, and buried them three and four deep.[44]

The shocking scenes of combat and duties necessitated in its aftermath completely destroyed some boys' desire to play war if they were fortunate enough to return home. Andrew Smith's grueling trial was at least safely endured.[45] Unlucky youngsters found plenty of time to reflect on their ordeals while wracked by painful wounds, lying in hospitals and hoping to survive. One underage recruit who was not spared such agony was Ezra Smith of the 95th Ohio.

Enlisting August 18, 1862, in Company F at Newark, Ohio, Ezra's military career transpired like a whirlwind. Within 24 hours he was mustered into service at Camp Chase in Columbus, and on the morning of the 20th outfitted and armed with the rest of the regiment. Without training, the 95th later that day was reviewed during its first dress parade by Governor David Tod, who delivered a stirring speech. Afterward, a flag was presented by ex-Governor William Dennison's wife while a throng of onlookers cheered. As soon as the ovations subsided orders were read at the governor's request, instructing the regiment to leave at sunrise by train for Lexington, Kentucky. The regiment was sent off so quickly it did not receive its tents or stores.[46]

The trip went well for the 900-plus buoyant men as they made their way south through Cincinnati to the Bluegrass. On the afternoon of August 22 the regiment arrived at Lexington, where it was issued tents and ordered to lay out its first camp. As the detail was completed new orders were received to march at sunrise for Richmond, Kentucky, 25 miles southeast. Confederate General E. Kirby Smith's approach via Cumberland Gap with 10,000 men necessitated the orders.[47]

As the eastern sky lightened the men formed ranks and set out on the limestone pike to Richmond. Even though they left their overstuffed knapsacks behind, the tramp was exhausting. By 5 p.m. the green troops

reached the Kentucky River after marching 15 miles. They were allowed to rest, but a courier arrived from Richmond urging haste and the march resumed. By 2 a.m. of August 24 the command arrived at Richmond, averaging only 20 men per company. The stragglers plodded on at a snail's pace but most showed up later in the morning. They happily learned the enemy was still some distance away, and finally were allowed to rest. For the next five days the regiment was instructed in a crash course of military basics while it awaited the Rebels.[48]

Just 10 days after being issued their uniforms and guns, Ezra Smith and his comrades were flung into battle the morning of August 30. Enemy cannonading began at 7:15, and by 9 o'clock the 95th and its brigade were ordered to the battlefield. The Ohioans led the way as the column marched to the sound of musketry. The 18th Kentucky's band followed close behind playing "Yankee Doodle." Every drum and fife of the 95th joined in, helping to build confidence in the ranks during the four-mile march. Part of that distance had been at the double-quick. The men were winded and thirsty, but surprisingly the regiment remained mostly intact.[49]

As it approached it was greeted by the sight of another Union brigade retreating rapidly toward its position, forcing the 95th to be placed in battle line while still advancing and within striking distance of the Rebels. This maneuver would not have been an easy one for veterans, let alone raw troops with minimal training. Confederate gunners began showering the Buckeyes with shell, inflicting the first casualties. Then an eerie silence replaced the cannons' reverberations. Wide battle lines of butternut could be seen pouring from the flanking woods and fence rows. Still the inexperienced troops were full of fight, and for the most part gladly accepted their brigade commander's and colonel's rash orders to fix bayonets and prepare to charge the cannons in front. Not all the fresh soldiers were eager to advance, prompting the 95th's colonel, William L. McMillen, to use his sword and fist on a few occasions to imbue fortitude in those lacking the quality just then.[50]

The Ohioans advanced in relatively good order toward their objective. Almost immediately they were engulfed in a torrential storm of musketry and artillery fire. Within minutes Colonel McMillen and a large percentage of the regiment turned and ran, leav-

Private Ezra H. Smith, Company F, 95th Ohio.

This inch-wide, silver-washed brass pin contains the pistol ball that wounded Ezra Smith in the battle of Richmond, Kentucky. It was kept with other war relics, including a tintype of Ezra's friend Stephen A. Ritter, below, also of Company F, 95th Ohio. Both teenagers enlisted the same day, were wounded at Richmond and mustered out together in August 1865.

Author's Collection

ing their dead and wounded among the Confederates and abandoning more than 200 who were compelled to surrender. The stampede covered two miles before Union forces attempted another stand, but again the Rebels prevailed. Before the day faded all but 237 men of the 95th Ohio were killed, wounded or captured.[51]

One of those sacrificed that day as fodder for the enemy's more experienced guns was Ezra Smith. Exemplifying the fury of the affair, his wound was caused by an antagonist so close that he was shot with a pistol. The small-caliber bullet pierced his right calf, disabling and forcing him to surrender. Considering that 32 of his comrades were killed outright, Ezra could count himself fortunate to have survived. Another lucky break was that the Confederates had no interest in caring for hundreds of wounded prisoners in the midst of a campaign, and therefore paroled them on the spot. [52]

Ezra's wound confined him to a host of hospitals for the next four months. During that period he had ample time to rethink the burning desire he had to enlist. Undoubtedly he never envisioned himself in the vortex of a full-scale battle without having proper training. The decisions made by those in command, including Governor Tod, were all responsible for the misguided efforts of the 95th Ohio during its first two weeks in service. For Ezra and his regiment the errors were costly. Although he faced a slow, painful recovery, his wound finally did heal. After medical release in early 1863 he rejoined his command and served the rest of the conflict unscathed. He returned to Newark where he became a schoolteacher and farmer. [53]

Early battle casualty lists were filled with more than a few boys who were killed or mortally wounded. John Baker of the 11th Ohio Infantry was among those who never made it home. Enlisting at 16, he was killed September 14, 1862, at South Mountain, Maryland — eight months to the day of joining the Army. [54]

The 1862 Maryland campaign also took the life of 13-year-old Charles Edwin King of Company F, 49th Pennsylvania. On the morning of September 17 the regiment marched to Antietam Creek, which it crossed in rear of the Army of the Potomac's right, and immediately was ordered forward near Dunker Church at the double-quick. It was needed to fill a gap created there and help support a battery taking position on a small crest. Fighting became severe to the 49th's left and the men had to "kiss the ground" to escape enemy missiles humming overhead. After lying down for a few minutes the regiment was ordered by General Winfield S. Hancock to fall back about 20 yards and use the crest's reverse slope as protection. It was a wise decision, for shortly after the move a Con-

federate battery opened heavy fire upon the crest until silenced by accurate counter-fire from Union guns posted there. During the rain of iron terror musician King was hit in the body and fell into the arms of Henry Bowles, another musician who belonged to the 6th Maine. His wound proved fatal three days later. Charles was one of only five casualties in the 49th at Antietam. Ironically, the regiment never was fully engaged and not one shot was fired from its muskets. [55]

Stephen Giles enlisted in the 8th Ohio Infantry in October 1861 at the age of 15. On March 23, 1862, the 8th was sent out as skirmishers to confront Rebels on the outskirts of Winchester, Virginia. Checking the enemy soon escalated into a full-scale battle as Confederate General "Stonewall" Jackson attacked the Federals with approximately 8,000 men. Lieutenant Colonel Franklin Sawyer of the 8th wrote:

Cannon balls were crashing through the trees, and the ugly rifle and musket balls were whizzing fearfully close to us. We were ordered to charge at once, and putting spurs to

12 YEARS 5 MO. AND 9 DAYS. OLD WHEN HE ENLISTED.

Charles E. King already was an accomplished drummer prior to joining the 49th Pennsylvania in September 1861. He was mortally wounded a year later at Antietam.

History of the 49th Pennsylvania Volunteers

77

old Timothy, [I] dashed up the hill with the line, and over the interval, an open space, under a terrible fire, which fortunately passed over our heads doing but little damage. The line struck the enemy at right angles with [a] stone wall, and a savage fight ensued. We were separated from the rebels by a rail fence, which was nearly demolished by the line as it came up, leaving us absolutely among the rebels. The fight was almost hand to hand, some of the men discharging and then clubbing their muskets.... The fire from both sides was intense, our men fell rapidly, but gallantly held their places, loading rapidly and firing with unerring certainty, as the dead in our front plainly showed. The rebels held out perhaps thirty minutes, when they broke and ran.... This was really our first battle, but veterans never behaved better than our men in this short but severe conflict, and it [has] seldom been the fate of troops to suffer greater loss in an engagement.

One member of the regiment struck down during the close-quarters mêlée was Private Giles, who lay mortally wounded on the field. He died four days later, his military experience lasting not quite six months.[56]

Edward Lee of the 1st Iowa Infantry fell during the first summer of the war. His story was written by an unidentified comrade years afterward for publication in a collection of veteran reminiscences, and details Edward's short tenure as a drummer in 1861.

Just a few days before our regiment received orders to join General [Nathaniel] Lyon on his march to Wilson's Creek [Missouri], the drummer of our company was taken sick and conveyed to the hospital, and on the evening preceding the day that we were to march, a negro was arrested within the lines of the camp and brought before our captain, who asked him what business he had within the lines. He replied: "I know a drummer that you would like to enlist in your company, and I have come to tell you about it." He was immediately requested to inform the drummer that if he would enlist for our short [three-month] term of service he would be allowed extra pay, and to do this he must be on the ground early in the morning. The negro was then passed beyond the guard.

On the following morning there appeared before the captain's quarters, during the beating of reveille, a good looking, middle aged woman dressed in deep mourning, leading by the hand a sharp, sprightly looking boy, apparently about twelve or thirteen years of age.

Her story was soon told. She was from East Tennessee, where her husband had been killed by the rebels, and all their property destroyed. She had come to St. Louis in search of her sister, but not finding her, and being destitute

of money, she thought if she could procure a situation for her boy as drummer for the short time that we had to remain in the service, she could find employment for herself, and perhaps find her sister by the time we were discharged.

During the rehearsal of her story the little fellow kept his eyes intently fixed upon the countenance of the captain, who was about to express a determination not to take so small a boy, when he spoke out.

"Don't be afraid, captain, I can drum."

This was spoken with so much confidence that the captain immediately observed with a smile, "Well, well, sergeant, bring the drum and order our fifer to come forward." In a few moments the drum was produced and our fifer, a tall, round shouldered, good natured fellow from the Dubuque mines who stood, when erect, something over six feet in height, soon made his appearance. Upon being introduced to his new comrade he stooped down, with his hands resting on his knees, and after peering into the little fellow's face a moment he asked, "My little man, can you drum?"

"Yes, sir," he replied. "I drummed for Captain Hill in Tennessee."

Our fifer immediately commenced straightening himself upward, when he placed his fife to his mouth and played the "Flowers of Edinborough," one of the most difficult things to follow with the drum that could have been selected, and nobly did the little fellow follow him, showing himself to be a master with the drum. When the music ceased our captain turned to the mother and observed, "Madam, I will take your boy. What is his name?"

"Edward Lee," she replied; then placing her hand upon the captain's arm, she continued, "Captain, if he is not killed —" Here her maternal feelings overcame her utterances, and she bent over her boy and kissed him upon the forehead. As she arose, she said, "Captain, you will bring him back with you, won't you?"

"Yes, yes," he replied, "we will be certain to bring him back with us. We shall be discharged in six weeks."

In an hour our company led the Iowa First out of camp, our drum and fife playing "The girl I left behind me." Eddie, as we called him, soon became a great favorite with all the men in the company. When any of the boys had returned from a horticultural excursion, Eddie's share of the peaches and melons was the first apportioned out. During our heavy and fatiguing march from Rolla to Springfield, it was often amusing to see our long legged fifer wading through the mud with our little drummer mounted upon his back and always in that position when fording streams.

During the fight at Wilson's Creek [August 10, 1861], I was stationed with a part of our company on the right of [Captain James] Totten's battery, while the balance of our company, with part of an Illinois regiment, was ordered down into a deep ravine upon our left, in which it was known a portion of the enemy was concealed, with whom they were soon engaged. The contest in the ravine continuing some time, Totten suddenly wheeled his battery upon the enemy in that quarter, when they soon retreated to the high ground behind their lines.

In less than twenty minutes after Totten had driven the enemy from the ravine the word was passed from man to man throughout the army, "Lyon is killed," and soon after, hostilities having ceased upon both sides, the order came for our main force to fall back upon Springfield, while a part of the Iowa First and two companies of a Missouri regiment were to camp upon the ground and cover the retreat next morning.

That night I was detailed for guard duty, my turn of guard closing with the morning call. When I went out with the officer as a relief, I found that my post was upon a high eminence that overlooked the deep ravine, in which our men had engaged the enemy until Totten's battery came to their assistance. It was a dreary, lonesome beat. The moon had gone down in the early part of the night, while the stars twinkled dimly through a hazy atmosphere, lighting up imperfectly the surrounding objects. Occasionally I would place my ear near the ground and listen for the sounds of footsteps, but all was silent save the far off howling of the wolf that seemed to scent upon the evening air the banquet that we had been preparing for him.

The hours passed slowly away, when at length the morning light began to streak along the eastern sky, making surrounding objects more plainly visible. Presently I heard a drum beat up the morning call. At first I thought it came from the camp of the enemy across the creek; but as I listened I found that it came up from the deep ravine; for a few minutes it was silent, and then as it became more light I heard it again. I listened — the sound of the drum was familiar to me — and I knew that it was our drummer boy from Tennessee beating for help the reveille.

I was about to desert my post to go to his assistance, when I discovered the officer of the guard approaching with two men. We all listened to the sound, and were satisfied that it was Eddie's drum. I asked permission to go to his assistance. The officer hesitated, saying that the orders were to march in twenty minutes. I promised to be back in that time and he consented. I immediately started down the hill through the thick undergrowth, and upon reaching a valley I followed the sound of the drum, and soon found him seated upon the ground, his back leaning against the trunk of a fallen tree, while his drum hung from a bush in front of him, reaching nearly to the ground. As soon as he discovered me he dropped his drumsticks and exclaimed, "Oh, corporal! I am so glad to see you. Give me a drink," reaching out his hand for my canteen, which was empty.

I immediately turned to bring him some water from the brook that I could hear rippling through the bushes nearby, when, thinking that I was about to leave him, he commenced crying, saying, "Don't leave me corporal. I can't walk."

I was soon back with the water, when I discovered that both of his feet had been shot away by a cannon ball. After satisfying his thirst he looked up into my face, and said, "You don't think I will die, corporal, do you? This man said I would not. He said the surgeon could cure my feet."

I now discovered a man lying in the grass near him. By his dress I recognized him as belonging to the enemy. It appeared that he had been shot through the body, and had fallen near where Eddie lay. Knowing that he could not live, and seeing the condition of the boy, he had crawled to him, taken off his buckskin suspenders, and corded the little fellow's legs below the knee, and then lay down and died.

While Eddie was telling me these particulars, I heard the tramp of cavalry coming down the ravine, and in a moment a scout of the enemy was upon us, and I was taken prisoner. I requested the officer to take Eddie up in front of him, and he did so, carrying him with great tenderness and care. When we reached the camp of the enemy the little fellow was dead. [57]

With youngsters returning in pine boxes, or news of their deaths reaching home by other means, many Northern parents realized the Army was no place for boys and tried hard to keep them from going. This was no easy task. Parents and children often were pitted against each other with the outcome up for grabs until the war ended or the boys escaped parental hold. Finding a child had enlisted without permission was quite common. As soon as most parents discovered their underage son had joined they attempted to have him returned. The quickest means was to ask the recruiting officer to release the youngster. On occasion that was all that was necessary as many of the parties involved knew each other. Sometimes officers released a boy if they believed they errored accepting him in the first place.

An example of such consideration was relayed to the parents of James King, a Newark, Ohio, lad who made his way to Columbus and enlisted underage without parental consent. They in turn requested help from a man named Marsh to find their son. After locating him, Marsh informed the Kings:

I have just had an interview with your son James. I found him at the barracks on Broad St. near High St. He

Lotz House Museum

Unidentified.

told me his health was good and that he had enlisted and been sworn in and expected to leave here in a week or two.

As I was leaving the Captain of the barracks said he wished to talk with me. He asked me if I was personally acquainted with James. I told him of course all that I knew. I said to him that Mrs. King told me this morning that it would not be possible for him to pass an examination. The Capt. said he had already passed and drawn his ration and clothes. I told him I would write to his parents our conversation and he told me to say to you that after what I had told him of James that it was left all entirely with you whether he remained in the army or not for if you desired it he would be discharged without the least trouble.[58]

On other occasions officers who were more skeptical asked for proof or a legal ruling before they considered releasing a boy.

Habeas corpus had long been the legal term for bringing someone unlawfully detained before a judge

so that he could be released. It primarily was used for persons held for some infraction who, by new evidence, could prove their innocence. During the war courts were inundated with *habeas corpus* cases initiated by parents trying to gain release of young sons from military service. If they could prove their son was underage and had enlisted under false pretenses or without signed permission, the courts then would stand with them and issue a *habeas corpus* writ. These were readily accepted by the military if a boy had not been in the service very long. As the war progressed it became increasingly difficult for parents to effect release without producing a wealth of documents to substantiate their claims. If bounties had been given to a youngster, all money had to be paid back before the military would relinquish its hold over him. This could be a problem if the boy had squandered the money. It also was hard for parents who learned the whereabouts of their son many months after he left and already was in the field. In such instances the military would not provide transportation home. A family with little or no financial means could not possibly pay for the fare without saving for a long period of time.

In cases where the military was reluctant to let loose of a boy, politicians were asked to intervene. Mayors, governors, congressmen, senators — even President Lincoln — were deluged with letters by concerned parents asking for help. Politicians, in turn, fired off correspondence to the military branch and unit commanders involved. Numerous records reveal that youthful soldiers were discharged "by order of the War Department." Many of these cases were cleared because someone with connections spoke or wrote to the right officer to have a boy discharged without legal proceedings.

Because the Navy was so eager to enlist boys its officers constantly were plagued with official letters and requests to release youngsters. Samuel Galloway, working as a special commissioner at Camp Chase, tried using his clout to secure discharge for a relative's son by penning the following letter to a Navy official.

September 16, 1863

Dear Sir,

I write to apply for the discharge of William Walton, a minor, who enlisted under Captain Bowen of the gunboat *Keenwood* in Mississippi Squadron. The boy has been wounded and is probably now at some hospital. I know the facts that he is under 16 and that he enlisted against the expressed opposition of his father. His mother is a sister of my wife and therefore I write intelligently in regard to him. He ought to be at home under the guardianship of his parents. If within the scope of your jurisdiction I will be obliged, and his parents consoled by his release. Accompanying I send the affidavit of his father.[59]

Boys caught in the pull between factions found the prospect of being sent home unbearably humiliating. One 13-year-old boy whose enlistment was discovered by his parents was James H. Moore of the 3rd New Hampshire. On September 3, 1861, the 3rd broke camp at Concord and began its train ride south. While laying over at Worcester, Massachusetts, where the hungry soldiers were treated to sumptuous fare presented by the townsfolk, Colonel Enoch Fellows was handed a telegram from Nashua. By court authority Moore's parents had sent the telegram, demanding "Jimmie's" return. This created quite a stir among the men to think that one of their drummer boys would be taken from them. Due to the document's legality the colonel had no recourse and young Jimmie was sent home.

He was not disheartened, however, and within a year was serving as a musician in the 9th New Hampshire at age 14. Discharged at the close of the war, he returned to Nashua and resided there the rest of his life. Like many boys who were caught the first time, Jimmie did not give up. It is not known whether his parents finally consented because of his persistence, or he happened to elude them.[60]

In September 1861 John Dirst, 15, enlisted in the 16th Ohio, but was forced to abandon his plans when his parents obtained a writ of *habeas corpus* on November 22. John, like Jimmie Moore, was not discouraged and tried again. When the 121st Ohio was being formed during the summer of 1862 he enlisted as a musician in Company A. This time he succeeded and remained in the ranks until discharged June 8, 1865.[61]

William Crosby was just as single-minded. "When the Civil War broke out I was very enthusiastic about going to the front," he explained. "But as I was not of legal age, my father hesitated about giving his consent; however, I enlisted in the Ninth [Vermont] regiment and drilled under Captain [George A.] Beebe, but was taken out by my father just as we were ready to start for the front. My second attempt to enlist was in the First Vermont Cavalry, which also proved a failure, but my parents finding I was so determined to fight for

An unidentified lad photographed by W.E. Prall in Knoxville, Tennessee.

my country they gave their consent and I, at the age of sixteen, enlisted in the 13th Vermont." At Gettysburg William was wounded in the head by an exploding shell during fighting on the third day. He eventually recuperated but was plagued with painful headaches throughout his life.[62]

Stanton Allen, the New Yorker who so proudly wore a discharged friend's cavalry jacket to school in 1862, experienced the humiliation of *habeas corpus* after Union victories at Gettysburg and Vicksburg goaded him to become a soldier despite his father's wishes. Wrote Allen:

I made up my mind that the crisis had arrived. I said to

[my friend Nathaniel] Bass: "Nat, our time's come."

"How so?"

"We've waited a year, and they've called for another regiment of cavalry."

"Then I believe I'll go."

"So'll I."

"Where's the regiment being raised?"

"In Troy."

"Will your father let you go?"

"Of course not — don't say a word to him. But I tell you, Nat, I'm going. The Union armies are knocking the life out of the rebels east and west, and it's now or never. I can't stand it any longer. I'm going to war."

I was only a boy, born February 20, 1849, but thanks to an iron constitution, splendid health and vigorous training in farm work, I had developed into a lad who would pass for nineteen almost anywhere.

To Stanton's disappointment, a few days later his father took Nathaniel to Troy, where he was mustered. Stanton believed his own chance had been robbed. Later that week while at a circus he met another under-age recruit who had managed to enlist in the same cavalry regiment as Nat. The boy, Henry Tracy, agreed to help him escape to the regiment and enlist. That night the two boys headed over the mountains where Henry lived, and the next day visited the mustering officer's quarters. At the time the Griswold Cavalry [21st New York] was paying two dollars for each recruit brought in, so Henry sold Stanton to one of the sergeants and received his pay. Henry then entered the recruitment tent and vouched for Stanton's stretched age of 19. In fact, whenever the subject of age was mentioned Henry spoke up so Stanton would not have to lie during questioning. Allen continued:

I did not contradict what my soldier friend had said, and the sergeant made out my enlistment papers, Tracy making all the responses to my age. After I had been sworn in for three years, or during the war, I was paid ten dollars bounty. Then we went up to the barracks, and I was turned over to the first sergeant of Captain George V. Boutelle's company. I drew my uniform that night, the trousers had to be cut off top and bottom. The jacket was large enough for an overcoat. The army shirt scratched my back, but what is the use of reviving dead issues.

One day orders came for Capt. Boutelle's company to "fall in for muster." The line was formed down near the gate. I was in the rear rank on the left. The mustering officer stood in front of the company with the roll in hand. Just at this time, my father with a deputy sheriff arrived with the *habeas corpus*, which was served on Capt. Boutelle, and I

was ordered to "fall out."

Then we went to the city, to the office of Honorable Gilbert Robertson Jr., provost judge, and after due inquiry had been made as to "the cause of detention by the said Capt. Boutelle of the said Stanton P. Allen," the latter "said" was declared to be discharged from Uncle Sam's service. My father refunded the ten dollars bounty, and offered to return the uniform, but Captain Boutelle refused to accept the clothes, charging that I had obtained property from the Government under false pretenses.

A few days later on September 1, 1863, the *Troy Daily Times* published the following account:

More Than he Bargained For.

A few days ago one Stanton P. Allen of Berlin, enlisted in Capt. Boutelle's company of the twenty-first (Griswold) cavalry. We are not informed whether it was Stanton's bearing the same name as the Secretary of War, or his mature cast of countenance that caused him to be accepted; for he was regarded as nineteen years of age, while in reality, but fourteen summers had passed over his youthful, but ambitious brow. Stanton received a portion of his bounty and invested himself in one of those "neat but not gaudy" yellow and blue suits that constitute the uniform of the Griswold boys. A few days intervened. Stanton's parents, on the vine-clad hills of Berlin, heard that their darling boy had "gone for a sojer." Their emotions were indescribable. "So young and yet so valiant," thought his female relatives. "How can I get him out?" was the more practical query of his papa. The ways and means were soon discovered. A writ of *habeas corpus* was procured from Judge Robertson, and the proof was clear that Stanton was only fourteen years old; he was duly discharged from the service of the United States. But the end was not yet. A warrant was issued for the recruit, charging him with obtaining bounty and uniform under false pretenses, and a release from the military service proved only a transfer to the civil power. Stanton found that he had made a poor exchange of "situations," and last evening gave bail before Judge Robertson in the sum of five hundred dollars.

The magistrate told Mr. Allen not to worry about bail, for Boutelle soon would be sent to the front and the matter forgotten. The two men then devised a scheme to teach Stanton a lesson, as the boy related:

As we were leaving Judge Robertson's office, a policeman arrested me. He marched me towards the jail. Pointing to the roof of the prison he said, "My son, I'm sorry for you."

"What are you going to do with me?" I asked.

"Put you in jail."

"What for?"

Two decades after the war Avery Brown billed himself as "The Drummer Boy of the Cumberland," even though he was discharged from the Army for incompetency. Born in September 1852, he hailed from Delphos, Ohio.

Author's Collection

"Defrauding the Government. But I'm sorry to see you go to jail. They may keep you there for life. They'll keep you there till the war is over anyway, for people are so busy with the war that they can't stop to try cases of this kind. You are charged with getting into the army without your father's consent. Maybe they won't hang you, but it'll go hard for you, sure. I don't want to see you die in prison. If I thought you'd go home and not run away again, I'd let you escape."

That was enough. I double-quicked it up the street and hid in the hotel barn where my father's team was until he came along. I was ready to go home with him. I did not know it at the time that the arrest, after I had been bailed, was a put up job. It was intended to frighten me. And it worked to a charm. It was a regular Bull Run affair.[63]

Legalities and threats of jail were only temporary

obstacles for those dead set on enlisting. Some youngsters unable to join due to their tender age in 1861 and 1862 waited until 1864-1865, having reached legal status in the interim. Most were forced to stay in school and follow the conflict's progress in the newspapers, while their parents kept a close eye on them whenever squads of men left for the war.

Fear of having parents return them home was constant for youngsters who enlisted without consent. Boys also had to contend with superiors being dissatisfied with their performance of duties. Worse than being dragged off by a mother or father was the ignominy of being tossed out by a commanding officer while comrades watched.

George Meyer suffered the humiliation of being sent home in July 1862 from the camp of the 55th New York. The 16-year-old had enlisted the previous November as a drummer in Captain George Williams' Company K. Putting up with the boy for eight months, Williams endorsed his discharge with the words, "Incapacity, the Drum Major pronouncing him altogether useless." Whether due to ineptitude, laziness or just plain homesickness, George and others simply were unable to perform a soldier's duties.[64]

Avery Brown served with Company C, 31st Ohio. On August 18, 1861, he enlisted at the age of eight years, 11 months and 13 days. Just four foot six, red-headed Avery had a difficult time from the beginning, falling ill before the regiment left the state. Throughout his service he was absent sick much of the time. Finally his commanding officer reached the limits of patience and sought to have him discharged. In December 1862 Lieutenant Abram Barber signed Avery's certificate "in consequence of being no musician and unable to bear arms." Since it was a disability discharge the boy needed a doctor's examination. Assistant Surgeon James L. Mounts found him "incapable of performing the duties of a soldier because of his age, [and] unable to undergo the fatigues of marches or active duties in the field." Because of the unusual circumstances the certificate had to be reviewed carefully as it passed higher in the chain of command. It finally was placed before General William S. Rosecrans, who agreed that Avery should be sent home. He endorsed the discharge on February 26, 1863.[65]

There were hundreds of extremely young boys like Avery Brown who had no business being accepted by recruiting officers in the first place. Guidelines had been formulated for that purpose. When boys far be-

low the minimum age were allowed to enlist they usually became a burden to their commands instead of an asset. Captain Nathan Pickett of the 63rd Ohio accepted two young drummers in 1861 for his company. George M. Gould and Elbridge Mick were 13 and 14, respectively, when Pickett let them enlist on August 19. Both boys received disability discharges by the spring of 1863, leaving a drummer vacancy for more than a year until Company A received a replacement.[66]

Excitement in forming a regiment caused fathers who enlisted to allow their small sons to join, too. Once emotions calmed down and everyone was acclimating to camp life, the fathers often realized their mistake by seeing how out of place the youngsters were in a military setting. Physical limitations became clear at the outset, but there were those whose lack of maturity was exhibited first. One observer described the May 1861 send-off of an Ohio regiment that contained a lad who may have belatedly thought he was not ready to leave home after all. "I witnessed the departure of three companies of 80 men each from Sandusky City for Camp Taylor at Cleveland; the scene will not soon be forgotten. The multitudes who were witnesses, mothers, sisters & wives, weeping as they bade their friends 'farewell,' but yet they seemed to let them go willing. One patriotic lady said, 'I would rather be the widow of a brave husband than the wife of a coward.' Most of them were noble looking young men & we think patriotic hearts moved them to make

Born November 15, 1852, at Newark, Ohio, Albert C. White and his family resided in Marion, Ohio, when the war began. According to an 1893 biographical sketch in *Blue and Gray* magazine, Albert "was of very delicate health. His mother, thinking that outdoor camp life might prove beneficial to her little son, induced [her husband] to let her accompany him to Camp Buckingham. In a few months she found that the frail, delicate little fellow had gained much from open air and the food furnished 'raw recruits,' and was now quite strong, and the roses were in full bloom on his cheeks."

The Story of the Sherman Brigade

84

such a sacrifice. Most of these left cheerfully, but my feelings were touched, when I saw the big tears stealing down the cheeks of a young drummer boy (thirteen years old) who had enlisted with his father and brother."[67]

From Camp Buckingham at Mansfield, Ohio, Lieutenant Cornelius C. White was accompanied south by his nine-year-old son Albert. The elder White belonged to Company D, 64th Ohio, and Albert acted as company drummer until officially mustered when the regiment left for Kentucky in December 1861. They learned the rudiments of soldiering at Louisville and Bardstown, where their stay in January 1862 was summed up by two words — "drill and Diarrhea."[68]

February was little improved. Some time was occupied by corduroying a road knee deep in mud. On the 24th the Ohioans crossed the swollen Green River after dark during a violent storm which frightened both mules and men. Reaching the other side, Albert and the rest of the wet, weary troops were forced to sleep without tents. As thunder boomed and lightning crashed through the eerie night, Lieutenant White may have thought his small boy would be better off back home.[69]

If inclement weather, mud and diarrhea were not persuasive enough, the battle of Shiloh convinced him. On the afternoon of April 7, 1862, the 64th Ohio disembarked from a steamer on the Tennessee River, just in time to advance on a disorganized enemy who was in flight. Viewing the battleground strewn with the worst carnage imaginable must have been an eye-opening experience for the green Buckeyes. It was not surprising that within three weeks of the fight Lieutenant White sent Albert home. He did not even procure a discharge, he just sent him. At the next muster Albert was marked absent without leave, but the company officers all knew their drummer boy was safe in Ohio.[70]

Albert officially was listed as a deserter on December 31, 1862. If authorities wanted to retrieve the musician they easily could have done so, but arresting a nine- or 10-year-old boy would have pointedly illustrated how foolish it was that he was permitted to join the Army at all. By December his father also had his fill of soldiering and resigned.

Twenty-three years later the records were amended. Albert was dropped from the rolls as a deserter and issued a disability discharge dating to April 26, 1862, when he left the regiment. In his case a young soldier's record was reviewed and changed with few problems. But others were not, and these unfortunate veterans ended up shamefully categorized with men who were bounty jumpers and cowards.[71]

Not all youngsters who enlisted during the war's early days were killed, died of disease or shipped home broken in health from wounds. Few wanted to return home when their intentions were exposed, and hundreds actually convinced parents to let them stay and continue soldiering once their whereabouts were known. The young boys of 1861-1862 who were able to join, pass muster and serve creditably became inspirations for all who followed during the remainder of the war. Red-headed Edmund Dodge who enlisted at age 12 in the 47th Ohio, and Edward Deck, 11, who began serving with the 14th Kentucky in September 1861, were examples of resilient youths that served their full terms before mustering out. John J. Falkenstine was a member of the 7th West Virginia Infantry when just eight years and 10 months old. On December 10, 1861, he was transferred to Company C, 3rd Potomac Home Brigade (Maryland infantry), and served until discharged March 16, 1865. At the time of his enlistment young John stood an inch over four feet tall, epitomizing the public perception of a drummer boy. As a class, these boys and many others left a legacy larger than life.[72]

CHAPTER 5

'More or less frolic and fun to enliven the dull routine'

One motivation of nearly every youngster joining the Army during the Civil War was adventure. Few if any had formulated political convictions strong enough to die for, and doing so was the last thing on their minds when enlisting.

The adolescent generation of 1861 was brought up surrounded by military pageantry. It viewed parades with veterans of the War of 1812 waving from carriages. It watched local militia units drill and maneuver in town squares. It listened to Mexican War exploits described by fathers and grandfathers. There were even a few Revolutionary War veterans still living for youngsters to idolize. Children grew up with the prospect of war a common topic of discussion at the dinner table. For some time citizens believed a conflict over states' rights and slavery would erupt one day. When it actually began Northern boys were ripe for recruiting officers, and off to war they went. Some served for the duration.

Having to act as men no matter their ages, a vast majority was still just boys at heart. Amid the horrors of battle there were occasions when youngsters somehow found humor or engaged in impromptu shenanigans. During the battle of Chancellorsville the drummers of the 153rd Pennsylvania, almost all aged 14 to 16, left their place in line and ran through the woods chasing frightened rabbits. A shell landed nearby, causing them to scamper to the rear for a moment as General Charles Devens looked on disapprovingly.

After a few yards they stopped and returned to the line, where they guyed each other over their temporary departure. Even the most arduous detail could not squelch indomitable youthful spirit from making the work fun, to the chagrin of overseeing officers. They left home in search of the adventure of a lifetime. Boys who were mentally and physically strong enough to withstand a rigorous soldier's life, or fortunate to survive the battlefield, easily found it. [1]

Quite a few already displayed stubborn spirit or manipulative power by circumventing obstacles to enlist. Now that they were soldiers the same traits at times were used against each other or toward their superiors. Fighting landed more than one youngster in trouble as new-found strength acquired with puberty required periodic outlet. "Under arrest" and "to the guardhouse" were terms learned all too well owing to youthful indiscretions. Being away from home and enveloped in a man's world full of adult temptations was more than many boys could resist. They soon were entangled in vices never before contemplated or experienced. They were boys and they were soldiers, and in

OPPOSITE: An unidentified boy soldier photographed in West Lynn, Massachusetts.

Author's Collection

the latter capacity many took their first alcoholic drink, embraced their first woman, placed their first bet, smoked or chewed tobacco, swore as never before, hit their first man and for some, killed their first enemy. Growing up with death close at hand made them realize how every moment counted, as well as the importance of friendship, teamwork and having fun. Some claimed much later to have lived more fully during their service years than they did the rest of their lives. The war was an exhilarating time for its young participants. Viewed through the eyes of a naïve young boy it was enormously so.

Being in the Army did not just entail work and fighting. Boredom and inactivity of camp life were almost more unbearable to front-line soldiers than an active campaign. Thousands spent practically their entire enlistments far from dangers of the battlefield protecting forts, rail centers, depots, prisons and training facilities. To entertain themselves, whether in a bomb-proof at the front or a rear-echelon barracks, they contrived and played a wide variety of games to help pass the time.

The number one pastime for soldiers young and old was cards, first invented in France about 1390 during the reign of Charles VI. From France the game rapidly spread through Europe and eventually to the Americas. Being a game of chance led to abuse by gamblers, and caused persons of a puritanical bent to look down upon it. In 1845 a new American edition of Hoyle's Games was published, containing descriptions and rules for a variety of popular card games as well as billiards, backgammon, dominos, draughts (checkers), tennis, horse racing and more. In the introduction editor Henry Anners warned of the evil of cards. "So many fatal examples have occurred of the ruinous effects resulting from the abuse to which cards, like various other amusements in themselves innocent, are liable, that it seems unnecessary to give any caution against fostering the growth of the spirit of gambling. We would, however, advise our young readers never to play for money — at least with persons whose characters they were unacquainted with; and seriously warn them, that if ever they feel an anxiety to meet a card party in the hope either of retrieving losses or repeating gains, however small, they are then on the verge of a precipice which has hurried thousands to irretrievable ruin, to despair, to madness, and to death." Anners' sentiments were shared by a majority of

Americans as the Civil War approached, and cards generally was not accepted in most Christian homes.[2]

Soldiers often played their first game of cards in the Army far from home and disapproving onlookers. Asa W. Bartlett, in writing the history of the 12th New Hampshire, entitled one of his chapters "The Boys." He recalled youthful days playing cards and how the game's reputation changed because of the war. "With so large a sprinkling of beardless humanity in the make-up of the army," Bartlett wrote, "it is easy to imagine that there must have been more or less frolic and fun to enliven the otherwise dull and monotonous routine of camp life. One of the principal sources of amusement among them was card playing. This was so universally common that few, even including the chaplains, did not learn to 'call, pass, beg' or 'peg' in the different games of poker, euchre, high-low jack, cribbage, etc. Many, who had been brought up to look upon a pack of cards as a bunch of fifty-two free passes to eternal ruin, soon forgot or reasoned away their early home instilled prejudice, and became adept euchre players. This was the great game in the army and did not lose its hold upon the 'boys' when the war ended, but it soon became so universally popular that a well worn 'euchre deck' could be found in almost every house. The good old father and mother looked on, at first, with fear and trembling, but they could not deny what seemed to afford so much pleasure to their boy for whose safe return they had so long waited and prayed; and, beside, whatever of evil there was, it was too late to avert, for he had already learned to play. And so, not only were the long winter evenings made merry by boys and girls playing four handed games of euchre, in many houses where a game of cards was never played before; but, stranger still, such is the power of example, upon the old as well as the young, to influence for good or evil, that in many pious homes the game was admitted and entertained as a welcome guest where, a few years before, it would not have been allowed an introduction to any of the family."[3]

Euchre may have been the favorite game played by those who saw cards only as an amusement, but poker and other card games of chance eagerly were played as well. Gambling for rations, tobacco or money, whenever the paymaster had visited, was a pastime that gripped individuals just as Henry Anners warned. Charles Bardeen, who enlisted at 14 in the 1st Massa-

Three unidentified comrades. The sword and Spencer rifle may be photographer's props.

Richard F. Carlile Collection

chusetts Infantry, remembered well his experience of gambling fever. His story is representative of those finding themselves under the spell during the war.

I had in me nothing of the gambling spirit. I was fond of all games, and of cards with the rest. As appears in [my] diary I twice sat up all night playing cribbage. I whittled out a set of chessmen and played with everybody who knew the game or would learn it. I played checkers so much that when the officers had finished their tournament the winner sent for me to play for the championship of the regiment, and won two games out of twenty. Cards mean a good deal to the soldier. They while away many an hour that would otherwise be tedious, and a pack of cards will be about the last thing thrown out on a long march.

I was as fond of cards as anyone, but it had always been motive enough to win without the inducement of gain, and I had hitherto refused to play bluff. This pay day everybody was playing that game and I could find no one for checkers or cribbage or seven-up or forty-fives. It is so in all armies, probably. So I was in a way forced to play bluff, and as the limit was small and as I began like all tyros by winning, I found it not so very bad after all.

This night Nick Dranger[4] came into my tent and proposed a game, and I played with him alone all evening, losing steadily. During the game Charley Tillson crawled into the tent, looked on awhile, and went out again without remark. But the next day he got me off at a distance from camp and said, "I was surprised to see you playing cards with Nick Dranger last night."

"Why?"

"He is a notorious gambler, and was cheating you out of your eye teeth."

"Cheating me? A boy? In his own company?"

"Every hand he dealt."

"How could he do it?"

"Easily enough: he stacked the cards."

"What do you mean?"

"He fixed the cards so that he could get what cards you had."

"I don't see how."

"Suppose he had two aces and you had two kings. As he gathered up the cards to shuffle he arranged them alternately, so that he gave you a king, himself an ace, you another king, himself an ace."

"But I cut the cards every time."

"You didn't cut those cards. He has a big hand, and when he passes the cards over for you to cut he keeps the half-dozen top cards inside his hand, and lays them down again on top. He is playing now in Jim McCrea's tent. Come over and watch him."

As we played the game the deal did not pass but stayed with the winner, so a man who once got hold of a pair of aces, a pretty good hand with two playing, could keep them indefinitely, showing them only when he was called, and taking most of the pots by his bets without exhibiting his hand.

Nick Dranger was not trying all the transparent cheating on Jim that he had on me, but I saw enough to be convinced my money had been stolen, and it made me angrier than I had been since I enlisted. What had been a pastime, indulged in only because I could get no other game going, became a study. I played whenever I could get a chance, for money if we had it, "on pay day" if we hadn't. On the march to Gettysburg I played at every halt with little John Turner, who got to owing me more money than he ever tried to pay or I to collect.

For I became classed among the expert players. Every pay day the loose money in each company would get into the hands of one or two of the better players, and then these men would form little parties and the winnings would gravitate into the pockets of half a dozen of the most skillful. The weaker players would have stopped gambling because their money had given out, but these regimental survivors of the fittest always had money or could get it, and played the year round. Eventually I got into this crowd, of which Nick Dranger was another. But he did not stack cards or hold out an ace or deal from the bottom in this party. It had to be a square game, for every man knew all the tricks and would have made it uncomfortable for anybody who tried them. The best player in this crowd was one of the hospital men. His hand always trembled, so that there was no guessing at his hand from that indication, and he never spoke an unnecessary word. He watched the cards and he watched the players, and his luck had to run hard to make him quit a loser.

The one thing I wanted was to break Nick Dranger, and at last the time came when I did it. I even lent him twenty-five dollars, and should have been gratified if I could say that he never paid it. But he used it as a stake in another game and paid me back within twenty-four hours. After that the game was never quite the same to me, and I quit it for good long before the regiment came home.

The stopping was as sudden and as unpremeditated as was the beginning. Ten months later than this, pay day had come and I had started out intending to play first as usual in the company. I met Johnny Turner. "Let's get up a game," I said.

"I believe I won't play this pay day," he replied.

I thought nothing of it until I saw him playing in another game. Then I recognized that I was looked upon as a professional, with whom the ordinary player did not have a fair show. It set me to thinking and to comparing these good fellows in my own company with the disreputable set I had lately played with mostly. I saw that I could not belong to

both sets, and I recognized that in my heart for a long time I loathed these greedy gamblers. As usual with me the turn was radical, and I never bet a dollar on cards or anything else again while I was in the regiment.[5]

Bardeen was lucky not to end up fighting with his friends when he regularly began taking their money. The nature of the game led to many quarrels among contestants who felt they were dealt a bad play. Drummer Andrew J. Smith of the 104th Pennsylvania stood only four feet 10 inches, but that did not prevent him from scrapping with a fellow musician over a card game in the late fall of 1861.[6] After the war he became a preacher in the United Brethren Church, and wrote of his tailspin in morals that led to so much trouble:

With my separation from home friends, and the sad scenes of death and burial all around me, with the early prospect of perhaps fatal conflict with the enemy, all of these considerations should certainly have awakened and continued serious emotions. Very soon, however, I could say, "None of these things moved me." I was fast becoming an unprincipled and hardened boy. I was in that school least of all suited to myself, and where thousands, for time and eternity, were hopelessly ruined. Card playing, the soldier's curse, as well as the fatal curse of society at home, and penny poker, became my daily amusement. At first there were scruples of conscience, remembering the aversion of my parents to this habit, and the convictions of my own heart. Soon, however, these were stifled, and I felt little trouble in doing as others did. A few faithful men admonished me, and for a day or two I would regard their counsel and heed their warnings, but soon the jeerings of comrades would rally me again to their sports. At the card-table I soon learned its usual language, and became at last a profane swearer. This was wholly against my purpose, but when once angry I found that I could go any distance.

My drummer-mate, Cochran, was a catholic boy raised in New York. I did not like him any too well, but our service threw us together, and as mates we would often share the social game of cards, even to the extent of gambling. One day we became enraged, and a fight was the concluding episode of the game. We were arrested and taken to the captain's headquarters for punishment. We were handcuffed hand to hand and face to face. This was too much for foes and a nearness of communion that neither of us admired. For an hour or so we kicked at and spit upon each other, until at last we were both exhausted and ashamed. Anger ceased, and friendship became cordial and permanent from that hour. Toward night, after being thus handcuffed for nearly an entire day, we were released on the promise that

An 1891 oil painting by Julian Scott depicting a group of young musicians engrossed in a card game.

U.S. Military Academy Museum

we would play penny-poker no more. The promise, though made in good faith, was soon broken, and the exciting game renewed with more interest and enthusiasm for a time. Meanwhile letters were arriving every week from home; and though I ever rejoiced in their coming, yet it seemed as though they had eyes to see and lips to declare my conduct to mourning ones at home. Hardened as I had already become, I was far from willing that my folks should know the condition of my heart and recklessness of my conduct.

Several times while in this camp boxes from the loved ones at home arrived, laden with rich and enjoyable tokens of comfort. Once I was deeply affected in being thus remembered by my Sabbath-school mates. While these delicacies comforted, they also condemned me, as I felt myself wholly unworthy of the bestowments. I had come to enjoy camp life. My improvement on the drum had made of that labor a pleasure, while boxing, card playing, pitching pennies, smoking, etc., had become fixed and foolish habits with me. I ever thought that I would leave them all in camp, and that I should never wish to indulge them when again at home. But habits formed, I was to learn, were not so easily broken, and though adopted for a day might continue for a lifetime.[7]

Not only were habits acquired that stayed with youngsters as they aged, on some occasions frolic at the card table led to devastating events. On April 24,

91

1862, Wallace Smith and his close friend Elderkin Rose, both members of Company A, 60th New York, sat down for a game as they often had done in the past. While it was in progress 16-year-old Elderkin playfully accused Wallace of cheating and threatened to shoot him with an old-fashioned pistol that lay on the ground nearby if he did it again. A few hands later both boys tired of the game and threw their cards on the table without caring who won. As they stood up Elderkin saw the pistol and thinking it was unloaded (some of the boys had fired blank caps with it during the day), picked it up and pointed it at Smith. Jokingly, he asked Wallace if he remembered his threat and pulled the trigger. To the horror of bystanders the gun discharged, sending a ball into Smith's chest. He exclaimed, "Oh, Rose," collapsed and died.[8]

Elderkin's pain in the knowledge he had been the instrument of his best friend's death enveloped him in deep depression. He served most of his term, then was transferred to the Veteran Reserve Corps for other medical reasons in 1864. Following the war his life remained troubled. Fifteen years after the tragic event he was admitted to an insane asylum, and those acquainted with him were glad he was finally committed. Herman Giffan, who had known him since childhood, stated he came home from the war "not regular in his mind," and recalled a neighbor asking what kind of "crazy men" roamed the streets of their town. After spending a year in the institution Rose died in 1878 at the age of 32.[9]

Not all pranks attempted near a card table led to such horrific endings. Most were harmless in nature and generally were contrived in fun to pass time. Delavan Miller wrote about an incident that happened in the camp of the 2nd New York Heavy Artillery early in 1862, when the officers ordered restrictions placed on card play after lights out. At the particular location where the event occurred the cook shacks were situated behind camp over a ridge. The ridge blocked any view from the officers' quarters, providing the men a place to play cards undetected. After some time Major Henry P. Roche became aware of the nocturnal poker games and took it upon himself to end the frivolity. Roche was an officer who could not grasp the proper way to deal with volunteers. He had been a subaltern in the British Army years before and because of his attitude toward the men was much disliked. On the night the major selected to surprise the boys they were

gathered as usual playing five-cent ante with sutler notes.[10] As Roche approached the alarm was sounded by a lookout whose job was to announce the presence of unwanted parties. Hurriedly the men stashed away all evidence of their game and concluded to surprise the major, who thought he was going to surprise them. As he made his way silently up the steps to the shanty's rear door, one of the players opened it while another tossed the contents of a kettle of old bean soup on the bewildered officer. Before he could recover the card players escaped through the front door and disappeared over the ridge into camp. Soon, however, the guilty men were ferreted out and Roche dealt them due punishment.[11]

Being an officer made it easy to seek revenge on boys whose indiscretions aroused their wrath. Stripping of rank, guardhouse sentences, work details and other penalties were held over their heads to keep unruly boys in line. Sometimes officers abused the advantage, which led to confrontations with hard-headed youngsters. Adept poker player Charles Bardeen recalled an episode that occurred in September 1862 between his 15-year-old drummer mate and fellow orderly, Joseph W. Phillips, and the 1st Massachusetts' adjutant.

When I was put on orderly I supposed this meant orderly sergeant and was looking around for some light blue cloth to sew stripes on my sleeves, but I soon learned it meant only to be an errand boy for the adjutant, Charles E. Mudge. I had this detail every week all the time I was in the regiment, so I got pretty well acquainted with Lt. Mudge. I can see his swagger now and his self-satisfied smirk. As I look back I think he was good-natured, not too exacting, pompous and conceited but meaning to be kindly and fair. He had to look so far down at us little drummers, however, that he sometimes forgot we had some pride of our own. One day when Phillips was orderly, the adjutant whistled for him but Phillips paid no attention. Lt. Mudge came to the door of the tent and saw Phillips nearby.

"Didn't you hear me whistle for you?" he asked.

"I heard you whistle, sir," replied Joe sturdily, "but I am not a dog."

"Do you mean to disobey me?"

"I mean that I will not answer to a whistle."

"We shall see about that," Lt. Mudge said, and had Phillips tied to a tree. Joe stayed there till he was released at night and then went to the colonel's tent, and told what had happened.

"Call Lt. Mudge here," said Lt. Col. [Clark B.] Baldwin, then in command, and when the adjutant came he said to him, "Lt. Mudge, when you want dogs, whistle for him; but when you want men, call them."[12]

Others who were insubordinate were not as lucky to have an officer of higher rank side with them and reprimand the overbearing officer at fault. Elbridge Copp was acting as orderly for Adjutant Alfred J. Hill of the 3rd New Hampshire when Hill abused his privileges after a night of heavy drinking in an adjoining camp. Shortly after returning to quarters drunk he found he was missing an article of his uniform, and immediately questioned his orderly in an unbecoming manner. During the interrogation Elbridge declared no knowledge of the item's whereabouts, and commented that he did not believe it was his duty to watch over the adjutant's clothing. This infuriated Hill, who proclaimed, "I want you to understand that when I am away you are to look after my things." Elbridge rebuffed, "Mr. Adjutant, I want you to understand that I am not your nigger; I am a clerk in this office and not your servant." To the adjutant the orderly's remark sounded like rank treason. He swore at and belittled Elbridge, ordering him back to his own company to serve in the ranks.

"I was crying with rage and indignation," Copp recollected, "and I have no doubt that I used insubordinate language. I remember telling him I would go back to my company, and much preferred doing duty in the ranks than being in his office. I immediately gathered up my baggage, which consisted of a knapsack and contents, and went with it to the tent of Capt. Randlett, and reported to him...."[13]

Conversely, Captain James F. Randlett appreciated the worth of a good orderly and assigned him to that position in his own command. Elbridge Copp and Joseph Phillips were normal kids who, in the course of certain circumstances, became entangled in confrontations with an officer. Both boys actually were very good soldiers. It is safe to say that almost every soldier for one reason or another was chastised for some offense during his term of service. On the other hand, there were plenty of youthful soldiers that regularly required scoldings, some needing them constantly.

Years later Luther S. Dickey readily admitted to and cherished Captain Simon P. Townsend's characterization of him as the "worst boy" in the 103rd Pennsylvania's Company C. Another officer, James S.

Mackey, confided that the youngster caused him more trouble than his entire company. Mackey's Company H was next in line to Company C, the two being separated by the color guard. Since 16-year-old Luther was the smallest in Company C's ranks he was placed at the end of the line (companies being formed from the tallest to shortest man, according to regulations). This arrangement placed him in closer proximity to Company H's officers than his own. Luther recalled an incident during 1862's Peninsular campaign where he knew he was pushing his luck with the hapless Captain Mackey. "One chilly night going up the Peninsula, when we were without overcoats and rubber or woolen blankets, and were compelled to stand and sit around wood fires, shifting positions occasionally to get away from the smoke, I decided to seek cover under Capt. Mackey's blanket. As he was sleeping soundly no protest was made until after I had awakened him by monopolizing more than a fair share. However, he then only accused me of being selfish and let me share it until morning. At no time can I recall that either Capt. Townsend or Capt. Mackey ever gave evidence that they had any dislike for me, although I was constantly doing things with no other purpose than to irritate and aggravate them."[14]

One method Luther and his Company C compatriots used in agitating officers was storytelling late at night. Dickey explained:

When bivouacking in proximity to the enemy it was customary to stack arms as they stood in line of battle, and for the men to retain positions close to their guns as they rested during the night. When everything was quiet one of the boys would single out some individual who could hear us, and make him the object of our remarks, acting as though we supposed he were asleep. Of course, we either manufactured tales, or exaggerated incidents in which the object of our gibes had been implicated. I have a vivid recollection of engaging in this kind of sport the night after the battle of Seven Pines at the expense of Capt. Townsend and Corp. [William] Leech of our company, and Capt. Mackey. I had overheard the two former expressing something like abhorrence of war, and so tales were invented and whispered so they could be heard beyond the limits of the Co. Capt. Mackey was also guyed that night by the boys of Company C. Among the things invented on him that night was that he exclaimed when the enemy opened fire on the Regiment in the woods, "Boys, do your duty; I have a wife and family at home." This would be followed by someone telling of seeing the Captain in some ludicrous position to

93

Luther S. Dickey of Company C, 103rd Pennsylvania, was promoted corporal in January 1865 in spite of owning a mischievous reputation.

History of the 103d Regiment Pennsylvania Volunteer Infantry

camp.... The next morning he [Wilson] ordered me to clean it up. I declined. A little later he returned and said that he would give me fifteen minutes to clean it up. I emphatically told him I would under no consideration clean it up. He ordered me to get my gun and accoutrements; I obeyed and was taken to the guard quarters and relieved George Forward, who was then on post. I stood guard in Forward's place that day. When the time came for court-martial boards to convene Capt. John Cochran sent for me. He told me that he was very sorry, but serious charges had been preferred against me. After lecturing me at length he asked me to apologize to Sergt. Wilson and he would have the charges withdrawn. I refused. He argued with me, calling attention to the disgrace attached, &c. I stood firm and told him that I could go to Fort Totten for six months and wear a ball and chain, but I could not say I was sorry for refusing to clean up the dirt of a drunken shirker who evaded duty all the time. I told him that every man in the company knew who had committed the nuisance, but Sergt. Wilson merely wanted to humiliate me. I then recounted incident after incident in which I had gone on picket duty after a hard day's march through rain and mud out of my turn, when my messmates asked me to come to him and protest. As I talked to Capt. Cochran the tears rolled down his cheeks, but when I left him he said he would have to forward the charges. "All right, Captain, I can stand it if you can," I replied, and left him. I was not court-martialed and from that time on I never again had an acrimonious word with Sergt. Wilson. From that time he became one of my staunchest friends.[17]

Although Luther's version ended in a way where he bested Sergeant Wilson, he did not earn the title of "worst boy" for nothing. In fact, there were many occasions he was out of line dealing with those in command — kicking coffee cups and throwing tantrums — which would not have been tolerated if he was a little older. One of the worst things he did was going on picket without his rifle being loaded. When reprimanded and asked why he had not done so, he quipped, "Because I had no orders to load my gun." This

escape the enemy's fire; by another who saw him fleeing rapidly to the rear, &c., &c.; perhaps a half dozen or more describing various ridiculous predicaments in which they had seen him; at times, someone would strike such a happy remark that everyone in hearing joined in laughter. This badinage was confined exclusively to the boys of the Co., and I think I was the main instigator. My enemies in the company received frequent verbal castigation in this way.[15]

Perhaps it was such shenanigans by Luther and his friends that caused others to dislike them. In an army where those with rank were better friends than enemies, Luther's attitude caused trouble that might have been avoided had he been more conciliatory. One of his constant antagonists was First Sergeant James M. Wilson,[16] who in Luther's mind picked on him unmercifully. One incident in North Carolina almost led to a court-martial.

We were encamped east of the Trent River at New Bern. One of the company had been on a drunk and had emitted the contents of his stomach on the street of our

provoked an angry Captain Townsend, who was questioning him, to draw his sword above Luther's head and exclaim, "I command you to load your gun!" In the midst of the conversation enemy cannons signaled a Confederate advance, forcing the captain and Luther to attend to more pressing matters.[18]

Sly remarks and vulgarity were common in the ranks, especially when large numbers of men from varying backgrounds were thrown together. Youngsters listening to such crude talk mimicked older soldiers as a way to fit in and appear more like men themselves. George Ulmer wrote of meeting a Pennsylvania drummer boy whose profanity shocked and appalled him. His encounter occurred during the September 1864 battle of Chafin's Farm, Virginia. As the fight intensified George's brother, who also served in the 8th Maine, yelled at him to leave ranks and head for the rear. Even though the air was filled with lead and iron, George stayed. Finally he became scared and heeded his brother's advice. "I saw men fall so thick and fast that there didn't seem as if there was any of my regiment left, and I made up my mind it was too hot for me, so started on the dead run to the rear for a place of safety, and didn't stop until I was pretty sure I was out of harm's way."

His scramble ended in an open field about a mile from his regiment, where he sat down exhausted in tall grass amid an artillery position that had been abandoned when the cannoneers advanced. As he caught his breath and noticed multiple bullet holes in his drum, the Pennsylvania drummer ran over and joined him. Both boys talked of their battle exploits and discussed what they should do next. Throughout this exchange, George recalled, "I thought he was the most profane lad I had ever met. Most every other word he uttered was an oath." Ulmer confronted him by asking if he was not afraid to talk in such a way.

"What the hell should I be afraid of?" he smarted back.

The area where the boys sat was littered with all sorts of ordnance and camp equipage. As the Pennsylvanian prattled on he picked up a discarded tent stake and tried to drive it in the ground with his boot. The earth was too hard, so he tried using an unexploded shell found lying nearby as a hammer. "I wonder if this was fired by those damn rebs?" he asked.

George replied, "I guess it was, and you better look out or it might go off."

The Keystone drummer casually rebuffed him, as George recalled: " 'Off be damned, their shells were never worth the powder to blow 'em to hell. See the hole in the butt of it? It would make a goddamned good mawl, wouldn't it?' Looking around at the same time he found an old broom. Stripping the brush and wire from the handle, he said, 'I'll make a mawl of it and drive that damn rebel stake into the ground with one of their own damn shells, be damned if I don't.' Inserting the broom handle into the end of the shell he walked over to a tree stump. 'Damned tight fit,' he hollered to me, and the next instant I was knocked down by a terrific explosion. I came to my senses in a minute and hastened to where he had been standing. There the poor fellow lay unconscious and completely covered with blood, there was hardly a shred of clothes on him, his hair was all burned and both hands taken completely off, as if done by a surgeon's saw."

George realized something had to be done quickly to stop the blood flowing from the boy's wrists. Ripping the snares from his drum he wound them tightly above the stumps and hailed a passing ambulance to carry him to a hospital farther back. He thought he would never see him again. A few weeks later George also was badly wounded by a Rebel shell that exploded near him. After transportation to Portsmouth, Virginia, he was taken to a hospital established in the old Balfour Hotel. When he was placed in a third-floor bunk he discovered the Pennsylvania drummer lying on the bed beside him. His attitude had changed dramatically since the accident, and he was content knowing he would soon die. His language remained somewhat amiss, but he was not as earnest in his vulgar speech. Several days after George's arrival he asked him to read a few verses from his Bible. Hearing the soothing words the boy's thoughts "carried him home to his mother [as] his breathing faded away."[19]

Not thinking of the consequences, youngsters perpetrated many similar acts that could have ended in disaster, but instead only landed a boy in trouble with his superiors, or humiliated him in front of his peers.

Charles Bardeen practiced sword fighting with his friend and fellow drummer Joseph Phillips one day in September 1862. As they parried with their musician swords the swinging and lunging intensified to an inappropriate point, considering they were not playing with toys but weapons of war. Suddenly, amid the noise of clanging steel and the boys' laughter, Joe stopped, turned and walked to camp without saying a word. When Charles made his way back a little later he found Joe had moved all his belongings out of their tent and moved in with another drummer. Being too proud to ask why he switched, Charles did not learn the reason for more than a year until excitement of narrowly eluding some Rebel cavalry together rekindled their friendship. As they sat catching their breath from the exertion of the escape, Charles finally inquired why Joe had moved out so long ago.

"It wasn't fair of you to pink me," he answered.

"Pink you? What do you mean?" asked Charles.

At this Joe realized his chum was completely ignorant of the event that caused him to walk away from their sword play. To explain his action he unbuttoned his shirt and exposed his chest, which showed a large scar close to his heart. In his clumsiness Bardeen had cut Phillips, who wrongly assumed the injury was inflicted on purpose. With the truth out in the open both boys apologized and continued to be friends the rest of their time in the Army. [20]

Elbridge Copp experienced quite a scare during another favorite soldier pastime, horse racing. Races were held for money with men betting freely on the speed of their regiments' champion or for the plain thrill of running a horse with comrades. The following incident narrated by Copp occurred in late February 1864 on Morris Island, South Carolina, after he had been promoted to adjutant of the 3rd New Hampshire.

Elbridge J. Copp, 3rd New Hampshire, mounted on his horse "Don."

Reminiscences of the War of the Rebellion

On one occasion a number of mounted officers, including Colonel [Aaron F.] Stevens and myself, had ridden up to the "front," as the line nearest the enemy is always called, and riding back down the broad beach, some two or three miles to our camp, without prearrangement we tried the speed of our horses. "Don," the horse I had purchased from the heirs of Adjutant [Alvin A.] Libby, had proved a thoroughbred. I was proud of his qualities, but here another phase of his character developed, showing his mettle and testing my own. In this race I won by a long distance, but this is not the whole story. I soon found myself leaving the other officers in the rear as we flew down the beach, and turning to them, I waved goodbye, and then gave attention to my horse, which was fairly flying through the air, and for two miles or more without lessening his speed, but rather increasing it, we sped along the hard sands of the beach.

In approaching the camp I pulled upon the reins, but made no impression upon the speed of my horse — faster and faster I seemed to go. Passing our own camp and on with increased speed, as it seemed to me, I could not make any impression upon the bit, the beast evidently having it between his teeth. Pulling upon the reins having no effect, my own mettle began to be stirred, and I put my spurs into the sides of the runaway. On we flew into and through the camp of one of the New York regiments, knocking down one of their tents in the wild course. The men, surprised and angry, of course, I could hear swearing about the damned drunken officer riding through their camp, who would kill someone before he knew it, not knowing the fact that it was an involuntary ride on my part. My horse finally, in the soft sands, became winded and concluded to let me have my way, and I rode back to camp.[21]

Boys and animals go hand in hand. Hundreds of boy soldiers found and secured all sorts of varmints to tame, race or play with while in the Army. Harry Kieffer recalled numerous occasions trying to catch a pet during the fall of 1863. One time he and his drummer mate observed a squirrel living in a tree near their camp and decided to capture it the next day. That night as they lay in their tent they fantasized about training the animal to ride atop their drums while on the march. When morning came they put their plan in action. First, they tied a bag over its hole and then began cutting the tree down, thinking the squirrel would be snared in the bag. After sawing for a half hour it came crashing down, but to their chagrin the squirrel escaped from another door of his home. Both boys watched as the frightened critter then leaped from tree to tree toward the 150th Pennsylvania. Shouts rang through the regiment's camp. "A squirrel! A squirrel!" Instantly, dozens of men were on their feet, charging through the woods in pursuit of the poor animal racing for its life. Leading the pack was Sergeant John C. Kensill's terrier "Little Jim." More than 100 men encircled the squirrel in a small tree, which they began shaking while yelling as if going into battle. After a few moments the terrified squirrel lost its grip and tumbled down to the mob below. The men were unable to grab it, but "Little Jim" pounced on the animal and broke its neck before the crowd knew what happened.

Harry and his mate decided capturing a squirrel was too difficult and instead turned their energies to catching something else. Not long afterward Harry was helping unload stores from a wagon. In the bottom of one of the boxes he uncovered three small mice and deposited them in his coat pocket. They were so young their eyes were still closed and fur had just started to develop. Finishing his detail Harry returned to his tent and fashioned a container from a bottle and can to house them in. Throughout the winter the two boys played with their trio of mice, naming them Jack, Jill and Jenny. They became quite tame and crawled all over the boys, in and out of their pockets, looking

for hardtack crumbs or seeds. Occasionally "Little Jim" snooped around their tent, but the boys were determined to keep the dog from killing their "mousies," and chased him off. With the arrival of spring the boys knew winter camp would be dismantled, so they carried the mice back to the teamster in whose wagon they were found and talked him into taking them along.[22]

Wild game of every description was consumed in camp or on campaign. Whether it ran, flew or swam did not matter to hungry soldiers. In a wooded area near Fredericksburg, Peter Grove of Company D, 150th Pennsylvania, and Harry Kieffer spent a whole afternoon shooting frogs along a stream bank. At the time it had been raining for several days and they were compelled to abandon their normal diet of hardtack because the crackers had been transformed to a mushy, moldy mess in the bottom of their haversacks. With some well directed shots the two boys headed back to camp with a sufficient supply of frog legs, which they boiled in their tin cups and speedily devoured.[23]

Farm animals and livestock also were at risk of ending up on soldiers' plates whenever found. One unidentified drummer boy in the Army of the Potomac nearly fell into serious trouble after a successful foraging excursion. Later in the day the officers were reviewing his regiment. As the companies marched by, all the drummers were beating their drums except the happy forager. Seeing him tightly grasping the instrument, the colonel sent the adjutant to inquire why the lad was not playing with the rest of the boys. Replying loud enough to be heard for some distance down the line, the boy said, "Tell the colonel that I can't beat my drum now. I have two live turkeys in my drum — and one of them is for the colonel!"[24]

Musician William Bircher of the 2nd Minnesota found himself in a fix with his commander, Lieutenant Colonel Judson W. Bishop, after foraging beyond the lines against orders. In December 1864 William obtained at a Georgia plantation some potatoes and eggs from the black inhabitants who lived there. While leaving he happened to notice two cows tied up in the barn and thought they would be nice to procure for the regiment's cook, Sam Bowler. Bircher's first concern was to get back to camp without being observed.

In a short time I arrived in sight of the regiment, and carefully looked up and down the line to see that the colonel was nowhere near. Not seeing him, I marched up to about where our left flank would be and tried to get around on the other side of the track where the band boys were; but what was my surprise when I ran right onto the colonel, sitting down behind a pile of railroad ties. I came up to within ten feet of him.

He looked at me and saw that I had a rubber blanket over my shoulder with something in it, and asked, "What have you got in your blanket?" I answered, "Potatoes."

"What have you got in your handkerchief?"

"Eggs," I replied.

"Where did you get them?"

"Oh," said I, "about two hundred yards from here."

"Is that so?"

"That's so," said I.

"About two hundred yards from here?" he remarked.

I answered with a nice little "Yes sir," and commenced to tell him about the two big fat cows that I had seen, hoping he would forget about the potatoes and eggs, but he didn't forget worth a cent. He told me he would talk "cows" a little later, and ordered me to put my potatoes and eggs on the ground, and go down on the railroad and go to work tearing up track. I never got humpbacked from the amount of work I did. I principally kept one eye on the colonel and the other on the potatoes and eggs.

It was not long before the colonel's cook (Place, I think his name was) came along and gathered up the aforesaid articles. I knew the colonel did not know anything about it, of course not. Colonels don't eat eggs. I did considerable talking to Place about it, but he took them all the same, saying, "I can't see potatoes and eggs lying around loose, when I know the colonel is just suffering with hunger." Well, that was the last I saw of the eggs and yams.

We encamped close by for the night, and it commenced to rain with thunder and lightning. Anybody who has been in the South knows that it is dark at such times. I had just got nicely curled up in my blanket in my shelter-tent, when the colonel's orderly came to me and said, "The colonel wants to see you." Throwing my poncho over my head, I proceeded to the colonel's tent, thinking, probably, he had some difficult military problem he wanted me to solve. But my consternation was depicted on my countenance when he asked me if I had not told him during the day that I knew where there were two nice fat cows. I drawled out a mighty long "Yes, sir," after which he said, "You will now report to Lieutenant [Jacob T.] McCoy, who is officer of the day, and he will take two men besides yourself and bring those cows into camp, and turn them over to Bowler, and tell him to have them killed and issued to the men in the morning, after which you will report to me again."

I bid the colonel goodnight and, in the darkness and rain, hunted up the guard-tent. I found Lieutenant McCoy, gave him my orders, and got a good damning from him for

telling the colonel about the cows. We finally got started, and I, as the guide, directed them through the dense pine forest the best I knew how, having been over the road but once myself. Fortunately, I found the plantation all right, also the cows, but we had no ropes. Now here was a quandary. We had no lanterns, and how were we to lead the cows back to camp? In feeling around in the dark I found an old harness and took the lines out of it, and with these we led them back to camp, but before we got there a sad calamity befell me.

Surrounding the plantation was a wide and deep ditch, over which a bridge was made to raise and lower whenever in use. In going over this, the cow I was leading, being wild, started and ran diagonally across the bridge, and it being so dark that it was impossible to see your hand before you, every vivid flash of lightning would so blind us that for a few moments we were, as it seemed, in the inky darkness.

As the cow ran she dragged me along, but I hung on to her like grim death, and ran off the bridge, falling into the ditch, down at least eight feet. I clung to the bank or side of the ditch the best I could, it being soft and slimy from the rain, until my comrades helped me out. The leather strap with which the cow was tied was wet and slippery, and, of course, I could not hold her. The other cow was held by one of the other boys, who was fortunate enough not to fall off the bridge. She continued to bellow, which kept the one which got loose from getting far away from us. In a short time we had caught her again, and succeeded in arriving in camp without any further mishap.

I then proceeded to notify Sam Bowler, who by this time was sleeping soundly in his tent. After waking him up and giving him the colonel's orders, I received another cursing and damning for telling the colonel about the cows. I waited to see that Sam got up, and then turned our stock over to him. Afterwards, according to orders I reported to Colonel Bishop, and informed him that we had returned with the cows.

The colonel being in bed, rose to a sitting posture and remarked, "Hereafter, when I give the regiment an order, I want you to understand that it includes you as well as any other member of the regiment; and sending you after the cows you may consider your punishment for your offense." He bid me goodnight, and then said, "Go and tell Bowler to give you a piece of the liver."[25]

James Shanklin, in a humorous anecdote published in *The National Tribune,* described foraging with his brother Jacob. James was born August 19, 1846, and was barely 15 when he and Jacob were mustered into Company C, 41st Ohio, in September 1861. "I was one of a detailed party to go as a train guard, as was my brother, from Chattanooga to Bridgeport, Alabama. When we left Chattanooga we were without rations of any kind. My brother and I were quite fortunate, as we were assigned to the blacksmith wagon, and they had plenty of hardtack, but that was all. The blacksmith said, 'Boys, we will furnish the hardtack if you can furnish the meat.' That was our only hope. I answered that we would try and do that. For dinner we had a great feast of hardtack and water; but for supper, oh, my! Well, brother Jacob (the poor soul was killed at the taking of Orchard Knob) and I started on a little expedition to get some meat. Fortune was in our favor, and we had to go but a short distance when we ran on a litter of nice fat pigs about two or three months old. Somehow my gun went off and two pigs died. We took pity on them and took them to camp, put them in camp kettles and boiled them, and so we had meat for supper. The next day we started on a long march. The day passed slowly, but towards evening we wanted more meat. We started ahead and came to a log house. There was a rail pen in front with a large hog in it. My gun went off again, and for supper we had more meat, and it lasted the remainder of our trip." [26]

An unidentified "Bucktail" drummer, photographed at Lochman's Gallery in Allentown, Pennsylvania. The 13th Pennsylvania Reserves (42nd Infantry) was the original Bucktail regiment, so named for the deer tail or fur worn on its members' caps and hats. In August 1862 two other Bucktail regiments were organized, the 149th and 150th Pennsylvania.

Courtesy of Thomas and Crystal Molocea

Youngsters even found amusement with creatures that normally caused them irritation. William Bircher won $100 on December 5, 1863, racing lice. On that date the regiment received a large mail and was spending a quiet day in quarters reading letters and newspapers. William recalled that lice, or graybacks as the pests were known, were especially plentiful. Before long the boys had their shirts off and sat half naked in their tents, picking and killing all they could find. Someone hollered that he would bet $100 on the well-fed specimen he was holding between his forefinger and thumb if anyone wanted to race. William also had captured a monstrous fellow and agreed. "Now," he wrote, "the question was, how would we get them to run? This matter was soon settled. We took one of our tin plates and held it over the fire until it was very warm, and at a given signal dropped our racers on the hot plate. Wag's jumped the track before he got half over, and mine went over the entire width of the plate, winning the stakes and the entire gate receipts. This was the only time on record where a grayback was known to have paid his board. After the race I had a kindly feeling for him, but was compelled to sacrifice him with the rest."[27]

Highest on the list of things sought by most teenage boys walked on two legs. Joining the Army did not deter the age-old phenomenon one bit. Being secluded from females only seemed to fuel the fire within boys to long for them more. Girls visiting training camps or garrisons were always the center of attention; at times, perhaps, more than they would have liked. At the 13th Vermont's camp near Brattleboro in the fall of 1862, 15-year-old George F. "Cooney" Harvan was detailed as a guard. When assigned the duty he was instructed to be suspicious and check all wagons leaving camp to make sure no soldiers were stowed away. He was described as "a wild boy, but a good soldier" who reportedly "knew no fear" and was never tired. "He would march all day and raise Ned all night." While acting as guard that day and being faithful to orders, Cooney stopped an open-air buggy containing two well-dressed young ladies. The girls were indignant. Cooney explained to them it was his duty to inspect all wagons thoroughly, and proceeded to feel around below the seat and the young ladies' feet under their hoop skirts. Aghast, the girls quickly figured out it was nothing more than a boyish prank and began laughing. They admitted they enjoyed the manner in which he performed his duties, and said if all soldiers were as conscientious the country would be saved.[28]

For youngsters who left girlfriends at home the separation could be intolerable as months turned to years. Letters were the sole means of communication. Some soldiers placed advertisements in Northern papers soliciting young ladies to start up correspondence, even though they were strangers. From this scores of relationships began during the war.

The sight of any girl to soldiers near the front sparked interest no matter what political or moral views she held. Delavan Miller wrote how one Southern belle caused a fellow drummer to fight for the principle of honor:

Pete Boyle was the largest boy of the drum corps and he was a born swell. His home was New York. He had been

USAMHI

Elbridge J. Copp, 16, enlisted as a private during his second year of high school. Rising in rank to first lieutenant and adjutant of the 3rd New Hampshire, he managed to find time to regularly correspond with his hometown sweetheart S. Eliza White, below. They were married after the war.

Reminiscences of the War of the Rebellion

a newsboy in the Bowery district. He was a clog and jig dancer equal to many professionals and when it came to sparring and wrestling he was the champion light-weight of the regiment.

After Pete had taken part in one "Virginia reel" which gave him the opportunity to show off some of his fancy steps he could have had anything he wanted from those Maryland farmers, and the girls, why they were just falling over each other to get a chance to dance with him.

As I stated, Pete was a swell and would never wear government clothes without having them cut over and made to fit, and he would not hide his shapely No. 5 foot with a government brogan.

The girls were all watching Pete from out of the corners of their eyes, but it was noticed that one in particular was his favorite and that he danced with her quite frequently, which was not looked upon with favor by her Maryland escort who was big enough to eat Pete up.

The next morning ... a darkey approached our party and asking for "Mistah Boyle" handed Pete a note which after looking over, Pete read to us. It was in substance as follows:

> Mr. Peter Boyle:
> I thought you might like to know, being as you are a Union soldier, that the young lady you have been paying so much attention to is a se-cesh sympathizer and has a brother with Mosby the rebel guerrilla. A word to be wise is sufficient.
> Joe Yardsley.

Of course I am not giving the real name that was signed but it will answer for the purpose.

Pete called the darkey, gave him a quarter and said, "You can go and tell Joe Yardsley that I said that if he was half a man he would be with Sue's brother. Tell him that I think he is a sneak and a coward and if he will come over in the grove about 5 o'clock this afternoon I will slap his face."

The darkey showed his white teeth, scratched his head and digging his big toe in the sand said, "I reckon I bettah not tole dat to Joe. Dem Yardsleys got a powahful temper, dey hab, an dey boss all de young fellahs roun' here."

"All right, Sam," said Pete. "You tell him just what I told you."

That afternoon Pete and Sue were inseparable. They made themselves conspicuous everywhere.

The darkey brought Pete another note during the day and it simply said, "I will meet you in the grove. J.Y."

Of course all of us boys went over with Pete and the Marylander brought three companions. The two principals stripped to the waist and I confess I was fearful of the result when I saw how much larger Pete's antagonist was than he.

When they got the word Yardsley made a spring at Pete who dropped his head and butted the big fellow below the wind and slid him over his back. He got up and came furiously at our Pete again. But he knew a lot of Bowery tricks and quick as a flash stepped aside, caught him around the neck, whirled him around and threw him, slapped his face smartly and then let him up. The fellow rushed at Pete again, who now thought it about time to quit fooling, and he landed a good hard blow on the fellow's nose and mouth, which staggered him and made the blood fly.

The spectators on both sides thought that the affair had gone far enough and called for a cessation of hostilities. Pete offered to shake hands with his antagonist, but he declined and went away muttering threats.[29]

William Bircher visited Nashville in January 1864 during his regiment's trip north for veteran furlough. As he and his comrades waited for rail transportation, passes were issued to the city where they met and saw many young women. William recalled that "Among the novelties we saw here were the ladies, of which we had seen very few since our long and tiresome marches through the South. As they passed us on the streets, we were compelled to stop and gaze after them as if they were fairies."[30]

Not all were "fairies." Nashville and Washington were especially crowded with prostitution houses where soldiers old and young could spend time with the opposite sex if they wished. A separate hospital for soldiers infected with venereal diseases was established at Nashville, as well as one for prostitutes. During the winter of 1862-1863 the prostitute population there became so large that local officials, with help from the Army's provost marshal office, gathered 1,500 "ladies of the night" and shipped them to Louisville.[31]

If prostitutes were not readily available, liquor was. Whiskey, usually referred to as "commissary" by the men, was issued as a stimulant — the soldiers saying "in quantities large enough to cheer, but too small to inebriate." Inebriety was only a question of management. Most non-drinkers passed on their allotments to friends, who then consumed enough to bring forth their hilarious side. For regular imbibers a variety of means kept the flow open. Friends at home sent desired liquids in well-soldered cans disguised as fruit, condensed milk or other non-suspicious articles. False requisition papers occasionally slipped through channels, allowing liquor to be consumed by daring parties

> ## "Our adventures were chiefly of the disorderly kind. How to get out of camp, take in the city and then get back without being arrested, was the question."
>
> — Melvin Grigsby, 2nd Wisconsin Cavalry

bold enough to acquire it in such a manner. In many instances smaller, younger boys fell under alcohol's intoxicating effects because they were not accustomed to drinking and their diminutive size required far less for them to become drunk.[32]

Charles Bardeen had grown up in the prohibition town of Fitchburg, Massachusetts. He was raised believing alcohol was evil and that it was a sin to consume it. Whenever whiskey was dispensed he felt so strong in his beliefs he spilled his issue on the ground instead of sharing it with those who were in earnest need. One day in February 1864 he was feeling rather blue when the whiskey ration was being served, and uncharacteristically decided to take his full allowance. From that night forward he heeded the officers' remarks and abstained from trying the experiment again. But thereafter he shared his ration with those who were more accustomed to the beverage.[33]

Few youngsters away from home for such long periods of time were as steadfast in their convictions as Bardeen. Byron Fairbanks, who enlisted at 14 in the 12th Wisconsin, made a notation in his diary every time alcohol was dispensed. On January 6, 1864, he wrote, "We got some beer and had a spree."[34]

Private Melvin Grigsby of Company C, 2nd Wisconsin Cavalry, was another underage Badger boy who enjoyed the spirits issued. He commented: "Soldier life at Memphis was nearly a repetition of that at Helena [Arkansas]. Our camp was surrounded by a chain of guards and we were not permitted to go away from camp without a pass. Our adventures were chiefly of the disorderly kind. How to get out of camp, take in the city and then get back without being arrested, was the question. I went to the city three times as often as I would have gone had there been no camp guard to prevent it. The selling of liquor to the soldiers at the saloons, or by anyone, was forbidden. Before that order was issued I seldom thought of drinking anything. After the order was issued I never went into the city without finding a place where the order could be evaded. Such rules and orders have that effect on most young men. When we were at Helena, rations of whiskey were issued to us, and half the soldiers wouldn't touch it. Most all of them who refused whiskey at Helena drank every time they could get anything to drink at Memphis."[35]

Fourteen-year-old James Dickinson mentioned a "spree" in his diary that landed him in considerable trouble when he missed getting back aboard his gunboat stationed on the Mississippi River. "Weather awful sharp. A bad day for me. Called away in cutter early this a.m. Ran up and down the levee until I got tired[,] then went into a rum den and drank two glasses of rum. Made me drunk, I puked on deck and could not stand up. Anderson got Isham to clean it up, but I was caught and my warrant as coxswain taken away from me. I am now degraded to 1st Class Boy."[36]

Hundreds of boys drank and, according to Pennsylvania drummer Andrew J. Smith, some found it extremely hard to give up intoxicating beverages once they were used to the effects. This led to addiction in post-war years. Alcoholism not only created undue strain on marriages and personal lives, it made it difficult to stay employed. Veterans' organizations fueled the problem by offering an outlet where men could sit around the "campfire" and exchange war stories over drinks. In fact, during Grand Army of the Republic national encampments liquor was not only freely available, but prostitutes used the gatherings to ply their trade as well.[37]

On the other hand, youngsters also derived much pleasure from acceptable activities. Sports such as baseball, boxing, racing and wrestling were popular and indulged in whenever possible. Sporting contests often pitted individuals, sometimes entire regiments, against each other. Bets usually were placed but with most events regimental pride was the incentive.

102

Fort Pulaski near Savannah, Georgia, hosted the 48th New York from June 1, 1862, until June 18, 1863. During the 12-month garrison detail the regiment, known as "Perry's Saints," enjoyed a full complement of two drummers per company, seated here on both sides of their stacked drums, and a brass band for entertainment.

U.S. Army Military History Institute

The 12th New Hampshire possessed a young drummer nicknamed "Libby" in whom a great deal of pride was entrusted whenever a wrestling contest was challenged. In unison its members boasted, "There he is, match him if you can." Libby could handle his legs and feet as quickly as his drumsticks, while his strength and body elasticity allowed him to intimidate opponents. He never lost a match during the war. [38]

Musician Abraham J. Palmer proudly recalled how he and a number of comrades in the 48th New York performed on stage in theaters the regiment built. Their troupe was named the "Barton Dramatic Association" in honor of the regiment's second colonel, William B. Barton. The 48th's first theater was constructed at Fort Pulaski, Georgia, where the regiment spent an entire year of its enlistment. Colonel Barton granted permission for an unused outbuilding to be converted for the purpose, and detailed his own men to have it built. At first the 20-man troupe and regimental band performed comedy, but when their audiences tired of that they selected popular dramas to enrich the programs. Palmer, who was 15 when he enlisted in Company H, always was cast in the role of a girl or young woman. During a production of Shakespeare's "Othello" he played Emilia, causing Major James A. Barrett to remark, "Our two leading ladies were said to be the handsomest women in the Department." [39]

Storytelling, singing, Bible reading and church services also were part of a boy's experiences in the Army. At the end of almost every day when not campaigning, activities around the campfires were full of fun and frolic. Every company possessed a favorite storyteller, jokester, singer, dancer or champion of some sort. Many were boys like Alfred P. Hayden of Company F, 3rd New Hampshire, who was considered the best dancer of his regiment. Alfred was noted for maintaining good spirits no matter how adverse the situation confronting him. He enlisted at 16, and as late as 1911 was still carrying mail at Nashua, walking more than 10 miles a day. His youthfulness kept him a favorite at regimental reunions, where he danced for his comrades for years.[40]

CHAPTER 6

'Appealing to the mercy of the court'

During the Civil War punishment in the Union Army easily could be described as harsh. On occasion it was meted out quickly with little time allowed for defense preparation, and in other cases offenders locked away waited months for their trials. Through bad judgment even the Army's youngest members often found themselves at the mercy of military justice.

Military court proceedings are called courts-martial. Soldiers could be brought before general courts-martial, which followed strict guidelines, and usually were necessitated for cases of murder, rape, arson, desertion, striking an officer, or the all-purpose offense of "conduct prejudicial to good order and military discipline." A general court-martial was the highest military tribunal during the war. After such trials were held the verdicts and sentences were forwarded to the respective headquarters for approval or recommendations. Defendants not receiving favorable sentences then could appeal to Washington through the Adjutant General's office. Further appeals reached the desk of President Lincoln, who with his two personal secretaries reviewed thousands of cases. A general court-martial board usually consisted of eight members, but specifically was to contain 13. If fewer than 13 were present the minutes had to explain why.

Besides general courts-martial there were less formal hearings held at regimental or garrison level for such offenses as having a dirty gun, being late at roll call, drunkenness, fighting, etc. At the regimental level sentences consisted of extra fatigue details, fines, stripped rank, confinement to quarters or the guardhouse, and any number of lesser penalties designed to keep men in line.[1]

"Drum head" courts-martial were trials of cases that demanded immediate attention, due to the Army's imminent movement or proximity of the enemy. These affairs usually were not recorded. Some should have been sent to a general court-martial. Adjutant Elbridge Copp of the 3rd New Hampshire witnessed a "drum head" proceeding in April 1864, and best described this part of military life in his post-war reminiscences:

A drum head court-martial is called in emergencies requiring immediate action; it gets its name from the supposed use of a drum as a court table upon which to do business. We had a drum head court-martial in our regiment when in Florida, for the trial of a deserter. Recruits had been sent to us from the North, and there were always more or less bounty jumpers, called so from having received a large bounty to enlist, then took the first opportunity to desert, finding their way to the North to again enlist, to receive another bounty. We had numerous desertions of this kind. Colonel Plimpton [Lieutenant Colonel Josiah J. Plumpton] was in command of the regiment, and was the kind of an officer who could not be trifled with. He determined to put a stop to desertions. One night he secretly placed the second picket line outside of the first. During the night a recruit escaped from camp, found his way through the first picket line, and approached a post of the second or outside picket line, supposing it to be that of the enemy. When challenged he replied, "Hullo, Johnnies, I am a Yank and am coming over to your side."

"All right," the sentinel said, "come on," and he fell easily into the trap. He was immediately taken into camp and to Colonel Plimpton's tent.

The colonel was awakened, the officer making his report of the capture of the deserter. The colonel immediately ordered a court-martial. It was then about midnight. The officers detailed organized the court and the prisoner was brought before them. Short work was made of the trial; the evidence was direct and there was no defense.

The prisoner was declared guilty of desertion, and under the rules of war and military law, he was sentenced to be shot. The report was made within the hour to Colonel Plimpton, when he ordered that he should be shot at sunrise, and in the presence of the whole command the sentence was executed. The man was shot and buried within six hours from the time he left camp.[2] Colonel Plimpton then made a full report of the affair to the department commander, asking that the proceedings of the court-martial and the sentence be approved. We had no more desertions in our regiment for many months.[3]

Desertion, the term given to any mustered soldier who abandoned his comrades or post, was a major problem. In the Army regulations' 20th Article of War the death penalty for desertion was clearly stated. After Fort Sumter was bombarded the death penalty was applied approximately 165 times during the war.[4] Considering that in a study of the first 42,000 Union courts-martial 14,146 were for desertion, the number of executions was small.[5] The reason for the disparity between the number tried and those executed was based on different factors. Deserters were by definition soldiers who left their commands with the intent of never coming back. Some soldiers due to calamities at home, boredom in the winter months or drunkenness, vacated their posts with intentions of returning in a short while. Being absent without leave was the category most offending soldiers found themselves in after sneaking to a nearby town to drink or fool around. Many accused deserters simply were absent without leave, but were charged with the more serious or both offenses. If a court determined a soldier did not intend to desert it could find him innocent of that charge, but still find him guilty of the second, lesser charge and administer punishment accordingly.

Knowing the number of court-martial cases involving desertion, and considering thousands of un-

derage soldiers were in the ranks, it stands to reason that some faced tribunals for the charge. In cases where extremely young lads were tried courts usually were lenient in view of their age. Sometimes a boy simply was issued a discharge.

Private John Moore of the 2nd West Virginia Cavalry was sent home after being arrested in Nicholas County, West Virginia, for deserting his command. Sergeant Asa Rusk of Company E, a prosecution witness, testified that on the morning of February 12, 1864, John wanted a pass to visit his home. Unable to obtain it he hopped a coal wagon on its way to Cannell's Creek and disappeared. The court asked the sergeant to state John's approximate age, height and weight. Rusk answered he came to the regiment a year before, and was now 14 years old, about five foot two and weighed 110 pounds. The boy offered no defense.

The court found Moore guilty of desertion and ordered him to be discharged with a loss of any pay due him. Colonel Rutherford B. Hayes of the 23rd Ohio, president of the court-martial, noted on the trial transcript: "The court is thus lenient in this case owing to the youth of the prisoner[,] he not being in appearance more than fourteen years of age, and should never have been enlisted as a soldier."[6]

Frederick Herzog was charged with deserting Company B, 98th Pennsylvania, in January 1862. He was turned over to the provost marshal by a bounty hunter in Philadelphia the following October. On December 7, 1863, Frederick was brought before a court-martial, during which he adamantly declared his innocence and personally represented himself. Captain Francis Fisher opened the prosecution's case.

"I am captain of Company B, 98th Pennsylvania Volunteers. Know the accused. He had been enlisted as a private and placed among the drummers. He was enlisted in Philadelphia on or about the 17th of September 1861. He deserted the company on or about the 12th of January 1862 when the Regiment lay at Tennallytown [Maryland]. I was present with the company at the time. We missed him at roll call in the evening, and made search for him but did not find him. I have not seen him since until the present time."

Frederick questioned the captain: "Was not the accused enlisted and mustered as a drummer?" Fisher replied, "No, he was enlisted as a private and was found too small and too weak to carry a musket, and at the first muster for pay he was put on the rolls as a drummer."

Frederick then asked, "A short time before he left the company was not the accused ordered to carry a musket?"

Fisher: "I heard the Captain say that he would return the accused to duty with the company. The accused said he was too small to carry a musket. I was 1st Lieutenant at the time. When the accused enlisted his mother was present and gave her written consent. I have not got that paper in my possession now. I don't think he would have deserted had it not been for one of his mess-mates who had great control over him and deserted afterwards himself." Finishing his testimony, Fisher told the court Frederick was between 14 and 15, and was a drummer when he deserted.

At the close of the prosecution's case the boy presented a statement which was read aloud.

Mr. President and members of the court:

I was enlisted and mustered into the service of the United States as a drummer. I was but two months more than fourteen years of age and entirely too young to enlist as a private and carry a musket. My mother would not give her consent for me to enlist as anything else than a drummer. When my enlistment papers were made out both myself and mother understood that I was to be a drummer.

A short time before I left the regiment I was ordered to return to duty with the company to carry a musket, and several of my friends, among them the Drum Major, advised me to go home, that I was too young to do duty as a soldier. I did not think I was doing wrong, and would not have thought of leaving had I been permitted to remain with the Drum Corps. I am too weak now to do duty as a private as I have the heart disease very severely.

After deliberation the court found Frederick guilty, sentencing him to forfeit all pay and five dollars for the next month after being returned to his company. Once again the lenient sentence was due to "the extreme youth of the accused." The verdict was approved by General Henry D. Terry, who recommended the boy be discharged. This was done as Frederick and his mother wished.[7]

Musician George Held also was discharged after going before a court-martial board on April 18, 1864, charged with desertion. He had enlisted in October 1861 in Company G, 99th Pennsylvania. About August 25, 1862, while at Alexandria, Virginia, George deserted and was gone for 20 months until found at Fort Ethan Allen outside Washington. His father was stationed at the fort as a member of the 112th Pennsylvania [Battery K, 2nd Pennsylvania Heavy Artillery]. George, hearing of his enlistment and nearby location, left his command to be with him.[8] In his defense he provided the court with a written statement:

The accused drummer George R. Held[,] 99th Pa. Vols.[,] a mere boy of 14 summers[,] enlisted at the tender age of 12 as a drummer in the above mentioned regiment. He was urged at the time by older boys and was no doubt captivated by the inducements held forth of travel and much fun. His father being applied to for permission reluctantly consented to let him go.

The boy has always been sickly, and a short term of service discovered to him his inability to perform his duties. He was never able to keep with his company on the march, and has been permitted much liberty on account of his youthfulness. Upon arriving at Alexandria Va. with his regiment he learned that his father had enlisted in one of the Penn. Regts. (112th) and was stationed in the defense[s] of Washington. He took the earliest opportunity to visit him, and he has been with his father ever since.

It is evident the accused did not know the penalty of the crime of desertion, and that he had no intention of such a crime in the act of visiting his father who it seems should be held responsible for the conduct of his boy. Appealing to the mercy of the court in this case, the accused respectfully submits this statement.

George R. Held (X) his mark.[9]

Drummer John Teniss was sentenced to be publicly reprimanded at dress parade of his regiment, the 35th Illinois, and discharged for being away four weeks. He enlisted September 1, 1861, when only 13. His youth caused General Jefferson C. Davis, in reviewing the court's findings, to remit the sentence and have the boy returned to duty. Teniss served for another year and a half before being discharged for disability in August 1864.[10]

Fourteen-year-old John Craddock of the 28th Pennsylvania was charged with desertion following a trip home to see his sick mother. He stayed three months before going back to the regiment. Because he returned voluntarily John was found not guilty of desertion, but guilty of absence without leave. Loss of pay while gone was all he had to surrender, and once again the court stated its leniency was due to his age.[11]

Other youngsters retained in the service after being returned to their commands were not as well off.

The Army was fond of imposing fines for infractions against its system. John Craddock's sentence of pay loss really was no penalty at all considering he was not present to earn it in the first place. John R. Thompson and Alexander Daugherty were both fined after deserting their respective commands. Thompson enlisted in the 102nd Pennsylvania on August 6, 1862, when 12 years old. After soldiering more than two years he learned a sister was deathly ill with smallpox, and went home with a group of men from his company in November 1864. Two months later he was arrested by a Pittsburgh policeman and remanded to the city's provost marshal. Guilty of desertion, he was returned to his regiment and ordered to forfeit $10 of his pay for the next 12 months. Additionally, the time absent had to be served at the end of his enlistment.[12]

Musician Daugherty of Company D, 10th Missouri, also was ordered to make up six months he was absent as well as lose eight months' pay. His case is interesting in that he enlisted with his father, Captain D.C. Daugherty, a witness for the prosecution, who also was retained by Alexander as his counsel. The younger Daugherty wrote:

I beg leave to submit to the court the following defense in relation to absenting myself from my company and regiment on the 1st day of March 1863.

I enlisted in Co. D, 10th Regt. Mo. Vol. inf. on the 25th day of July 1861. When I enlisted it was my belief, based on information received from officers recruiting companies that each enlisted man would be entitled to forty days furlough every year during their term of service, but after having served one year I applied for a furlough but it was refused me, and after repeated applications I became satisfied that no furlough would be granted me during my term of service, and having observed that a large number of enlisted men belonging to the different Regiments composing the division to which my Regt. belongs had returned home without proper authority and remained there a short time and not punished on their return to their companies, led me to believe that the penalty for being absent without leave was not so great as I now know it to be. Therefore I do acknowledge that I absented myself from my company and regiment on the 1st day of March 1863 for the purpose of returning home for a short time to visit my mother, after which I intended to return to my regiment, it never having been my intention to remain absent a longer time than would be required.... But after arriving at home (which required over a month to go, I having walked the entire distance from Memphis) and remaining there ten days I be-

came alarmed in consequence [of] the authorities arresting men absent without leave & I crossed the Mississippi River to Hamilton[,] a small town opposite my mother's place of residence, but soon after I received a letter from my mother requesting me to return and give myself up to Lt. Ball[,] military commander at Keokuk[,] Iowa, to be forwarded to my Regiment, which I eagerly sought to comply with as what I wished was to return to my Regiment & while on the ferry boat for the purpose of crossing the river to report I was arrested and forwarded to St. Louis. My mother had me detained in order to procure my discharge from the service in consequence of my minority[,] I being at that time but 4 months past 16 years of age. While at the barracks (Schofield) I did guard duty during the entire period of my detention there as the commander of the same said he knew of no charges against me.

In conclusion I hope the honorable court will deal with me as lightly as the circumstances and the good of the service demands, taking into consideration my long term of service, my youth, I being but four months past fourteen years of age at the time of my enlistment, and my conduct as a soldier since my return.

First Lieutenant Marcus Frost of Company D was asked by Alexander, "How did I perform my duty as a soldier prior to my desertion?" Frost responded, "Well, you was always a good soldier. At the battle of Corinth you was a musician & left back at camp, but you got a musket & came out to us & done as well as any soldier in the field." The lieutenant also declared he had "done very well at the battle of Chattanooga" after his return to the company. Several statements from others heralding his worth followed before the court adjourned for deliberation.

Alexander's defense was strong enough to warrant a not-guilty-of-desertion verdict, but being absent without leave cost him his sentence and fine. In summary, the small boy was caught between his mother who had written President Lincoln about procuring a discharge, and his father who returned him to the regiment.[13]

Albert C. Meady's mother got involved with his case after he was arrested, tried and sentenced to one year of hard labor without pay. Albert's woes began when he was confined in the 14th Massachusetts' guardhouse for fighting. Soon afterward he escaped. On February 7, 1863, he was found at a convalescent camp where he was placed in custody and charged with desertion. His mother, Elizabeth Meady, was a widow with three other children at home depending

**"Wearing the barrel" — Union soldiers
stationed at the Point Lookout, Maryland,
prison receive a dose of military punishment.**

Author's Collection

on Albert's pay for support. Eventually she appealed
in writing for her son's release. Her letter illustrates
the harsh punishment courts could impose in contrast
to those affording leniency.

Salem Sept. 1st 64

Col. Tufts

Sir — Permit me to address you on behalf of my son
Albert C. Meady, formerly a private in the 14th Mass. Regt.
Co. E, who is now a prisoner at Fort Jefferson[,] Florida.
His regt has been discharged but his sentence extends to
Feb. 13th 65. It has now been more than two years since he
has received any pay & I was dependent on him for support.

I am a widow with three younger children to provide
for, and we have suffered much already, in consequence of
his pay being stopped. And now since the Regt has been
discharged even our one dollar a week state pay has been
withdrawn. And now we have come to actual want. At the
present high prices it is impossible for me to earn enough to

keep them from hunger. My next to Albert in age, a daughter 13 years old, has been obliged to leave school & go out
to service, but the two younger ones, one a daughter 11, and
a son 5 years old, must be provided for. And now I have not
a dollar in the world and we see nothing before us but suffering, unless Albert's leave can be obtained....

Albert enlisted March 4th 1862 without any bounty &
has never received but four months pay. He was but a boy
only 14 years and 8 months old when he enlisted but he was
smart, and would have made a good soldier if Henry N.
Dyke [of Company E] had let him alone.

Dyke was the instigator of the quarrel and any unpreju-
diced person would say wholly to blame, for my son injured
him only in self defense, but Albert was a stranger in the
company [recruited from Amesbury, Massachusetts] and
Capt. Sargent was a hard man. If Albert had been in a Salem
Co[mpany] amongst friends it would have been different.
Isnt it a pity that a boy like him should be so severely punished because he had spirit enough to defend himself
against a mean overbearing fellow like Dyke.

If I am not mistaken I think the law allows a widowed
mother her son whom she is dependent on for support. But
he was patriotick enough to join the army, before bounties
were given and proud to become a soldier and [assume] the
responsibilities of a man at so early an age and so I let him
go little thinking my support would be cut off and his energies & prospects would be crushed at so early an age. He
has had a hard sentence and been severely punished for one

so young. And now Sir, if you will present his case to the President & try to obtain his full pay and pardon, I trust you will not lose your record.

I hope and trust his pay will not be refused me for that would be depriving me and my children of every comfort in life. And render life a burden to me. I will send you a copy of the charges against him which were sent me from the Fort. You will see there are two charges[,] both of which are more severe than the case will warrant without any allowance being made for his youth. He was arrested for injuring private Dyke and had been confined in the guard house for more than a month when he found he was not to receive his pay with the rest. He was so disappointed that it made him reckless. He didn't consider or think of the consequences so he left & went to convalescent camp where he stayed until he was caught and brought back again under guard to Fort Albany where he was tried and received this severe sentence. He was sentenced to fort Delaware where I hoped he would remain till he was released but has since been sent to Fort Jefferson[,] Florida. Will you be so kind as to write me in a few days & let me know what can be done. I shall await with interest and anxiety a reply.

Yours truly Elizabeth E. Meady

In spite of his mother's impassioned plea Albert served his entire term of confinement and was discharged March 7, 1865. Fortunately for his younger siblings the loss-of-pay sentence was remitted as long as the money was sent directly to Massachusetts for the family's support.[14]

Severe sentences, including death, could be inflicted on soldiers who fell asleep on duty, according to the 46th Article of War.[15] With prolonged activities many were asked to perform it was relatively common for weary, overworked soldiers to commit this offense.

Royal Seeley, Company E, 16th New York Cavalry, was charged with sleeping on post after officer of the day Charles S. Eigenbrodt of the 2nd Massachusetts Cavalry found him asleep on the outskirts of their cavalry camp. In accordance to orders three men were to constitute each watch. One man was to be mounted, one was to stand to horse and the third was permitted to lie down and even go to sleep, but was required to rise at anyone's approach. In this instance it was Royal's turn to be the third man. Eigenbrodt contended he was slow to awaken, and after mounting was still in a semi-stupor. Royal's defense was simple and to the point. "I was the man who was permitted to lay down. I had the reins in my hand. I was fourteen

years old last June." His arguments and other testimony earned an acquittal and he was returned to the ranks.[16]

Private John Horrigan of the same regiment's Company F was not as lucky falling asleep on top of a haystack while detailed as company stable guard. After pleading guilty he was ordered to clean four horses twice a day for two months, and also forfeited two dollars of pay for four months. In sentencing the 14-year-old boy the judge advocate wrote, "The extreme youth of the prisoner leads the court to inflict this punishment."[17]

James Lebarre's "extreme youth" spared him harsher treatment for inappropriate behavior on May 2 and August 10, 1863. The 61st Ohio private was part of a sharpshooter detail ordered to take a Confederate battery the evening of May 1 at Chancellorsville. The attempt was unsuccessful and James rejoined Company C after dark. Early the next morning he left for the rear where he was found by First Lieutenant William H. Kirkwood, sent by the company's captain to retrieve him. Abandoning one's command with a battle imminent was reason enough for the death penalty, but James' antics only became worse. As a prosecution witness at Lebarre's court-martial Lieutenant Kirkwood described events surrounding the 16 year old's immature actions:

I had warned him two or three times that if he ever went off again [Lebarre apparently was a habitual straggler] I would tie him and lead him. I found him about half a mile in rear of the line of battle. I asked him what he was doing there and he said he was looking for the provost guard. I tied his hands behind him and led him with me back to the regiment. After I took him to the regiment the captain told me to tie him to a tree right in rear of the line of battle. After tying him, he got his hands loose and commenced tearing his cartridges behind him and strewing his caps on the ground. I warned him several times to stop or I would buck and gag him. He refused to stop and swore he would be goddamned if he would shoulder his gun or shoot with it and swore vengeance at me. He said he carried a gun and I carried a sword and he would make me pay for it. He used very abusive language toward me and bit my thumb and bit the corporal's fingers and kicked at me. I left him bucked and gagged [for] a time and then loosed him and told him to go back to his line of battle. He refused. I told him several times and he refused. I then bucked and gagged him again. I left him so an hour then again loosed him and told him to go back to his line, but he swore and would be damned or

110

die before he would do it or shoot his gun. Then the Colonel sent him to the provost marshal. He did at this time and I have very frequently heard him threaten to desert, cursing the President and the war and the generals. When we first went on duty where we now are [in August 1863] Lt. Col. Bown gave the orders that no man was to leave camp without a pass approved by him. The accused disobeyed the orders and was caught outside the lines. Col. Bown then told me to prefer charges and also prefer the old charges. He has been doing duty since Chancellorsville. He came back to the regiment from the provost guard while we were in the breastworks.

The provost guards likely had enough to do May 2 at Chancellorsville with the retreat of the Eleventh Corps, to which the 61st Ohio belonged. At any rate, James was returned to his regiment as the battle opened. Private John Brown, also of Company C, testified the teenager was in the breastworks firing at Confederates and "did his part" during the retreat. Although lauding Lebarre's behavior during the actual battle, Brown stated he heard James say on occasion that he wished he was out of "this abolitionist Army." The court obliged, finding him guilty of all charges and pronouncing sentence of hard labor for the remainder of his enlistment and forfeiture of six months' pay. Approving the sentence, General Hector Tyndale noted that only extreme youth would be accepted to warrant the "light" punishment instead of death. Lebarre was detained at Fort Delaware until discharged May 19, 1865.[18]

Paulis Van Versen was incarcerated for permitting a prisoner he was guarding to escape. Paulis enlisted at 14 in Company E, 131st New York. When his right arm was seriously wounded and rendered useless in 1863, he transferred to the Veteran Reserve Corps and was stationed in New York City. In August 1864, while detailed to accompany prisoners to Governors Island, he was accused of taking a $40 bribe and allowing a soldier named Timothy Daly to run off. Paulis conducted his own defense at court-martial, producing recommendation letters from officers and other witnesses to substantiate his innocence. Despite solid arguments he was found guilty, but the prosecution's claim that he accepted the bribe was not proven. In the court's opinion his age did not become a factor. He was sentenced "to be confined on bread and water diet for the period of 14 days," and fined $40 — the same amount he was accused of taking.[19]

Stealing and robbery were other crimes placing boys before the courts. James Murphy was 14 when he crept into the officers' quarters of the 168th New York and stole a revolver. He offered no defense, pleaded guilty, and due to "extreme youth" was assigned to one month of hard labor.[20]

Murphy admitted he knew his actions were wrong. But determining right from wrong while foraging was another matter. Depending on the area of operations or a commander's ideas of what was considered foraging and stealing, the act could be interpreted differently. Sixteen-year-old Melvin Grigsby of the 2nd Wisconsin Cavalry found himself in an interpretive dispute on the subject with his commanding officer in Mississippi. He wrote:

We camped [one] night in a little place called Vernon. In an abandoned house I found a trunk addressed to the captain of a rebel regiment; broke it open, and among other things that were evidently intended for a soldier in camp there was a pair of fine woolen blankets and a little bag of silver. These I took. I presented the blankets to our colonel [Thomas Stephens] and kept the silver, four or five dollars.

A few days after that Uncle Tommy, as the boys called the Colonel, got on his ear because so many of us left the ranks to forage. Had he kept us where there was fighting to do he would have had no trouble, but fighting wasn't in his line, and we all knew it. I had been scouting on my own hook one day and, on coming to camp, found a camp guard out. Not expecting anything of the kind, I was captured and taken before Colonel Stephens. He was in a great rage. Had my forage, of which I had a load, taken from me, and ordered me to get off my horse and be searched. I told him I had not taken anything but forage, and was not in the habit of taking anything else. Adjutant [Joseph P.] Scott asked to see what I had in my pockets. As the colonel, who was a rank englishman, saw the silver he fairly frothed at the mouth.

"Where did'e get that?"

"In a house in Vernon," I replied.

"Been a-burnin' 'ouses, 'ave 'e? Been a-robbin' of people and burnin' 'ouses, 'ave 'e? I'll teach 'e to break horders and burn 'ouses, so I will. Hadjutant, send this man to his company under harrest."

I tried to explain but he ordered me off. Lieutenant [Daniel L.] Riley saw Adjutant Scott next morning, and together they pacified the colonel. Nothing further would have been said or done had I been content to let the matter rest. The colonel called me hard names, had taken money from me that he had no better right to than I had, and, as I did not have much respect for him anyhow, the more I thought of it the more I thought I had been misused.

Examining the army regulations, I found that valuables taken from the enemy should be turned over to the hospital department. From Adjutant Scott I learned that the colonel had kept my silver and made no report of it. After talking the matter over with Captain [William] Woods, who was then acting as major, I concluded to ask the colonel for the silver. So one day when we had halted for a noon day rest, I walked up to the colonel, who was lying in the shade surrounded by other officers, and asked him to return the silver that he had taken from me. He reached for his sabre, jumped up and made for me as though he meant to run me through on the spot. Captain Woods and the other officers stopped him and reminded him that he had no right to use his sabre on a soldier for asking a question.

I was subsequently tried before a [drum head] court-martial on charges preferred by Colonel Stephens. The trial was in the colonel's tent. I did not hear the evidence submitted against me, but I was called in and asked to explain how and where I obtained the silver, and why I asked the colonel to return it to me. I sat on a cot in the colonel's tent, and turning up the blankets, noticed the very same white blankets that I took from the trunk in which I found the silver. When I told where I had got the silver, I said: "Gentlemen, I took a pair of white wool blankets from the same trunk and presented them to Colonel Stephens. He thanked me with great kindness and made no inquiries as to where I got them. I think these are the same blankets."

I uncovered a pair of white blankets on the cot. The officers of the court smiled; the colonel got red in the face and tried to explain, but about all that he could say was that he did not know that I was the boy that gave him the blankets. As I never heard any more from the court-martial I suppose that the charges were not sustained.[21]

Peer pressure coaxed two 14-year-old soldiers of the 4th East Tennessee Cavalry to participate in the armed robbery of citizen R.H. Askins. While Privates Joseph Cuppels, William Anderson and J.C. Jackson guarded cattle on October 27, 1864, outside Nashville, Askins rode up in a wagon and offered the boys a drink. During conversation he bragged about a large amount of money he had, showing it to the trio. He then asked if he could accompany them to town when their watch was up. They agreed and soon all four started. Passing an old house a shot was fired in their direction, causing the boys to draw their pistols and poke around the dwelling. As they searched, Jackson suggested divesting Askins of his money. Cuppels and Anderson were against the idea, but before both knew it Jackson pointed his gun at the man and demanded his cash. Askins pulled the wad from his pocketbook, threw it on the ground and began running for the woods. Jackson fired, claiming he killed him. The boys split the money at Jackson's insistence and rode on. Early the next day they were arrested. Askins was alive and brought forth as a witness. Cuppels and Anderson cooperated with the prosecution, providing details of the incident to the court. All three boys were sentenced to five years in Nashville's military prison, but because Cuppels and Anderson were 14 their terms were reduced to two years. They actually were released early, in October 1865.[22]

It can be surmised Jackson's bad aim prevented him and his comrades from a military execution. Sixteen-year-old Ephraim Richardson and Abraham Purvis, 18, both of Company C, 21st Missouri, were not treated as lightly. At a general court-martial held January 9, 1865, the two were found guilty of murder for shooting "with gunpowder and leaden bullets" civilian Dominick Patton while on the march from St. Charles to St. Louis, Missouri. Ephraim had enlisted November 16, 1862. No reason for the killing was stated in court papers, but of all the boys who went before various court-martial boards his sentence was one that perhaps should have been remitted due to the prisoner's "extreme youth." Instead, he dropped from a St. Louis jailyard gallows on January 13, 1865. Ephraim Richardson holds the distinction of being the youngest soldier executed by the United States military.[23]

CHAPTER 7

'Covered with dirt if not with glory'

Young soldiers participated in nearly every battle of the Civil War, and each experienced a fight like no other. A boy's senses keenly absorbed the sights, sounds and smells of the battlefield — searing impressions that lived long in memory if he survived. Accounts of combat by or about the youngest warriors in the ranks share common threads, yet all are as diverse as the participants themselves.

The 12th New Hampshire was one of those regiments that contained a large number of underage soldiers. At the battle of Cold Harbor, Virginia, these boys and their comrades led an assault by Colonel Griffin Stedman's brigade of the Eighteenth Corps against strong Confederate fortifications along their part of the line. The futile charge was devastating, causing 167 casualties in the 12th, of which 23 were killed outright.[1] For the boys June 3, 1864, was an unforgettable, exceptionally trying day. As they advanced from a stream bed where their brigade formed for the charge, they cried out, "Huzzah! Huzzah!" and rushed forward 10 lines deep. Instantly the regiment was splattered with iron and lead. Those still standing pressed toward the earthworks that spewed fire through the smoke, only to be struck themselves as they clambered over bodies already dead and dying at their feet. The attack faltered and the survivors instinctively began to dodge, recoil and lie down. It lasted less than half an hour. Most casualties had been inflicted within the first 15 minutes.[2] Of the 12th New

Hampshire's losses a good many were young boys. Some had enlisted underage in 1862 when the regiment was formed. Others had waited patiently until they aged sufficiently, or had grown enough to become replacements in 1863-1864. All were still too young for what transpired that day.

Orrin G. Colby enlisted in the regiment at Concord 10 days prior to his 17th birthday in 1862 and returned there in 1865. At Cold Harbor a Confederate shell almost took his life, grazing him as it screamed by. One witness said it "knocked him heels over head." Adrenalin pumping from the narrow escape, he regained his feet and moved on, being among the last to leave the field when the assault bogged down. As he retreated over the corpse-strewn ground he was struck again, this time in the back by an explosive musket ball. In extreme pain he still summoned the strength to make it to the stream bed's protective bank, where comrades administered aid.[3]

James F. Marshall also was an early recruit, enlisting in 1862 at age 15. Described as one of the "bravest and best soldiers of the regiment," he never was known to leave the colors during a march or battle. On June 3 he was shot through the shoulder, the wound disabling him for a number of months. With "invincible determination" he fought through the pain and healed in time to return to the regiment to see final victory in 1865.[4]

William O. Bryant had just celebrated his 16th birthday in 1862 when he enlisted in Company I with

Orrin G. Colby   **James F. Marshall**   **William O. Bryant**

Among the 167 casualties of the 12th New Hampshire at Cold Harbor were the five teenagers pictured here. The regiment began its assault June 3, 1864, with fewer than 300 effectives, according to historian Otis F.R. Waite. "Many of the wounded were left upon the field between the two lines of works, not more than seventy-five yards apart, for three days, before they could be taken away. Twenty of the dead of this regiment were found within five yards of the enemy's works."

Samuel H. Roberts

Charles H. Heath

his father Sullivan. He, too, was reputed to have been an exceptional soldier, steadfast in the execution of his duties. During the battle of Gettysburg William was detailed to the 1st New Jersey Battery, its ranks being insufficient to man its guns. The battle was absorbing for father and son, each narrowly escaping death. Sullivan, wounded in the hand by a ball, felt a shell fly by so close that it tore off his knapsack. William miraculously was unscathed when another shell killed two battery horses he was holding. At Cold Harbor fate was not so kind. Mortally wounded in the bowels, William lingered until 6 p.m. His last hours were spent quietly talking with friends. Suddenly he exclaimed, "Oh, dear, I shall die!" and expired. When the news reached his mother she tearfully sighed, "He was a good hearted, dutiful boy." [5]

Samuel H. Roberts joined the 12th during January 1864, having run away from school in Massachusetts to escape his parents. Only 14, he was enrolled as a musket-carrying infantryman in Company D. Samuel also was injured at Cold Harbor, but the wound proved too slight to leave the ranks. His boyish face later caused a Confederate picket at Petersburg to yell across the lines, "Go home, kid, and nurse your mother," to the laughter of all who heard. [6]

Charles H. Heath, born July 24, 1848, was yet another young recruit accepted in December 1863 to fill the regiment's depleted ranks. He was struck three times at Cold Harbor — in the back, knee and severely through the right ankle. This last wound incapacitated him, and he was discharged for disability after spending more than a year in the hospital.[7]

For all five boys the battle was costly, especially so for William Bryant, who that day donated his youth and his life. It can be assumed that some level of fear was present as they ran forward, surrounded by comrades being slaughtered at their sides. Accounts written by underage participants of battles clearly state that fear was always a factor when confronting the enemy. Many declined to deny it, perhaps because they knew fear kept them alert.

Controlled fear could be described as bravery, but even the bravest experienced anxiety during a fight. There were instances when uncontrollable fear gripped an individual, but after a short period he regained his composure and never was afflicted again. One unidentified soldier in the 27th New York was seized in such manner as the regiment approached Hanover Court House, Virginia, in May 1862. The recruit notified his captain he did not want to go to the front. He was taken to General Henry W. Slocum, when he began to cry and begged to be sent home. The general chastised him, calling the young man a big baby. "I wish I was a baby, and a girl baby, too!" whimpered the soldier. His words and tears were ignored, and he was returned to his company.[8]

Most individuals declared their first battle was the most unnerving, even if it was not the hardest fought. Charles Willison wrote of his first encounter at Chickasaw Bayou, Mississippi, with the 76th Ohio on December 29, 1862: "Here I was initiated to the terrifying, bloody realities of warfare, far different from anything I had yet experienced. No engagement in which I was afterward involved impressed me with the nightmarish sensations of this one." After jockeying around the field the regiment ended up lying in reserve to one of the main assaults. In that position it suffered a few casualties from a Confederate barrage, but was only lightly engaged. As night enveloped the bayou Charles was posted on picket. Rain cascaded in torrents and enemy shells continued searching the woods. Willison reflected: "While standing lonely and forlorn at my picket station, carefully scanning the sandy waste between me and the rebel lines, a screech owl suddenly flew up near me with one of its unearthly cries and almost scared the wits out of me. I had never heard anything of the kind before and must admit it almost made my hair stand up."[9]

George Ulmer of the 8th Maine recalled his first battle was a terrifying experience:

After a long, tedious march across pontoons [and] over corduroy roads, we confronted the Johnnies at Cold Harbor. It was here that I found myself in a real, genuine battle. I got lost in the scuffle. I found myself amidst bursting shells and under heavy musketry fire. I was bewildered and frightened. I did not know which way to go. I ran this way and that, trying to find my brother and regiment. Every turn I made it seemed I encountered more bullets and shells. Soldiers were shouting and running in every direction, artillery was galloping here and there, on every side it seemed they were fighting for dear life. On one side of me I saw horses and men fall and pile up on top of each other. Cannon and caissons with broken wheels were turned upside down, riderless horses were scampering here and there, officers were riding and running in all directions, the shells were whizzing through the air, and soldiers shouting at the top of their voices. Everything seemed upside down. I thought the world had come to an end. I tried to find shelter behind a tree, away from the bullets, but as soon as I found shelter on one side it seemed as though the bullets and shells came from all sides, and I lay down in utter despair and fright. I don't know how long I was there, but when I awoke I thought the war was over, it was so still. I thought every one had been killed on both sides, excepting myself. I was just thinking I would try and find a live horse, ride back to Washington and tell them that the war was over, everybody was killed, when my brother tapped me on the shoulder and asked me where I had been. He had gone through it all, escaped with the loss of a toe, and had come to the rear to have it dressed and find me.[10]

On many occasions youngsters concealed their fright so they would not lose face. At Fredericksburg on December 12, 1862, Charles Bardeen broke ranks in the 1st Massachusetts Infantry to have a look at the desolated city. He watched other Federal soldiers plunder houses, but kept out of trouble himself and soon returned to his company. Since it was the closest he had been to a battlefield, he picked up a few spent bullets and an enemy bayonet, which he proudly showed his comrades. They belittled his treasures, asking instead to see flour or tobacco they knew should have been easily found. Thinking about what

William Young, a 13-year-old Detroit schoolboy, enlisted August 15, 1862, in Company G, 24th Michigan. The musician was in the Army two months shy of three years and was present at Gettysburg, where his Iron Brigade regiment sustained 363 casualties of 496 present. During the summer of 1864 he spent some time sick at Washington's Armory Square General Hospital. "Dead beet" was noted on his bed card.

David D. Finney Jr. Collection

other we were scared we pretended to deliberate. "Do you think we ought to go on?" I asked, and like the heroes in the Aeneid who were scared my voice stuck in my throat.

"P-perhaps they won't let us in," he replied with similar indistinctness.

"Maybe the regiment will be moving," I added.

"Yes, I think we had better go back to it," he assented.

By this time the gunners had got the range and the shells were coming fast.

"Perhaps the regiment may charge these batteries," I suggested, "and we shouldn't want to miss that."

"No, we shouldn't want to miss that," Prest agreed, his teeth chattering. "We'd better start right along," and with lengthy strides made back up the hill.

"Hold on," I cried, "you're right in range. Come down the river a piece before we start back."

But if he heard me he did not turn, and he made a bee-line for the regiment. I went down the river almost to the Lacy house before I turned up the hill and was soon out of the line of shells.

But I was certainly scared. One shell had exploded near enough so that I could realize its effects, and one thing I wanted was to get where no more shells could burst around me. This patriotic hero who had declared in front of camp-fires how he longed for gore would have liked to be tucked up once more in his little trundle bed. Bomb ague is a real disease and I had caught it.

they said he decided to go back and relieve the city of a more practical crop than what he procured the previous visit. A fellow drummer named "Prest" accompanied him. When they neared the Rappahannock River pontoon bridge Confederate batteries, which had been quiet for some time, came to life. The first shell careened overhead. Both boys stared awestruck as they watched it land among troops marching toward the river. Everyone halted and searched for cover or dropped to the ground. At that point Charles became indoctrinated to fear:

Then occurred one of those psychological inconsistencies of which life is so full. I was scared, Prest was scared; I knew he was scared, he knew I was scared; I knew he knew I was scared, and he knew I knew he was scared; yet though either of us if he had been alone would have lost no time in getting to a place of safety, rather than acknowledge to each

Returning to the regiment, Bardeen was scolded by his commanding officer for sightseeing when he should have been at his post. He was more concerned his comrades would chide him for coming back empty-handed because of a few shells. He fibbed to his companions that they were not allowed in the city by the provost guard as an excuse for not returning with the desired goods. Prest had told them the same story. "But we deceived no one," Charles wrote. "Cowardice is like seasickness — you may keep your voice cheerful but the color shows."

The next day brought the horrendous battle of Fredericksburg to a climax. Bardeen and his comrades watched from the east side of the river as the Irish Brigade made its famous forlorn assault up Marye's Heights. At 2 p.m. the 1st Massachusetts crossed the Rappahannock. After the morning's slaughter there were few who relished the idea. During the march Charles discovered fear's place on the battlefield. As it happened his regiment had the right of column, so the drummer boys led the way. As they advanced their principal musician fell out of line, saying that nature was calling. Charles admitted he would have done the same, but "scared as I was it would have taken more bravado to sneak out like that than to walk straight up to a cannon." He took particular interest in one of the captains he held in high esteem and thought was a brave fellow. He noticed the

officer was blanched and nervously dug his fingernails into his palms. Reflecting on this for a few moments, Charles concluded that "the good soldier is not the one who is not scared but the one who holds his post whether he is scared or not. That helped a good deal, and I saw that I was going to get through without disgrace, scared as I was. So when we started again and came under fire, though I was alert I was reasonably cool."[11]

C. Perry Byam of the 24th Iowa also was frightened more than once by shell fire. His experiences took place during the siege of Vicksburg, where both sides filled the air with exploding terror.

I vividly recall the incident of the first shell that screamed over me. I turned and flew in the same direction it had taken. I say "flew" understandingly, being certain at the time that I passed the shell, for upon suddenly slowing down, it again passed me. Envious persons, as I believed, meanly insinuated that it was another shell, but I stood stoutly by my own convictions.

On the crest of the hill which sheltered our camp was located a battery of heavy siege guns, which I spent much time enjoying the privilege of "pulling off" these heavy guns after they had been charged and sighted. This must have been a very annoying battery, for the sharpshooters were continually "plugging away" at it, and one day, without the seeming slightest regard for my presence, the enemy dropped a "long rakish" shell right into the works unreasonably close to me. In striking it tore up the earth, throwing it all over me, made one mighty bound and lay exposed in all its fearsome nakedness. It was a percussion shell, and of course should have exploded when it struck; but shells in any form or condition were always very discomposing to me, and not waiting for an explanation of any kind respecting this one, I tore off down the hill at a rate of speed that would have done credit to an antelope, covered with dirt if not with glory. I frequently thereafter viewed this fort from a distance, but was never stimulated with sufficient interest to approach or enter it again.[12]

This image of C. Perry Byam, Company D, 24th Iowa, was taken October 13, 1863, and sold during the late 1880s in cabinet-card format to raise money for distressed veterans in St. Paul, Minnesota.

National Archives

"The day after a battle is always a sad one in a regiment," reflected musician Delavan S. Miller of Company H, 2nd New York Heavy Artillery. "Men search for missing comrades and some are found cold in death who were full of life the day before. No jests are spoken. The terribleness of war has been forcibly impressed on all participants."

Drum Taps in Dixie

On the morning of May 18, 1864, the 2nd New York Heavy Artillery serving as infantry advanced with the Second Corps to the battlefield of Spotsylvania. The New Yorkers were stunned by the gruesome sight of hastily buried corpses protruding from the reddish-brown clay. They further were demoralized by shirkers and wounded men streaming from the front, which was getting closer with every step. Young Delavan Miller wrote: "It surely began to look like real warfare. Our men grew silent and their faces took on serious expressions. We knew that our time had come and that the regiment with its full ranks was to strengthen the thin line in front." The drummers became increasingly nervous and one of them asked Harry Marshall, the drum major, if it was about time they should fall out. There was "no use of us going up to be shot at when we had nothing to shoot back with." At the next halt Marshall approached Colonel Joseph N.G. Whistler and inquired if there was any purpose in the boys needlessly exposing themselves. "Needless exposure?" yelled Whistler. "What in the hell did you enlist for? Your place is with the regiment and I'll see that you are instructed as to your duties." He turned to the surgeon and continued, "Major, I want you to take charge of the musicians and in case of a fight see that the young rascals do their duty."

At the command Surgeon O. Sprague Paine pulled the boys aside and told them to follow in rear of the regiment. After the men passed Delavan and the others trailed behind until a halt was called under the brow of a slight hill, where they were held in reserve for two hours. The whole time the air was filled with metal fragments, showering leaves and tree limbs on those below. The drummers secured water for the men from a small spring nearby. As Delavan went down the line laden with canteens, he came to his father. Tears streamed down his cheeks. It was the only time during their service that Delavan recalled him being so touched.

At 10 o'clock the regiment was moved some two miles and positioned in a wood. Slowly the sounds of fighting fizzled out and the men relaxed through the night, thinking they had missed the fight. Nibbling hardtack and drinking coffee, some of them the next morning were upset they had not taken part in the fray. Unknown to these brave talkers the time to ante up was close at hand.

Around 2 o'clock a rider on a lathered horse galloped up and delivered orders to Colonel Whistler, who in turn formed the regiment in line. It advanced some distance, was placed behind a low stone wall and ordered to fix bayonets. "If you have 'been there' yourself you know all about it," Delavan wrote. "If not, let me tell you in all sincerity that the clicking of the cold steel will make an impression on one that will

A wicked looking saber bayonet wielded by an unidentified adolescent private. As a Union veteran observed, "His young blood had been curdled by reading harrowing descriptions of bayonet charges. He had seen pictures of long lines of gorgeously dressed soldiers advancing upon the enemy with their bayonets sticking out in front, and he imagined that when they reached the other fellows they just used their bayonets like pitchforks, tossing about their unhappy foes as he had pitched pumpkins from a wagon. He thought this was the way fighting was done. [But] only in very rare cases was the bayonet long enough to reach for purposes of blood-letting." Far more often it was employed as a candle holder or to impale fresh mutton, beef or ham and carry the meat conveniently to camp.

Author's Collection

send the chills down his spine every time he thinks of it in after years." For 10 minutes they awaited orders, once again subjected to watching a steady stream of wounded and demoralized men passing to the rear. The suspense finally was broken by word to advance toward a Union battery positioned in an open field. At the guns two companies were halted and stationed in support, but the drummers were ordered to continue with the remaining companies. They soon began taking casualties. Delavan recalled being mesmerized by a blood-smeared officer shot in the forehead, who rode through their lines on an uncontrollable horse until he tumbled off dead a few moments later.[13] This and other sights were too much for one drummer, as

Delavan afterward wrote: "The contortions of one of our drum corps boys who was badly demoralized by the flying bullets was so ludicrous that I should have laughed if I had been killed for it the next minute. Every time one of those 'z-z-ping' minies came near him he would leap in the air and then fall flat on the ground. Was I frightened? I will admit in strict confidence that I was never so scared in all my life. But I felt somewhat as one of our boys expressed it when he said, 'By the great horns spoons, they'll never know I'm afraid if I can help it.'"[14]

Elbridge Copp of the 3rd New Hampshire would have empathized with Miller's attempts at hiding fear, especially during his first major battle at Secession-

Neophyte warriors

Unlike comrades who chose to be photographed informally, the young recruit at left and those on the facing page opted for more warlike poses, displaying weapons and accouterments in their newly issued uniforms of varying patterns — frock coat, blouse and jacket.

Before they could fight they first had to learn to drill. The neophyte soldier, mused Ohioan Wilbur Hinman, "knew that a 'drill' was something to make holes with, and as he understood that he had been sent down South to make holes through people, he supposed drilling had something to do with it. He handled his musket very much as he would a hoe. But [his] ignorance was no indication that he would not make a good soldier. He was more than willing to learn — his heart was burning with a desire to know all about the mysterious things of which he had heard so much, that he might speedily attain to the fullest measure of usefulness in his humble sphere of martial life."

Grizzled sergeants, detailed to teach the lads how to handle their arms, "fully realized [their] important and responsible functions as instructor[s] of these innocent youths, having at the same time a supreme contempt for their ignorance."

Carte de visite image
by M.M. Griswold,
post photographer
at Camp Chase, Ohio.

Author's Collection

Jon Miller Collection

Author's Collection

Author's Collection

ville, South Carolina, on June 16, 1862. An assault on the Confederate stronghold, a hamlet on James Island, failed completely, and for members of the 3rd it was well remembered as their baptism of fire. Copp, the regiment's 16-year-old sergeant major at the time, later wrote:

There had been firing on the picket line all the morning, and now a detail of skirmishers was sent forward, under the command of the proper officers, and had disappeared in the woods. The regiment was then ordered to "stack arms" and wait for further orders. Now was our test of courage — waiting in line for the opening of the fight.

Upon breaking ranks most of the men threw themselves to the ground. Firing was heard from the skirmishers, with a ping, ping following the crack of the rifle, and at almost the same instant a shell exploded over our heads.

A feeling of horror, dread and fear came over me — I was faint, and only too glad to sit down and find a place against a tree. I questioned myself as to whether I was faint from fear, or from not having eaten anything so far that morning. I reached into my haversack, took a biscuit, attempted to eat it, but could not swallow the first mouthful. I took a drink of water from my canteen but to no purpose. Then the conviction came to me that surely I was a coward, and what was I to do? I shivered as with the ague. I got to my feet, but there was no escape. I must face the danger.

The firing was increasing upon the skirmish line; another shell from the rebel battery came screaming over our heads, and exploded beyond us, the rattle of musketry in the woods in our front increasing all the while.

Orders were given to "Fall in!" Every man was on his feet in an instant. A glance along the line satisfied me that I was not alone in my terror; many a face had a pale, livid expression of fear. A solid shot came bounding through the woods in front of us; several men were coming from the front, wounded. One man in the path of this shot or unexploded shell threw himself to the ground to escape, but was directly in the path of the shot, which struck the man, killing him instantly.

"Take arms!" was the order from Colonel [John H.] Jackson, repeated by acting Colonel [John] Bedell on the right and acting Major Plimpton [sic] upon the left, and by every company commander, each man taking his rifle from the stacks.

I was able to keep on my feet, pride coming to the rescue. I determined that if I was a coward, no one should know it.... As we approached the enemy I was getting command of myself, fear growing less and less....

The full attention of the rebels in the fort was now turned upon our regiment. The order to commence firing had been given, and a deadly fire from the guns of the Third

New Hampshire swept the rebel infantry from their parapet, and silenced their guns in our front, but their fire was soon renewed and with deadly effect. At the same time fire was opened upon us from a rebel battery from our rear, a battery concealed by the woods, and our men were falling upon my right and left, killed or wounded, sometimes throwing up their arms with a fearful shriek, pitching forward to the earth, and sometimes dropping to the ground without a groan.

Upon coming into the field we found the ground irregular, broken by clumps of bushes here and there, and the colonel finding the impossibility of making the charge, located the companies of the regiment in position for the best possible advantage. In executing the orders the adjutant and myself conveyed them to the different company commanders from the colonel. Returning to the colonel after delivering each order, and saluting with my sword, I reported with the same precision that I would have done upon carrying out the orders upon any ceremony. I do not think I should take any special credit to myself in this; I simply had no fear. The men falling killed and wounded around me, and the shrieks of the wounded and groans of the dying, made no impression. Is there a psychological explanation of this unnatural and practically inhuman mental condition?

This was my experience throughout the war; it was the fear of what was coming. The knowledge of an impending battle always sent that thrill of fear and horror, but once fairly in the fight and under fire, all fear was gone. The struggle to overcome the first tremors of fear was sometimes greater than at other times, the physical condition probably had its influence, and this varied with individual soldiers. I have seen men so overcome with fear when moving up to the front that they fell out of the ranks, and in spite of orders and threats of their officers, laid themselves upon the ground in perfect helplessness.[15]

On June 11, 1863, a hopeless situation confronted Willard H. Peck and his brother Corporal William E. Peck of Company A, 108th New York. When William enlisted in the summer of 1862, 15-year-old Willard followed him into the Army as a private. The boys were very close and wanted to be together during their service. A year later the two were still inseparable as the regiment stopped for a quick lunch near Stafford Court House, Virginia, on its march from Falmouth to Gettysburg. While filling their canteens at a spring the brothers were quietly captured by a band of Rebel guerrillas. They were marched to a secluded spot about a mile away, then were ordered to face about by their captors, who at that moment cocked their guns. There was little time to be afraid, for as soon as they

Private Luke Dickerman of Company A, 33rd Illinois, as he appeared in 1861. Three months prior to his October 1865 discharge he was promoted to sergeant.

History of the Thirty-third Regiment Illinois Veteran Volunteer Infantry

supporting them many performed their assignments well, even with fear gnawing inside them.

Luke Dickerman was the youngest member of Company A, 33rd Illinois. Because of this novelty and the fact he was well liked destined him to become company "pet." In the course of the 1863 Vicksburg campaign he shared many hardships with his comrades. Soldiers unabashedly stated that one of the most trying times in warfare is lying in reserve under enemy fire without being able to retaliate. During such an episode Luke hugged the ground as close as possible to evade Confederate shells sent his regiment's way as it approached Jackson, Mississippi. A cannonball burrowed itself a few feet from where he lay clutching his gun and exploded. The whole area was enveloped in flying dirt, shell fragments and dust, but Luke was unhurt to everyone's disbelief. For him it was just the beginning of a long series of memorable exploits of the campaign.

The day following the battle of Champion's Hill in May 1863, Company A was selected to lead the regiment, which took it through a relatively open field. Only a few tree stumps and brush offered any concealment. While advancing quietly near some slave shanties at the field's edge, Luke heard a commotion in one and slipped alongside, capturing three Rebels hiding there. Turning the trio over to Corporal John D. King, he continued moving forward with the others. The company reached a knee-high cornfield. Despite caution it was spotted and immediately the Confederates began sending shot and shell as an unfriendly welcome. The Illinoisans were ordered to lie down in the corn. Being a wet morning the field was a quagmire and everyone became thoroughly covered with mud. As Luke stated, "We were a sorry looking set." Cannon fire searched for the men as they longed for the few places of cover present. David Shaw and another comrade found a small stump and crawled behind it. Shortly, a solid shot split it in two, wounding Shaw

turned both were shot execution-style in the back of their heads. William died instantly and Willard also was thought to be killed by the guerrillas, who disappeared into the woods. Unbelievably, the younger boy was only knocked unconscious, in which condition he remained until the next day. Awakening, he wandered around dazed until two young girls found him and helped him to their home. Once there the girls' father used a pair of shears to shave his head and pulled from the wound five buckshot and an embedded lead ball. After regaining his strength somewhat he made it back to the Army, then was sent home to recuperate following time spent in various hospitals. He never returned to duty but eventually recovered fully, and in later years became a lawyer and pension agent.[16]

Unlike Willard and his brother, youngsters going into battle or an active campaign usually had plenty of time to consider their fate. Like most everyone they knew a job had to be done, and with comrades

Two mud-spattered friends took time to stand before a field photographer's canvas backdrop.

slightly and causing the other to lose his hat. While in camp witnesses to the scene debated if it was the shell or his nerves that forced the hat to fly in the air.

Luke wondered, too, even years later when thinking of his own wounding a few days after the advance through the cornfield. On May 22 the 33rd Illinois participated in a charge on Vicksburg's earthworks. Company A was the third one in line. It had to traverse a road on which the Confederates adjusted their guns in anticipation of an attack. While in the act of crossing Luke was injured: "Just then [William] Biggerstaff fell in front of me; I saw the blood come out of his left ear and knew there was no help for him. I jumped over him and in an instant I was struck in my

left leg, half way between knee and thigh, just enough to cut the flesh. It felt as though a hot iron had been drawn across my leg. The next instant another ball struck my gunstock, one splinter hitting my right leg and another my right thumb. Both scars show yet, and while I am very proud of them, I never show them for fear people would think I was striking for the rear, not knowing, as we do, that the rebs had a cross and rear fire on us."

In spite of his wounds Luke continued on. His comrades attested his youthful age was no detriment to soldiering, and he was as apt as anyone in the company to see a detail through no matter how dangerous or difficult.[17]

Knowing who would stand straight and stay by one's side during a battle was an important quality to consider when picking friends or tentmates. Bernard Matthews, who joined the 108th New York when 16, firmly believed that if not for comrade Timothy Keefe he would not have survived the war. On July 3, 1863, at Gettysburg, Bernard received a wound to his leg that was severe enough to warrant an amputation. He thankfully recalled that Keefe was the one who helped him off the field that day.[18]

After spending countless frigid nights trying to find warmth or being tested on a long, fatiguing march, most tentmates got to know each other quite well. Because they usually were together during a fight it was common for them, as close friends, to share common fates.

Ira Odell and Ovid Webster were 16 when they ran away from their homes and joined the 45th Pennsylvania. A number of their school chums in Tioga already had enlisted in Company H, and they were added to the muster roll. John C. Roosa, who became Ira's bunkmate, was one of the older boys among their acquaintances, having celebrated his 17th birthday 10 days before enlisting. As members of the 45th they participated in their share of combat, and all were considered stand-up soldiers. Ira recalled that at the battle of South Mountain, Maryland, they saw the first of their classmates fall, which helped them realize what war was about. Seven members of Company H were killed that day. As the war progressed the 45th and Company H's boys became hardened soldiers. After returning from veteran furlough in 1864 they fought in the grueling battle of Cold Harbor. It was a trying and costly day for the regiment, which lost approximately

Ten-year-old William Lawn lost part of his right arm to a wound suffered April 23, 1863, near Suffolk, Virginia. Attired in a Zouave-style jacket and armed with a militia sword, Willie posed at Kimberly Brothers National Gallery, Fort Monroe.

Author's Collection

181 of 315 engaged. Of that number 45 were killed or mortally wounded.[19]

A few days later Eugene Beauge of Company G wrote home: "At daybreak Friday morning, June 3d, our brigade under command of Colonel John I. Curtin, with Lieutenant-Colonel F.M. Hills in command of the Forty-Fifth, formed line of battle and advanced upon the enemy in their entrenchments in our front. The line was met by a murderous fire of musketry and grape and canister but never wavered, moving forward steadily under a deadly direct and cross fire until within less than a hundred yards of the enemy works, when the command 'halt' was passed along the line, and there, keeping close to the ground for protection, what was left of the Forty-Fifth held their part of the advance line under fire all day."[20]

Companies H and G fought in a ravine running partially at right angles with the Confederate line. Their approach allowed their opponents to fire on them with a high rate of execution. All officers and non-commissioned officers but one were either killed or wounded in the attack. Lieutenant George Scudder, Company F, was temporarily in command of Company H during the battle. Not being well acquainted with the boys, recalled John Roosa, the lieutenant told them not to fire unless ordered. John saucily rebuked him even though Scudder was an officer. "I said that I didn't care, and that I came out for that purpose and when a man steps out to shoot us and I have a good shot, I will take it, orders or no orders."

The company advanced and the argument ceased. At the Confederates' third volley Lieutenant Scudder fell mortally wounded at Roosa's side. Soon Levi Robb was wounded by a Rebel that John reciprocated in shooting, giving him "his discharge." Within five minutes of Scudder's death Roosa himself received a shot in the right breast, the ball traveling through a lung and exiting slightly below his shoulder blade. Almost simultaneously his bunkmate, Ira Odell, was shot through his left wrist, the ball shattering the bones. Both boys had stood fast together during one of the bloodiest battles of the war. Carried to the rear they began the dismal experience of hospitalization.

Ira was laid on one of the many operating tables in use that day, and there had his arm amputated four inches below the elbow by Surgeon J.T. Lanning. He eventually recuperated and after a few months was sent home. John also endured a long hospital stay, and despite his wound gained strength enough to be accepted with other invalids in the Veteran Reserve Corps. Both had no idea when they began soldiering their Army careers ultimately would be finished the same day.[21]

125

Otis Smith, whose story of Cold Harbor was preserved in the regimental history, was another runaway in the 45th Pennsylvania. He recollected:

On the 3d of June, 1864, Joseph Walton, Company B, had served within a few days of three years. The poor fellow came to me as we were forming and said: "I do not feel like going into this engagement." Knowing that he was a brave fellow and had lost a brother [Amos] at South Mountain, the 14th of September, 1862, I advised him not to go in. He replied that it would reflect on him if he did not. The order was given to advance over the open field. We charged up to the line to within 80 yards, our company covering an angle of a battery of about six guns. It was not long before we silenced the battery with a loss to our company of 14 wounded and two killed. Poor Joe fell, as nearly as I remember, about ten o'clock that day and I picked up the ball that killed him. I handed it to Captain Diebler and said, "Do you want this?" He looked serious and replied, "No."

I was firing at a man who exposed himself on the rebel works from behind a big oak tree. We exchanged three or four shots at each other and they were coming pretty close, one through my sleeve, one through my forage cap. I spoke to Lawrence M. Small. He was the only man in the company who had his knapsack. "Lawrence, throw your knapsack here quick," I said. I made a breastwork of it and it was fortunate that I did for the ball went into the knapsack. I said to Lawrence: "Load both guns and I'll fire them." The rebel did not know that I had doubled up on him and when he exposed himself to look for the result of his last shot, I let go and got him.[22]

Abraham Palmer wrote of his 1864 experiences in Petersburg's trenches, where he and fellow 48th New York musician George W. Richman were losers during a similar shooting match while on picket. "At that time our pickets were posted in lines of little rifle-pits, hastily dug among the trees in the woods in front of our works. But two men at a time were placed in these little holes, and so hot was the fire that the reliefs were only made at night. Whoever ventured to stand up a moment in sight of the enemy, either in the rifle-pits or upon the fortifications, was sure to be picked off by sharpshooters. Sometimes the boys would rig up a dummy upon a pole and lift it to the top of the parapet; it was sure to be riddled with bullets in a moment. The two personal friends with whom [I] shared a shelter tent in those days [John H. Graham and Richman] were thus killed by sharpshooters — Graham on June the 30th, while trying to run to the rifle-pits with some coffee for the men; Richman the very next morning

while we were together and alone in a rifle-pit on picket. That was a terrible day, from the early morning till it grew dark at night, which [I] spent by the side of [my] dead friend...."[23]

Soldiers detailed to serve with other commands did not have the comfort or help of comrades to sustain them through an ordeal. Hugh Craig was 16 when he ran away from home in Lockport, New York. He had tried to join a regiment forming there, but after rejection traveled to Rochester and was accepted in Company F, 108th New York. Hugh was detailed from his company more than once — at one time he was attached to Professor T.S.C. Lowe's balloon corps — and after Gettysburg was sent as a guard with a contingent of prisoners to Elmira, New York. During the Petersburg siege on August 8, 1864, a reconnaissance party was organized by selecting a few men from several regiments. Hugh was one taken from the 108th. The detail was instructed to ascertain enemy strength in front of a section of the Ninth Corps by sneaking under cover of darkness to the Confederate works. During the advance the Rebels were alerted and sent a shower of lead in the Federals' direction. One of the balls struck Hugh's gunstock and passed through his right hand. Damage also was inflicted from wood splinters that impaled his wrist. Returning to the Union lines he was shuffled from hospital to hospital for the next few months. The whole time he was mixed in with strangers, being the only casualty from the 108th that day, and therefore was with men of other regiments involved.

At a Beverly, New Jersey, hospital doctors noted the gangrenous condition of his wound and told Hugh they would have to amputate his arm. He was not that easily persuaded and ran off, making his way to Rochester, where he checked into another hospital. After five months his wounds healed sufficiently for him to conclude to return to the New Jersey hospital before he was branded a deserter. Before leaving, he asked for a note to take along explaining his case.

U.S.A. General Hospital
Rochester, N.Y. Feb. 17, 1865

The bearer Hugh Craig, Pvt. "B" 108th N.Y.V. was admitted to this hospital Aug. 29, 1864 with gangrenous wound of right hand and stated that he had left U.S.A. General Hospital at Beverly N.J. without leave as surgeons were intending to amputate his arm. He has been unable to return there until now, and he now is ordered to return there and will do so. His character has been good while in this Hospital and I trust he may be dealt with as leniently as possible.

Azel Backus
A.A. Surg. U.S.A. In charge.

Hugh remained in the hospital for six more weeks. When he heard of Confederate capitulation at Appomattox in April he again left without orders to join his regiment in the field, though still unfit for duty. But at least he was back among comrades and friends. During the Grand Review in Washington he was forced to sit and watch as a spectator because he could not muster enough strength to carry a gun.[24]

Unlike Hugh Craig, who was wounded away from his command, Sergeant Samuel P. Snider of the 65th Ohio was the subject of talk around his regiment's campfires after he received a wound near Murfreesboro, Tennessee, the night of December 29, 1862. The Union Army of the Cumberland and Confederate Army of Tennessee were jockeying for position prior to the battle of Stones River, which started on the 31st and culminated January 2, 1863. On the 29th rumors kept Union commanders guessing what moves to make. One rumor that surfaced late in the afternoon said the enemy was retreating from Murfreesboro. This news caused commanding General William S. Rosecrans to order an advance of one of General Thomas L. Crittenden's divisions across the river toward the Rebels. Crittenden selected General Thomas J. Wood's division. Colonel Charles Harker of the 65th Ohio immediately called forth skirmishers and ordered his brigade to follow. As the men waded through Stones River's thigh-deep water and gained the opposite shore, they disappeared into an almost impenetrable, bramble-infested thicket. Realizing the extreme danger to his troops going forward over unknown ground toward enemy positions at dusk, General Wood began protesting. Crittenden, however, refused to suspend the peremptory order, which he had received from Rosecrans.

While commanders continued arguing the situation, their troops broke through the undergrowth and emerged in a large cornfield. After moving ahead some distance a terrific volley suddenly crashed from the far end of the field, the bullets passing overhead. At about that time new orders were received from the rear. Rosecrans had countermanded his previous directive and now wished a withdrawal across the river. As the order was passed from command to command, the men turned and double-quicked back over the field, through the tangle of briers and brambles, in utter darkness, and plunged into the river without hesitation. During the retreat Confederate lead whistled past, hastening their departure. Although not well versed in warfare that early in the conflict, most in the 65th Ohio agreed the advance was a mistake, and realized if they had continued they surely would have sustained many casualties. As it was few in Harker's brigade were struck. Samuel Snider was the only casualty in his regiment. Enlisting at 16, he had volunteered as a mounted orderly that night and was wounded while carrying dispatches between the skirmish line and regimental staff. Sam was considered a universal favorite in the 65th. Word quickly spread of his wounding and everyone wanted to know what happened to their boy in Company D. He narrowly escaped death when a bullet clipped his nose. Patched up by doctors and with Mother Nature lending a hand, Sam was back on duty in short time, despite his visage not being quite as appealing as before.[25]

John F.W. Mains likewise had his face disfigured during the war. In August 1861 the diminutive 13 year old quit school and mustered into Company I, 11th Indiana Infantry, as drummer. The regiment saw its fair share of early fighting in the West at Forts Henry and Donelson, Shiloh and the siege of Corinth, before being ordered to Helena, Arkansas, on July 24, 1862. While at Helena the 11th was sent to the countryside west of town to investigate suspicious enemy movements and help keep the area under Federal control. During an expedition toward Little Rock in August, a small party including Mains became entangled with Confederates near Clarendon on the 13th. In the short encounter he absorbed a blast of buckshot in his face, neck and shoulders. Although the wounds bled profusely no bones were struck. After the confrontation the Hoosiers returned to Helena, where musician William Armstrong dressed John's cheeks and neck, then accompanied him to Cairo, Illinois. He recuperated in a Northern hospital and returned to the 11th Indiana in November. This absence was the only time John was away from the regiment during his service, which was quite outstanding considering his age.[26]

No part of the human anatomy was immune to bullets or shell fragments. Otho Gash, who joined the

108th New York at age 15, was wounded in the hand so severely at Chancellorsville that his thumb was amputated. He served the remainder of the war in the Veteran Reserve Corps.[27] Ohioan Charles F. Kimmel, 16 when he enlisted in Birge's Western Sharpshooters, was wounded three different times within six weeks during 1864's Atlanta campaign.[28]

John D. Nelson was born March 3, 1847, in Monroe County, New York. At 15 he quit school and joined Company F, 108th New York, then recruiting in the county. After the battle of Antietam he was assigned to work at one of the field hospitals. "I was detailed as a nurse to care for the wounded, which was by no means a desirable job for one so young and inexperienced," he explained. "The duty was, nevertheless, performed to the best of my ability, and seemed perfectly satisfactory to the wounded rebels, about forty in number, whom it became my duty to administer to." Nelson himself was slightly wounded in the leg at Gettysburg by a ball from an exploding spherical shell. He was hit again in the leg during the battle of the Wilderness. This second wound was more severe and he was hospitalized until almost the end of the war.[29]

Sergeant Sam Snider's facial wound received near Murfreesboro was inconsequential compared to the life-threatening one he suffered in the battle of Chickamauga. Because of outstanding conduct at Stones River Sam was recommended for promotion to second lieutenant, but due to the understrength condition of the regiment a commission was never issued. Early in September 1863 he went before an examining board and was appointed captain in the 2nd Regiment United States Colored Troops. While awaiting orders to report and his commission to arrive, Sam led Company D at Chickamauga although just 17 years of age.

A native of Highland County, Ohio, John F.W. Mains, 11th Indiana, suffered for three decades from the effects of his August 1862 wounds. He died of pneumonia in September 1892 at the age of 44. Carte de visite image by Apple & Thorn National Photograph Gallery, Indianapolis.

Author's Collection

Captain Thomas Powell reported that young Snider "bravely led his men, whom he encouraged by precept and example, to stand by the flag." Lieutenant Brewer Smith of the 65th Ohio wrote that "Late in the day on Sunday the 20th of September 1863, he [Snider] was severely wounded while taking a leading part in repelling one of the last assaults of the enemy on our line." Sam's wound was nearly fatal, as General John Beatty recalled: "I saw him lying on the field in the afternoon of the second day of that battle bleeding and helpless, and supposed at that time he could not live. I know from my own observation, as well as from testimony from his comrades, that he behaved most gallantly in that engagement."

Sam fell into Confederate hands along with others who were unable to retire. After 11 days he was paroled and sent through the lines. "October 4 1863 I

128

was hauled in an ambulance from the battlefield," he wrote, "where I had lain a supposedly mortally wounded prisoner, since [the] previous Sept. 20th. The enemy paroled all prisoners who were so badly wounded that they would not bear transportation to Southern prisons. It was my fortune, good or ill, to be in that class." In such a state the teenaged sergeant reached the hands of Union doctors who set about

Corporal Albert C. Matthias
Company K, 65th Ohio

saving his life. The ball, as described by Assistant Surgeon Phillip Musgrave, "enter[ed] the deltoid muscle of the left arm causing atrophy, fracturing the humerus, passing through the left lung, [and] was extracted near the sixth dorsal vertebrae." Surprisingly, eight months later Snider was able to assume his position as captain, but struggled with his health through the summer of 1864. He resigned due to the arm wound and went home in October, having just passed his 19th birthday.[30]

Albert C. Matthias, a member of the 65th Ohio's Company K, also was noted for bravery and recommended for promotion. Like Snider he, too, was wounded, and owing to its debilitating effects was unable to take advantage of a commission.

Albert was born May 19, 1845, in Stark County,

Ohio. In November 1861 he enlisted at age 16.[31] On May 10, 1864, near Rocky Face Ridge, Georgia, the 64th Ohio, brigaded with the 65th, was ordered to assault a hill swarming with Confederate soldiers. The attack lasted less than 30 minutes when the Buckeyes fell back. It was at this time Matthias drew the attention of his commanding officers. Brigade historian Wilbur Hinman detailed his actions that day:

Sergeant Samuel P. Snider
Company D, 65th Ohio

When the Sixty-fifth was ordered to cover the withdrawal of the Sixty-fourth, it was halted some three hundred yards from the rebel works, and so disposed as to be in position to check the enemy, should he attempt a counter-assault. Officers and men were directed to shield themselves as well as possible behind the rocks and trees. Corporal Albert C. Matthias, of Company K, who was scarcely more than a boy, observed a squad of Union soldiers, with a regimental flag, a considerable distance in front. Matthias crept forward and joined the squad, which belonged to the One Hundred and Twenty-fifth Ohio, Lieutenant Colonel [David H.] Moore being in command. The men remained there until dark, sheltered by rocks, keeping up a brisk fire upon the enemy. Rebel bullets flew thickly about, and several of the party were wounded. Corporal L.S. Calvin, of the One Hundred and Twenty-fifth, while in the act of discharging his piece, was struck by a ball which entered his head near the left temple and passed out through the right lower jaw. He fell into the arms of Corporal Matthias, who was at his side. His musket was empty, showing that he and the rebel had fired at the same instant. Under cover of darkness the men withdrew. Calvin, who had lain unconscious, was left for dead. The next morning he was found alive and sent to a hospital. Strange to relate, he recovered and is now living in California.

About the same time that Calvin was struck, Corporal Matthias had an exceedingly "close call," a bullet clipping a lock of hair from his temple, as he peeped over a rock looking for somebody to shoot at. The next day Lieutenant Colonel [Horatio N.] Whitbeck, of the Sixty-fifth, warmly commended Corporal Matthias for "gallant conduct in the face of the enemy." Colonel Whitbeck directed that [a letter he received from Lieutenant Colonel Moore] be read to the company, and that Matthias be promoted to sergeant as soon as there was a vacancy. Colonel [sic] Harker learned of the incident and informed the corporal that he should recommend him to the governor of Ohio for a commission. Five days later Matthias was severely wounded at Resaca. He was entirely disabled for further duty, and early in the following year was discharged.[32]

Albert kept a copy of Moore's letter for the rest of his life as a prized memento of the war. It read:

> Camp of the 125 O.V.I.
> May 11th 1864
>
> Colonel
> I take pleasure in recommending Corporal A.C. Matthias of Co. K of your Regt. for gallant conduct on the night of the 10th inst. He joined my command of some 20 men within 20 paces of the enemys works[.] after firing his piece till it became heated He drew his Revolver and fired some 40 Rounds and only desisted when Strictly ordered.
>
> Yours truly D.H. Moore
> Lt. col. 125th O.V.I. [33]

"While nobly doing his duty" a minie ball passed through Albert's elbow on May 14.[34] Six days later his cousin, Captain John C. Matthias of the 65th, informed Albert's parents of his misfortune. "I hast to convey the sad entelligence [sic] that your son ... was severely wounded in the late battle of Resaca fought on the 14th and 15th of May. Albert was wounded about 2 p.m. threw his elbow[.] from the reports I am afraid his arm was broken[.] I didn't get to see him after he was wounded but I am afraid he will lose his arm as it apeared to be shattered."[35] Feebly using his left hand, Albert wrote home on July 9, updating his condition. "Still in bed. my arm is doing well. the gash was 5 inches long and it is all heald up but one little hole where the matter runs out. there is a pretty strong grissel in my arm. I do not think the doctors will let me leave here till my arm is well so I can not come home till some time in August any how."[36]

Getting back to Stark County that month was wishful thinking for he remained in a host of hospitals until discharged in February 1865. His arm was permanently paralyzed from the wound. Later in life the limb was finally removed and kept in a bottle until his death, when it was buried alongside him.[37]

As diverse as the location of a wound was the mental attitude displayed by soldiers who were injured. Some wailed and carried on, swearing and complaining violently even if the wound was slight. Others hurt seriously often endured it calmly. Delavan Miller wrote of such a display occurring after the battle of Cold Harbor. "I recall how little Will Whitney, one of the 'ponies' of our company as the boys were called, lay there on the ground shot clear through the body, patiently waiting his turn [at a field hospital], while a big fellow with a wounded hand was dancing around and making a terrible fuss until Whitney, thoroughly disgusted, spoke out. 'Shut up, there, old man, you're not the only one that got scratched in this fight.' "

"Scratched" was putting it mildly. Whitney, who enlisted at 15, was hit in the groin by a minie ball that traveled through his pelvic bone before exiting. An attending physician in a letter trying to have William's 30-day furlough extended wrote on August 15, 1864, that particles of bone were still surfacing from the oozing wound. But the boy continued to improve and finally was discharged September 29, 1865.

Miller also wrote about a second young Cold Harbor victim. "I assisted to the rear another of the lads of Co. H, Henry C. Potter, a former schoolmate at Carthage, and as bright and promising a young man as any who went to war. His left arm was badly shattered, necessitating an amputation. There was not a murmur, not a regret. He was glad it was not his right one, for with that saved he could be of some help to his father in the store." Unfortunately, Potter succumbed to the injury on August 2, 1864.[38]

In an addendum to his Chancellorsville battle report, Captain Frank Gibbs of Battery L, 1st Ohio Light Artillery, drew attention to the *sangfroid* of a teenaged member of his command. "At 4 o'clock p.m. [May 3, 1863], during one of the artillery duels, a shell struck the limber of Detachment B, broke the iron axle, exploded, killing Lieut. [Frederick] Dorries, Corpl. [Frederick] Koehler, and taking the right leg off of private Cassius Edmonds, a driver, who, when his team was ordered to the rear, volunteered to help work the gun. He is a little fellow, about sixteen years of age, and when carried from the field whistled as if nothing had occurred; he did not shed a tear."[39]

Diarist Osborn Oldroyd of the 20th Ohio, while in the Vicksburg trenches, wrote on June 17, 1863, of an-

Private Michael Rentz of Company G, 39th Ohio, sat for this portrait within six months of his July 1861 enlistment. During the battle of Atlanta three years later he was badly wounded, and succumbed to his injuries July 29, 1864, in a Marietta, Georgia, field hospital. He lies buried in Marietta National Cemetery, Section J, Grave 315.

Courtesy of Peg McFarland

other fearless youngster. "A ball struck a little drummer boy a while ago, and he limped off whimpering, 'I wouldn't give a darn, but my other leg has been shot already.' Some of the boys went to his assistance, and then they had to hurry towards the hospital, for the rebels got range of them and began firing quite briskly." [40]

Some soldiers were more afraid of hospitals than anything else. In spite of illness or minor wounds, they cared for themselves and stayed in camp. Ebenezer Foster was 15 when he enlisted in July 1862 as a musician in the 10th Vermont. His stature was unusually small, slight and fair, much like a little girl. These traits were so marked his comrades called him "Little Nellie," the daughter of the regiment. Ebenezer possessed a sunny disposition, always smiling and chumming around. In the spring of 1863 he fell sick but was not totally incapacitated. The surgeon visited him and after noting his slight build and youthfulness, declared he should be sent to the hospital to recuperate. As soon as the doctor was gone the men of his com-

pany, not wanting to lose him, smothered Ebenezer with all sorts of horrifying stories of hospital life, convincing him to stay. Once he consented they took turns administering to his needs until he recovered. After the short illness he served to the end of the conflict and never left the company, except during veteran furlough. [41]

Others looked at being sick or wounded in a nonchalant, cavalier way. Byron Fairbanks was 14 when he enlisted in Company D, 12th Wisconsin, on October 4, 1861, as a musket-toting private. In the rear of his 1864 diary he summarized his service up to June of that year, when he commenced keeping daily entries:

This is the 3rd year of my service in & for the Government of the United States of America. I enlisted again on the 4th of Jan 1864 in the Veteran Volunteers as musician of Company D 12th Wis – this was wrote on 16th of Jan 1864 – We think now that the war will be ended in about 8 months – I am 16 years old and will be 17 years old the 23d of this month – Our regt helped to take Vicksburg Miss – When I enlisted in this regt I was 14 years old – carried the musket one year and then was appointed fifer of company D the company I belong to. Since then I have learned to play the high key on fife. We have marched and traveled about 5000 miles in all. We have seen seven different states since we started out – over 560 of our regiment has enlisted in the veterans volunteers – We stayed at Natchez Miss. about a month. I was 17 years old the 23d of Jan. 1864. We left Natchez on the 23d of Jan and came up to Vicksburg and marched out to Hebron 9 miles from Vicks and camped – We have been home in the month of April and May on Furlough, we had a very good time. We stayed 50 days in Wisconsin. Came back to Cairo and then went to Sherman's Army at Ackworth [Georgia], got there on the 10th of June 1864. We moved with the Army under Sherman on the 10th June and up with enemy same day. Up to the 20th of June

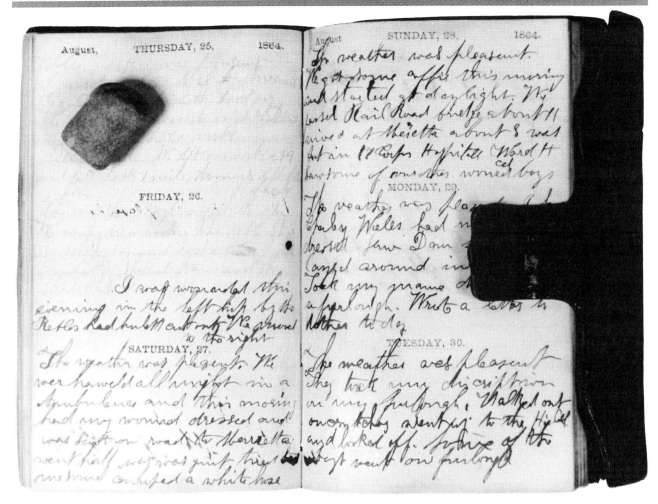

have advanced 5 miles. Our regiment has lost 27 men killed[,] 25 on the 15th of June. Have marched nearly 500 miles since we came back from furlough.

Despite the regiment's heavy losses sustained in June at and near Kennesaw Mountain, Byron seemed to enjoy himself. On June 11 he bragged, "I had 12 shots at the rebs on picket line," and again on the 13th he wrote, "I was up in picket line and shot at rebs." His June 15 entry stated, "drove rebs from picket line, cannon opened on them & scattered them then our whole line of skirmishers advanced, the rebs opened cannon, 25 killed and wounded men of our regiment."

The months of July and August also were costly for the 12th Wisconsin. Byron wrote of the hotly contested battle of Bald Hill outside Atlanta on July 21, "There was a charge made of the 4th Division and our 1st Brigade on rebs, take their works, hard fight. Our regiment lost 155 killed wounded and missing, our company lost 15 killed and 15 wounded." But he retained a boy's good spirit and curiosity. On August 17

Twelfth Wisconsin private Byron Fairbanks' 1864 pocket diary, opened to the August 26 entry mentioning his leg wound. At upper left is the Enfield bullet removed from the limb prior to his admission to the Seventeenth Corps hospital in Marietta.

Author's Collection

he noted, "climbed a tree and looked at Atlanta, the rebs opened on us and we replied." As much as Byron enjoyed being at the front shooting at Confederates it seemed only a matter of time before his name was added to the long list of casualties. Sure enough, before the month ended he was wounded.

August 26 began like any other day during Atlanta's siege. Using a pencil, Byron wrote, "The weather is pleasant today. We occupy new works. The Rebel skirmishers advanced[,] had a little fight, our battery shelled them and they skedadled." With that he concluded his daily entry. Unknown to him when he laid aside his pencil, his work for the day was not finished. Whether he was sent on outpost duty or remained in the breastworks cannot be determined, but late that night he resumed writing, this time with a pen. "I was wounded this evening in the left hip by the Rebels. Had bullet cut out, we moved to the right." His matter-of-fact notation was no more detailed than other events he had witnessed and written about. He worded it almost as if he expected it to happen. Byron was placed in an ambulance and sent with other casualties of the day to Marietta.

Two days later he was admitted to the Seventeenth Corps hospital, where in Ward H he saw other wounded boys of the regiment he knew. The next day he was pleased when issued a pass permitting him to leave the hospital and go to town, as he was feeling pretty good. Soon, however, he became sore and took to his bed. On September 3 he wrote, "my wound bled a little tonight, had the artery stopped up and my wound dressed." By the 6th he was quite sick and his diary entries were shortened to being "in the hospital" until month's end. Occasionally he mentioned how bad his leg was looking, and that he was concerned with the outcome. Finally, on October 2 he walked a little and started to feel better. On the 23rd he was issued a 30-day furlough and started north, although the wound was still seeping.

November 3, 1864 was a special day for Private Fairbanks. After lying in hospitals for more than two months wondering if he would ever see his family again, he reached home. "Mother was very glad to see me as was me to see her, she had gave me up." The remainder of the war was spent in Wisconsin recuperating from the wound he at first thought was so slight that he casually wrote of it the day it happened. In 1865 Byron returned to his command in time to be mustered out with his comrades July 16, a battle-hardened veteran at 18.[42]

Fairbanks not only kept a diary, he faithfully sent letters home to his family, sometimes twice a week. He likewise received many from his mother and father. In his diary he noted the mail arriving whether he received anything or not, eagerly awaiting each shipment in hopes of a parcel. Letters were an important morale booster for soldiers during the war. Like Byron, almost all soldiers sent and received their share.

The government realized its importance early and allowed Army correspondence to be sent home with postage due. A soldier's lack of money never was a factor, but writing paper often was in short supply.

Charles Bardeen was a boy who kept the mail clerks busy, writing continuously to his parents while away. Afterward, when publishing his wartime diary, he included two of only three letters preserved through the years. One written during the 1863 Mine Run campaign provides good insight into the thoughts of a youngster during active operations.

Wilderness, Nov. 29th 1863

Dear Folks

I don't know where we are, what we are doing, where we are going, what we are going to have to eat or anything else.

Thanksgiving reveille was beaten at 8 a.m. and at daylight we started going S.E. until we reached Jacob's Ford on the Rapidan between Raccoon and Germania Ford. Here we stopped and sent skirmishers out ahead. We worked along slowly until about dark when we halted for two hours; then moved back a little way and stopped for the night about 8 p.m. Thus passed Thanksgiving. The next morning we started early and went off two or three miles when we ran on the enemy's pickets. Our Reg't. was ahead and Co. D acting as skirmishers. They went out and returned reporting the enemy in force. So our Reg't. was formed and the fight commenced. About 2:00 the first heavy firing began, and the first man brought in was Billy Evans of Co. C. The firing soon became very heavy; indeed the musket firing (no artillery of consequence was used) almost equalled Chancellorsville. But the Rebels could not move our line and dark found us as we commenced. The next morning we moved down to the left. It rained hard, and the mud was awful. But we were not engaged again and have not been since, though we are at the rear and the Regiment is ahead reconnoitering. We have no rations and have got to live on half rations, Gen. French says, till this move is over as our communications is destroyed. The [wagon] trains were sent back across the river. Some say we are going to Dobbs Court House, some to Fredericksburg but we can't believe anything. If I get a chance to send this I will but I think not.

Your affectionate son
Charles W. Bardeen
Co. D First Mass. Inf.

No opportunity presented itself, so Charles added on December 4:

We crossed the river yesterday and are at our old camp. Monday morning preparations was made for a grand charge

Phillip "Jimmy" Doyle, 14, of Mount Vernon, Ohio, enlisted October 3, 1861, in Company F, 1st Battalion, 18th U.S. Infantry. At Chickamauga the Irish-born musician was among the 1st Battalion's 145 casualties. Though slightly wounded he continued serving with the Regulars until mustered out September 2, 1864. Six months earlier his younger brother John M. Doyle enlisted as a musician in the 61st Ohio before transfer to the 82nd Ohio.

Author's Collection

of the whole line upon the rebel breastworks. Our Regiment all had white faces. Never saw them so dreading anything before. It was a long distance to charge and the muzzles of the Rebs guns loaded with chainshot & cannister struck terror into the hearts of all. All the men put their money into the hands of the Chaplain or those not forced to go into the fight. I staid with the Reg't until the order was given to "Fix Bayonets" and was starting for the rear, in a secluded spot far from shot and shell when the order was countermanded. If ever I saw happy faces it was then.

We staid over the river and recrossed Wednesday. We have been gone from camp 8 days and only took 3 days rations and had one days issued, and the men were almost starved. The Army was never so short before. For four days I lived entirely on fresh meat (a cow some of us killed) without salt, just boiled over the fire. I never knew hunger before. I guess our campaigning is over for the winter. If that charge had been made it would have taken all winter to reorganize the army. [43]

Charles Goddard of the 1st Minnesota also was elated when the attack was canceled. On November 30 Charley and his companions serving in General G.K. Warren's Second Corps were to lead the charge. As they scanned the horizon a hastily-built line of earthworks bristling with abatis was revealed, stretching as far as each soldier could see. Confederate cannon muzzles poked through epaulments, stirring thoughts that serious losses would be incurred. Some Union soldiers were so moved by a sense of foreboding they pinned notes to their blouses providing names and regiments, with the additional words "killed in action, November 30, 1863." The assault order had been issued by Army of the Potomac commander General George G. Meade, but after General Warren viewed the fortifications he called off the attack on his own

initiative. "The works cannot be taken," he told an infuriated Meade. "I would sooner sacrifice my commission than my men." [44]

In a December 4 letter, Charley told his mother he had seen "some fighting, been in some hot places, but never in my life did I think I was gone up the 'spout' until the order came to charge those works and I was shure as I set here writing to you that if I went up in that charge Chas. E. Goddard would be no more.... Such awful suspense I never experienced before in my life, I thought it was the longest day of my life." [45]

Everyone had opinions about their commanders, war strategy, and battles and campaigns they participated in or heard about. When a futile attack was made soldiers were quick to point fingers. If they wanted to belittle or praise a commanding officer, their feelings often were expressed in letters home. Charley Goddard inserted all sorts of opinions in his correspondence. Shortly after the disastrous battle of First Bull Run a sense of disloyalty to 1st Minnesota Colonel Willis A. Gorman manifested itself with his troops. Charley wrote, "There is men in the Reg. that hate him [enough] to shoot him as quick as look at him — he is an old tyrant.... if there is any little thing goes rong he will throw down his cap and curse and sware so and when our Reg was coming down the river he got as drunk as a fool and hardly could stand up." [46]

If he did not like his colonel, Goddard was always faithful to General George B. McClellan. Shortly after McClellan was dismissed from command of the Army of the Potomac, Charley fumed, "I hardly feel any interest in this war since General McClellan [was] removed — it was a grand mistake and I think they will rue the day they took him from the command.... They will keep general Burnside in a little while and then the Editors of the papers through the country will raise the cry, _he is doing nothing_ and the people will take it up after them until the President thinks he had better put another one in and let old stone wall Jackson get after him and chase him back to Washington. Then they will begin to think there is no man in the world like little McClellan after all." [47]

It was "Little Mac" who came upon the regiment after the Confederates were repulsed at Fair Oaks in May 1862, and received "six cheers and two tigers." While riding through Companies E and B, McClellan responded by looking down at the men still in line. Raising his hat he asked, "Well, lads, are you prepared for everything that comes? I trust this point to you.... All goes well everywhere." Charley prophesized, "How very plain to be seen General McClellan is a General that econimizes life — Mother you mark my word General Mc will be recorded in history [as] one of the greatest Generals that ever lived not excepting Napolion Bonipart." [48] In the same letter written after Charley viewed the battlefield, he added, "Never saw such sights in my life. Rickets grape & canister done good execution. The most of them seemed to be shot in the head a very few in the breast." [49]

The war was filled with so many memorable events that it stands to reason hundreds of youngsters wrote about them during the conflict. They were plied for news by family members and friends. Sometimes words simply failed. After Chickamauga, Albert Matthias was asked to recount the battle by his younger brother at home. Albert replied: "Well Frank ... that is impossible for me to do[.] I might tell you some things

that happened but that is all[.] a man that is to his post all the time using his musket has not much time to look around and take notes. A battle is the hard[e]st thing in the world to discribe[.] it cannot be did with pen and ink." [50]

Prosecuting the war could not be done by "economizing life," and boy soldiers continued to be found on growing casualty lists. Andrew Routt was among those who perished. At 16 he enlisted in the 63rd Ohio, and nine months later received a mortal wound near Battery Robinett during the October 1862 battle

Stephen Altic Collection

Late-war recruit David R. Seville, 15, was a drummer in Company F, 5th Maryland Infantry. At Petersburg on July 6, 1864, he was struck in the right shoulder by a Rebel bullet. The photograph was taken while he recuperated at Lovell General Hospital in Portsmouth Grove, Rhode Island.

of Corinth. He lingered long enough to be removed to a field hospital, but died within hours. While recording his death for the Army, Captain Charles Brown of the 63rd certified "the deceased left no effects, except the clothing in which he was buried." [51]

Musician Thomas Dalton was 15 when he enlisted in the 12th New Hampshire and participated in several hard-fought engagements. At the siege of Petersburg June 30, 1864, he was sitting behind a second line of earthworks playing cards with comrades when fragments from an exploding shell shattered his thigh. Asked if he wished to send any word to his mother, he murmured, "Tell her I am dead," and immediately expired. Gilman Smith, born in April 1846 and also a member of the 12th New Hampshire, received a fatal wound at the battle of Chancellorsville. He was injured by a ball that lodged in his chest after entering his neck. He lived for two days in great agony, and died at Falmouth while being carried to Potomac Creek Hospital. [52]

Charles H. Howard survived the war, only to die shortly after returning home. He gave his age as 17 when enlisting in the 13th Vermont, but the six-footer was actually only 15. Howard was noted for keeping himself and his equipment meticulously clean. Coupled with the fact he was a strikingly good-looking young man, other boys in the company called him Lieutenant Howard, even though he never rose higher in rank than private. At Gettysburg he received a wound which led to complications and his discharge. On the day after John Wilkes Booth shot President Lincoln, the handsome teenager was arrested and detained for more than 24 hours as government officials mistook him for the alleged assassin. In 1866 Charles died at his New York home. It was believed at the time his Gettysburg wound killed him. [53] He was a casualty of the war as surely as those shot dead on the battlefield.

CHAPTER 8

'The world's commiseration their only reward'

Sixteen-year-old William M. Child was listed as missing in action after the May 25, 1864, battle of New Hope Church, Georgia. Only three months earlier he had enlisted in the 73rd Ohio as a replacement in Company A. Being a new face in the regiment was likely a factor in his body not being recognized on the field. Today he lies in one of thousands of unknown graves throughout the South.[1]

It is estimated that more than 200,000 Union soldiers were taken prisoner during the war. For 15 percent of these the end result of being captured versus being killed was the same. More than 30,000 died while incarcerated.[2] In 1864 and 1865, when prisoner exchanges had all but stopped, it was well known in the ranks that being captured inevitably would lead to a miserable and trying ordeal.

Among the long rolls of Union prisoners were many beardless boys. Their experiences as prisoners and tales of capture and escape attempts are as varied and colorful as their stories of battle. Musicians serving as medical attendants often fell prey to capture when field hospitals were overrun. On such occasions they could have left their posts and made a hasty retreat, but even with capture imminent most remained with their patients. Youthful couriers sometimes were "gobbled up" while carrying dispatches over unfamiliar terrain, finding themselves among the enemy instead of the command for which they searched. Once in custody they could be "paraded" because of their youth and in rare instances given special treatment, but for the most part were delivered to stockades with others where survival became paramount.

Seldon B. Kingsbury was born October 29, 1846, in Lorain County, Ohio. When Fort Sumter fell he was a 14-year-old student at Oberlin College. Flushed with patriotic fervor, he helped organize the 7th Ohio Infantry's Company C, which was composed almost exclusively of students. The 7th participated in its first battle on August 26, 1861, at Cross Lanes in western Virginia. During the engagement Seldon and 116 comrades were captured. Elias W. Morey of Company C explained the shock of being taken prisoner: "This was one of the exigencies of war which few, if any of us, had counted on. Most of us had realized that we were liable to be sick, wounded, or killed, but had not dreamed of the possibility of being captured; but here we were at the very beginning of our term of service in the hands of the rebels, deprived of arms, accouterments, and liberty itself."

Kingsbury and the others started on the long journey to captivity. Their experiences mirrored those of most that followed, as Elias Morey recalled. "The guards treated us like men and soldiers, but some of those in camp took every opportunity to show their contempt of us by taunting, insulting and cursing us indiscriminately. 'What you'uns all come down here to fight we'uns for?' was a question so often repeated all along our route that it became a by-word with us. The oft-repeated statement that 'one Southerner could whip a dozen Yanks' showed the estimate they placed upon our fighting ability...."

After marching more than 100 miles during the next four days the prisoners entered Staunton, Virginia, and were led to the train depot. While on the boarding platform a large crowd gathered and someone, noticing the preponderance of captured youngsters, bellowed, "I guess you'uns would like to see your mamas about this time." Quickly, one of the boys responded, "Oh, we were weaned some time ago." The retort was too much for a large, burly Rebel major standing nearby. He immediately stepped forward and chided the wag. "You are a prisoner and a Yankee. You had better understand that. We've had enough of your damned insolence. Shut up and behave yourself as a prisoner should, or I'll rope you. I have the authority and I'll do it."

After days of traveling the boys reached their destinations. Kingsbury first was incarcerated in Richmond, then New Orleans, and finally Salisbury, North Carolina, where he was paroled in July 1862. Following his exchange he went home to Camden, Ohio, for a 60-day furlough. But he was so beset with chronic diarrhea acquired in captivity that he was granted a disability discharge.[3]

Henry S. Redman was one who was badly wounded and in that capacity captured. His desire to become a soldier kindled as soon as the smoke cleared over Fort Sumter, when he and a number of other young boys formed a Zouave company in Penfield, New York, while attending school. In the summer of 1862 16-year-old Henry enlisted at Rochester in the 108th New York. After a few days his Zouave training became evident and he was appointed corporal. Like many others, however, his glory was short-lived when his father, with the influence of a judge, procured a discharge due to his age.

As soon as his 18th birthday arrived he enlisted in Company L, 21st New York Cavalry, and again was promoted to corporal. During an engagement at Ashby's Gap, Virginia, on July 18, 1864, a bullet tore through his left lung, entering an inch left of his heart, and passed out under the left shoulder. He spent the night on the ground with other severely wounded men, but the next day was shoved in a wagon and carried over the Blue Ridge Mountains to the village of Paris, Virginia. Henry and two other injured soldiers were laid in a grocery store because the officers thought they were too weak to travel further. Before

Musician Charles Smith was 14 when he enlisted in the 49th Pennsylvania's Company C in August 1861. On June 29, 1862, he was captured in the sundown engagement of Savage's Station, Virginia, one of the Seven Days battles near Richmond. English-born, Smith spent 73 days in captivity at Libby and Belle Isle prisons. After his 1864 discharge from the 49th he reenlisted for one year in the 3rd U.S. Veteran Volunteer Infantry, Hancock's Veteran Corps.

History of the 49th Pennsylvania Volunteers

leaving the brigade surgeon advised him to give his colonel things he wished to be sent home, including any message for his parents, as he believed the teenager would not last another 48 hours.

Shortly after the Union cavalry departed, a contingent of Mosby's Confederate rangers under Captain Walter E. Frankland entered the town. Frankland assured the wounded Federals they would be cared for and placed a guard at the door to watch over them. Henry takes up the narrative:

We were fortunate in having the services of a doctor in the village, by the name of Paine, who was a Union man and a true friend to us in our need. During our stay in Paris we had the opportunity of getting acquainted with a number of Mosby's men, among them a sergeant ... who was largely instrumental in aiding John Brott and myself to escape. Brott had volunteered to stay behind and care for us wounded men. Confederate clothes were secured for us by a Union girl, not yet sixteen years of age, whose name was Kendall, and left in the sugar boxes of our prison (which continued to be the old grocery store). On September 17th, 1864, our friend the sergeant came riding up to our door in great haste and told me that that night was the time for us to make the attempt to reach our own lines. He was to be in command of the pickets at the Gap that night, and promised that he would so post the guards that they would not be able to hear us working our way past on the turnpike. We at once set to work to carry out the project, and succeeded in passing the lines with safety that night about eleven o'clock.

During our tramp of twelve miles, we had to hide three times to avoid being discovered by scouting parties. We reached General Sheridan's pickets about six o'clock on the morning of the 18th, when I removed two pieces of bone from my side, which were the first of twenty four pieces that were eventually taken from me.

Redman fully recuperated by mid-January 1865 and was sent to Annapolis, Maryland, to guard prisoners until he was discharged that August.[4]

Abraham Palmer included his own experience of captivity in his published history of the 48th New York. In July 1861 15-year-old Abraham, just five foot two, signed the muster roll as a musician in Company D. He quickly came to the conclusion that beating a drum all day was not exciting enough, and was detailed as Colonel James H. Perry's personal orderly. After the colonel's death he continued as a staff orderly, serving with Lieutenant Colonel William Barton, until captured July 18, 1863, during the Union assault on Fort Wagner near Charleston, South Carolina.[5]

Although an earlier attack by Colonel Robert Gould Shaw's 54th Massachusetts failed, the 48th New York and 6th Connecticut spearheaded a second assault on the fort's sea-face side. They attacked in column of companies in close order, scrambling up the most precipitous parapets of the fort. Their objective was to take the sea-face bastion, which they did in a hand-to-hand encounter with the 31st North Carolina, and gained possession of the entire salient. Palmer estimated 800 men from the two regiments actually entered. They were holding it against counterattack when, to their horror, the 100th New York as part of the third wave came up from behind. Supposing them Confederates, the 100th delivered a full volley into the backs of their own troops. "It was then that Colonel Barton fell," wrote Palmer, "and hundreds of brave fellows who had survived that storm of fire in their front went down before the volley of their own comrades from the rear. It was one of those mistakes never to be accounted for, nor atoned for, in war. I have no doubt that, exasperated by such a stupid blunder, some of the men within the fort fired back at their assailants on the parapet behind them. At least they broke and retreated, and left us there, still holding the salient, but greatly reduced in numbers."[6]

After the New Yorkers' departure the survivors held the salient and awaited help, but it never came. Palmer continued:

The ground ... was piled with the dead and dying in some places three feet deep; the wounded cried for help; our numbers had been greatly reduced, both by the fire from the rear and by the retirement one at a time, as best they could, of many who thought the attempt to hold the bastion was folly. After all had gone, however, there still remained, scattered along the inside of the superior slope, 140 men. They were mainly of the Sixth Connecticut and Forty-eighth New York, although there was hardly any regiment that had participated in either of the three assaults, some of whose men had not forced their way into the bastion, and did not join that little stalwart company who was determined to defend it to the last. In the darkness they did not know each other. They only knew that they were lying on top of heaps of dead, and could tell from their own fire that they were well distributed, and that they had made a common resolve that they would hold what they had taken to the end. When their ammunition was exhausted they robbed the dead for more; when they were assaulted at one point, they rushed together there and defended it. They were actuated by the noblest spirit that ever prompted soldiers to valorous and desperate

In March 1864, George W. Raymond presented this photograph of himself taken in Brooklyn to fellow 48th New York musician Frank Cady. Both were home on veteran furlough and George evidently was proud of his new uniform. The 48th's musicians did not participate in the assault on Fort Wagner, preventing them from sharing their comrades' fate.

Author's Collection

deeds; they helped each other automatically, for there was no one to order them. They were not like a single company or the remnants of a regiment, properly officered and ordered what to do, and yet they did not know until the next morning, when they looked into each other's faces in the prison, that there was not among them a single commissioned officer, that to a man they were private soldiers....

Moments passed — dreadful moments of intense anxiety. What instant the rebels would rush down upon them in overwhelming numbers in the darkness, and at what point, they could not know. One terrible assault upon them ... they successfully repulsed; many minor assaults also. Thus hours passed, terrible hours of suspense, but of unrelenting fidelity. The heavens were black with clouds; not a single star would look on a scene of blood like that. The only light was the flash of the guns from Fort Sumter above, and the embrasures on either side. For more than three hours that defense of the fort within the fort was kept up. A mere handful of men did it. They were surprised the next morning when they counted each other, to know that they had numbered only one hundred and forty. They became conscious towards midnight that they were being surrounded; they saw faintly in the darkness lines of rebels passing down the seashore in their rear, on the right; others that they did not see crossed the face of the curtain behind them on the left. Seventeen hundred men on their own ground had failed for more than three hours to dislodge 140 abandoned men from the mighty salient they had captured. But at midnight the Confederates, by suddenly rushing in upon them from the front and flanks and rear, did finally overwhelm them; then they surrendered. The writer never can forget the instant when the mass of rebels from all directions, yelling "Surrender! Surrender!" rushed in upon us; he fired his last cartridge into one of them, then broke the little carbine he had been given at [Fort] Pulaski upon the cannon by his side, and held up his hands and surrendered. He was at the time but a boy, and he claims now to have been but the least, and the least worthy, of that immortal band of 140 who defend-

ed that salient till midnight; and it is an inexpressible sorrow to him to this day to remember that it was the unhappy fate of many of those 140 private soldiers who survived the carnage of that battle, to live to become idiots for their country, and to starve and freeze and die at last at Belle Isle and Andersonville, with the world's commiseration their only reward.[7]

The next morning the captives were led through Charleston's streets amid jeers. Of 140 prisoners, 28 belonged to the 48th New York, and of that number 22 never saw home again.[8]

Palmer was paroled April 16, 1864, and recovered at Patterson Park Hospital in Baltimore. In June he returned to his regiment and began clerking. He was discharged September 20 at age 18 with three years' service behind him.[9]

With the 48th New York's core used up at Fort Wagner its ranks were filled with replacements. It was the fault of some of these, believed Otis B. Smith of Company B, that he was captured in the fall of 1864. His colorful record was published in the 45th Pennsylvania's history.[10]

I enlisted the 15th day of February 1864, running away from home. My first initiation was the 6th of May 1864 at the battle of the Wilderness. During the charge in the afternoon on the enemy, Longstreet's Corps was driven quite a distance. We were going down to the creek to fill our canteens, when a rebel soldier, who was wounded in the abdomen, asked me to give him a drink of water. Returning from the creek with my canteen full, I raised his head and saw that he was not long for this world. I gave him a drink of water. "Is there any way I could aid you?" I said, knowing well there was not, and he replied, "No." I am not superstitious but I think it carried me through the campaign of 1864 without a scratch. But they got me at last as a prisoner of war.

On the 30th day of September 1864, near the Weldon Railroad, they broke through the Forty-eighth New York regiment, composed mostly of foreign substitutes, and then [it was] every man for himself. Major [Roland] Cheeseman, the color sergeant and I all got together. We were behind an old abandoned log house. The major commanded the ser-

Richmond's Libby Prison actually was three connected brick buildings used as a warehouse prior to March 1862. It originally housed both commissioned and enlisted prisoners, and became the Confederacy's most photographed structure.

U.S. Army Military History Institute

geant to step out into the road and rally the colors, thinking our men were firing on us. It happened to be the Rebels. We abandoned our place then and went to the left. Major Cheeseman was wounded in the neck and also captured. They took us to Petersburg, to Richmond (Libby) and then to Salisbury prison, North Carolina. There they commenced to starve us. I soon saw the rations we were getting would not sustain life and I commenced to scheme.

The guards were from 60 to 75 years old, not fit for active service but could do garrison duty. I noticed that they had their clothes fastened with thorns and strings instead of buttons. Knowing these were products of the North, I got busy. I went to one of the guards about nine o'clock at a reasonable distance from the dead line. "Johnny, how are you on the trade?" "What have you got?" he replied. "Buttons." "How many?" "Two dozen, what will you give me in return?" "Hoecake, sweet potato pie, meat, tobacco and confederate scrip." I met him when he came on the next relief with the supply and I had [a] package of dirt clods and pebbles, representing the size of about two dozen buttons. "Lower the commissary and here are your buttons." I threw them up so that he could not catch them, although they fell on his side. He told me that he would get them in the morning when he got off duty. I carried this on for about two weeks until they commenced to find my packages. One night I went out to the guard and said: "How are you on the trade?" He did not reply, and thinking the old fellow was hard of hearing I jumped the dead line and repeated my question. He answered me: "Get back there you ——, I'll give you dirt clods and pebbles." I got back.[11]

On March 10, 1865, when Otis' physical condition led Confederate authorities to consider him no threat, he was paroled and sent north. Soon after his arrival he received a furlough and returned home to regain his strength. During May and June he was detailed as a provost guard at Alexandria, Virginia, and in July was discharged.[12]

Fortunately, some young boys were only detained a short while before being paroled, and were not subjected long to the horrors of prison life. Born April 30, 1850, Lucius Hull went off unmustered with the 116th Ohio when that regiment was formed late in 1862. At Winchester, Virginia, in June 1863, he was captured and sent to Richmond's Belle Isle prison. Perhaps being just 13 or because he was never mustered, he was paroled after limited imprisonment. Undaunted by the experience he enlisted in Company G, 18th Ohio, that December and rose to the rank of principal musician by May 1865, in which capacity he was serving when mustered out. While he was with the 18th his father had a discharge sent to the regiment, but when Colonel Charles Grosvenor presented it to Lucius he tore it up in the colonel's presence.[13]

William Jewell, also of the 18th Ohio, enlisted as a Company I drummer at age 15, and was captured during the battle of Stones River. The December 1862 fight was costly to the regiment. It sustained 170 casualties of 446 who went into action. Twenty-three were missing, including Jewell, who was shipped to Richmond. The 19-day trip lasted longer than his imprisonment. After eight days in confinement he was sent to City Point, Virginia, and paroled. His health may have contributed to the early release. William was so incapacitated upon arrival at City Point that he

spent seven weeks in the hospital. He then was sent to Camp Chase in Ohio and forwarded to his command in June. During July the five-foot-two drummer was appointed chief musician, but this position of honor was not held long due to another attack of diarrhea. Not until March 1864 was he able to return to the regiment. Delinquent in getting back, he was brought up on formal charges of being absent without leave. At his court-martial held in April, Jewell's actions were vindicated by the 18th's lieutenant colonel, who testified on the boy's behalf. The court judged his leave was justified and he was found not guilty. He served the rest of his term, but chose not to reenlist and was discharged November 9, 1864.[14]

Along with a detachment of his regiment 11-year-old John Walker, 22nd Wisconsin, was captured March 25, 1863, at Brentwood, Tennessee, by General Nathan Bedford Forrest's cavalry. When it became obvious the Badgers were surrounded, John sounded the long roll, kicked both heads from his drum and began smashing band instruments to keep them from the Rebels. Because of his age he was released unconditionally at Tullahoma and given a pass through the lines to Vicksburg, but Army of Tennessee commander General Braxton Bragg countermanded the order when he learned Walker was regularly enlisted and subject to exchange. The boy was shipped instead to Libby Prison, arriving there April 9. He was paroled within five days and rejoined his comrades on May 13. His brief experience of captivity did cause some medical problems, however, and on December 28 John was released from the Army. In validating the drummer's discharge the 22nd Wisconsin's surgeon wrote, "... general inability to withstand the hardships and privations of camp life since his return to the regiment after a long march as prisoner to Richmond and much suffering while in prison."[15]

Parole was the magic word that kept spinning through the mind of every prisoner. While some contrived plans to escape, most, after watching others' unsuccessful attempts, wisely placed hope in the word "parole" and their energy into procuring food and caring for physical needs.

Charles A. Storke was born November 19, 1847, in New York. At a young age his family moved to Oshkosh, Wisconsin, where his father died in 1855. From that time he alternately attended school and worked to support himself and his mother. In February

Eleven-year-old John D. Walker posed in a gray uniform with his rope-tension drum shortly after enlisting in the 22nd Wisconsin. The oversized instrument accentuated his bantam size.

Racine Heritage Museum

1864 he could stand staying at home no longer and at 16 ran off with two underage friends to enlist in the nearby town of Fond du Lac. After looking the boys over for a few minutes the recruiter accepted two of them, including Charles. He was assigned to Company G, 36th Wisconsin, which had a number of youngsters in its ranks. The regiment left Camp Randall at Madison by train for Washington on May 10, and from there was forwarded as part of the Second Corps to Spotsylvania Court House. The march from Belle Plain, Virginia, to the front was far more taxing than the young boys expected. Charles and his fellow recruits spent the next few days learning what soldiering was all about, occasionally skirmishing with the enemy before arriving at Totopotomy Creek. On May 30 he lost one of his good friends, Theodore V. Wortman of Sheboygan Falls, and later wrote of his death: "Poor Wortman, he was shot next to me, and I hear the bullet to this day, as the dull thud came from the stroke of the ball.... He was shot in the mouth and the ball

lodged in the skull; there was no wound of entrance or exit visible. I recollect when the detail was sent out to bring his body back a few rods for burial, and how thankful I was that the detail did not include me. Something akin to stage fear had seized me. After I became used to danger it did not phase me much."

On June 2 the 36th Wisconsin participated in the doomed assault at Cold Harbor. Charles and 43 of his comrades were captured and sent to Libby Prison. By the 14th all but one were transferred to the dreaded Southern prison pen at Andersonville, Georgia. When they reached the stockade it was bulging at the seams with more than 30,000 Union prisoners. Although the 36th boys were relatively healthy when they arrived it was not long before their numbers dwindled. Within two months eight of 12 members of Company G died. On September 30 Charles and another comrade, John Adams, were transferred to Savannah, and then to Millen prison during the middle of October. At the time of their arrival Millen was a new stockade and the boys, having learned the value of wood at Andersonville, gathered all they could find and built a small hut with two other young prisoners. Rations consisted of two ounces of bacon or four of beef, and a half-cup of cornmeal per day. Once a week molasses was substituted for the meat. One of the other boys in the hut had been a candy maker in Pennsylvania, so he and Charles decided to go into the candy business with the molasses. They soon made $40 selling their sweet concoction, using the money to purchase half a blanket from a guard. With some boards it was employed to cover their little hut's roof.

Shortly after Thanksgiving 1864 the prisoners were turned out one rainy night and herded into box cars. After four days of travel with no rations the train stopped at a place called Blackshear near the Florida state line. About 6,000 captives were gathered in the woods without a stockade or fence to enclose them.

143

One day an order announced that a third of the prisoners was to be paroled, and through trickery Charles made sure he was included. Happy with the proposition of going home, he gave away his half-canteen, small cup and prized half-blanket before heading for the train. Swearing not to take up arms against the Confederacy, the select prisoners again boarded cars and started toward Savannah. When it was reached, to their mortification, the train continued on to Florence, South Carolina's military prison. Hopes of parole all but vanished. Charles' spirits were crushed.

Here I [was] about as forlorn as one possibly could be. Hope left me, and I should have died had not [Addison] Chaplin, of Company E of our regiment, been exceedingly kind and let me live with him, and draw rations in his little utensils. I had none of my own. Poor Chaplin, I owed my life to him. Here also I found [George W.] Whipple [of Company G] on parole carrying in wood for the prisoners. After a few days Chaplin handed me a small bar of lye soap about a foot long and an inch and a half square, and told me to cut it up into thirteen pieces, if I would trade the other ten for him. I did so and earned the three pieces, which, by the way, was the only soap I saw in the Confederacy. Then came the order to select a thousand of the worst cases for parole. I had failed rapidly at Florence, and then weighed less than a hundred pounds. I waited until the thousand that I belonged to, the third, had fallen in over the dead line. I went down to the creek and broke the thin covering of ice, and washed myself thoroughly; then hovered over a pitch pine fire until I had blackened myself up again; then carelessly washed so as to leave the dirt in streaks on my face; and then, dressed in all the clothing I had, a pant leg tied into a turban for a hat, a coat without sleeves, and with but one tail, pants with one leg mended with the coattail, and with the other so torn that every time I stepped forward my knee would come out half way to the thigh, with shoes, one

Lanky Charles A. Storke, 36th Wisconsin, weighed just 95 pounds when he left Confederate captivity, then spent five months in parole camps before being discharged May 28, 1865. He afterward became a prominent Californian — founding the *Los Angeles Herald* and serving in the state legislature and as mayor of Santa Barbara.

The Thirty-sixth Wisconsin Volunteer Infantry

of which had a top and no sole, and the other a sole and no top, I presented myself to the sergeant of the thousand, and said I belonged to his thousand. At his order, I fell in where I would be the first one of the thousand that would be seen by the inspecting officer. He came along, looked at me and said, "What is the matter with you?" I replied with a shiver, and quaking, not forced for it was very cold, "I–I–I don't

144

Distraught with concern over missing soldiers, loved ones at home anxiously waited for news. The parents of Private Edward C. Middleton, Company I, 4th Ohio Cavalry, took it upon themselves to solicit information about him with this unusual notice, printed in Cincinnati. Middleton, 15 years old when captured, remained a prisoner until war's end.

Courtesy of Gary Delscamp

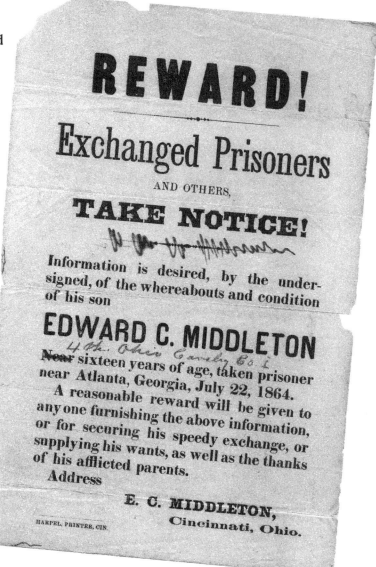

REWARD!

Exchanged Prisoners

AND OTHERS,

TAKE NOTICE!

Information is desired, by the undersigned, of the whereabouts and condition of his son

EDWARD C. MIDDLETON

4 th. Ohio Cavalry Co. I.

Near sixteen years of age, taken prisoner near Atlanta, Georgia, July 22, 1864. A reasonable reward will be given to any one furnishing the above information, or for securing his speedy exchange, or supplying his wants, as well as the thanks of his afflicted parents.
Address

HARPEL, PRINTER, CIN.

E. C. MIDDLETON,
Cincinnati, Ohio.

know." "How long have you to serve?" "My time will be up in February." I lied like a trooper. Said he, "I guess you will not enlist again; you may go out," and I went out.[16]

A number of prisoners were not content waiting for parole, and devoted all energy and thought to escaping. Few actually made it from a Confederate stockade, but that did not stop the planning and attempts.

Second Wisconsin cavalryman Melvin Grigsby was consumed by the desire to escape after being captured in February 1864 while foraging 12 miles from Vicksburg. The day he was captured he and seven comrades had just sat down to eat in a country house when they heard the Rebel yell outside. All went for their guns but defending themselves was futile and short-lived. Surrounded by a band of independent scouts, Melvin's first few hours of captivity were tense. Earlier that day a confrontation with a nearby resident over a horse prompted him to inquire of the man's loyalties, at which time the Mississippian displayed a Union pass. Now the man wanted to make sure he never made it back to his own lines, where he could expose him as a Confederate spy. Fortunately, Melvin pleaded his case to the scouts who protected him from harm.[17]

His first escape attempt came during the trip to prison. The Rebel scouts with captives in tow stopped at a small town where dances were held nightly. Since there was a shortage of men and an abundance of young ladies, some of the prisoners were "forced" to attend. Melvin and a comrade asked two girls to help them escape by dancing with the guards, keeping them entertained while they climbed out a window. The girls agreed, but as soon as the pair were half way out the belles cried, "They are getting away! The Yanks are getting away!" The guards grabbed their guns and rushed out the front door. At the same time the two prisoners clambered back in. Although evading punishment they were not invited to any more dances.[18]

The destination was Andersonville, and Melvin described their memorable arrival. "The gates were thrown open. On each side of what seemed a street, leaving room for us to pass in column of twos, we saw a dense mass of beings. Those in the front rank held in their hands cups, cans and little pails, and chunks of bread. They are there, we thought, to hand us food as we pass. We entered. The line on either side was a line of living, human skeletons, walking mummies; ragged, many nearly naked, all skin and bone, black as Indians, not exactly smoked Yanks, but the skeletons of Yanks. We were hungry. These men seemed to be starved. There they stood, their great eyes protruding beyond their gaunt and bony cheeks; their limbs, half covered, showing great, swollen joints, black, bruised-looking elbows and knees, and great puff-balls for feet. The feet of many looked like boxing gloves. All this we saw in sections, as it were, by the uncanny, flickering, smoking light of a pine knot torch or a 'fat' pine stick, that here and there one of the creatures held in his hand. Yes, nearly every one of the front rank had food or wood in his hands, but not to give. They were there to barter or to sell. The majority of us had nothing with which to buy or trade. We did not ask for anything. There was that in these surroundings which, if it did not make us forget our hunger, made us feel that our misery was not worthy of mention." [19]

This indoctrination solidified Grigsby's quest for freedom. "I tried many plans for escape. In fact, there was not a day from the time I was made prisoner that I was not looking for a chance to get away."

Not until being moved to South Carolina and Florence prison was a good opportunity of escape presented. He eluded his guards while getting water outside the containment area and actually reached the Atlantic coast, where he hoped to find a Union vessel. Instead, after all his efforts he was recaptured by a citizen guarding a bridge, a mere boy not noticed until he was half way across. The youngster marched him to his home, leveling a double-barreled shotgun at his back. In his travels Melvin had secured a Confederate jacket and forged a pass for such an occasion, but when talk turned to hanging the "rebel deserter" he decided it best to show his true colors and divulge he was an escaped Union prisoner. He spent a day locked in the town jail, then was shipped back to Florence. [20]

Returning to dull prison life Melvin was favored by being assigned to a wood-chopping detail. The choppers went out daily to a forest near the stockade, where each man was required to cut a cord of wood per day. In exchange for the work they received extra food and the right to as much wood as each could carry. The extra wood then was traded for even more food or other items. The prisoners were allowed out on their honor and had signed paroles. One day one of the choppers made his escape. When the Rebel officers were alerted the rest of the detail was returned to the stockade, and the next day another party was selected to go out. Earlier, Melvin had studied the surrounding countryside, anticipating the need for such knowledge in case he wanted to run off. Chopping duty had been a good job, and as long as he was favored the need to escape was not worth the risk. With his parole of honor now gone and facing bleak monotony, he started working again on a plan to get away.

"Aside from the danger involved, this was to me a critical moment," he recalled. "For ten months my thoughts by day, my dreams by night, had been of escape. I was about to try. Succeed, and home and mother, father, brothers and sisters, and all that life gives promise to a boy, were before me; fail, and tortures and hunger were sure, and perhaps starvation, sickness and death." [21]

Using another man's pass Melvin managed being placed on a work detail outside camp, but never returned. He traveled a mile overland, then walked a mile or more through a swampy creek to camouflage his scent. A cold, steady rain began to fall, further dissipating his scent. In this manner he passed through the area the dogs patrolled, which was the biggest obstacle for escaped prisoners. It was January 10, 1865.

Melvin traveled north, aided by negroes along the way. At one point he acted the part of a slave owner by walking through a town with a small black boy trailing behind him; in reality the boy was his guide. On February 1 he heard in the distance a brass band playing "The Girl I Left Behind Me," and the rumbling of wagon wheels. "I ran on for nearly a mile through thick woods. Coming to an opening in the woods I climbed on to a fallen tree, and there across a field, marching in the road, with band playing, and colors flying, go the boys in blue. I take off my hat and try to shout. I cannot. My heart is in my throat. My strength is gone. I recline against the limbs of the tree and sob and cry like a child, and wonder whether my strength will come back, or whether I must sit there helplessly and let that army go by."

Two cavalrymen spotted him and with guns drawn they approached. He stated he was an escaped prisoner. The passing troops belonged to General William B. Hazen's Fifteenth Corps' division of Sherman's command, and soon Melvin was seated at a campfire telling Hazen's orderlies his story of escape. He stayed with his new friends until Sherman's forces reached Goldsboro, North Carolina. There he was permitted to take the first train to New Bern, and eventually reached Washington, where he received his back pay, discharge and transportation home.[22]

Thousands who dreamed of escape or parole never left the prison stockades alive. Rashio Crane was among those perishing at Andersonville. Born November 13, 1848, he was forced to remain at home in Wisconsin when older brother Richard marched off with Company D, 7th Wisconsin, early in the war. By February 1864 he had waited long enough and enlisted as a drummer in Richard's company at the age of 15. Three weeks later a third brother, Stephen, followed suit, also enlisting in Company D. The Cranes were afforded little time together after Rashio and Stephen reached the front. Less than three months from the day he arrived in camp, Rashio was captured May 5 in the Wilderness.[23] A memorial composed by an unidentified writer, and found tucked inside brother Richard's wartime diary, tells his story:

> To the memory
> Of Rashio Crane,
> Co. D, 7th Reg. Wis. Vol.
> who died July 23rd 1864 aged 15 years.

The subject of this brief notice was the youngest son of George W. and Mary Ann Crane, and was a native of the town of Mt. Pleasant, Racine Co. Wisconsin. Some years since, his family removed to Rutland, Dane Co. Wisconsin, where they have since resided.

At the first outbreak of the rebellion, he would readily have responded to his country's call, but his youth, and other considerations deterred him from taking any decided stand until the winter of 1863-4 when he enlisted in the Federal Army and joined his two brothers in the field, where the brave sons of the Northland were nobly striving "to steady the rocking pillars of the republic."

In the hard fought battle of the Wilderness while assisting in carrying a wounded

Rashio Crane visited J.S. Anderson's Racine photography studio shortly after his enlistment in Company D, 7th Wisconsin. Within five months he was captured, sent to Andersonville prison and died there July 23, 1864.

Author's Collection

Bugler Josephus Gephart, 24th Indiana Battery, spent the last five months of 1864 in captivity. The Germantown, Ohio, native was photographed wearing a non-regulation musician's jacket at the Indianapolis gallery of Howard & Davies.

Author's Collection

comrade from the field, he was taken prisoner and removed to that theatre of the darkest rebel atrocities, the prison stockade at Andersonville Ga. Here he lingered enduring patiently the most intense suffering and deprivations until the 23d of July when quietly and almost alone he fell asleep, far from the loved ones at the old home.

Gladly would they have watched beside him and caught the language of his spirit in those last sad moments which to them will ever be shrouded in uncertainty. Yet his widowed mother recalls with a mournful pleasure many casual circumstances and expressions which indicated a determination to do right, a strong desire for a higher nobler life and the attainment of goodness and truth.

The headboard bearing the number 3878 which marks his grave, points out the last resting place of a hero and a patriot; for through the whole of his prison life one thought seemed to overcome all else: his love for his country, and concern for the honor of the old flag.[24]

Fifteen-year-old Thomas M. Hale enlisted August 27, 1861, in the 33rd Ohio. After two years campaigning he was captured on the first day of fighting at Chickamauga. Despite the fact his disappearance coincided with a major battle, he was listed as absent without leave because no one knew his whereabouts. In February 1864 his command finally learned his fate through correspondence between the War Department and Confederate authorities. By that time, however, Hale had died while a prisoner at Danville, Virginia.[25]

News of high mortality rates and wretched conditions at Andersonville by the summer of 1864 generated thoughts of rescuing the prisoners there. As Union forces converged on Atlanta, General George Stoneman won approval from General Sherman to take his cavalry command south to liberate Andersonville's captives, as well as those at Macon, Georgia. Before heading to Macon he was to unite with General Edward M. McCook's troopers, who were destroying railroad track below Atlanta, and then proceed togeth-

er. But Stoneman decided his mission was more glamorous than cutting rail lines. Despite orders he rode straight for Macon without waiting for McCook. On July 30 McCook's men were told to make their way back to Union lines as best they could after nearly being surrounded by Confederate cavalry under General Joseph Wheeler. Stoneman's jaunt proved no more fruitful.

On July 27 the general, with three brigades and a two-gun battery totaling more than 2,000 men, headed for Macon. By mid-afternoon of the 31st he retained just over 200 men belonging to the 5th Indiana Cavalry and the two guns of the 24th Indiana Battery. The rest had been driven back or scattered. Stoneman and his little band held out as long as possible to give his other brigades time to extricate themselves, regroup and return to safety. As the day waned his staff officers and those of the battery and 5th Indiana persuad-

Farm boy William W. McDonald of Perry County, Ohio, enlisted in February 1864 to fill a musician's vacancy in Company I, 31st Ohio. During General W.T. Sherman's celebrated "march to the sea," McDonald was captured just outside Milledgeville, Georgia, on November 24, 1864. He was paroled in North Carolina three months later.

Author's Collection

Charleston, his youth presumably a factor in persuading Confederate authorities to free him.[28]

Although this raid and others failed to free any prisoners, a mass release never occurred until the Confederacy capitulated. During February 1865, when the Union noose was tightening and Sherman started marching north through the Carolinas, prisoner exchanges were renewed for the first time since General Ulysses S. Grant stopped the practice in the summer of 1864. On March 20 the first large batch of prisoners at Andersonville and some from Cahaba prison in Alabama were sent to Union lines to be exchanged. Traveling over a rough line of track the emaciated captives reached Camp Fisk near Vicksburg. As they waited Lee's army surrendered in Virginia. Word of the victory spread from squad to squad and a general celebration took place. Then the men were told by authorities they would have to remain in camp until the huge task of filling out paperwork was completed. Since everyone was anxious to leave it was decided to let them start on their way and the paperwork would follow. Happy and relieved, the ex-prisoners marched to Vicksburg's wharf to board transportation north.[29]

One of the boats chosen for the trip was the side-wheeler *Sultana*. It was overcrowded with some 2,500 passengers and crew on April 24 for the journey up the Mississippi River. Legal capacity was only 376, but because the government was paying so much per head the *Sultana's* owners decided to forego safety in favor of making a heavy profit. Transportation officers in charge, some of whom were said to have received kickbacks, were ambivalent to the fact another boat, the *Pauline Carroll,* was lying empty alongside, its captain pleading to take some of the men. In spite of reason the *Sultana* shoved off. Near Memphis about 2

ed him to give up, as ammunition was almost gone and escape seemed futile. Stoneman agreed and surrendered his existing command. Ironically his men, who had seen themselves as great liberators, were imprisoned at Macon with the very captives they hoped to release.[26]

On August 6 Stoneman, via flag of truce, was able to send a report to Sherman, in which he summarized the affair: "Without entering into particulars, we were whipped." At the end he added, "I feel better satisfied with myself to be a prisoner of war, much as I hate it, than to be amongst those who owe their escape to considerations of self-preservation."[27]

One who stood by General Stoneman as he satisfied himself capitulating was the 24th Indiana Battery's young bugler, Josephus Gephart. He and all 49 artillerymen who began the raid were surrendered together. Gephart was paroled December 13, 1864, at

a.m. April 27, 1865, the sidewheeler's boiler exploded, and what ensued remains the worst maritime disaster in American history. As many as 1,800 died.[30]

Among the youngest soldiers on board was Stephen M. Gaston, who at the time of the explosion was 15. In October 1863 he joined Company K, 9th Indiana Cavalry, at age 13. Eleven months later Forrest's cavalry captured Gaston with a portion of his regiment at Sulphur Branch Trestle, while the Hoosiers were on their way to relieve troops at Athens, Alabama. During April 1865 he was formally exchanged and sent to Camp Fisk, where with 16 others of the 9th he boarded the *Sultana*. On the trip north he and a friend, William Block, found a cask of sugar which they freely consumed. Stephen remembered:

Our evening dreams were sweet, for we had eaten about two pounds of sugar each, and then were we not going home to see our loved ones who had mourned us for dead? We dreamed the soldier's dreams of home and loved ones, of camp life, of the battle and the prison, the scanty fare and the cruel guards, when, suddenly, our dreams were broken. I felt myself raised to a height and then a crash came; the smokestack had fallen directly on the pilothouse, crushing it down almost on us. I felt for Block and called his name but no answer came.[31] The cries of the wounded were heard all around me. I was a prisoner again, for a network of rubbish surrounded me. The stack above the remnant of the wheelhouse behind the boat was on fire, and directly below some poor fellows were wedged in at my right hand and begged for help. I was helpless and could render no assistance. They soon smothered from the heat and smoke. After trying again and again I finally extricated myself and, going to the hatchway or steps, I found my way obstructed and debris scattered everywhere.

I finally concluded to jump to the lower deck, but found I could swing down on to the breaching of the stack. I did so, and oh God! what a sight. I was on the bow of the boat and could not see aft, but what misery I did see was enough for me. Men were crying, praying, swearing, and begging. Wounded in every shape, some with broken legs and arms, others scalded, burnt and dying, their cries made the already dark night hideous, lighted up by the now fiercely burning boat.

My senses remained and I thought it would be best to try some mode of escape (I was wounded and badly scraped from my exertion to get from under the smokestack). On looking around I found an empty flour barrel, and divesting myself of clothing I jumped into the chilling waters. Taking the precaution to see that no person was near I was fortunate to get clear of the boat without encountering anyone,

although two or three tried to get to me, but drowned before reaching me. I saw at least twenty drown at once. As fast as one would feel he was drowning he would clutch at the nearest, and I believe many a bold swimmer was drowned that night who could have saved himself if alone. I was finally rescued by a life-boat from the steamer *Bostonia* and taken to the cabin of that steamer in a cramped and exhausted condition, and was then taken in an ambulance to Overton Hospital [in Memphis].

After a short stay Stephen made his way home to Terre Haute, Indiana. He was discharged June 28, 1865.[32]

Emaciated as many of the prisoners were made swimming almost impossible. Most, like James K. Brady, realized that before jumping into the river while the boat burned around them. They knew their only hope was to salvage something that floated, and hang on.

Brady was 15 when he marched off to war with the 64th Ohio in the fall of 1862. As a private he fought in every engagement of the regiment, receiving a scalp wound in front of Atlanta and a flesh wound to his hip on November 30, 1864, at Franklin, Tennessee. There, he and five members of his company were captured while falling back to the main Union breastworks. His *Sultana* ordeal was not only a struggle against the river but against others trying to survive as well.

My friend, David Ettleman, and I went up to the hurricane deck and made our bed, as we were too much crowded below, and laid down. That was the last that I knew until the explosion, which occurred about two o'clock a.m., at which time I was suddenly awakened to my senses, as the fire was all over me and my friend was trying to brush it off; it had already burned most of the hair off from the top of my head. We finally got the fire out and began looking around for some means to save ourselves, for we could see that the boat was on fire. We could see nothing to get, so we went to the front end of the hurricane deck and took hold of some ropes and went down to the bow of the boat, and oh, what a sight met our gaze! There were some killed in the explosion, lying in the bottom of the boat, being trampled upon, while some were crying and praying, many were cursing while others were singing. That sight I shall never forget; I often see it in my sleep, and wake up with a start.

After looking for something to save ourselves with in vain, we had about given ourselves up as lost, when all at once we saw a crowd with something which proved to be the gang plank. As this seemed to be our last chance my

Private Christian Knudson was 16 and residing in Fillmore County, Minnesota, when he enlisted in Company K, 15th Wisconsin, in February 1862. He was one of 13 members of his company captured at Chickamauga. He died at Andersonville on June 28, 1864, and is buried in the national cemetery there, Grave 2498.

State Historical Society of Wisconsin

some more of our passengers. I looked back and saw that there were two men on the plank behind me, how many were in front of me at this time I could not tell, but I knew that my friend was there as every little while he would call out some encouraging word to me to keep up my spirits. The two men on the plank behind me would crawl up on top of it and finally upset it again, and one of them lost his grip and went down to rise no more. Then the other fellow seemed to get crazy, for he not only climbed upon the plank behind me but reached over and tried to grab me by the shoulder. Just as his fingers were touching my shoulder I dropped under the water and he went right over me into the river like a big frog, turning the plank over with the force of his plunge, but I came up on the other side of the plank, grabbing it with my left hand. I never saw that man again.

friend and I both grabbed hold of it, just as it was going over the side of the boat, and we all went down together. I think not less than forty or fifty men had hold of that plank, at least there were as many as could crowd around it when it went into the water, and it was very heavy. I ran beside it. It struck the water end first, and I thought it would never stop going down, but it finally did, and slowly arose to the surface. I think there were about fifteen or sixteen of us that had stuck to the plank. But now a new danger had seized me, as someone grabbed me by the right foot and it seemed as though it was in a vise; try as I would, I could not shake him off. I gripped the plank with all the strength I had, and then I got my left foot between his hand and my foot and while holding on to the plank with both hands I pried him loose with my left foot, he taking my sock along with him, but he was welcome to the sock. He sank out of sight and I saw him no more.

By this time the plank had been turned over and we lost

I was now getting very tired in my weak state, as I only weighed 96 pounds when I came out of prison (I weighed 154 pounds the day before I was taken prisoner). I was almost ready to give up when I heard my friend Ettleman say, "Now boys, this plank is able to carry fifteen or twenty men if properly handled, and there are but five or six of us; now I will steady the plank while the rest of you get on and lie flat, then I will get on." We all got on and laid flat down and paddled with our hands. It was not long after this that one of the men in front said that he could see a house, and for us to paddle on the left side. We did as we were told and soon had our plank along side of the building.

Shortly after sunrise a patrol boat rescued Brady and his companions.[33]

Charles Myers, who had joined the 15th Ohio at age 16 in 1861, was not as lucky. The gray-eyed teen captured at Chickamauga survived more than a year

During the summer of 1864 more than 100 Union soldiers died each day inside Andersonville's overcrowded stockade. In mid-August nearly 33,000 prisoners were confined on 26 acres of the prison.

of hell at Andersonville before being paroled and sent aboard the *Sultana* — only to disappear in the muddy Mississippi.[34]

In his classic narrative *This Was Andersonville,* John McElroy of the 16th Illinois Cavalry wrote of a young drummer there who became one of the most well known Union boy prisoners.

One of our best purveyors of information was a bright, blue eyed, fair-haired little drummer boy, as handsome as a girl, well bred as a lady, and evidently the darling of some refined loving mother. He belonged, I think, to some loyal Virginia regiment, was captured in one of the actions in the Shenandoah Valley, and had been with us in Richmond. We

called him little "Red Cap," from his wearing a jaunty, gold-laced crimson cap. Ordinarily, the smaller a drummer boy is the harder he is, but no amount of attrition with rough men could coarsen the ingrained refinement of Red Cap's manners. He was between thirteen and fourteen and it seemed utterly shameful that men, calling themselves soldiers, should make war on such a tender boy and drag him off to prison. But no six-footer had a more soldierly heart than little Red Cap, and none was more loyal to the cause. It was a pleasure to hear him tell the story of the fights and movements his regiment had been engaged in. He was a good observer and told his tale with boyish fervor.

Shortly after [Henry] Wirz assumed command [at Andersonville] he took Red Cap into his office as orderly. His bright face and winning manners fascinated the women visitors at Headquarters and a number of them tried to adopt him, but with poor success. Like the rest of us, he could see few charms in an existence under the rebel flag and turned a deaf ear to their blandishments. He kept his ears open to the conversations of rebel officers around him and frequently secured permission to visit the interior of the stockade, when he would communicate to us all that he had heard. He received a flattering reception every time he came in, and no orator ever secured a more attentive audience than would gather around him to listen to what he had to say. He was, beyond a doubt, the best known and most popular person in the prison.[35]

The boy not only was a good storyteller while in prison, but years after the war wrote of his thrilling experiences for the *Frostburg Mining Journal* published in western Maryland. Little Red Cap's name was Ransom T. Powell.

"On the 14th of May 1862 I enlisted in Captain James A. Jarboe's company, which was recruited under the pretense of being an independent scouting company to remain in the counties of Hampshire and Hardy, W.Va. I was a drummer boy. After remaining around Piedmont and New Creek about one month, we received orders to go to Beverly, W.Va., there to become Company I of the 10th W.Va. Volunteer Infantry."

Mustered in at Beverly, the four-foot-tall recruit accustomed himself to Army life of that mountainous region. The 10th West Virginia's primary objective was to keep bushwhackers in the area under control. It was not an easy job. The region was sparsely settled, making it a perfect setting for bushwhackers to operate. After nine months of this work Powell was captured on January 3, 1864, while escorting a wagon train. He related:

We were encamped in a block-house nine miles below Petersburg, West Virginia. The wagon train was returning after having taken supplies [there]. Our Lieutenant, then in command of the company, received orders to take thirty men and go in advance of the train one mile until it passed Moorefield Junction, which was three miles below. I obtained permission to go with this detachment, thinking it would be a Sunday evening recreation for me. I procured a cap-box, being too small to carry a cartridge-box, put ten cartridges in it, and got one Sharps carbine and started.

We had not gone more than a mile before I became tired and lazy, and waited for the wagons to come along to have a ride. Instead of getting into the wagon, however, I got on the seat which the driver used, situated above the rubber block, as he was walking. While sitting there I occasionally pointed my carbine over to the woods and boasted of what I would do if the Rebels should appear.

Presently they came riding out of their hiding places by the hundreds. When they first appeared our little force, numbering about two hundred, rallied and began firing at them. I sat down and fired two or three shots. By this time all my comrades were on the double quick striving to get to the woods. I started across the hill but did not get very far before I met a Yankee. I observed from his movements that something was wrong. Looking behind here was a Rebel almost at my heels. When he saw both of us going to fire at him he jumped off his horse, and making a breastwork of him, laid his revolver on his saddle and fired all his loads at us. I never shall forget how near he came shooting me. I would see where each ball would tear up the dirt around me. During this time I could not get my carbine to fire; something had gotten between the tube and cartridge. I again turned and ran, but soon heard someone laugh in my rear. I looked and saw four Rebel cavalrymen. One of them ordered me to surrender. He cursed me and inquired, "What are you doing here?" I replied, "Fighting for my country." He said, "You have no country." I was conveyed down to the road. In a few minutes all was over.[36]

After his capture Ransom was looked upon as many young Union boys were by Southerners. He was called one of "Abe Lincoln's puppies" and "a little Yankee pet," made to sing and whistle, and at one point was asked if he wanted to go to a Southern home, providing he promised to stay there. At Richmond, Ransom and his party were taken to Belle Isle. Soon after his arrival his youth was noticed and special favors were granted.

[There was] quite a number of little Yankee boys. We had the privilege to run around in the enclosure, where the bakehouse, cookhouse and headquarters were, and we frequently sailed around on the James River in small skiffs. We were enabled to get enough to eat, and have good times.... I stayed on Belle Isle four or five weeks when there came orders for so many hundreds to leave daily. I tried to get away with the first squad but failed. I succeeded on the second day. I was under the impression that we were going to be paroled, but was told differently by the Confederates.[37]

Instead of going home Ransom, by insisting on leaving when he did, was sent to Georgia. The trip ended at the gates of Andersonville. He was part of the second squad delivered there while the stockade was being built. After two months' imprisonment his diminutive size caught the attention of a guard named Lewis Jones of the 26th Alabama. Jones proposed that Ransom become its drummer and promised to have him removed from the stockade to perform the duties. The boy declined, but Jones arranged to take him out anyway and moved him to his quarters. He was free to roam as far as a mile from camp on a pledge that he would not run away.[38]

Six weeks later the 26th Alabama was detailed to the front and replaced with Georgia Reserves. That morning Ransom was summoned to Commandant Wirz's headquarters. Lying on a cot in the office was a young Union boy who was very ill. Ransom and another prisoner were asked to care for the boy, but by the next morning he was dead. Wirz then proposed that Ransom should act as headquarters' messenger, which he accepted. In that capacity he was able to enter the prison, as McElroy mentioned, and became so universally known.

Wirz was so impressed with young Powell that he moved him into his own home for about six weeks. While there the boy did chores and ran errands between the house and headquarters, nightly taking supper with Wirz's family.[39]

The commandant demanded promptness from his subordinates. If a soldier hesitated even slightly performing his duties, a pistol was poked in his face. With an explosive temper it was only a matter of time before Wirz and Ransom had a falling out.

Captain Wirz sent me over to the depot one day with a message to General Winder's headquarters. His mare was over in a stable. I hurried over and back, as I was barefooted, and had been quite a while. The ground was sandy in this part of the state. I never saw a stone while I was there. The sand was terribly hot as it was about noon. There was a creek which crossed the road about half way, to which I would run as hard as I could, then cool my feet and hurry on. This was an every day practice of mine, as I was sent over there daily with messages. When I returned this day he was in an unusually bad humor. He asked, "Why did you not bring my mare over with you?" I replied, "You did not tell me to bring her over. I would have been glad of a ride back." He flew into a rage. He called me a "liar," cursed me dreadfully, threatened to shoot me if I contradicted him again, and called for a guard. Without any ceremony whatever, he ordered me taken and put in the prison.[40]

By this time conditions in the stockade were intolerable. Vermin and filth were everywhere, and each day the dead were carried out in droves. Ransom fortunately still had friends on the outside, and at times they brought him an extra scoop of meal, a piece of meat or some other item. Finally, on September 8, 1864, he and a squad were called from the stockade. As they stood in front of Wirz's headquarters the commandant walked out and addressed the boy, "Well, Ransom, you are going home now. Goodbye, and when you get there, stay with your father at home." Ransom recalled that "he said this in a loud tone and it had the desired effect. We were all sure then that we were going home."[41]

But after three days traveling by rail, the prisoners were deposited in the stockade at Savannah. Luck once again followed Red Cap. Samuel B. Davis was the commandant. He had been in charge at Andersonville for a short period and knew Ransom quite well. He allowed him to stay in a little building situated inside the stockade for clerical purposes, along with two clerks who lived there.

Early in October orders were received to parole all Navy personnel. One of the clerks had learned of the order and intended to assume a dead seaman's name and fall in with the lot. Ransom decided it was a "good go" and took the name of a cabin boy who was missed while at Andersonville. On the morning the group gathered to depart it was formed in line outside the prison and Davis called roll. The affair lasted more than two hours as the commandant dismissed those who could not give proper account of themselves. Ransom recalled shivering with fear. When Davis finished he walked to the column's rear where the anxious boy was standing, and called out, "Ransom."

"My heart was almost in my mouth. I began to think he was going to put me back into the prison. He repeated my name. I was then compelled to answer. Greatly to my surprise, he said, 'I am going to let you go home now. I know all about you being out here. When you get home, stay there. Do not go back in the army anymore.' Then shaking hands with me he said goodbye."[42]

Leaving Savannah, Ransom spent a few days in Richmond and was paroled October 8, 1864. Returning north, he was admitted to a hospital and never rejoined his regiment. In post-war years he became a miner, raised a family and eventually was appointed a U.S. pension agent and examiner. It is assumed there were not many ex-prisoner claims he denied.

CHAPTER 9

'That begrimed, hungry family of Uncle Sam'

One thing consistently found in the Union Army was family members serving together. Savvy recruiters targeting a particular locality convinced thousands of fathers and sons, brothers, cousins and brothers-in-law to enlist at the same time in the same company or battery. Of those who joined together many were mere boys who otherwise would have been turned away if a father, uncle or older brother was not by their sides swaying recruiting officers. Scores of boy soldiers also were allowed to serve because a relative happened to be the recruiter.

The Eber C. Byam family of Mt. Vernon, Iowa, represents well how familial ties were used to gain admission for underage recruits in addition to other favors. The first member to follow the flag was Charles L. Byam, who joined the 6th Iowa in 1861 at age 15. He was severely wounded at Shiloh and discharged in August 1862. At the same time his 36-year-old father successfully solicited permission from the War Department to recruit a "temperance regiment," with a rendezvous of September 15. Eber Byam was appointed colonel of the newly formed 24th Iowa. Within a month all three of his sons became members of the regiment. William W. Byam mustered as a 14-year-old drummer in Company G, and nine-year-old Commodore Perry Byam followed suit the next day as drummer for Company D. With Charles' wound nearly healed his father appointed him regimental adjutant on September 17 at the modest age of 17.[1]

Unlike so many early-war appointees, Eber Byam stood up well to the task of leading the regiment. At Champion's Hill, Mississippi, in May 1863, he personally led his regiment's assault, in which the 24th Iowa sustained 189 casualties, the third highest Union loss in the battle.[2]

Unfortunately for the 24th and the Byam family, tragedy soon struck, ironically at home. During that summer Eber's only daughter died of diphtheria and a week later his wife also passed away. Eber resigned, returning to Iowa to attend the funerals and take care of pressing family matters. Perry Byam noted years later, "She [his mother] was only in her 37th year, the mother of three sons, all of whom, together with their father, were serving in the army at the time of her death; this, finally, being bitterly illustrative of the irony of fate: in that the father and sons should survive the carnage of war, whilst the mother and daughter who grieved for them should perish in a haven of supposed safety."[3]

Eber Byam's resignation took effect June 30, 1863, just as the siege of Vicksburg was coming to a close. Within a few weeks of his father's leaving Charles submitted his own resignation due to complications stemming from his Shiloh wound. The paperwork took effect July 22, and four days later the youngest of the boys, Perry, was gone, too. William Byam detailed his brother's departure in Perry's pension application. "I remember he was discharged at Vicksburg, Mississippi, on account of his age as he was too young for that character of service. Our brother Adjutant Charles Byam had been wounded in the leg at Shiloh and resigned at Vicksburg, and wanted to take [Perry] home with him. Our father had resigned prior to that time and brother Charles wanted to take brother Perry home as the surgeon of the regiment told Charles it was not right for him to go ... and leave that child Perry in the service." The surgeon no doubt did not wish to become a baby-sitter for the 10-year-old soldier.[4]

Perry was indeed a handful, even while his father was present. The regiment's officers were quite aware of his immature behavior, but felt constrained to curb it because his father was colonel. Detesting discipline, Perry admitted his shortcomings years later. "Reaching the siege of Vicksburg, a great change came over me. I was still exceedingly active, but my energies were usually applied in a manner that resulted in trouble. It was a season wherein drummers were in little demand, and a laxity in discipline prevailed among them. So far as I was personally concerned, I reached a stage where I was reliable only in my absolute unreliability. Regarded from my standpoint of view, my chief source of annoyance, and one which I bitterly resented, arose from the alleged friendship of a certain set of officers, whose system of espionage continually conflicted with my own private arrangements; and more especially pronounced was my loathing of their attentions when, upon occasion of the disappearance of any trifling luxury, or small article of military adornment, they would invariably cross-examine me in a most aggravating manner, rendered all the more embarrassing to me by reason of their views being usually secretly shared by myself. At night, in my bunk, I frequently destroyed these inquisitive officers, by methods which would have appalled the Spanish Inquisition."[5]

One of his boyish stunts illustrated why officers were eager to send Perry home after the fall of Vicksburg, as he explained: "Towards the close of the siege, so great was my desire to be in the van when the surrender took place, that I spent much of my time in the rifle pits. With a borrowed musket and ammunition I would load and fire with 'the best of them,' and this brings me to my last exploit, which is well known to many men still living, and was no less an achievement than my prematurely entering the enemy's works slightly in advance of the surrender. Not at all cast down by being held a prisoner for a few minutes, I

Private Marion McMillin
Company C
2nd West Virginia Cavalry

was soon out, and loudly boasting of having been 'the first man' to enter Vicksburg."[6]

With Perry's departure William was the only Byam still with the regiment. He campaigned and fought for the remainder of the war, returning home in mid-1865. Even then he was just 18 with three years' service behind him.[7]

Considering the number of large families typical of the 1860s, it was common to find three and even four family members serving together or separately during the war. The 2nd West Virginia Cavalry boasted six brothers of the McMillin family in its ranks. The McMillins lived near Buckeye Furnace in Jackson County, Ohio. When the war began three of the younger boys, Andrew, Emerson and Murray, enlisted in Company H. Marion, due to his age, was not permitted to go until December 1, 1863. He was the "baby" of the family. Milton and Harvey, the oldest, later joined when Company M was formed during the fall of 1864. Of the six it was the "baby" who never returned home.

As it happened, a battery was captured near Hanging Rock, Virginia, on June 21, 1864, by a 60-man detachment of Confederate guerrillas that swooped out of a mountain defile onto the unsuspecting artillerymen. The raiders rounded up prisoners and destroyed as much property as time allowed before nearby Union cavalry heard the commotion. It was not long until the battery's escort arrived at the scene of the short fight. Some artillerymen who had escaped to the woods by that time had set fire to remaining equipment so the Rebels would not be able to take it after dark. The conflagration had spread considerably by the time the cavalrymen returned, and a large area of underbrush was burning. Here and there rounds of ammunition and other explosive ordnance lay near the flames. When General George Crook's troops neared the site he stationed a guard on the road and detoured his command around the blaze. Colonel William H. Powell leading the 2nd West Virginia did likewise. But when the major in command of the column's rearguard came along, he seemed to "completely lose his head," for with loud and angry oaths he led his men directly through the burning area. In passing the major noticed a wagon full of powder and ordered it destroyed by some Company H boys of the 2nd who were with Lieutenant James W. Ricker nearby. Ricker argued that it was too dangerous, and pointed out the powder soon would be burned up anyway. The major insisted, calling Ricker's men cowards as he rode off a short distance to safety.

The lieutenant and his detail began offloading the powder, carrying it to an adjacent creek where it was dumped. Hot embers filled the air around them as they worked. In a few minutes an explosion occurred, and a few seconds later the powder still in the wagon blew up with shattering effect, killing and injuring more than half the detail. One of the dead was "baby" Marion McMillin. When he first enlisted Company H's roster was full, so he was mustered into Company C. Since three of his brothers were in Company H he often rode with that command, and was doing so on the day of the explosion. Within moments of the blast Emerson and Murray McMillin hurried to the scene, but all they could do was gaze at his lifeless body.[8]

It was natural for older brothers to watch over younger siblings. For the McMillins, losing their youngest must have been a horrible shock. Not only were the remaining brothers consumed with grief, they were obliged to inform family members back home of the tragic news.

Richard M. Crane was faced with this heartbreaking task in 1864. He had enlisted in Company D, 7th Wisconsin, at 18. At Gettysburg he was captured, sent to Richmond, and paroled a month later. On October 7, 1863, he returned to the regiment. His two younger brothers, Stephen and Rashio, were added to the 7th's roster as replacements early in 1864. At the time of their reunion Richard was the oldest at 20, and Rashio the youngest at 15.[9]

As the Army of the Potomac moved south of the Rapidan River that May, Richard kept a diary of daily events. On May 5, after being heavily engaged in the Wilderness, he wrote: "Moved soon after daylight. Advanced in line of battle about a mile and a half. Our Brig. suffered severely. Our Co. lost twelve men. Brother Rashio missing. Moved to the left this evening to support the second Corps. Did not get engaged. On the skirmish line, till after midnight. Heavy fighting."

The 6th was "a terrible day. No news from Rashio. Fear he is a prisoner." After marching toward Spotsylvania Court House more fighting took place. On the 9th Richard again wrote, "Can learn nothing about Rashio."

More fighting transpired on May 10. "Another bloody day. Our line advanced about M. Woods thick. The enemy in strong breastworks. Our Co. lost four wounded and three missing. Brother Stephen wounded. George Kocher missing. Nothing gained here on the right. Gen. Rice wounded. Reported that Gen. Sedgwick and Robinson killed. Had my gun stalk shot off. Lay in our breastworks."

On the 11th he scrawled, "This is the eleventh day of the fight. Probably the greatest of the war. Stephen returned to the Co. His wound not bad." The next day he noted they fought five hours and he fired about 200 cartridges. On May 16 a member of Company A told Richard he saw "Brother Rashio dead on the field," to which he responded, "Can it be possible? I can't believe it. Another tells me that he saw him after the fight was over." The anxiety worsened when he learned Stephen was "quite sick" and had gone to the hospital.[10] In a letter Richard relayed the unsettling information to a relative in Wisconsin.

In line of Battle near Spotsylvania
Court House May 19th 1864

Dear Cousin,

I will write you a line to let you know where I am. You have heard of the hard fighting that has been going on here for the last two weeks and I presume you will be anxious to hear from us. I have some bad news[.] Brother Rashio is missing[.] he went into battle with us on the 5th of the Month and has not been seen since. We think he is a prisoner[.] While we were fighting on the 5th Rashio was with the other drummers carrying off wounded. We drove the Enemy about a mile and then they turned and drove us back again. I did not see Rashio after the engagement commenced. The Drummers all think that he must have tired out on the retreat – and been taken prisoner. We have done some very hard fighting and lost very heavily. I have not got room to give you anything of a description of it. We left Culpeper on the 4th inst. and have been marching and fighting ever since. We have been in eight engagements. Our Co. has lost twenty-two men wounded and missing and have ten left. Our Regt. has suffered in proportion. Stephen was slightly wounded in the side on the 10th but he did not leave the Regt. he staid with me until the 15th when he went away sick. Our hard marching used him up[.] I fear that he will have a run of fever. Scott Bell is the only one of the boys that was at Racine with Rashio that is left and he has been slightly wounded. George Kocher was wounded in the heart. We have had some very hard fighting but I believe it has been a big victory to us. We have gained considerable ground. We are about two miles south of Fredericksburg. We are in line of battle and may fight at any time. I have been through all our fighting so far and have not got a scratch[.] I don't know how it is that I am so lucky. It may be my turn next. See Aunt Susan and let her know how we are up to the present. I shall write as often as possible. I have written to Mother twice since we left camp. We have not had any mail for nearly three weeks.[11]

Richard's premonition of "my turn next" proved true six days later at the North Anna River, where he was wounded severely in the left leg. In less than three weeks all three brothers became casualties — Richard and Stephen wounded, and Rashio, as everyone thought, a prisoner of war.

Mary Crane, their mother, was at wit's end. Worried about Richard's wound, which in a gangrenous state had eaten away much of his leg muscle, she traveled east seeking permission to have him transferred to a Wisconsin hospital. A letter she mailed to medical Inspector General Joseph K. Barnes got right to the point.

New York City, August 13th 1864

Sir

Please pardon a stranger for intruding on your time. I would say without further remarks, I am directed by the Medical Directory of this city to address a few lines to you, in regard to a transfer for my son R M Crane of Co D 7th Regt Wisconsin Volunteers who was wounded the 25th of May (last) in the Army of the Potomac Whare he has served one term and reenlisted. I am a Widow[,] have three Sons, and they are all in the service of their Country[.] one of them has been taken Prisoner and is now in the hands of the Rebels. An other that was wounded Before Spotsylvania, and has since became helpless and this one R M Crane is at Portsmouth Grove Hospital R.I. I want to get him transferd to our own state Wisconsin[.] We have a good Hospital at Madison Wis[.] I can only get him transferd to the Hospital now[.] I would be greatly Obliged to you[.] I have two little daughters at home and am needed there every moment. I have often been told it was not my duty to let all my sons go in the Army but they was an[x]ious to do something for our Country in this our time of trouble and I could not say "No" and now I am left, as you see, to do the best I can. I will close least I weary you[.] Please make my case your own and assist a Mother in this her time of need.

Her request was granted. Richard was sent west to

A January 1862 visit to a portrait gallery by 12-year-old musician George W.M. Masury of Company H, 60th New York, and Second Lieutenant Marcellus L. Fitch resulted in this striking image.

Author's Collection

Madison, where he convalesced until discharged May 20, 1865. Stephen, after months of hospitalization, was discharged the previous month. But even as Mary Crane penned her letter to Colonel Barnes, 15-year-old Rashio was dead, a victim of Andersonville.[12]

Mrs. John Masury of Brownsville, New York, allowed all four of her sons to join the Union Army, the youngest at age 11. When the 60th New York was formed during the latter months of 1861, her two youngest volunteered their services to Captain James M. Ransom's Company H and were mustered October 17. William T. Masury, standing only four foot eleven, was 14. George W.M. Masury, born October 20, 1849, celebrated his 12th birthday three days after enlisting and stood slightly shorter than William at four foot nine. Only a few months elapsed before the service's hardships sent both boys to the hospital. George fell sick first in August 1862 and was admitted to a Baltimore hospital. William lasted a month longer, ending up in the same infirmary September 14. Eventually the brothers were sent to the Army's general hospital at Steuart's Mansion. While there the matron of nurses gave them special care. Despite the extra attention they were discharged in December 1862 because they had been disabled for more than 60 days.[13]

Surprisingly, the following March they were mustered into Company A, 106th New York. The youngsters were readily accepted because an older brother, John, was a sergeant in the company. But little George once again could not endure soldiering. In November Surgeon Thomas R. Crosby found him "incapable of performing the duties of a soldier because of Debility and a delicacy of organization which renders him unfit for service having existed since August 15, 1863. This soldier is not physically suitable to enter or reenlist in the invalid corps." George still was not willing to give up, no matter what the doctor said. In February 1866, at age 16, he joined Battery K, 3rd U.S. Artillery. Ironically, a year later he was discharged on the technicality of being a minor, five and a half years after he was accepted as a drummer boy during the Civil War.[14]

Brother William also was plagued by illness, spending more than eight months in various hospitals while with the 106th. His maladies may have stemmed from his capture at Martinsburg, Virginia, on June 14, 1863. Enduring 30 days in prison, his health wavered for two years until he was discharged after hostilities ended.[15]

John C. Masury was listed as 18 on his company descriptive list, but mustered with parental consent — an indication he was underage when enlisting in August 1862. John, who worked for a dentist prior to his enlistment, was well liked by his superiors and soon promoted to corporal and general guide of the regiment. In that position he carried a small pendant or flag to help the men keep alignment during maneuvers. In early 1863 he was further promoted to sergeant. At Spotsylvania May 12, 1864, he received a gunshot wound to his left leg, almost destroying the ankle joint.[16]

That summer, with two sons lying in hospitals, their distressed mother pleaded by mail to have William returned home.

> Brownsville Jefferson Co. N.Y.
> August 30, 1864.
>
> Surgeon G.S. Parmler
>   Dear Sir,
>   We are very anxious to have our son William T. Masury, fifer, come home for a short furlough. His father has been an invalid for many years and he has had many severe spells of sickness than usual this summer, which has discouraged him about living to see his dear boys again. We have given all our sons (4) to fight in this great struggle to preserve the best government the sun ever shone upon, and the eldest we hear is dead, and the second badly wounded. These are the circumstances and we feel that you will be pleased to gratify us in seeing William if possible. If you are obliged to refuse us make the denial as pleasant and kind for him as possible. With many wishes for your health and safety with much respect I am Mrs. John Masury.[17]

In William's case it appears the request was denied, but John was given a 60-day furlough on October 10. At its expiration he still was unable to return to the regiment. For a while he was listed as a deserter. In time it was shown he was permanently incapacitated and never again soldiered. As for the oldest Masury son who died during the war, his name and record cannot be traced.[18]

Whenever brothers, or fathers and sons, were united in the field it was a special, joyous occurrence. "I would join my brother at all hazards," thought 14-year-old George Ulmer shortly after his sibling Charles reached legal age and enlisted in Company H, 8th Maine, in October 1862. George persevered in spite of his parents' wishes, and on March 23, 1864, was accepted as a recruit in his brother's company at age 16.[19] After an adventuresome sojourn he arrived May 16 at the 8th's camp in General Benjamin Butler's Army of the James. Years afterward he described the emotionally charged night finding his brother at the front.

> I started out across the fields in the direction of a light — on, on I tramped, into ditches, through mires, over fences. The farther I went the faster I went. I was so impatient I could not hold myself to a walk; it was a dog-trot all the time. I was heedless of every obstacle, till I began to near the front. I realized the danger by the whizzing of shells, and the zip, zip of bullets. I found myself among lots of soldiers, and how ragged and dirty the poor fellows looked. I asked the first man I came to where the Eighth Maine was. He looked at me in perfect astonishment. "This is the Eighth, what's left of it." I asked him if he knew where my brother was. Charlie Ulmer? "Oh, yes," he said, pointing to a little group of men, who were round a wee bit of a fire. "There he is, don't you know him?"
>
> I hesitated, for really I could hardly tell one from the other. He saw my bewilderment, and took me by the hand and led me over to the fire. They all started and stared at me, and to save my life I could not tell which was my brother. But one more ragged than the rest uttered a suppressed cry, rushed forward, and throwing his arms about my neck, sobbed and cried like a child. "My God! My brother! Oh, George, George, why did you come here?" His grief seemed to touch them all, for they all began to wipe their eyes with their ragged coat-sleeves. This began to tell on me, and for the next ten minutes it was a kind of blubbering camp. After a while they reconciled themselves, and began to ply me with questions faster than I could answer. My brother sat down with me and lectured me very soundly for coming, as there was no need of it. He gave me such a graphic description of the hardships they had endured, and I can never obliterate the picture he presented that night. His clothes were ragged and patched, begrimed with smoke, grease and dirt; his hat an old soft one, with part of the rim gone and the crown perforated with bullet holes; his beard scraggly and dirty; his big toes peeping out of a pair of old boots with the heels all run down; in fact, he was a sight —

Brothers Martin B. and Augustus B. Gilbert served respectively in Companies C and H, 91st Ohio. Martin, 13, enlisted three weeks earlier than his 18-year-old sibling in the summer of 1862. Augustus died of disease at home in Portsmouth, Ohio, on March 27, 1864. Martin continued drumming until his June 1865 muster-out. Nicknamed "Jude, the old soldier" a quarter-century after the war, he was murdered September 25, 1893, in a Mississippi River fishing camp north of St. Louis.

Alan E. Hoeweler Collection

that begrimed, hungry family of Uncle Sam was on the march to the river. We were marched on board an old ferry boat, and crowded so thickly that we could scarcely stand. My brother seemed now to feel that he had the responsibility of my comfort, even my life, on his hands. And being a favorite he elbowed me a place at the end of the boat, where we could sit down by letting our feet hang over the end of the boat. In that position we remained. We didn't have room to stand up and turn around. I was awful sleepy, but dared not go to sleep for fear I would fall overboard. Finally my brother fixed me so I could lay my head back, and he held on to me while I slept.[20]

When Albert Roberts of Company K, 45th Pennsylvania, enlisted as a drummer at the age of 13, he was the first of three brothers to join the regiment. Oldest brother William, 22, joined Company K as a private in August 1862, and Edward, 15, obtained their father's consent to enlist in the 45th in March 1864, also as a drummer.[21] On Albert's enlistment day his father, Edward Roberts Sr., accompanied him to camp

a strong contrast to my tailor-made suit. I will never forget the expression on my brother's face when about half an hour after my arrival he looked up to me with his eyes half full of tears glistening on that dirty face, and with a kind of cynical smile, asked, after looking me over: "What are you, anyhow?"

I told him I didn't know.

"Well, after you have been here a while, those pretty clothes won't look as they do now, and you will probably find out what you are after you have dodged a few shells."

Our conversation was brought to a climax by orders to break camp and fall in. We learned we were going to embark somewhere on a boat. Everything was hustle-bustle now; little shelter tents were struck, tin cups, canteens, knapsacks were made ready, and in about fifteen minutes

161

Illustration from the December 19, 1863, issue of *Harper's Weekly*.

and asked Captain Thomas Welsh "to take good care of Rollie," as the boy was nicknamed by family and friends. Albert stood less than five feet tall and labored with a mild speech impediment.[22] Nonetheless, he soon became the regiment's pet.

His bravery at times was almost too much for comrades to behold, and more than once during his service childish behavior caused him harm. The 45th's chief musician, Abraham Girod, recollected that "He was a very useful and good soldier and courageous to the full extent of a boyish waist. At Pleasant Valley near Antietam he was blowed up by a bag of powder captured from a Rebel caisson. His youth and thoughtless courage made him the subject of the care of our officers and older soldiers. I remember seeing Major

[Edward A.] Kelsey of our regiment 'spank' him with his scabbard at the battle of Blue Springs, East Tennessee, because he insisted upon staying in danger at the front of the line." [23]

Following Albert's powder mishap William Roberts wrote their parents describing his foolishness. "Brother Albert met with a serious accident while we lay in camp at Pleasant Valley, and came near losing his eyesight. He gathered a lot of cartridges and poured the powder into an empty sardine box. He then got a coal of fire and carried it between two sticks, when it fell into the powder before he was ready, and while his face was directly over the box, with the result that his hair and eyelashes were singed off and his eyes filled with the burnt powder. He was in the hospital several weeks and it was thought that he would lose his sight, but he came out all right."[24]

In a letter composed July 24, 1863, William provided another tale involving Albert's indiscretions which landed him in the hospital again. "Brother Rollie met with an accident on the 3d of July. He was swinging on a grapevine, when he lost his hold and fell about 15 feet into a ravine, breaking his right arm near the wrist joint, and otherwise injuring himself. Dr. Horace Ludington, the brigade surgeon, dressed his injuries, and he has been in the hospital ever since. I understand he is improving rapidly." On August 23 he mentioned the boy's "arm is almost well from the accident he met with in Mississippi, and he is able to use the drumsticks again, though his arm is crooked at the wrist."[25]

Albert's injury became an issue years later when he tried to obtain an invalid pension. Before the pension commissioner would grant it he had to prove the accident occurred in the line of duty. His voluminous pension file contains differing views from different comrades. At the time of the mishap Company K was detailed at division headquarters. It had just arrived at a new camp situated on uneven, heavily overgrown terrain. The area had been quarried for slate years before and was riven with large holes. Albert claimed he "had been frying some crackers in fat, and his hands were greasy, and catching hold of a grapevine on the bank of an old quarry to save himself from falling his hands slipped and he fell down the quarry some thirty feet, falling on his right side with his right arm under him.... It was dark at the time of the accident."[26]

The tumble momentarily knocked him unconscious, as William's affidavit stated. "... someone told me that my brother Albert had fallen. I discovered him at the bottom of a stone quarry and I hastened to pick him up believing him to be killed. When I reached him he was in a senseless condition and had fallen almost perpendicularly about 40 feet. He was unable to tell me how he happened to fall. There were soldiers nearby but no one seemed to know much about it and their statements conflicted. As near as I could understand it was owing to the dangerous condition of the camp which was full of pits and rough places.... He had occasion to go out on a call of nature and he may have gone into the brush on that account." Others corroborated this theme, but Lieutenant Ephraim E. Myers, when questioned by the pension board, avowed, "I

will state here about the way he received his injury. While laying in camp near Mill Dale Landing, Miss. he got upon a large grapevine and commenced to swing and he fell down." With that, Albert argued his case in another direction. "I was injured in the 'line of duty' and on the same principle which has entitled hundreds of soldiers to receive pensions for injuries received from runaway horses, falling branches, accidental discharge of firearms, falling stacked guns, wrecked ships and [rail] cars, etc."[27]

After soliciting recommendations from two generals, he finally received his pension. For brother William, procuring one was much easier due to the battle of the Wilderness.[28]

On May 6, 1864, Companies K and A of the 45th Pennsylvania were chosen as skirmishers to advance into the Wilderness' thick underbrush. As William related, they soon encountered resistance. "The first man I saw fall was Simon Sanders of Company K. He was the second man from me on the left, Frank P. Swears being between us. Major Kelsey ordered Frank and myself to go see how badly he was wounded. We both went to him and called, but received no answer. We turned him over and found a bullet had pierced his heart, killing him instantly. After pronouncing him dead the Major ordered us back to our respective places. As Frank and I were exposed to the full view of the enemy we expected the same fate, but for some unexplained reason they did not fire on us. After resuming my position and firing three or four shots a bullet pierced my left arm near the shoulder and the Major ordered me to the rear." At a field hospital the regimental hospital steward dressed the wound. Later in the day a surgeon wanted to amputate, but William refused so vehemently the doctor dismissed him and went to the next case.[29]

On May 13 he informed his parents how their three boys fared in the fight. "When I left the regiment at Chancellorsville, Va., last Sunday morning, Edward and Albert were both sound and well. Being drummer boys they are not necessarily exposed to the dangers of the battle, as their duties as musicians are to assist in attending to the wounded in time of battle; but they are exposed more or less."[30] Abraham Girod recalled that Albert was "generally employed in holding the funnel for administering chloroform after engagements as he was not regarded as strong enough to carry a stretcher."[31]

163

Knox County, Ohio, resident Benjamin Knox of Company H, 20th Ohio, died in his company's quarters after receiving a gunshot wound August 10, 1864, in the trenches before Atlanta.

Jeffrey S. Creamer Collection

engaged July 22 in the battle of Atlanta, fending off repeated Confederate assaults while fighting on both sides of its breastworks. During the mêlée Robert Elliott of Company F discovered his brother Mathias of the same company lying dead on the works. Robert was so incensed he stood beside his brother's body, loading and firing at the Rebels until he, too, was struck down and died at Mathias' side.[36]

In the weeks following the battle both sides kept up a steady fire of small and large calibers, settling down to siege-style warfare. Private Ira S. Owens of Company C, 74th Ohio, described the front during that time in his diary: "Went on picket at night, it being dangerous to relieve pickets in the daytime, the picket-line being within a few rods of the rebel line. It was very disagreeable ... raining a good portion of the time, so as to render sleep impossible. When we got into the pit, it was nearly filled with mud and water, and after daylight it was very risky standing up. We could not stand up, lie, or sit down, but had to remain in a crouching position, which was very tiresome." Other days the sun baked Unionists and Confederates alike, as Captain Isaac J. Rogers of the 27th Alabama wrote: "The weather was extremely warm and the troops suffered very much being continually in line of Battle exposed to the hot rays of the sun. Working and picketing all day and night. I had four holes Shot through my clothes and one through my cap while on this line."[37]

Such were the conditions on the day Benjamin Knox's name was added to the list of those whose lives were sacrificed for Atlanta. He was shot by a musket ball and died shortly afterward in his company's quarters. It is not known if his brothers were at his side to provide words of encouragement and hope, as he had done when Edward was wounded the year before.[38]

During the summer of 1861 Wesley T. Fissell en-

In June, Edward was wounded in battle at Bethesda Church, Virginia. By war's end all three Roberts brothers were healthy enough to go home.[32] Considering the 45th Pennsylvania was among the top 25 Union regiments suffering the greatest number of men killed between 1861 and 1865, it is remarkable they survived.[33]

The 20th Ohio's ranks included the three Knox brothers — Charles (Company H), Edward (Company E) and Benjamin (Company H). Edward was wounded in the leg near Vicksburg on May 29, 1863, and that day inscribed in his diary: "We arose this morning early. I was detailed to go after water. I was wounded by one of our own men; I had to get in a ambulance as there was no hospital there. I rode over a rough rode and suffered much." While recuperating he mentioned several visits by his brothers and how glad he was to see them. He eventually returned to his company.[34]

Fifteen-year-old Benjamin enlisted in November 1861. He was present for duty every day as a musket-carrying private until August 10, 1864, when he was shot near Atlanta.[35] The 20th Ohio had been heavily

listed in Company H, 30th Ohio.[39] Ten days later his 21-year-old brother John joined Company C of the 20th Ohio.[40] Two other brothers, George and Joseph, were forced to stay home due to their age. For a year the younger siblings, enthralled by newspaper stories and correspondence from their brothers at the front, became more determined to enlist. At this time Captain George E. Ross began recruiting for the 45th Ohio in the Fissells' hometown of Darbyville, Pickaway County, Ohio. Joseph was the first to step forward. For the next seven days he played a drum for Ross to help in the company's recruitment. By then he had persuaded the captain of his usefulness and was allowed to join. Two days later his 18-year-old brother George also signed the list of Company A's recruits.[41]

After formation it headed to Camp Chase for inspection and muster on August 19, 1862. Joseph, born September 1, 1851, was just shy of his 11th birthday. A family story relates that when his mother learned her husband allowed her youngest to enlist, she became frantic and ordered him to Columbus to bring Joseph home. By the time the boy's father arrived the regiment and her boys already were on their way to Kentucky.[42]

Through the remainder of 1862 the 45th Ohio was stationed south of Cincinnati, defensively posturing against any attack on the Queen City. In February 1863 the regiment was issued horses and served as mounted infantry for the next year. During that period it saw hard service, including pursuit of General John Hunt Morgan when his Confederate cavalry raided Ohio in July 1863. The chase was so aggressive that one 45th Ohio trooper, Silas J. Mann, wore out seven horses and traveled the last few miles on foot before Morgan's surrender.[43]

For most of the time the regiment was mounted Joseph was home on extended sick leave. He was allowed to remain there until February 1864, when he returned to his company. It seems no coincidence that as soon as the 45th received its horses he was sent home, then rejoined as quickly as it was dismounted. How well an 11-year-old burdened with a drum could have managed an animal over Kentucky's rugged countryside can only be surmised. During Joseph's furlough his mother once again urged his father to visit Ohio's governor to secure his discharge. Upon being interviewed by Governor David Tod in the presence of his father, the boy was asked if he wanted to stay

Drummer Joseph Fissell, 45th Ohio, was the youngest of four brothers who served the Union. While visiting one of them in front of Atlanta, he was instructed to keep his head down. "Boylike," Joseph recalled, "I became careless and looked over the trench rim. Whizz! A bullet embedded itself in a tree behind the rifle pit."

Ohio Historical Society

On April 20, 1865, Illinois brothers James, left, and Luther Backus reunited to be photographed at Dalton, Georgia.

Author's Collection

home or return to the Army. Joseph chose the latter and the affair was settled.[44]

In September 1864 he was detailed as an orderly at Fourth Corps headquarters, acting in that capacity until mustered out with brother George and the rest of Company A on June 12, 1865.[45] When they reached Pickaway County they were greeted by Wesley, John and their elated parents. John had been wounded in the shoulder in May 1863 at Champion's Hill, and was discharged a year later.[46] Wesley decided not to reenlist as a veteran volunteer, and came home in August 1864.[47] Mrs. Fissell, who worried so much about her boys, was gratified to see all of them return.

The mother of David, James and Jacob Shanklin of Wooster, Ohio, was not as fortunate. Only James, who enlisted in the 41st Ohio shortly after turning 15, survived. At Orchard Knob two days prior to the storming of Missionary Ridge outside Chattanooga, James and Jacob were wounded. Jacob's injury proved fatal four days later. With his older brother dead, James declined reenlistment and was discharged in September 1864 at the end of his three-year term. Five months later, however, he and brother David joined Company F, 187th Ohio. Although the war ended within two weeks of the regiment's departure south, its members were obligated to serve their one-year enlistment. While performing provost duty near Macon, Georgia, David fell ill and died six months after hostilities ceased. Jacob returned to Wooster in January 1866 and a well deserved welcome.[48]

Luther Backus was another recruit who enlisted during the Confederacy's twilight. In August 1862, when older brother James joined Company A, 75th Illinois, Luther was 13 — too young to persuade his parents in Dixon, Illinois, to let him go. As the war progressed Luther watched for news from the front. James, serving as a fifer, had plenty to write home about. His regiment was heavily engaged at Perryville, Stones River and Chickamauga. Finally, in February

1865, Luther, now 16, obtained permission to enlist as a drummer in the newly-formed 147th Illinois. In three months the rebellion was over, but his obligation was not. Luther performed provost duty in northwest Georgia for nine months. His war record was highlighted by no battles or exhausting campaigns, but he served his country well nonetheless.[49]

Hundreds of young boys also served with their fathers. Among the first and youngest to take up arms was Thomas L.F. Hubler of Indiana. Three days after Fort Sumter's shelling "Little Tommy" and his father Henry enlisted in the 12th Indiana Infantry. At enlistment Tommy, born October 9, 1851, was nine years, six months and six days old. Interestingly, his father marked his age on the parental consent form as 14. Tommy served the entire war, mustering out June 8, 1865. Of all underage boys it is probable he was the youngest to spend the most time in the Union Army. He participated in more than 20 battles and skirmishes, and was the pride of his regiment.[50]

On September 30, 1862, seven days after John C. Foster was appointed principal musician of the 92nd

Ohio, his 13-year-old son Eben enlisted as a musician in Company I. Eben served throughout the war while his father was discharged for disability in the spring of 1864. John B. Wood Jr. was 14 when he and his father enlisted together in November 1861 in Company K, 76th Ohio. John Jr. served two and a half years as a musician after John Sr., 44, went home with wrecked health in October 1862.[51] Fifty-year-old William Lyons took along his 12-year-old son, John, when enlisting in the 81st Ohio. Father and son were both accepted despite being outside age standards set for recruits. Unable to withstand the rigors of soldiering they each received disability discharges in 1862.[52]

When First Lieutenant William Ambrose of Company G, 22nd Ohio, was dismissed for drunkenness in December 1862, he asked to take his 13-year-old son William H. Ambrose with him. The younger Ambrose, a drummer in Company E, was quite ill for a two-month period but improved during July 1862. From that time he served well, but with his father returning home others agreed it would be best for him to go, too. To obtain leave for the boy his company commander made the following appeal.

Camp 22nd Ohio Infantry Vols.
Jackson Tenn. March 15th 1863

Major Henry Binmore A.A.G.

Sir

I respectfully ask that leave of absence for twenty days be granted to William H. Ambrose Musician Co. E, 22 Ohio Infantry Vols. for the following reasons. He is very young and in delicate health[,] his age being but thirteen years and he is unable to take the necessary care of himself with the Regiment to restore his health. Also his father William Ambrose[,] recently a First lieutenant in the Regiment[,] has been dismissed from the service and desires to take his son ... home with him for the time above specified.

Respectfully
Wm. E. Lockwood Capt.
Comdg Co. E

By day's end the request was granted. William's father secured for him a disability discharge with the certification: "General debility from chronic diarrhea and from mere youthfulness being only 13 years of age." [53]

William H. Howe was another father who allowed his very young boys to enlist at his side. In June 1861 William and 10-year-old son Lyston joined Company

Illinois State
Historical Library

Musician Lyston D. Howe of Waukegan, Illinois, soldiered three and a half years with the 15th and 55th Illinois before mustering out at age 14.

I, 15th Illinois Infantry, as musicians. Lyston's stay was short, being discharged for minority on October 21, but after William was transferred to the 55th Illinois and appointed principal musician, he procured Lyston a position in Company B as drummer. Seven months later older brother Orion joined the ranks of Company C. Orion, also a musician, was born December 29, 1849, and was just eight months older than Lyston. After campaigning together for a few months father Howe was discharged in February 1863, leaving his two boys in the Army.[54]

Lyston served his complete three-year enlistment and mustered out February 28, 1865. The 55th Illinois was a hard-fighting unit in which one of three members was killed or died of wounds or disease. Two-thirds of its enrollment were wounded in 31 different engagements. Lyston could have been proud of his service if he was a full-grown man, but to have been present between the ages of 10 and 14 was remarkable. At the time of his departure he was the last of the family in the Army, but not the most notable.[55]

Orion P. Howe, right, was the celebrated "drummer boy of Vicksburg" and the subject of the poem "Calibre 54," describing his brief encounter with General Sherman on May 19, 1863. Howe's regimental commander, Colonel Oscar Malmborg, joined him for this photograph.

U.S. Army Military History Institute

Orion Page Howe's conduct May 19, 1863, at Vicksburg earned national attention. Captain Henry S. Nourse of the 55th detailed the day's events and their aftermath:

Among the several boy musicians of the regiment the youngest were two sons of Principal Musician Howe.... They were both small for their years. Our "infant drummers" attracted much attention on dress parade in the great camps of instruction, at Camp Douglas [in Chicago], even rivaling our original "giant color-guard." [56] The little Howes drummed well, proved hardy, never seemed homesick, were treated as regimental pets, and passed through battle after battle, and march after march, untouched by disease, unscathed by bullet and shell.

In the charge of May 19th [Orion] Howe, like the other musicians, with a white handkerchief tied about the left arm to designate him as a non-combatant, followed in the rear of the line to assist the wounded. At the advanced position finally held by the regiment, it was essential to our safety not to allow cessation in the firing, and cartridge-boxes became rapidly depleted. Ammunition, from the difficulties of the ground, could only be brought to us by special messengers and in such quantity as they were able to carry about the person. Sergeant Major [Joseph] Hartsook was instructed to go back to the regimental ordnance wagon, take command of the musicians and such other men as he might find detailed near our camp, and send them to the front one by one with cartridges. This dangerous duty was promptly and well performed.

The little drummer, by his own statement, was not at this time with the other musicians, but in a ravine just in rear of the regiment, having been ordered back from the front to be out of danger, by the colonel. About him were several dead and wounded men. Collecting the ammunition from their cartridge-boxes, and using his blouse for a sack, he carried this up to the command. Flattered with some praise then received, he started for the ordnance wagon and returned in safety, with his small but valuable contribution. Again he sped down across the ravine and up the steep opposite slope. We could see him nearly the whole way as he ran through what seemed like a hailstorm of canister and musket-balls, so thickly did these fall about him, each throwing up its little puff of dust where it struck the dry hillside. Suddenly he dropped, and hearts sank thinking his brief career ended; but he had only tripped over some obstacle. Often he stumbled, sometimes he fell prostrate, but was quick up again, and finally disappeared from us, limping, over the summit, and the Fifty-Fifth saw him no more for several months. As the boy sped away the last time the colonel shouted to him, as he alleges, "Bring caliber fifty-four." General Sherman's letter to the War Department will best tell the rest of the story:

Headquarters Fifteenth Army Corps,
Camp on Big Black, Aug. 8, 1863.

Hon. E.M. Stanton, Secretary of War.

Sir: I take the liberty of asking through you that something be done for a young lad named Orion P. Howe of Waukegan, Illinois, who belongs to the 55th Illinois, but is at present absent at his home, wounded. I think he is too young for West Point, but would be the very thing for a midshipman.

When the assault on Vicksburg was at its height, on the 19th of May, and I was in front near the road which formed my line of attack, this young lad came to me wounded and bleeding, with a good healthy boy's cry: "General Sherman, send some cartridges to Colonel Malmborg, the men are all out." "What is the matter my boy?" "They shot me in the leg, sir, but I can go to the hospital. Send the cartridges right away!" Even where we stood the shot fell thick, and I told him to go to the rear at once, I would attend to the cartridges; and off he limped. Just before he disappeared on the hill, he turned and called as loud as he could, "Calibre 54!"

I have not seen the boy since, and his colonel, Malmborg, on inquiring, gave me his address as above, and says he is a bright, intelligent boy, with a fair preliminary education. What arrested my attention there was, and what renews my memory of the fact now is, that one so young, carrying a musket ball wound through his leg, should have found his way to me on that fatal spot, and delivered his message, not forgetting the very important part even of the calibre of the musket, 54, which you know is an unusual one.

I'll warrant the boy has in him the elements of a man, and I commend him to the government as one worthy the fostering care of some one of its National institutions.

I am, with respect, your obedient servant,
W.T. Sherman. Maj. Gen. Commanding.[57]

Orion's meritorious deed not only secured Sherman's endorsement, it also generated poems and songs about the incident. The most well known verses were composed by George H. Boker and published in the September 1864 *Atlantic Monthly.* Captain Nourse pointed out that caliber "54" was incorrect, as the rifle-muskets the 55th Illinois carried used .58 caliber ammunition. But he observed it was more important that Orion's attitude and actions were being recognized and commended.[58]

The boy's leg wound earned him a furlough on June 5 for 30 days; however, it was extended until his return August 27. For a Christmas present that year he was sent north again on recruiting service, and also about that time was promoted corporal. When he returned in early April 1864 he was attached to the headquarters of General Morgan L. Smith as an orderly. On October 1, 1864, by order of the Secretary of War, he was discharged to prepare for the U.S. Naval Academy as requested by General Sherman. Orion attended the school for two years before failing to make the grade. Afterward he joined the merchant marine and almost was drowned in a shipwreck off the Irish coast in 1867. Having enough of the sea he tried cowboy life, chasing Indians in the West for a few years until finally settling down back in Illinois, where he remained.[59]

On April 23, 1896, Orion was awarded a Medal of Honor for his Vicksburg heroism, the citation reading: "A drummer boy, 14 years of age, and severely wounded and exposed to a heavy fire from the enemy, he persistently remained upon the field of battle until he had reported to Gen. W.T. Sherman the necessity of supplying cartridges for the use of troops under command of Col. Malmborg."[60]

More common than fathers leaving early and sons staying were cases of a father seeing his mistake and sending the youngster home. The service of John Mackey, 103rd Pennsylvania, and Albert White, 64th Ohio, abruptly ended when their officer-fathers realized the Army was no place for children.

Drummer George S. Canfield was 13 when he and his father, Captain Silas S. Canfield, were mustered in Company K, 21st Ohio, during the fall of 1861. The senior Canfield was taken prisoner at Chickamauga with 115 fellow officers and men on Horseshoe Ridge when they exhausted ammunition for their Colt's revolving rifles. He was sent to Libby Prison in Richmond.[61]

The captain's capture eventually led to George's discharge in January 1864. By then he was 15 but extremely small and slender. As the regiment prepared to veteranize, its commander, Captain James L. Curry, requested George's discharge due to his frail constitution and his father being at Libby. With approval George was permitted to travel home with the men who were going north on furlough. Captain Canfield eventually was released and mustered out with the 21st. After the regiment's experience at Chickamauga it is likely he served the rest of the war well satisfied his boy was safely back in Ohio.[62]

Motivation for fathers taking young sons to the Army was varied. One father, perhaps thinking his son was safer by his side, was principal musician Edwin Harris of the 133rd Ohio. In April 1864 Edwin was shot through the arm and body at his home near Gahanna in Franklin County, Ohio, by a member of a secret, pro-South organization known as the Sons of Liberty. He already had thwarted two previous attempts on his life, and had been warned repeatedly because of his political beliefs. Within two hours more than 200 armed Union men appeared at the house in support of the Harris family, and to let Peace Democrats know such actions would not be tolerated.

At the time of his wounding Edwin was a member of the Ohio National Guard. When the Guard was called for duty and federalized as the 133rd Ohio Infantry during May, he was appointed principal musician despite his injuries. Fearing for his 11-year-old son Lucious' welfare, and knowing most Union men would be away with the Guard, Edwin enlisted him as drummer of Company F. Father and son served their 100-day term in more relative safety than perhaps they would have at home, where they returned in August 1864.[63]

At times it was a boy's inspiring zeal that caused his father to enlist. Fifteen-year-old Albert Busiel enticed his father Harrison to join the 12th New Hampshire, as did William Bircher his father in the 2nd Minnesota.

The younger Bircher, 15, caught war fever while smoke still drifted over Fort Sumter. When the 2nd Minnesota was recruiting near his home in the summer of 1861 he tried repeatedly to enlist, but was rejected because of his diminutive size and age. "But Captain J.J. Noah, of Company K, seemed to think that I would make a drummer," he reflected, "as the company was in need of one. I was then taken to the office of mustering-officer Major Nelson, and, after being questioned very carefully in regard to my age, was not accepted until I should get the consent of my parents. On the receipt of this decision I immediately walked to St. Paul and broached the subject to my parents, who of course objected, but after seeing that I was determined in my idea of becoming a soldier, my father also took the patriotic fever and we both enlisted in K Company of the Second regiment."[64]

Levi Leach recalled years after the war that his 15-year-old son, William, chastised him by saying, "Father, this rebellion must be put down, and we must go and help do it." William enlisted in Company I, 12th New Hampshire, on August 14, 1862. The next day Levi, moved by his son's words, followed suit and became a member of the same company. His wife, Catherine, related that even as a young boy William possessed a serious disposition. He was more interested in study than play by age seven. But soldiering got the best of him during General Ambrose Burnside's "mud march" near Fredericksburg. Severe exposure brought on typho-malarial fever, causing William's death February 17, 1863.[65]

The 12th New Hampshire contained a number of young boys and their fathers. George H. Fowler became the regiment's adopted son. His father, Hadley, was surgeon. Instead of enlisting the 14 year old, he took him to the field as his private orderly. George served unmus-

William S. Leach, left, and George H. Fowler, 12th New Hampshire.

sion and signature. Charles went back to the front a regularly mustered trooper, receiving pay and an enlistment bounty. By the time of his discharge in August 1865 he had been appointed chief bugler with the rank of corporal. In every respect he was a veteran, but never was able to wear the veteran's chevron.[67]

Some boys lost their soldier-fathers. In August 1861 William H. Seekell joined Company E, 11th Michigan, as a fifer. Enlisting beside him as drummers were his 12-year-old twin sons, Charles and James. The 11th performed relatively safe duty guarding rail lines through the summer of 1862, with a few forays pursuing Confederates in Kentucky. The Seekells, however, would not all see the year end. In late September the boys' father came down with fatal typhoid fever. He was buried in Nashville's city cemetery. For Charles and James his death meant the eventual end of their military experience. On February 4, 1863, both were mustered out and sent home by order of the War Department.

Another Wolverine, 14-year-old George Lutz, had the misfortune of losing his father while serving together in Company E, 22nd Michigan. John Lutz was 38 years old when he mustered in August 1862. His initiation to soldiering was rather uneventful. After leaving Pontiac the regiment headed for Kentucky, where it was stationed near Lexington and Danville

tered for two and a half years before his father decided to send him home. By that time Surgeon Fowler had seen enough sorrowed fathers in the regiment and thought it best to throw down his hand and not press luck.[66]

Charles Oliver Brown left Ohio with his officer-father, though not mustered. Company C, 3rd Ohio Cavalry, was formed in the fall of 1861 and Oliver M. Brown was appointed second lieutenant. He allowed Charles to become a bugler for the company at 13. The boy served until the regiment returned to the Buckeye State for veteran furlough on February 9, 1864. By then it was obvious to everyone the young bugler was worthy of becoming a soldier, so while at home he officially enlisted. In spite of his prior service the recruiting officer still required his father's permis-

until the following March. The time spent there was without incident, which might explain why the elder Lutz signed George's consent form at Lexington, allowing the boy to enlist as a musician in his company. The inactivity bred a false sense of security.[68]

On September 20, 1863, at Chickamauga, John Lutz was one of 389 casualties sustained by the 22nd Michigan on Horseshoe Ridge. Two and a half months after the battle his young son, still unaware of his father's whereabouts, expressed concern in a letter from Chattanooga.

Dear friend Sara,

I now take my pen in hand to inform you that I am well[.] I wish I could say so of Father but he is wounded and perhaps dieing at this hour. Perhaps you have heard of the great fight of Chicamauga, well our Regiment was in the hotest part of it and lost many men. I was not in it but was in Camp about 3 miles from the battle-field but we could hear the musketry very plain[.] it was brack brack brack all the day long. We could also hear the cannon[.] Oh it was dreadful to hear. Towards night some of our men came in all covered with blood and dust[.] many of them were wounded but I could not hear anything from Father nor have I heard anything from him since except that he was a prisoner and paroled. He is also wounded as I was afterward told but where he is now I cannot tell....[69]

Unknown to George his father already had died October 12 in a Stevenson, Alabama, hospital. On February 29, 1864, the young Lutz was transferred as an orderly to General George H. Thomas' Army of the Cumberland headquarters, where he bunked with another 22nd Michigan boy, John Clem, and served until war's end.[70]

John A. Cockerill thought his own father was killed in the battle of Shiloh. Shortly after his brother Armstead was appointed first lieutenant of Company D, 24th Ohio, in June 1861, John also joined the regiment as a musician at age 16. Their father, Joseph R. Cockerill, soon afterward organized the 70th Ohio and was appointed its colonel in October. Meanwhile, his boys were in West Virginia learning warfare at Philippi, Rich Mountain and Cheat Mountain. In the winter of 1861 the 24th Ohio was transferred west to Louisville, and the next spring was ordered to assist in the campaign against Fort Donelson. The fort was captured before the regiment reached it, so the Ohioans were detoured to Paducah, Kentucky. During the trip John fell ill. As his father was then at Paducah with his new regiment, John was left in his care while the 24th went on to Nashville. Though not completely healthy, the boy asked permission to join his command. He was told to remain with his father until thoroughly well.

Because of these chance occurrences John found himself in the 70th Ohio's camp next to Shiloh Church on Sunday

Brian Boeve Collection

Unidentified.

morning, April 6, 1862. The musician later wrote:

The headquarters mess of the Seventieth Ohio Regiment had finished its early breakfast, and I had just taken my place at the table ... when I heard ominous shots along our adjacent picket lines. In less than ten minutes there was volley firing directly in our front, and from my knowledge of campaigning I knew that a battle was on, though fifteen minutes before, I had no idea that any considerable force of the enemy was in the immediate front of our cantonment. The Seventieth Ohio and the brigade to which it was attached, commanded by Colonel [Ralph P.] Buckland, of Ohio, formed on its color lines under fire, and, although composed entirely of new troops, made a splendid stand. At the first alarm I dropped my knife and fork and ran to my father's tent, to find him buckling on his sword. My first heroic act was to gather up a beautiful Enfield rifle, which he had saved at the distribution of arms to his regiment, because of its beautiful, curly maple stock. I had been carrying it myself on one or two of the regimental expeditions to the front, and had some twenty rounds of cartridges in a box which I had borrowed from one of the boys of Company I. By the time I had adjusted my cartridge-box and seized my rifle, my father was mounted outside, and, with a hurried good-bye, he took his place with the regiment. By this time the bullets were whistling through the camp and shells were bursting overhead.

The enemy was pressing closely on my left flank, and Shiloh Church, with its ancient logs, was no more a desirable place for observation. I hurried over to the headquarters camp of the Seventieth Ohio, taking advantage of such friendly trees as presented themselves on the line of my movement, and there found a state of disorder. The tents were pretty well ripped with shells and bullets, and wounded men were being carried past me to the rear. As I stood there debating in my mind whether to join my father's command or continue my independent action, three men approached, carrying a sorely wounded officer in a blanket. They called me to assist them, and as my place was really with the hospital corps, being a non-combatant musician, I complied with their request. We carried the poor fellow some distance to the rear, through a thick wood, and found there a scene of disorder, not to say panic. Men were flying in every direction, commissary wagons were struggling through the underbrush, and the roads were packed with fugitives and baggage trains, trying to carry off the impedimenta of the army. Finding a comparatively empty wagon, we placed our wounded officer inside, and then, left at liberty, I started on down toward the Tennessee River.

Before John had gone far a young lieutenant of an Illinois regiment temporarily "enlisted" him to fight. The Illinoisans' immediate front was relatively quiet, but before long they were fully engaged with the enemy. Waving his sword above his head, the lieutenant was shot dead at John's feet. Soon the fire became so heavy the regiment retreated to a ravine. While crouching in the declivity John began thinking of his mother and home. He had fired his last cartridge and sat motionless, holding his prized Enfield. A sergeant brandishing a revolver asked why he was not firing. A dead soldier nearby was pointed out, and the boy was told to secure his cartridge box and commence shooting. Before John could argue that the man's ammunition was the wrong caliber, the Rebel yell was heard approaching the ravine. Young Cockerill bolted rearward with the others, Confederate flags closely following their flight.

It was at this point that our thin blue line first wavered. Out of this ravine, over the bank, we survivors poured, pursued by the howling enemy. I remember my horror at the thought of being shot in the back, as I retreated from the top of the bank and galloped as gracefully as I could with the refluent human tide. Just by my side ran a youthful soldier, perhaps three years my senior, who might, for all I knew, have been recruited as I was. I heard him give a scream of agony, and turning, saw him dragging one of his legs, which I saw in an instant, had been shattered by a bullet. He had dropped his rifle, and as I ran to his support he fell upon my shoulder and begged me for God's sake to help him. I half carried and half dragged him for some distance, still holding to my Enfield rifle, with its beautiful curly stock, and then, seeing that I must either give up the role of Good Samaritan or drop the rifle, I threw it down, and continued to aid my unfortunate companion. All this time the bullets were whistling more fiercely than at any time during the engagement, and the woods were filled with flying men, who, to all appearances, had no intention of rallying on that side of the Tennessee River. My companion was growing weaker all the while, and finally I sat down beside a tree, with his back toward the enemy, and watched him for a few moments, until I could see that he was slowly bleeding to death. I knew nothing of surgery at that time, and did not even know how to staunch the flow of blood. I called to a soldier who was passing, but he gave no heed. A second came, stood for a moment, simply remarked, "He's a dead man," and passed on. I saw the poor fellow die without being able to render the slightest assistance. Passing on, I was soon out of range of the enemy. I then realized how utterly famished and worn out I was.

At the rear with other refugees, John saw a familiar face belonging to his father's regiment. "I recognized him by the letters and numbers on his hat. Inquiring the fate of the regiment, he told me that it had been entirely cut to pieces, and that he had personally witnessed the death of my father — he had seen him shot from his horse. This intelligence filled me with dismay, and then I determined, non-combatant that I was, that I would retire from that battlefield."

Sneaking aboard an ambulance carrying wounded to the river, John escaped the cavalrymen rounding up skulkers. The wagon made its way to an improvised hospital where he jumped out, walked to the riverbank and sat down, pondering his next move. On the opposite shore he noticed a blue column being loaded on a steamer.

I knew that this was General Nelson, commonly known as "Fighting Bull Nelson." I ran down to the point where I saw this boat was going to land, and as she ran her prow up on the sandy beach, Nelson put spurs to his horse and jumped him over the gunwale. As he did this he drew his sword and rode right into the crowd of refugees, shouting: "Damn your souls, if you won't fight, get out of the way, and let men come here who will!" I realized from the presence of Nelson that my regiment (the Twenty-fourth Ohio) was probably in that vicinity. I asked one of the boat hands to take me on board, and after some persuasion he did so. The boat recrossed, and as soon as I got on shore I ran down to where the troops were embarking to cross the river to the battlefield. I soon found Ammen's brigade and my regiment. Hurrying on board one of the transports, I climbed to the hurricane deck, and there found my brother with his company. He was looking across the river, where the most appalling vision met our sight. The shore was absolutely packed with the disorganized, panic-stricken troops who had fled before the terrible Confederate onslaught, which had not ceased for one moment since early that morning. The noise of the battle was deafening. It may be imagined that my brother was surprised to see me. I made a hurried explanation of the circumstances which had brought me there, and gave him news of [our] father's death. Then I asked him for something to eat. With astonishment, he referred me to his negro servant, who luckily had a broiled

Unidentified.

chicken in his haversack, together with some hard bread. I took the chicken and as we marched off the boat I held a drum-stick in each hand, and kept close to my brother's side as we forced our way through the stragglers, up the road from the landing, and on to the plateau, where the battle was even then almost concentrating. Right there I saw a man's head shot off by a cannon ball, and saw immediately afterward an aide on General Nelson's staff dismounted by a shot, which took off the rear part of his saddle, and broke his horse's back. At the time I did not stop eating. My nerves were settled and my stomach was asserting its rights. My brother finally turned to me, and giving me some papers to keep and some messages to deliver in case of his death, shook me by the hand and told me to keep out of danger, and, above all things, to try and get back home. This part of his advice I readily accepted. I stood and saw

174

the brigade march by, which in less than ten minutes, met the advance of the victorious Confederates, and checked the battle for that day.

John wandered along the riverbank until darkness and rain settled in. He met another soldier of his father's regiment who corroborated earlier reports of disaster for the command. The two sat or slept on a hay bale. All the while gunboat shells shrieked overhead and more troops disembarked at the landing.

As morning light began to fill the sky, stragglers uplifted by music from the 15th U.S. Infantry's band began to reform and head forward in search of their commands. John and his comrade did likewise. Among the journey's sights was one of a young dead Confederate. "Further on I passed by the road the corpse of a beautiful boy in gray, who lay with his blond curls scattered about his face, and his hands folded peacefully across his breast. He was clad in a bright, neat uniform, well garnished with gold, which seemed to tell the story of a loving mother and sisters who had sent their household pet to the field of war.... His waxen face, washed by the rains of the night before, was that of one who had fallen asleep, dreaming of loved ones who waited his coming in some anxious home. He was about my age. He may have been a drummer. At the sight of that poor boy's corpse I burst into tears, and started on."

That night John slept under a tree near Shiloh Church. With morning he made his way to the 70th Ohio's old ruined camp and remained there through the day, looking at the destruction. His father's tent had been ransacked and everything of value taken. Early in the evening he heard a body of troops marching toward the camp. "At its head rode my father, whom I supposed to be dead — pale and haggard, and worn, but unscathed. He had not seen me nor heard from me in sixty hours. He dismounted, and taking me in his arms, gave me the most affectionate embrace that my life had ever known, and I realized then how deeply he loved me." [71]

William L. Curry, a first sergeant with the 1st Ohio Cavalry, arrived at Shiloh the morning of April 9. Curry's nephew, Dunallen Woodburn, had run off from his Union County, Ohio, home at 14 and enlisted as a drummer with the 58th Ohio. The sergeant knew Dunallen was somewhere on the field, and as soon as he could set out to locate him.

"Knowing that the 58th Regiment was in the battle," Curry related, "and that his parents, John and Maria Curry Woodburn, would be anxious about him, I mounted my horse and after a search of several hours on the battlefield, strewn with the dead of both armies, I found 'Dun' as happy and unconcerned as if he had been at his home. I sought and found Colonel [Valen-

Runaway Dunallen M. Woodburn, 14, signed the rolls of the 58th Ohio using his middle name, Marion. Discharged in December 1864 after three years' service, he then was assigned principal musician of the 47th U.S. Colored Infantry.

History of Jerome Township, Union County, Ohio

tine] Bausenwein, who, in his fez cap, was enjoying his pipe, and requested that Dun accompany me to our bivouac, to which he readily consented. I took him on my horse and we made our way to my regiment. We had no tents and it rained almost continuously for two or three days, but I shared my blankets and rubber poncho with him. All around were dead artillery horses, and ambulances were busy gathering up our own boys in the dense woods."[72]

It was sad enough for a family to lose a son or father during the war, but there were instances when some were burdened by losses of both. In January 1862, 42-year-old Thomas K. Harper and his 16-year-old son Asa enlisted in Company C, 73rd Ohio. Thomas died that summer at Winchester, Virginia, of disease. Within two months Asa also was laid to rest under Old Dominion soil.[73] He was one of 164 casualties the 73rd suffered at Second Bull Run. The day following the battle survivors of the regiment searched the field for their comrades under flag of truce. Major Samuel Hurst noted, "They found our poor fellows stripped and robbed of almost everything, in the most approved style of Southern Chivalry."[74] As the burial crews toiled one wonders what thoughts filled their minds when they discovered the blue-eyed boy's body.[75]

Far more fathers and sons enlisting together served their terms and returned home to share memories for years afterward. John W. Messick was nine years old and stood just over four feet when he joined the 42nd Indiana with his father, Second Lieutenant Jacob W. Messick. At Chickamauga the regiment lost 93 officers and men, one-third of them as prisoners. It was a trying time, especially for a parent with a boy at his side. Near the battle's conclusion Lieutenant Spillard Horrall recalled seeing the older Messick carry drummer "Johnny" off the field on his shoulders. With his father's help the youngster was able to stay with the regiment through his 36-month enlistment. Jacob Messick served a year longer and was mustered out at conflict's end.[76]

Forty-year-old Freeman H. Sunderland permitted his 16-year-old son George to enlist with him in Company K, 13th Vermont. Both were well liked by their comrades. George was an especially shy boy who spoke little, but diligently executed orders. At Gettysburg his unflinching calm won admiration from all who witnessed the boy in action. His father, on the

other hand, had a hard time comprehending the manual of arms. Because of this he was appointed company "washerwoman." As he became adept at ridding his comrades' garments of lice, he soon was washing for most of the regiment's officers, charging a small fee for the work. When George came down with measles his father nursed him back to health in his tent instead of sending him to the hospital. Shortly after Gettysburg Freeman was discharged. George remained in the Army. When he made it home both were able to reminisce about a remarkable period in their lives.[77]

Even General Sherman allowed his sons William and Thomas to "act the soldier," as did General Grant and President Lincoln.

Michael Waskul Collection

John W. Messick, Company A, 42nd Indiana.

176

Adopted as a "little Sergeant," nine-year-old Willy Sherman became pet of the 1st Battalion, 13th U.S. Infantry. Before his untimely death in October 1863, Willy showed keen interest in his father's military exploits. According to his mother, Ellen, he followed Army movements by studying maps like "an old campaigner."

University of Notre Dame Archives

In May 1861 Sherman was appointed colonel of the 13th U.S. Infantry. Within four years he became one of the country's most famous military leaders, and by 1869 was elevated to full general. When the war started he and wife Ellen had just added a sixth child to their family. Of the six, their two boys were William, the oldest, and Thomas, the fourth child. In November 1861 Ellen and the two boys made their first trip from Ohio to visit Sherman at Louisville. During the autumn of 1862, while the general was stationed at Memphis, Ellen and Tommy visited him again. She stayed in a hotel, but Tommy enjoyed sleeping in camp with his father. An Army tailor even fashioned a child-sized uniform for him to wear.[78]

After the Vicksburg campaign Sherman convinced his wife to bring their four oldest children to his camp on the Big Black River 20 miles from Vicksburg. While there young Willy attached himself to a battalion of the 13th Regulars as one of its sergeants, if only in make believe. The battalion's officers reciprocated by letting him participate in drill and, since he had accurately memorized the tactics, allowed him on occasion to practice his knowledge with a squad of men. Unfortunately, camp life in disease-prone west Mississippi bayou country was more than the nine-year-old could handle. Willy caught typhoid and died after a brief struggle.[79] Shortly after his namesake and favorite son's death, Sherman penned a letter to the 13th's commander.

Gayosa House, Memphis, Tenn.
Oct. 4 [1863], Midnight.

Capt. C.C. Smith, Commanding Battalion 13th Regulars

My dear friend: I cannot sleep to night till I record my deep feelings of my heart to you and to the officers and men of the battalion, for their kind behavior to my poor child. I realize that you all feel for my family the attachment of kindred; and I assure you all of full reciprocity. Consistent with a sense of duty to my profession and office, I could not leave my post, and sent for my family to come to me in that fatal climate, and in that sickly period of the year, and behold the result! The child that bore my name, and in whose future I reposed with more confidence than I did in my own plans of life now floats a mere corpse, seeking a grave in a distant land with a weeping mother, brother, and sisters clustered about him. But for myself I can ask no sympathy. On, on, I must go to meet a soldier's fate, or see my country rise superior to all factions, till its flag is adopted and respected by ourselves and all powers of the earth.

But my poor Willy was or thought he was a sergeant of

177

the 13th. I have seen his eye brighten and his heart beat as he held the battalion under arms, and asked me if they were not real soldiers. Child as he was he had the enthusiasm, the pure love of truth, honor, and love of country which should animate all soldiers. God only knows why he should die thus young. He is dead, but will not be forgotten till those who knew him in life have followed him to that same mysterious end.

Please convey to the battalion my heartfelt thanks, and assure each and all that if in future years, they call on me or mine and mention that they were of the 13th Regulars, when poor Willy was a sergeant, they will have a key to the affections of my family that will open all that it has — that we will share with them our last blanket, our last crust.

Your Friend W.T. Sherman, Maj. Gen.[80]

Willy's death deeply affected the general and his wife. A year later, when Sherman had become a household name, Ellen expressed her feelings to him by writing: "Well have we been taught the utter vanity of human ambition. Here you have accomplished all that man could do in your position — you have won for yourself through merit a name which will be honored by the brave and true as long as history lasts and your oldest son, your darling, the one to whom that name would have been most dear is lying in the cold bosom of the earth deaf to all sound of human glory." In December 1864 Sherman's six-month-old child Charles also died, but his loss never was as keenly felt as that of little Willy.[81]

General Ulysses S. Grant had fathered four children by the beginning of the war. Frederick Dent, born May 30, 1850, Ulysses S. Jr. (known as "Little Buckeye" because he was born in Ohio in 1852, and afterward called Buck), and Jesse Root, born February 8, 1858, were his three boys. Only daughter Ellen [Nellie] was born July 4, 1855.[82]

During the 1863 Vicksburg campaign Fred was allowed to visit his father in the field, even though he was only 12 at the time and attending school in Covington, Kentucky. Arriving March 29, his young eyes were opened wide to warfare's realities over the next three months, as described by Fred in the following vignettes:

• April 30, we went on board the *General Price,* formerly a Confederate ram, and moved down to where Bruinsburg [Miss.] had stood. Now not a house was to be seen, fire had destroyed the whole town. The crossing of the troops continued vigorously, and, tired of watching them, I fell asleep on deck. Awakening the next morning, I found that my father had gone to the front, and the sound of cannon announced the progress of a battle [at Port Gibson]. General Lorenzo Thomas told me that father had given strict orders that I should not be allowed to go ashore, but he finally permitted me to join a party in chasing a rabbit on the land, and I took advantage of that permission to push my investigation over the hills. I fell in with a wagon train and secured a ride on a mule; and after going some distance in that way I joined a battery of artillery on its way to the front, and later followed a passing regiment – the Seventh Missouri – which was soon in battle. Presently my father appeared. My guilty conscience so troubled me that I hid from his sight behind a tree. Within a short time a mighty shout announced the victory of our troops, and the horrors of a battle-field were brought vividly before me. I joined a detachment which was collecting the dead for burial, but, sickening at the sights, I made my way with another detachment, which was gathering the wounded, to a log house which had been appropriated for a hospital. Here the scenes were so terrible that I became faint and ill, and, making my way to a tree, sat down, the most woebegone twelve-year-old lad in America.

• From the 7th to the 12th of May General Grant was constantly in communication with [Generals] Sherman, McPherson and McClernand, riding around from one to the other. This made his headquarters so uncomfortable and his mess so irregular that I, for one, did not propose to put up with such living, and I took my meals with the soldiers, who used to do a little foraging, and thereby set an infinitely better table than their commanding General. My father's table at this time was, I must frankly say, the worst I ever saw or partook of.

• After the battle of Champion's Hill [May 16], while riding toward Edwards Station, father suddenly turned back, and I went on into a house filled with Confederate wounded. They were not feeling very friendly toward the Yankees, and they threatened to kill me. Of course I decided not to intrude, and I passed on. Further down the road some of our own men, who did not know me, attempted to take me prisoner. Soon, however, an old soldier recognized me, and called for "Three cheers for young Grant," which were given with a will, and I began to feel more comfortable. About midnight I returned to the field, and reached a house in which I found my father and several of his staff officers, most of whom were greatly elated over their victory. I slept in the room with my father that night; he, even after the great battle and victory of that day, and with the expectation and cares of another battle on the morrow, was, as ever, most considerate of the comfort and welfare of his

General Ulysses S. Grant with sons Jesse, center, and Frederick. Though not soldiers, both boys spent time with their father's troops in the field. Fred wrote: "I remember with the utmost interest my life in camp, and with deepest affection the men whom I met in the army. Much of my time was spent among the private soldiers, who were never too tired or too worn out to comfort and pet the young boy – the son of the 'old man.' "

The general noted in his *Memoirs* that Fred "looked out for himself and was in every battle of the [Vicksburg] campaign. His age, then not quite thirteen, enabled him to take in all he saw, and to retain a recollection of it that would not be possible in more mature years."

Illinois State Historical Library

young son.

The next morning we made an early start, and moved toward the Big Black River. When we halted near the railway bridge, General Grant and his staff occupied the porch of a fine plantation house. Our troops were now moving on the enemy's line at a double quick, and I became enthused with the spirit of the occasion, galloped across a cottonfield, and went over the enemy's works with our men. Following the retreating Confederates to the Big Black, I was watching some of them swim the river, when a sharpshooter on the opposite bank fired at me and hit me in the leg. The wound was slight, but very painful; and I suppose I was very pale, for Colonel [Clark B.] Lagow came dashing up and asked what was the matter. I promptly said, "I am killed." Perhaps because I was only a boy the Colonel presumed to doubt my word, and said, "Move your toes," which I did with success. He then recommended our hasty retreat. This we accomplished in good order.

• The wound I had received early in the campaign now began to trouble me very much, and, under Dr. [Henry S.]

Hewitt's expressed fears of having to amputate my leg, I remained much at headquarters. Because of this I saw a great deal of my father's methods, his marvelous attention to detail, and his cool self-possession. I also witnessed the devotion of his men to him, and the enthusiasm with which they greeted "the old man," as they called him, when he passed along the lines. Father was a splendid horseman, and visited many points of his army every day.[83]

Fred's leg healed and he eventually witnessed the capitulation of Vicksburg's besieged defenders on July 4. "This ended my connection with the army for a while," he reflected. "From the result of exposure I had contracted an illness which necessitated my withdrawal into civilian life again, and on the 8th of July I was sent home to recuperate."[84]

After the city surrendered, five-year-old Jesse and Grant's wife, Julia, arrived for a visit. Years later Jesse reminisced about his Vicksburg sojourn:

As my earliest memories come back to me, [an] event that stands out clearly is of a steamboat journey with mother down the Mississippi, to join father at Vicksburg. I remember a joyous start, and next, a confusion of crashing noise, and mother striving to dress me, bewildered and cross, in the darkness. Although the Union forces were nominally in control of the Mississippi from St. Louis to Vicksburg, our steamboat had been shelled from the shore. Years later I questioned father how this could have happened. "Military occupation did not necessarily imply that we were in possession of all the light field pieces cached away on farms and plantations along the shore," he answered, smiling at the memory. "Such guns were often dragged out for a hasty shot at some passing boat."

But I reached Vicksburg to meet the – to me – great event of the war. As our carriage drew up before Army Headquarters I glimpsed a small Shetland pony standing [and] saddled at one side. Before the carriage stopped I had scrabbled out and was climbing into that saddle. Father had secured the pony, and a soldier had made the diminutive saddle and bridle for me. Life holds but one thrill such as mine as I sat in that saddle upon Rebbie in the first knowledge of possession. For years thereafter Rebbie was my most constant companion, and the pony lived until 1883.

Wonderful days followed. To the small boy it was "father's army," and the soldiers made me very welcome, carving all sorts of toys and regaling me with molasses candy made over the camp fires. The troops were encamped in and for a considerable distance around Vicksburg. Almost daily I rode with father upon tours of inspection, sometimes mounted upon Rebbie, but often perched behind him and clinging to his belt as we thundered along upon a big buckskin horse that had been presented to him, called, because of its viciousness, Mankiller.

One other incident of the days when mother and I were at Vicksburg stands out clearly. A committee from Congress arrived, bringing father a gold medal – now in the National Museum in Washington. Before the presentation they read some flattering congressional resolutions, followed by several laudatory orations delivered by various members of the committee. When the last speaker rounded off his peroration there was an expectant pause. Silence deep and heavy fell upon the assemblage. All were waiting, as was I, standing close at his side, for father to respond. Father remained silent. The situation grew more tense, until I could bear it no longer.

"Papa, aren't you going to make a speech, too?" I cried.

"No, my dear boy!" he answered with unconscious energy that carried to every ear. A wave of laughter swept the company as the tension broke, putting everyone at ease.

I remember leaving Vicksburg with regret. Recollection of where we went from there is dim and confused. Incidents stand out clearly, but the sequence is lost.[85]

Toward the end of 1863 Mrs. Grant and the children moved to Burlington, New Jersey, where the two older boys enrolled in school. Periodically she visited her husband after he established his headquarters at City Point, Virginia, as general-in-chief of all U.S. armies. With the other children in school Julia and Jesse moved to City Point for a season. During that time another indelible remembrance took shape for the boy concerning a visit President Lincoln made to the region. On an earlier occasion Jesse had made the acquaintance of Tad Lincoln, one of the president's sons, who was five years his senior.

President Lincoln and father, accompanied by a mounted escort, and with Tad Lincoln and myself, rode to an outlying fort. The escort was drawn in front of our cabin, the horses dancing impatiently during an unexpected delay, when Tad Lincoln, who was not a confident horseman, demurred at mounting a small, beautiful horse called Jeff, that had been provided for him. I can still hear the pride in father's voice as he said, "Jesse will ride Jeff." Then, at last, we were off, I riding upon Jeff and Tad Lincoln mounted upon my pony, Rebbie. Before we had cleared the reservation, Tad and I had forged ahead, Rebbie's diminutive hoofs ringing like the beat of a drummer's double time in his efforts to keep pace with Jeff.

But my satisfaction, and I fancy father's, was short. With a wild forward lunge, Jeff bolted. Instantly both father and President Lincoln were spurring in pursuit, accompanied by a young staff officer who proved to be better mounted than either of them. All the pull I could exert but steadied Jeff in his stride, and under my featherweight he was widening the gap between us and our pursuers at every bound. Father saw that the pursuit was but exciting Jeff to greater effort, and drew up, calling to Mr. Lincoln and the officer. Ahead of me men were shouting and running, and a double line of soldiers and teamsters formed as by magic, converging upon the open gate of a mule corral. Down this living lane plunged Jeff, and into the corral, and that excitement was over. But the rest of the way, chagrined and rebellious, I rode far in the rear, and an orderly rode at my side, a lead on Jeff.

But the disappointments of this memorable day were not over for me. We were but just dismounting at the fort when a Confederate battery opened fire upon us.... I have never known whether the rebels had knowledge of President Lincoln's coming, whether their lookouts noted the increased activity, and from this and the size and character of our escort suspected that there were visitors of importance, or whether it just happened. But the keen delight of Tad Lincoln and myself, when the rebels opened fire, I shall never forget.

Two small boys whose experiences were only of war, that had touched only to delight them, and in company with their fathers, whom each considered the greatest man in the world, were incapable of fear at a martial demonstration, regardless of its nature. The orderly confusion of perfectly

Lincoln's 'little lieutenant'

Author's Collection

A child-size uniform was tailored for Tad before war's end. Six years later he died at age 18.

Thomas D. Lincoln, the president's youngest son, was nicknamed "Tad" because his father thought he resembled a tadpole at birth. One of his mother's cousins described him as a "merry, spontaneous fellow, bubbling over with innocent fun." A White House employee recalled the boy possessed "a man's heart, and in some things a man's mind. I believe he was the best companion Mr. Lincoln ever had — one who always understood him, and whom he always understood."

Tad, it was universally agreed, pretty much did as he pleased. This sometimes irked older brother Robert, especially on one occasion in 1864 when the Harvard student was visiting his family in Washington. Robert alleged that Tad "went over to the War Department to-day, and [Secretary of War E.M.] Stanton, for the fun of the thing, putting him a peg above the 'little corporal' of the French Government, commissioned him 'lieutenant.' On the strength of this, what does 'Tad' do but go off and order a quantity of muskets sent to the house! Tonight he had the audacity to discharge the guard, and he then mustered all the gardeners and servants, gave them the guns, drilled them, and put them on duty in their place. I found it out an hour ago, and thinking it a great shame, as the men had been hard at work all day, I went to father with it; but instead of punishing 'Tad,' as I think he ought, he evidently looks upon it as a good joke, and won't do anything about it!"

trained discipline, the shrilling bugles, the sharp commands of officers, gun squads hurrying to their positions, and the shells screaming overhead, afforded us the sort of entertainment we most keenly enjoyed.

And then father hurried President Lincoln and us into a bombproof. For an eternity of time — I now imagine it to have been about twenty minutes — we huddled in the safety of that shelter, listening to the distant booming of guns, but able to see nothing. At first Tad and I begged to be allowed to remain outside, and then more earnestly, to be permitted

to stick our heads out. Gradually the bombardment slackened, and, our fort failing to respond, it ceased entirely....

I recall but little more of my life at City Point. I remember later my two brothers and sister Nellie came there and remained for a time. Then we all returned to Burlington.[86]

At the war's onset Abraham Lincoln's family included Mary, his wife, oldest son Robert Todd, born in 1843, William Wallace [Willie], born in 1850, and Thomas D. [Tad], born in 1853. Willie Lincoln, like

181

On June 26, 1861, Gustave Schurmann enlisted at Yonkers as a drummer in Company I, 40th New York. The Westphalia-born musician later picked up the bugle and transformed himself into one of the Army of the Potomac's premier buglers, serving with several notable generals. He performed creditably as an orderly for more than two years prior to his 1864 discharge.

William B. Styple Collection, U.S. Army Military History Institute

Willy Sherman, died of a typhoid-related illness February 20, 1862, at the White House. "It is hard, hard, hard to have him die!" lamented his father. Mary Lincoln was so devastated she lapsed into mourning for a year and a half. His death to some extent affected Robert's Army service as well.

For most of the war Robert studied law at Harvard University. Being of military age he — and his father — was criticized for not joining the Army. Robert wanted to, but his mother constantly discouraged it. During such debates Mary argued she already had lost one son. That was all that should be expected. Her husband pointed out that many mothers had given all their sons, and their boy was no more dear than others at the front. Finally, at the beginning of 1865, Robert was made a captain on Grant's staff for the remainder of the war, in spite of his mother's wishes.

Of the Lincoln boys, young Tad's story is worthy of inclusion here. He clearly was the president's favorite son. Tad was described as the life and the worry of the family. His outgoing, frolicsome personality also made him a favorite with White House employees, as well as the troops he regularly visited with his father. Jesse Grant was not the only youngster who came in contact with Tad during forays to the front. Quite a few were detailed to oversee or entertain the enthusiastic boy. Harry Kieffer recalled a presidential visit, with Tad and other dignitaries, to the Army of the Potomac in April 1863. Harry and the 150th Pennsylvania were cleaned, polished and aligned for a review. The day was intolerably hot, and as noon approached the waiting lines began grumbling. Finally the ranks caught a glimpse of dust rising in the air, moving their way.

"Fall in, men, for now here they come, sure enough," wrote Harry. "Mr. and Mrs. Lincoln in a carriage, escorted by a body of cavalry and groups of officers, and at the head of the cavalcade Master Tad, big with importance, mounted on a pony, and having for his special escort a boy orderly, dressed in a cavalry-man's uniform, and mounted on another pony. And the two little fellows, scarcely restraining their boyish delight, outride the company, and come onto the field in a cloud of dust and at a full gallop — little Tad shouting to the men, at the top of his voice: 'Make way, men! Make way, men! Father's a-coming! Father's a-coming!' "

William W. Sweisfort was the young orderly accompanying Tad. "I was detailed to take charge of

'Little Tad' during that visit of President Lincoln," stated Sweisfort, "and was responsible to headquarters for his safety. And I tell you I had a time of it. That boy was a lively boy. He kept me moving. He rode his horse half dead, up and down, hither and yon, into every camp, putting his nose into everything, investigated every artillery park, inspected every provision train, hardly slept at night. I believe I was just a little glad when his visit was at an end, and I turned him over to his father in good order."[87]

Of the boy soldiers detailed to escort Tad his favorite and admired hero was Gustave Schurmann. In June 1861 "Gus," barely 12 years old, enlisted with his father, Frederick, in the 40th New York as a musician. He was a bright, well liked member of the regiment. Within five months his father fell ill and was discharged, leaving Gus in the Army.[88] During the summer of 1862 General Philip Kearny called for a drummer boy to act as his orderly while the Army was reviewed by General McClellan. Gus was given the detail. Kearny handed a bugle to him for the occasion and mounted him on a great white mare named "Babe." As the general, a fine horseman, headed to the review, he took a direct route over rough ground, jumping a small ravine along the way. Once across he turned in his saddle to see if any of his aides would follow suit. All declined except Gus. "Babe" was a stable mate of the general's horse "Moscow," and followed close on his heels with the diminutive rider hanging on the best he could. "Babe" charged ahead, ears pointed back and fiery eyes scanning the path. When she came to the chasm she shot forward with a powerful lunge and pulled up as she neared the general and his mount. Kearny was so impressed by the spectacle he appointed Gus his permanent orderly.[89]

On July 5, 1862, Gus was detached as bugler on the general's staff. Kearny was reported to have written orders on his back during battle, and if the four-foot-seven-inch boy flinched too much he was ridiculed. After the general's death at Chantilly, Virginia, on September 1, 1862, Gus was transferred to General David B. Birney's staff. He next was detailed to serve with General George Stoneman, and on January 1, 1863, to General Daniel Sickles.[90] During one of President Lincoln's Army visits at Belle Plain, Tad spied Gus on his horse, acting larger than life. Tad immediately developed a fondness for the unknown boy bounding about in his blue uniform. Gus reflected:

As I look back I can see that I must have been an object of envy to Tad, as by that time I had become quite a horseman, could blow a bugle, beat a drum, and swagger about like the bigger ones. The men, with whom I was somewhat of a favorite, had presented me with a mustang that had formerly been ridden by Mosby, the guerrilla chieftain, and on him I cavorted about the field until Tad could stand it no longer, and persuaded a cavalryman to lend him his horse to ride. Finally the President and Mrs. Lincoln being ready to return to Washington called Tad and bade him take leave of me.

"Mother," says Tad, "I won't go home unless 'Gus' (as he already called me) can go along."

"Oh, no," interposed the president, "that won't do. This lad is a soldier, and must remain here and attend to his duties."

"I don't care, pop," responded Tad. "I want him to go home with me and teach me to ride and blow the bugle."

This appeal, and the tears which suffused his eyes, was too much for the tender heart of our president, who ever loved Tad as the apple of his eye, and to relieve the great and good man from embarrassment General [Sickles] said: "Mr. President, if you desire, the bugler may accompany you. I will give him a furlough."[91]

Tad, greatly overjoyed, thanked the general, while I returned to my tent and secured my knapsack. I rode to Washington in the president's carriage, and that night slept serenely in the guests' chamber at the White House. Tad slept in a crib alongside his parents' bed. The contrast of my new quarters with my humble and sometimes uncomfortable lodgings of the past year was so overwhelming that even now the thought of the beautiful chamber that I occupied awes me.

Tad was a generous-hearted, sweet-tempered lad, with an adventurous and inventive turn of mind. I well remember one Sunday afternoon when the rain kept us in doors, that Tad's budding genius took a particularly distinctive turn, when with his little hatchet — perhaps the same one used by George Washington — he hacked at various pieces of furniture, and finally sawed away the banisters of the main stairway. When this was reported to the president, he called Tad and myself into his room and entertained us with a story about the Black Hawk war, and showed us the sword he carried in that campaign of a company of volunteers. He did not allude to our vandalism.

Tad and I owned Washington for several weeks, doing pretty much as we pleased....[92]

Gus' White House interlude ended as abruptly as it began when he was ordered in June 1863 to report back to the Army. At that time General Lee and his Confederates were invading Pennsylvania and the

Union Army, requiring its full strength, was on the move. Gus served his full three-year term and was mustered out in July 1864 when only 15. Lincoln purportedly had promised him an appointment to the U.S. Military Academy, but the president's assassination the following April ended the prospect. Gus also hoped one day to reunite with Tad after the war, but a meeting never occurred. In 1871 Tad Lincoln, then 18, died of a disease contracted during a visit abroad with his mother.[93]

CHAPTER 10

'Every tender and humane feeling of the soul'

A common misconception during the Civil War, and today, was that drummer boys, enlisted as non-combatants, did not confront danger in battle. By definition a non-combatant is "a member of the armed forces whose activities do not include actual combat."[1] This falsehood unwisely led numerous parents to allow their sons to enlist in the first place. While it is true that some youngsters were protected by being sent to the rear, equal or larger numbers were in the front lines as stretcher bearers waiting to administer aid to fallen comrades. These boys were more exposed than the men fighting from behind trees, fences or breastworks. As battles raged boys sometimes sent rearward found themselves in peril, caught in a flanking movement or when lines were overrun. Descriptions of their exploits caring for wounded and dying men, and providing aid in the midst of shot and shell tell a much different tale. Not only did musicians acting as stretcher bearers valiantly carry out hazardous missions, some gave up their health and lives in the process.

Hendrick E. Paine, serving as a "non-combatant" drummer, would have agreed that he was exposed at times more than soldiers of the firing line. Because of his youth and delicate physique he was unable to enlist until 1862 in Company D, 105th Ohio. He was a universal favorite due to his appearance, obliging character and close attention to duty. Colonel William R. Tolles never tired of doing favors for his "pet," who was always at his side.

During the October 1862 battle of Perryville, Hendrick, born in 1845, was detailed as a stretcher bearer for the first time. He recalled that he and a fellow drummer were "half-compelled and half-persuaded" by an officer of another division to go into the fire-swept space between the contending lines to bring off his brother, who was badly wounded. The officer escorted them near to where he lay, but stopped short while within safety of some trees and pointed him out. The boys crept forward alone as balls whistled over their heads and retrieved the fallen man. When discussing the rescue years later, Hendrick said he was not sorry he saved the man, but realized only a new recruit could have been duped into such a foolhardy attempt.[2]

Complying with officers' orders, other ill-advised missions of mercy were carried out. Delavan Miller recollected that shortly after the 2nd New York Heavy Artillery assaulted rebel lines at Totopotomy Creek, Virginia, on May 31, 1864, the question of boys at the front was raised. "The musicians of our regiment were back under the cover of some woods, and while the engagement was at its height we saw big George B. — our sergeant major — coming across the field on a run toward us. George explained his mission in a few words, which were about as follows: 'Col. Whistler wants you boys to come up on the fighting line and help the surgeons take care of our wounded, and you better come p.d.q., too, for the old man was pretty mad when

185

he missed you.' It is needless to say we got there lively, but while we were carrying some wounded past our brigade commander he remarked that we were endangering their lives more by trying to remove them during an engagement than to leave them on the ground until the fighting was over. We thought it safest, however, to obey our colonel, and after that we took great care that he did not have to send an officer to hunt us up."[3]

Musician Loren Tyler was caught up in a similar situation after a member of his regiment was wounded near Nickajack Creek, Georgia.

Soon after sunrise [July 5, 1864], in response to word that one of the 15th [Iowa] had been severely wounded, at the first post on the right of the road [Henry] Metz, [Tilghman A.H.] Cunningham, [John S.] Bosworth and Tyler took a stretcher and hastened to the front. From a cut in the road at the edge of the timber they saw the rebel picket posts, and some 150 yards ahead were our skirmishers with rails and dirt thrown up in front. On the left of the road behind a tree in an old split bottom chair sat Lieutenant [William P.] Muir, of E Company, commanding our line, and feeling that he was Monarch of all he surveyed (he was – viewing the rear), he raised his hand and signaled the advance of the 15th (the four boys) to go back, but they had higher authority to bring the man in, and at the command "Forward, trot," they lit out, incited by the yells and balls from several rebel posts, but the bloodthirsty Texans were not good shots on the wing and they hit no one. In less than Maud S. time the four fell panting among the Vets, behind a rail pile. When time restored their breath they laid the wounded man on the stretcher, and on the command "prepare to git," they got up, and immediately the Johnnies greeted them with yells, and 50 of them (more or less), from posts on both sides of the road, opened fire and slung lead all around them, scattering dirt and gravel and accelerating the speed of the quartet, who ran like the devil yonder, until they

reached the protection of the cut, when they dropped again plum exhausted. On reaching the bivouac, Surgeon [William H.] Gibbon in strong terms censured the party who reported the man severely wounded, and had caused four others to risk their lives needlessly, when the wounded man could as well as not have walked back to camp alone.[4]

One dark night in 1865 near the Salkehatchie River in South Carolina, following some evening skirmishing, a man approached the 43rd Ohio's headquarters calling for stretcher bearers. Four boys — John McClay, David and Demas Auld, and William Brown — at once grabbed a stretcher and went forward. It was a disagreeable advance as they sloshed through mud and brackish water near the river. Occasionally the faint call "Drummers, drummers!" could be heard, toward which they directed their march. At last they discovered an Irish member of their regiment sitting at

William L.C. Atkinson enlisted October 21, 1862, in Company H, 12th Iowa, at Davenport. The 15-year-old served as a company drummer, in the regimental band and as an orderly while earning the right to wear veteran stripes displayed near the cuffs of each sleeve in this late-war photograph.

Author's Collection

186

thoughtful drummer boy.[6]

By the time of Gettysburg, Harry Kieffer of the 150th Pennsylvania had learned what was expected of a musician in the Army:

I suppose my readers wonder what a drummer-boy does in time of battle. Perhaps they have the same idea I used to have, namely, that it is the duty of a drummer-boy to beat his drum all the time the battle rages, to encourage the men or drown the groans of the wounded. But if they will reflect a moment, they will see that amid the confusion and noise of battle, there is little chance of martial music being either heard or heeded. Our colonel had long ago given us our orders — "You drummer-boys, in time of an engagement, are to lay aside your drums and take stretchers and help off the wounded. I expect you to do this, and you are to remember that, in doing it, you are just as much helping the battle on as if you were fighting with guns in your hands."

And so we sit down there on our drums and watch the line going in with cheers [July 1, 1863, west of Gettysburg]. Forthwith we get a smart shelling, for there is evidently somebody else watching that advancing line besides ourselves; but they have elevated their guns a little too much, so that every shell passes quite over the line and ploughs up the meadow sod about us in all directions.

Laying aside our knapsacks we go to the seminary, now rapidly filling with the wounded. This the enemy surely cannot know, or they wouldn't shell the building so hard. We get stretchers at the ambulances and start out for the line of battle. We can just see our regimental colors waving in the orchard, near a log house about three hundred yards ahead, and we start for it — I in the lead, and Daney [Strickland of Company G] behind.

There is one of our batteries drawn up to our left a short distance as we run. It is engaged in a sharp artillery duel with one of the enemy's, which we cannot see, although we can hear it plainly enough, and straight between the two our road lies. So, up we go, Daney and I, at a lively trot, dodging the shells as best we can, till, panting for breath, we set down our stretcher under an apple tree in the orchard, in which, under the brow of the hill, we find the regiment ly-

the base of a tree. The boys questioned him about his wound, when to their disgust he told them the Rebels had shot his finger off. Roasting him in a severe manner, David Auld broke in. "You darned old fool, did you fool us out here expecting us to carry you back to camp with only a finger off?" The soldier replied, "Be gobs, boys, I want you to earn your money." The quartet walked him back to camp, abusing him verbally along the way.[5]

For every soldier that could have helped himself there were those who truly benefitted from the stretcher bearers' actions. Joseph S. Delevau was wounded in a thigh at Antietam and placed by two comrades of the 108th New York in front of a straw-stack. Shortly afterward drummer Sanford Cassidy of Company D saw Delevau and remarked, "You are not out of range of the bullets and had better not ought to stay here." Sanford moved him to the other side of the stack. In about 10 minutes a large shell struck Delevau's previous position. He carried the bullet in his leg until his death, which occurred at a much later date thanks to a

ing, one or two companies being out on the skirmish line ahead....

[I am called] away for a moment to look after some poor fellow whose arm is off at the shoulder, and it was just time I got away, too, for immediately a shell plunges into the sod where I had been sitting, tearing my stretcher to tatters, and plowing up a great furrow under one of the boys who had been sitting immediately behind me, and who thinks, "That was rather close shaving, wasn't it now?"

With bullets zipping past Kieffer made his way to a small log house. Soon his comrades echoed the cry "the Rebels are coming." Curiosity overcoming fear, Harry crept to the structure's corner and was peering around it when he felt the strong hand of Colonel Langhorne Wister grasp his shoulder. The very man who detailed the youngsters to the front could also be compassionate, as he advised, "Keep back, my boy, no use in exposing yourself that way." [7]

Stretchers, like Kieffer's, had to be replaced for many reasons. John McClay related a sad story of making one with fellow drummer William Meek of the 43rd Ohio near Ruff's Mill, Georgia. On July 4, 1864, while the two were stitching up the new litter after discarding the old because it had become too bloody, Captain Charles A. Angel, acting major of the 35th New Jersey, rode up inquiring what they were doing behind the skirmish line, considering all the bullets and shells flying around. Meek remarked, "If you don't get off that horse, we are likely to carry you off on this." Angel jokingly replied that the bullet had not been molded to kill him. He continued on for only 30 feet when he fell from his horse, shot through the heart. He was the first to be carried on the new stretcher.

McClay had many interesting experiences tending the wounded. During the battle of Resaca he came across mortally wounded Franklin J. Russell of the 43rd's Company H, who requested water and for John to take his belongings and send them home. When Russell tried to take his ring off it would not budge. He instructed McClay to cut it off after he died. But with the aid of a comrade and a string they left the finger in place. Later, while carrying another man, a bullet struck the stretcher's handle he was holding, causing the man to topple to the ground. The next day John's reputation grew with the boys after he helped a wounded German of Company H who was shot in the face. McClay knew the man well. Finding him lying

in a pool of blood and noting a gurgling sound coming from his mouth, he surmised a plug of tobacco was the cause, as the man was an inveterate chewer. He dexterously ran a finger into his mouth to remove the tobacco when the man's jaw clamped down on John's finger and held it like a vise. The regiment's assistant surgeon came to his relief and pried the man's teeth apart with a bayonet. After the release the surgeon scolded, "Now you little fool, never try that again." For the next few days when the boys were out looking for wounded, they hailed McClay by calling, "Here is a man that has tobacco in his mouth!" [8]

When Walter Cheney enlisted in September 1862 in Company C, 125th Ohio, he inflated his real age of 13 by five years. Immediately after muster he was transferred to the drum corps and drew rations and tented with the other boys. During the battle of Dandridge, Tennessee, on January 17, 1864, Walter and Clinton H. Phelps were carrying mortally wounded George Beckwith from the field when a ball hit Walter in the leg, leaving Clinton to attend to both. Once in the rear Walter was placed on the ground and waited his turn with the surgeons. [9]

Whenever a fellow drummer was struck others took it personally. Delavan Miller described the wounding and salvation of a fellow musician in the 2nd New York Heavy Artillery at Cold Harbor:

A drummer-boy of our regiment who was carrying a musket was found wounded and left between the lines. There were many other of our comrades there, too, but somehow to us drummer-boys who had beaten the reveille and tattoo together and tramped at the head of the regiment so many long and wearisome marches, the thought that one of our number was lying out there in the blazing June sun suffering not only pain but the terrible agony of thirst, stirred our sympathies to the uttermost and we longed to go to his relief, but dared not for it was like throwing one's life away to show himself over the breastworks.

It was late in the afternoon that Peter Boyle, our "Pete," suggested a plan by which our comrade was rescued. Pete cut three or four scrub pine trees which abounded there and proposed that he and a couple of others should use them as a screen and go out between the lines.

"Why not wait till dark and go?" someone asked. But then it was feared he could not be found.

The bushes were set over the breastworks one at a time so as not to attract attention, and as there were many more like them growing they were probably not noticed. When the evening twilight came on Pete and two others crawled over the breastworks and got behind the trees. Each had a couple of canteens of water for they knew that there would be many to whom a mouthful would be so very acceptable.

The three boys crawled and wriggled themselves toward the rebel lines shielded by the trees. Their movements necessarily had to be very slow so as not to attract the attention of the enemy. The ruse was well planned and executed, but fraught with much danger. They found their comrade and had to lie behind their shelter until darkness concealed their movements, and then the wounded comrade was brought into the lines and his life saved. [10]

Nathaniel Carter Deane enlisted in July 1861 at age 14 as a private in Company D, 21st Massachusetts. During the war he was wounded twice and sent to field hospitals, where he observed a host of horrendous scenes:

[I] was wounded at Cold Harbor on June 2nd [1864]. I had no bones broken or artery severed; a shell splinter passed through my leg but I was crushed by dirt and logs falling on me from a hastily built breast work by a shell

explosion ... coming to at midnight with moans from the dark places about me; later I found myself outside a field hospital lying among hundreds of other wounded men on the ground waiting for my turn.

Surgeons were at work, sleeves rolled up, bloody and soiled like a butcher, with a rough knife, saw, and steel forceps, etc., the kind to scare. Water had to be brought from a distant slough, first used for slopping the tools then to wash the bloody board. Old wood buckets were receptacles for water and the ground around the board was wet and muddy, to be moved to a dry place from time to time, and all things dirty and with victims black, dirty and sour and sweaty, and their clothes filled with vermin, and suffering from diarrhea, and in the intense summer heat with a pile of arms and legs and old clothes and swarms of flies, and in the stench the work went on and it was a lucky man who received any attention whatsoever, as this was the flow point for many of the wounded who could take care of themselves.

I lay under a small tree, for my wound was slight in comparison to so many others. No one was put under the influence of an opiate, neither were their wounds washed before or after amputation. In the place of opiates was used the double cross to hold the patient down to keep the live patient still for the surgeons to do their work by four attending men, two standing at the head, one on each side and crossing the victim's arms across his breast, then reaching by the men standing opposite side, top of the shoulder, then laying their arms down and across the breast and throat, holding the patient in a vice like grip. If he struggled, they bore down and choked the patient still for the surgeon to do his work. Hence the oft-time expression, "They gave me the double cross."

Two days earlier Nathaniel's good friend John D. Reynolds was wounded at his side by a shell splinter. Reynolds' abdomen was torn open but his bowels remained untouched. Nathaniel and three others carried him to a field hospital, where they were told by the

Nathaniel C. Deane was so moved by unsanitary conditions witnessed during the war that he afterward became heavily involved with the American Red Cross. He was a lifelong friend of the organization's founder, Clara Barton, whom he met while a boy serving with her pet regiment, the 21st Massachusetts.

Author's Collection

189

'No need to go back to old Sparta for daring lads'

Nearly 179,000 African-American soldiers served in the Union Army, with an additional 9,600 in the Navy. A sizeable number of these troops and sailors was underage, as were thousands of young black non-combatants — many of them former slaves — that accompanied field forces as servants, cooks, teamsters and grooms.

A 7th Pennsylvania Cavalry officer stationed in Tennessee praised ex-slaves attached to his regiment for the care given its animals. He also believed there was "a natural affiliation between a negro raised on a cotton plantation and a mule. On one occasion [our quartermaster] had rigged out his train with a new supply of mules. When the train came to move, one team of four absolutely refused to do so. Drivers shouted, flogged and swore, but all in vain. Their feet were firmly planted; their ears assumed different angles, and their eyes rolled, searching for something to kick, but go they would not.

"The struggle continued for half an hour; the atmosphere became sulphurous, and the case seemed hopeless, when an innocent looking black boy, standing by, remarked to the quartermaster: 'Boss, I can drive dem mules.' 'Then do it, and you can have a job.' Quietly the negro approached the team, adjusted the harness and spoke to each mule, took hold of the line, and gave the signal to go and they moved off as readily and steadily as any wagonmaster could desire."

Black boys showed their mettle on the battlefield as well. In a sharp fight June 15, 1864, at Noonday Creek near Kennesaw Mountain, 12th Wisconsin private Hosea Rood, himself a teenager, witnessed two of them in action:

"We had several young boys attached to our regiment, some white, belonging to our drum corps, others

Courtesy of Don Farlow

As Union forces converged on Atlanta in the summer of 1864, a "contraband" named John Taylor ran off from a Georgia plantation and attached himself to Company E, 5th Connecticut, as a servant. Corporal Charles F. Hallock thought so highly of the ex-slave that he posed with Taylor for this quarter-plate tintype. At war's end Hallock brought John to Norwalk, Connecticut, where he became a church deacon.

Courtesy of Paul Gibson

Unidentified.

black, who did various jobs, such as cooking, tending officers' horses, etc. These boys caught the general spirit of the occasion, and, although being non-combatants, they felt they must do something or *burst* with the effort of keeping down the excitement that took possession of them. Seeing some of our fellows scattered on the ground beyond the rifle-pits, they seized a stretcher and started on a run for the front. Having reached one of the fallen men, they gently rolled him upon it. They picked him up and made quick time till they got him back in the rear, where he could be attended by the physicians. Back and forth they went several times, each time bringing someone to a place of safety. Two of them were white and two black, [and] they worked for humanity that day in spite of the great risk of losing their own lives. No need to go back to old Sparta for daring lads."

Robert Morton, right, servant of Captain Robert A. Potter, Company E, 2nd Connecticut Heavy Artillery.

In August 1862 George H. Sheffield enlisted as a private in Company K, 121st New York. He later served as a musician and was detailed to the 2nd Brigade band, 1st Division, Sixth Corps, in the summer of 1863. At brigade headquarters he also served as an orderly. In front of Petersburg in 1864 his left eardrum was shattered by heavy cannonading, rendering it forever useless. Here, he wears a Sixth Corps badge, identification shield and riding gauntlets.

Author's Collection

surgeon, "Take him away, I have too many others to care for; he has but a slim chance to live. Carry him back out of the way." The teenager was detailed to stay with Reynolds that night; however, there was little he could do but offer comfort. Nathaniel wrote that "The dark, underlying shadows from the light of the moon and with dead men lying about, their ghoulish grins, the spectered horror, imbedded deep in my fear. There I stood ... as he tried to relieve his sufferings by song and prayer." Reynolds' life slowly ebbed away in the cheerless night. For Nathaniel it was an emotional experience, and of his friend's death he wrote, "I stood for a time and cried as freely as boys do when things hurt most; alone among the dead, then covered his face with an old coat I ran away, for I was alone, passing dead men all about as I went." [11]

Joseph G. Patterson served as a drummer in Company G, 90th Pennsylvania. He, too, enlisted at 14 in 1861 and served his full three-year term. Like Nathaniel Deane, Joseph was horrified by the misery of the hospitals and also lost a good friend. In a letter written home two weeks following the battle of Gettysburg, he related: "... very sorry for not writing to you sooner, but to tell you the truth, I could not write after the battle. I undertook to write to you but I was so nervous I could not write a word. You could understand the reason of it. I am unable to tell you but I am well now and pearly. Mother we have a mighty small regiment now. Our regiment numbers 100 men.... I was detailed for 14 days at Gettysburg to take care of the wounded and help bury the dead, but my constitution could hardly bear the smell of the wounds. You have no idea how they smell.... All our brigade drummers

[were] taken prisoners but 3 or 4 but I was among the lucky ones. They were taking care of the wounded in the hospital when the rebels came in. But I just came off the field and the rebels was after us. There was no time to stay there in the town for the balls was flying thick. You would be going along and a poor fellow fall before you. I lost my best friend in this fight. He was killed dead, shot in the same part of the head as Jimmy Boyd was. His name was Frank Wise, Co. H, maybe you will see it in the paper." [12]

Charles Bardeen never relished nursing duty and forthrightly admitted it when he published his wartime diary. "No doubt the place for the drum corps in battle is at the hospital, and at [Fredericksburg] when we were ordered there I went. I staid through, and did everything I was asked to do as well as I was able. But it was the only time I did it. Thereafter, whenever it was possible I kept by my regiment in battle, not always on the firing line for I had no musket, but near enough to see what was going on, which when I discovered how practically useless I was without a musket, succeeded the ambition to do valiant deeds. I was always glad to help any of our wounded to the hospital, where I was willing to take care of men if they were our own, but I did no more service as a general nurse. I did not object to the work itself. I was not fond of pathology and unless I was needed would avoid as zealously as many others seek the sight of persons or animals badly injured. But I found that when I had some part to perform my attention was so concentrated on doing it well that the horrible aspect made little impression. Theoretically it would be a difficult thing for me to hold a man's leg while it was being sawn off. Practically I did it without shrinking, much more easily than I could have looked on without holding the leg."[13]

Battles and hospitals were mentally taxing for everyone, but especially so for boys. Asa W. Bartlett, who served as a musician in Company F, 12th New Hampshire, noted the extra strain his peers felt. "The soldier of the line, though he stands in the midst and takes an active part in the work of destruction, strange as it may at first seem, knows little of the real sufferings and horrors of the inhuman carnage that surrounds him. He hears, perhaps, the death shriek of a comrade as he falls by his side, and sees the blood oozing from the mortal wound. He heeds it not in the excitement of the hour for he is too intent in the work of killing the enemy to think of his comrades, or even the danger of being killed himself. But how changed and different with him whose duty it is to visit the fresh field of carnage where the pitiful cries of the wounded mingle with the groans of the dying, and where every tender and humane feeling of the soul is shocked with the heart-sickening scenes of blood."[14]

After days, weeks or months caring for wounded men, many young soldiers became numb to their surroundings. John D. Folsom, "a mere boy" when he enlisted as a musician in Company B, 11th New Hampshire, wrote of the phenomenon experienced at Spotsylvania on May 12, 1864. "We were obliged to carry our wounded to the Ny [River] bridge on the Fredericksburg road, a distance of nearly a mile, at every step sinking in the adhesive mud, characteristic of Virginia's sacred soil.... One man died after we had carried him a mile, just as we set him down at the field hospital. As I remember, we were highly incensed at his dying at that inopportune moment. War had pretty much blunted the fine edge of our sensibilities."[15]

In addition to tending wounded and bearing stretchers, another large percentage of boys served as orderlies — soldiers acting as attendants or messengers for superior officers. They could be detailed at company level on up, serving under a lieutenant or a general. In camp their quarters usually were placed close to the commanding officer, from where they could be called on quickly for all sorts of errands and missions. During active operations Article 36 of the 1861 Army regulations directed them to ride as escort following the officer who detailed them, or to walk at the head of the brigade or division to which they were attached. It also clearly stated they were to "carry dispatches only in special and urgent cases." All dispatch deliveries required the exact date and time at which they were conveyed to be marked on the cover, informing an orderly of the time frame necessary to perform the duty.[16] During battle, speed was essential as orders often were transmitted over wide areas and hostile terrain. Considering the importance of some dispatches one might wonder why so many orderlies were boys.

Gilbert Vanzant was detailed from the 79th Ohio to serve as an orderly on General William T. Ward's staff after the battle of Resaca. Strenuous marching had become too taxing for Gilbert, so he was detached from his regiment and thereby allowed to ride with Ward's division headquarters. During the 1864 Savannah campaign Gilbert was mounted on a captured pony and proved to be one of the most valuable aides at headquarters. Captain Ira N. Snell of the 79th believed it was due to his youth that the boy lacked the discretion of older heads and would take the most direct route delivering orders in spite of danger. Gilbert offered another reason for his actions, stating there were many times during his Army career when he would have given anything to be somewhere else, but pride kept him steady.

Gilbert lost his best friend William Baner of Company A, 79th Ohio, who was killed while carrying a message. "One of the great sorrows of my life as a soldier," he recalled, "was the death of my pal, Billy Baner. Billy was the colonel's orderly, and when possible we were together. When going with the colonel on a tour of inspection he would frequently get permission for me to ride with him, using one of the colonel's horses. During the battle of Peachtree Creek July 20,

The distinctive painted backdrop of Nashville photographer J.H. Van Stavoren's Metropolitan Gallery was used when Gilbert Vanzant, 79th Ohio, was photographed in 1863. That summer he was 11 years old. "The first time I had a razor to my face was while in camp," he mused. "Strolling down to the cook's tent one day, the cook, seeing me, called: 'Come in Gib, and let me shave you.' Setting me on a cracker box, he lathered one side of my face, when he saw my father walking down the company street toward the tent. Not wishing to be caught, the cook took his apron and wiped the lather from my face; I stepped down from my perch, and he went about his duty as if nothing unusual had happened."

Author's Collection

1864, Billy was sent away with a dispatch. Returning with the answer he approached the colonel, still sitting on his little gray horse. The colonel told him to get down, that he might be shot, but the warning came too late. A rebel bullet pierced his heart, knocking him from the saddle. He was carried to the rear and placed in the shade of a tree that stood behind our lines, and with many others who had met the same fate, among them my cousin."

Gilbert fulfilled his obligations well as an orderly, earning the respect of everyone with whom he served. Captain John Speed, assistant adjutant general of the

3rd Division, Twentieth Corps, explained that "We tried to be easy on the boy, but he always insisted upon doing his full duty, and he did it. At the investment of Savannah our division was on the left of the army on the Savannah River. Part of the command was sent over on the Ogeechee [River], twelve or fifteen miles away. It was to be recalled. I wrote an order and called for an orderly. It was, it seems, Gilbert's turn. The little fellow came at the summons. I told him to send me one of the men. He said he would go anywhere any of the men would go. So I gave him the envelope, and away in the night he brought back the receipt."

Captain William Hardenbrook of the 70th Indiana recalled that while chief of pioneers for the Twentieth Corps he sent Gilbert with an order to the pioneers during the battle of Bentonville, North Carolina, on March 19, 1865. "This noble, little, trusty and brave soldier took the order, and in less than thirty minutes returned with my Pioneers. Reporting to me during the thickest of shot and shell, just as he rode up to me, my horse being wounded by a piece of shell from the rebel guns, he took my wounded horse to the rear."

While serving on General Ward's staff Gilbert had the privilege of meeting some of the prominent commanders in the west. One occasion he cherished remembering occurred in front of Kennesaw Mountain when he was ordered to deliver a message to General George H. Thomas, the Army of the Cumberland's popular commander. He had a "nice talk" with the general, who at the time was scanning the mountain through a field glass. He described his view to Gilbert as if he was an officer or close friend instead of a child. On another occasion General Sherman rode up and began conversing with some officers. Reaching in his pocket he procured a cigar, but being unable to find a match looked at Gilbert, saying, "Son, you are younger than I am, won't you get me a light for my cigar?" The boy fetched one and was thanked for his efforts.[17]

Stanton Allen's good conduct with the 1st Massachusetts Cavalry earned him the honor of serving as General George G. Meade's orderly during the latter part of the war. While in the cavalry he shared in a variety of daring adventures. One night in the Wilderness he was ordered to ride 100 yards in front of his company to draw enemy picket fire in a search for the Confederate flank. In the midst of the dangerous work Stanton's horse began to neigh. After a few tense moments an officer approached and asked what was the matter with his horse. Having acquired the steed the previous day after his own was killed, Stanton could offer no reply. Fortunately, daybreak came and with the aid of field glasses no more forward observation details were needed. On another day while securing water, he and a comrade blundered directly into a Rebel infantry column. Bluffing that they were lost Confederate orderlies, they asked directions and spurred off before the ruse was fully discovered and a volley was harmlessly fired after them.

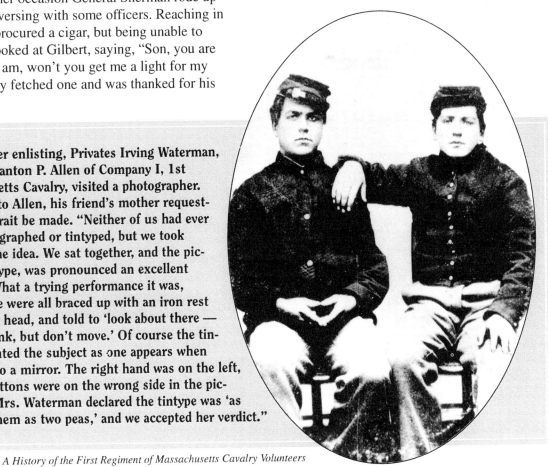

Shortly after enlisting, Privates Irving Waterman, left, and Stanton P. Allen of Company I, 1st Massachusetts Cavalry, visited a photographer. According to Allen, his friend's mother requested the portrait be made. "Neither of us had ever been photographed or tintyped, but we took kindly to the idea. We sat together, and the picture, a tintype, was pronounced an excellent likeness. What a trying performance it was, though! We were all braced up with an iron rest back of the head, and told to 'look about there — you can wink, but don't move.' Of course the tintype presented the subject as one appears when looking into a mirror. The right hand was on the left, and our buttons were on the wrong side in the picture. But Mrs. Waterman declared the tintype was 'as near like them as two peas,' and we accepted her verdict."

A History of the First Regiment of Massachusetts Cavalry Volunteers

As an orderly Allen was equally brave. On April 2, 1865, Stanton was detailed with a major from Meade's staff to deliver a dispatch to General Horatio G. Wright, commanding the Sixth Corps outside Petersburg. Stanton and the officer rode directly across a field as shells screamed around them. One exploded beneath the major's horse, but miraculously both rider and mount escaped unhurt. Stanton initially thought he was dead, but the major shouted, "Come on! I'm all right." They continued and successfully delivered the note.[18]

Stanton was arrested for enlisting under false pretenses his first try and stole away to enroll in the 1st Massachusetts Cavalry at age 14. From being a runaway to serving at the side of General Meade provided a good indication of his drive. Such vigor as he possessed elevated other boys during the war as well. One of Stanton's comrades in the 1st Massachusetts, Richard R. Walsh, served as cavalry General David

L.M. Strayer Collection

Bugler Charles O. Brown of Company C, 3rd Ohio Cavalry, was promoted to corporal in March 1865. He was born in Calhoun County, Michigan, in 1848.

M. Gregg's orderly. At 15, Richard had enlisted in August 1862 as Company A's bugler. In 1864 he was promoted to corporal and then quartermaster sergeant, despite being detached at Gregg's headquarters.[19]

Officers became quite attached to their orderlies, treating many as headquarters' pets. Henry Funk enlisted August 14, 1861, with his father Jacob in Company D, 49th Ohio. Jacob served as a brigade wagoner and his son as company drummer. When 12-year-old Henry joined he stood just four foot seven. Well liked, he was on duty as orderly at his division's headquarters by the end of 1862. His military records list more than 20 battles and campaigns in which he participated. When it was time for the youngster to reenlist as a veteran, Colonel William H. Gibson of the 49th personally witnessed his papers and submitted a sworn statement on his behalf for the mustering officer. Henry and his father were mustered out with their company on November 30, 1865, at Victoria, Texas. At discharge he was still two years underage.[20]

Bruce Miller also enlisted from Ohio at age 12. On October 20, 1861, he signed up as drummer for Company B, 80th Ohio. He was an orderly at Fifteenth Corps headquarters during 1863, but soon after was appointed chief bugler of the Seventeenth Corps' pioneers. In 1864 he returned to Fifteenth Corps headquarters and served until discharged at war's end.[21]

Another Buckeye sought by different commands was Charles O. Brown of Company C, 3rd Ohio Cavalry. Charles, 13, joined the Army with his father in December 1861 and served unmustered until the regiment returned to Ohio on veteran furlough. After his February 1864 muster he was considered good enough to be promoted corporal and chief bugler at regimental headquarters. He was detached from the 3rd Ohio on June 16, 1865, when Lieutenant Samuel S. Culbertson requested Charles to report as orderly at Cavalry Corps headquarters, Military Division of the Mississippi. The request was endorsed by General James H. Wilson, corps commander, through Special Order 109. When the officers of the 3rd, including his father, received the order they flatly refused to part with the boy. A reply was drafted and sent back, asking that the order be revoked as Charles "is the only bugler in the regiment able to sound the calls not already detailed." The young Buckeye was not relieved and five days later was ordered back to his regiment.[22]

Sometimes a transfer request was made to help a

boy. Hendrick Paine's uncle, General Eleazer A. Paine, sent the following letter to Colonel Albert S. Hall of the 105th Ohio after his nephew fell ill.

Col. Hall,

The bearer is my nephew. He is drummer in the 105th Regt. Ohio Vols. He has been sick with the measles and is still in poor health. Really not fit for field service. If you could have him ordered to report to me as an orderly you would confer a very great favor, for which I would be under lasting obligations. As soon as his health is fully restored I would order him to his duty if he was needed. Through your influence the detail could be procured and he ordered here. Have his captain give him his descriptive roll if he can come.

Very respectfully yours E.A. Paine Brig. Gen.

"The written communication from Brig. Gen. Paine is respectfully forwarded," wrote Colonel Hall,

Aide-de-camp William M. Dunn Jr., seated center, was surrounded by other officers belonging to the staff of Lieutenant General Ulysses S. Grant, seen wearing a felt hat to Dunn's immediate left. An employee of Mathew B. Brady's firm took this photograph in July or August 1864 at Grant's City Point, Virginia, headquarters.

National Archives

"with the request that the detail be made. The young man is in feeble health, and can perhaps serve the country as efficiently for the present in the capacity of orderly as any other." On January 15, 1863, Hendrick was transferred to his uncle's staff. In spite of the move his health declined to improve and he was discharged the following month for disability.[23]

William McKee Dunn Jr. ran away from home, enlisting on April 18, 1861, in the 6th Indiana Infantry when 17 years old. That August his father, serving as an aide-de-camp to General McClellan, had him discharged for minority after his whereabouts became known.[24] Will, undaunted by the setback, once more left home against his father's wishes. As months transpired the elder Dunn, then a major on the Judge Advocate General's staff, inquired everywhere for Will — with no results. At last, General Grant, a family friend, was informed that an officer by the name of Will Dunn belonged to the 83rd Indiana. Grant had the soldier brought before him and saw it was Will. After the meeting the general, as a favor, had him transferred to his staff as aide-de-camp.[25]

Of all boy soldiers who served the Union, Dunn, although not quite as young as others, was perhaps the most respected and shouldered the highest responsibility as one of Grant's trusted couriers. In this position he was in contact with numerous leading Federal commanders. Such high-ranking generals as Sherman, McPherson and Meade conversed with him freely about strategy and war news. Sherman habitually referred to Will as "Young Dunn" in his dispatches. When Sherman was nearing the Atlantic coast after his march through Georgia, Grant selected Will for the task of travelling south to greet him with communications. On December 13, 1864, Sherman's Army reached the sea. The following day Will personally handed him Grant's letters and orders. Sherman replied he would retain Dunn until notified that Savannah's Confederate occupants accepted his demands for surrender. Showing the confidence these men placed in Will, on December 26 General John G. Foster wrote Grant, "[Lieutenant] Dunn bears full dispatches from General Sherman, and will be able to explain to you fully the highly encouraging character of the situation in this department."[26] When the conflict closed William Dunn had blossomed into a man, coming a long way from the underage runaway he was four years before.

CHAPTER 11

Gallantry and valor
'in the very vortex of battle'

The assault lasted but a few minutes, remembered 37th Ohio drummer John S. Kountz. His regiment was part of General Sherman's forces attacking Tunnel Hill at the north end of Missionary Ridge east of Chattanooga on November 25, 1863. Their opponents were Confederates of the Army of Tennessee, primarily veteran soldiers belonging to the division of General Patrick R. Cleburne. So strong was Cleburne's position, Kountz believed, that "10,000 men could hold it against ten times their number."

As blaring bugles signaled the Union advance, young Kountz laid his drum aside to accompany his regiment unencumbered. He never forgot what happened next.

"The firing from the enemy's entrenched position [was] simply terrible — grape, canister, shot and shell rained upon us. The fire was so murderous that it fairly plowed up the leaves and made the very ground seem alive. Twice our forces charged upon the rebel works, and twice our bleeding lines were compelled to fall back. In this assault my regiment lost forty-one killed and wounded.

"I was hit by a rifle's ball in the left thigh and bled from the wound until the ground under me seemed saturated with blood. I became very thirsty, but fortunately had two canteens of water. At my side lay [Christopher] Weber, of Company A, who had been instantly killed. As we were not very far from the enemy's works and our men had fallen back to the

point from which the advance was made a few moments before, my position was not an enviable one, as I lay between the two fires. Capt. John Hamm, of Company A, who had always been very kind to me, having been told that I lay wounded in front of our line, went over to my company [G] and reported the fact, asking 'Who will go and get him out?' Wm. Smith [Schmidt] promptly answered, 'I will.' Another comrade pointing out the direction in which I lay, he went to the left of the line, and advancing some distance under cover of the hill, sprang forward, hurriedly placing me upon his back. Although there was much firing, we were soon under cover of the hill to the left of our line.

"I was then placed upon a stretcher and carried to the rear, where the boys gathered around me expressing their warmest sympathy. My leg was bandaged by Surgeon [Adolph W.] Billhardt and I was carried to a log cabin in the ravine, below the point from which we made the advance. I remained upon the porch with other wounded until dark, when I was placed upon a stretcher and taken some distance over the hill, where I was put into an ambulance and taken to a point on the Tennessee River near the mouth of Chickamauga Creek. Here I was laid upon the surgeon's table, and after an examination of my wound the surgeon informed me that my leg was so badly shattered that amputation was necessary, or words to that effect. I objected, but my objection was not heeded; I was then chloroformed and on awakening felt for my leg and it was gone.

Drummer John S. Kountz's regiment, the 37th Ohio, also was known as that state's 3rd German Regiment. John's mother died a few years prior to the war. During his Army service his father and sister also passed away.

L.M. Strayer Collection

"The next day I asked the surgeon for the bullet, and he told me it was in many pieces, being an English explosive rifle ball. After remaining here about ten days, I was with others placed in an ambulance and taken to the field hospital at Chattanooga. At this time I was 17 years of age."[1]

"Johnny" Kountz was allowed to enlist during the fall of 1861 at age 15. He met John Hamm, then a lieutenant in the 37th's newly formed Company G, who told the boy he would like to take him along as a drummer. "I was delighted," Kountz reminisced, "and going home I asked my father's permission. At first he hesitated, but finally gave his consent. On a Monday morning I bid adieu to home — to my father and sister it was the last good-bye ... and taking the train for Toledo, where we changed cars for Cleveland, arrived at Camp Brown the same evening [September 30, 1861]. I was pretty tired from the day's experience. A short time after our arrival in camp the bugle signal notified the men that supper was ready, and we formed in single file, marching to the kitchen, where I was given a large tin cup and a tablespoon. The cook with a long-handled dipper filled my cup with coffee, and I was given a slice of bread and a piece of baked salt pork, which constituted my first army meal."[2]

Johnny was a daring, popular boy. On one occasion in West Virginia during an early December 1862 cold spell, he went to the assistance of another soldier who had fallen through thin ice covering the Kanawha River. Lying on the uncertain surface and reaching with outstretched arm, he broke through himself when the man's weight proved too great. A rope was rushed to the scene and both were saved.[3]

As an orderly (all drummers served as orderlies in the 37th) he was called upon regularly. In July 1863 Colonel Edward Siber chose Johnny to accompany him on a night reconnaissance outside Jackson, Mississippi. After advancing in the dark for three hours the colonel insisted they rest and shared his blanket with the young drummer. Leaving the boy asleep, Siber crept forward to listen to the enemy's movements until satisfied of their departure, then awoke his orderly and they returned to camp. It was such high esteem he enjoyed in the regiment that induced a comrade to risk his own life to save Johnny's at Tunnel Hill.[4]

After the war Kountz's charisma propelled him far in business and politics. In 1885 he was honored with election to national commander of the Grand Army of the Republic, the country's largest veterans' organization. That same year Kate Brownlee Sherwood, wife of Brevet Brigadier General Isaac R. Sherwood, penned and published the touching poem "The Drummer Boy of Mission Ridge," by which Johnny was known for the rest of his life. With political clout, a decade later he was awarded the Medal of Honor, the military's highest decoration for valor, for his actions at Tunnel Hill.[5]

William Schmidt, the young comrade who rescued Kountz, also received the Medal of Honor for his heroics that day. He was a 16-year-old school chum of Johnny's and both mustered together in September 1861.[6]

With so many boys serving as stretcher bearers, orderlies or front-line combatants, gallant acts were abundant and did not go unrecognized. During the war 30 soldiers aged 17 or younger were awarded the Medal of Honor. Ten others were 18. The youngest recipient was William "Willie" Johnston of the Green Mountain State.[7]

In the summer of 1861 William H. Johnston, 40, enlisted in Company B, 3rd Vermont. That December young William followed his father and was added to Company D. Willie was 11 at the time of his enlistment, but was not allowed to muster in accordance with Army regulations. This proved no deterrent as he went along anyway and served in every capacity as a soldier. With the approach of his 12th birthday the next summer he officially was mustered. His service records indicate his muster was delayed due to the stipulation he could not draw pay because of his age. Musicians were not supposed to be accepted unless they were 12 years old or older. Willie's birthdate is unknown, but believed to be in July of 1850, according to his February 1864 veteran enlistment declaration form, where he stated his age as 13 years and seven months. It is likely his 12th birthday was near enough to allow his muster. The deed leading to his earning the Medal of Honor occurred almost immediately after his acceptance in the regiment.[8]

On June 26, 1862, the Army of the Potomac engaged the Rebels five miles outside its goal of Richmond. It was as close to the Confederate capital as it would advance. In a series of delaying actions and retreats, the Army fell back over the next week until it was able to batter the Rebels at Malvern Hill. The so-called Seven Days battles were too much for many Union soldiers, who gave way during the campaign. General William F. Smith, commanding the 2nd Division, Sixth Corps, was impressed with those who did not. In his after-action report he pointed out that "The cheerfulness with which the men and officers [in *his* division] endured the fatigues and watchings and privations of this terrible march, always forming their

Recommended for the Medal of Honor by General William F. Smith, drummer Willie Johnston of the 3rd Vermont received the award 15 months after his actions on Virginia's Peninsula. Here the medal is visible on his jacket just above the drumsling.

The Hartford, New York, Historical Group

lines with alacrity when threatened and always repulsing the enemy when attacked, is above all praise." [9] When Smith's division paraded at its Harrison's Landing camp soon afterward, Willie Johnston skillfully beat his drum while marching in the column. He was the only drummer in the division playing as all other musicians had discarded their instruments during the retreat. General Smith, noticing the small boy's singular accomplishment, ascertained his name and regiment, then forwarded the information to the Secretary of War with a recommendation for the Medal of Honor. On September 16, 1863, Willie received his medal. At the time he was just 13 years old. [10]

Young Johnston spent most of the remainder of his service either as a patient or attending others in Baltimore-area hospitals. Following a stint in the Veteran Reserve Corps he was transferred back to the 3rd Vermont in August 1865 and mustered out on the 31st. At 15, he was still three years shy of "military age." [11]

Benjamin B. Levy also was issued a Medal of Honor for conspicuous actions during the Seven Days battles. In October 1861, 16-year-old Ben enlisted in Company G, 1st New York Infantry. (His younger brother Robert, 14, previously had joined the 58th New York). Ten days after enlistment Ben was appointed company drummer and soon detached as an orderly for General Joseph K. Mansfield. One of his

The Army Medal of Honor was authorized July 12, 1862, and presented to non-commissioned officers and privates for gallantry in action. Officers became eligible for the award on March 3, 1863.

principal duties was carrying dispatches from camp at Newport News, Virginia, to Fort Monroe, situated to the north of Hampton Roads and guarding the sea entrance to the James River, which led to Richmond. General John E. Wool, stationed at Fort Monroe, sent and received numerous messages from Mansfield via Benjamin Levy. [12]

Almost daily the Union ship *Express* visited the fort with supplies, mail, munitions and men. Ben was a regular passenger as dispatch carrier. One morning as the *Express* was pulling a small schooner used to carry fresh water to blockade ships off the coast, the Confederate gunboat *Sea Bird* approached from the opposite side of Hampton Roads. Being a hazy morning, the *Express'* commander could not clearly distinguish the boat's flag and assumed it was delivering mail or official dispatches. Suddenly his error was made plain when a shot from *Sea Bird* screamed overhead. The unarmed *Express* tried to escape, but the Confederate vessel steadily came closer during the one-sided combat. As the chase progressed it occurred to Ben that the water schooner in tow was an impediment. Without orders he ran to the rear of the ship, concealed himself, and cut the heavy rope attached to the schooner. Once released, the *Express* gained considerable speed, allowing it to get away. Upon arrival at the fort Ben was complimented by all on board, and later by both Generals Wool and Mansfield. [13]

When General McClellan launched his 1862 Peninsular campaign toward Richmond, Mansfield appealed to the 1st New York's colonel to have Ben detached to his staff. The boy thanked the general, but asked to remain with his regiment. Back to his former position in Company G he drummed throughout the first five of the Seven Days battles. On the night of June 29 the 1st New York, detailed as pickets, covered the rear, which was an unenviable task knowing the Rebels were all too happy to "gobble" a private or two that fell behind. Ben's tentmate, sick with malaria, could not keep step in his weakened condition. When he was about to give up, Ben smashed his drum, seized his comrade's musket and equipment, and helped him escape.[14]

On June 30 the regiment fought at Glendale near White Oak Swamp. As a musician Ben was not required to go forward into battle. In spite of this, he reported to his captain the fate of his drum and volunteered to fight in the ranks. The 1st New York was heavily engaged while holding the left of General Hiram G. Berry's brigade. Berry extolled the New Yorkers' conduct, reporting that they "behaved handsomely. This regiment received a charge of a rebel regiment, and charged in turn and broke the enemy in confusion."[15]

At midnight Berry's troops were ordered to fall back with the rest of the Army to Malvern Hill, leaving their dead and wounded behind. Two abandoned casualties were the 1st New York's color bearers. During one of the regiment's charges both were shot down near Ben. Seeing the first man fall, he lunged to grab the flag's shaft. While in this act the other bearer was struck, leaving his flag to be cared for by the youngster as well. Throwing away his sick comrade's gun, he seized both colors, flung them over his shoulder and hastily dashed for safety in the Union line. As he ran the lead whirled past so close he received a flesh wound. Breaking through some woods in the rear he became disoriented, but stumbled into General Philip Kearny, commanding his division. Following the general's directions he located his command and turned over the flags to Colonel Garrett Dyckman. For Ben's gallantry Kearny promoted him to color sergeant on the spot and later recommended the Medal of Honor for his heroic actions.[16]

The next morning Color Sergeant Levy was called on to carry his flag for the first time as another day of battle dawned. As the New Yorkers marched toward Union soldiers already entrenching they were mistaken for Rebels because of their soiled appearance. A battery fired with effect on their position in an open field, causing the regiment's officers to command their men to conceal themselves in the grass. Colonel Dyckman ordered Ben to unfurl the flag and advance until the firing stopped. It worked, the cannons stopped, but his show also caught the attention of Confederate sharpshooters who pinned him down in the middle of the field. One bullet hit the flag staff, another his cap and a third his tin cup. Quickly he dropped to the ground as more bullets whistled overhead. To rise up meant certain death, so the clear-headed boy disconnected the flag from its staff and tied it in a bundle. He then laid parallel to his regiment and rolled over and over until he reached his comrades, who heartily cheered his audacious feat.[17]

Ben proudly carried the 1st New York's colors for the remainder of its two-year enlistment. After being discharged with his command in May 1863 he stayed at home until the following January. While the 40th New York was home on furlough he joined that regiment as a private, but was promoted to sergeant when his past valor became known.

The spring campaign of 1864 seemingly was one continuous battle for the Army of the Potomac. In the Wilderness Ben was severely wounded, suffering a compound fracture of his left thigh. Lying exposed on the field for a number of hours, he was removed to a tent hospital erected near the front line. The next morning a Confederate raid forced everyone into the open as the tents and supplies were torched. For two weeks the emaciated soldiers laid in the open field with nothing to eat but two crackers a day and water procured by those able to walk. Finally their dire situation became known when a nurse made his way to the Union lines. At once a force was assembled to retrieve the wounded men, who were taken to Fredericksburg-area hospitals. Ben's leg was infected with gangrene and he fought a long battle with doctors over its proposed amputation. When a New York hospital physician declared it must be done, he discharged himself and returned to a previous hospital where the doctors were not as intent on cutting off the limb. Eventually his leg healed enough to warrant his return to the 40th New York in March 1865. Soon after his arrival he received the Medal of Honor from Washington. Upon inspection it was found to be engraved, "For gallantry in the battle of the Wilderness." A little later a new medal with the correct inscription, "For gallantry at Glendale, Virginia," was sent in its stead. The error could have been caused because six different generals had recommended him for the decoration, and each for different acts.

Ben Levy was present during the last days of the Appomattox campaign, but due to recurring leg pain was sent home prior to the Grand Review in Washington in May 1865.[18]

John Cook's citation accompanying his 1894 Medal of Honor award for heroism at Antietam read, "Volunteered at the age of 15 years to act as a cannoneer, and as such volunteer served a gun under the terrific fire of the enemy." Cook was born in Cincinnati on August 4, 1847. When 13 he signed up as bugler for Battery B, 4th U.S. Artillery. After a year of relative inactivity in Washington's defenses, Battery B joined the Army of the Potomac and participated in almost every battle in the East. Besides bugle duties John became Lieutenant James Stewart's orderly. During a fight he dashed among the three two-gun sections of the battery with orders. One artilleryman recalled that his presence, at times, was not appreciated. "Johnnie rode a bob-tailed pony, which we always hated to see in the line of battle because she made a center target for the enemy's shells. Sometimes Stewart would send him to the rear, in order to get the pony out of sight of the enemy. 'Get that damn ghost out of sight!' the officer would yell sometimes when the enemy would begin to reach for little John and his white pony with their shells."[19]

At Antietam it proved fortunate that Stewart had the young bugler at his side, as Cook related:

General [John] Gibbon, our [brigade] commander, had just ordered Lieutenant Stewart to take his section about one hundred yards to the right of the Hagerstown Pike, in front of two straw stacks, when he beckoned me to follow. No sooner had we unlimbered, when a column of Confederate infantry, emerging from the so-called west woods, poured a volley into us, which brought fourteen or seventeen of my brave comrades to the ground. The two straw stacks offered some kind of shelter for our wounded, and it was a sickening sight to see those poor maimed and crippled fellows crowding on top of one another, while several stepping but a few feet away, were hit again or killed.

Just then Captain [Joseph B.] Campbell unlimbered the other four guns to the left of Stewart, and I reported to him. He had just dismounted, when he was hit twice, and his horse fell dead with several bullets in its body. I started with the captain to the rear and turned him over to one of the drivers. He ordered me to report to Lieutenant Stewart and tell him to take command of the battery. I reported, and, seeing the cannoneers nearly all down, and one, with a pouch full of ammunition, lying dead, I unstrapped the pouch, started for the battery and worked as a cannoneer. We were then in the very vortex of the battle. The enemy

Deeds of Valor

Bugler John Cook assists his wounded commander, Captain Joseph B. Campbell, from the field at Antietam. Campbell's Battery B, 4th U.S. Artillery, was nominally attached to the Army of the Potomac's famed Iron Brigade.

had made three desperate attempts to capture us, the last time coming within ten or fifteen [yards] of our guns. It was at this time that General Gibbon, seeing the condition of the battery, came to the gun that stood in the pike, and in full uniform of a brigadier-general, worked as a gunner and cannoneer. He was very conspicuous, and it is indeed surprising that he came away alive.

At this battle we lost forty-four men killed and wounded, and about forty horses which shows how hard a fight it was.[20]

John's mature actions prompted Stewart to recommend him for the Medal of Honor, stating, "His courage and conduct in that battle won the admiration of all who witnessed."

Cook served his three-year enlistment in the same manner. At Gettysburg he rode nearly a half mile one way dispatching orders to the battery's different sections. Each ride was hazardous with Confederate sharpshooters making him their mark. Shortly after his term expired in May 1864 he participated in the battle of Bethesda Church. The regimental historian commented:

It was at least his twentieth battle, and he was still less than seventeen years old. Literally, Johnnie had more battles than he had years. His time was out, he had his honorable discharge in his pocket, and was only awaiting transportation to go home.

But his bugle never sounded so loud and clear as it did when he followed the Captain and blew "Forward, trot!" and "Forward, gallop!" as our horses stretched their necks for that rebel battery on the pike. The Captain did not want Johnnie to go into action on that day. Maybe he had a superstition that a man or boy who went into a fight when his time was out would be killed. But Johnnie had got that old scent of powder up his nose once more, and nothing could stop him.

So away he went, following the Old Man along the pike and blowing his bugle as lustily as ever, while the enemy's canister cut down the brush by the side of the road or screamed over our heads. And when we finally unlimbered our guns and made them "talk," Johnnie was everywhere as usual, riding back and forth along the line of battle, as fresh and eager as if he were a tenderfoot rather than a veteran.[21]

The October 1862 battle of Perryville, Kentucky, supplied the opportunity for William H. Surles to unselfishly offer his life for his commanding officer, Colonel Anson G. McCook. The heroic deed placed his name on the list of Medal of Honor recipients 29

years later. In September 1861, when William enlisted with his brother Alexander in Company G, 2nd Ohio Infantry, he was 16 years old, weighed less than 100 pounds, and possessed a girlish countenance.[22] Of his regiment's fight at Perryville, Surles recalled:

We were forced to fall back. During the retreat Colonel McCook's horse was shot from under him. Arming himself with a musket taken from a dead soldier, he fought on foot and by his own gallant example, cheered the drooping spirits of his men. The ground we traversed was thickly strewn with the dead and wounded of our own army and presented a ghastly picture.

We observed with horror that our pursuers, with the cruelty of barbarians, were plunging their bayonets into the prostrate forms of many of our comrades. Colonel McCook himself noticed one of the ghouls, just about to extinguish the life of one of our boys with his bayonet. The Colonel halted, fired his musket and dropped the fellow before he could accomplish his dastardly deed.

The death of the rebel made the enemy still more furious. A Confederate soldier, a veritable giant in appearance, presently sprang from behind a tree close by and took deliberate aim at the colonel. I had observed this fellow's movements and realized the great danger my beloved commander [was in]. How I wished I could with a well-directed shot end this "Johnny's" life. But like the colonel himself I had just fired my musket and did not have time to intercept the shot. My blood froze in my veins as I saw the rebel raise his gun and take aim at our brave leader. Presently, on the spur of the moment and moved by the love and admiration I felt toward our commander, I sprang directly in front of Colonel McCook, ready to receive the bullet which was to strike him.

Happily the rebel giant was a little too slow in firing or hesitated to make sure of his shot; anyway, before he pulled the trigger he himself was shot through the head and rolled on the ground to die within a few seconds. One of the crack shots in our company had frustrated his plans. All of this happened while shot and shell were flying around us like hail, and within less time than it takes to tell it. I should not forget to mention the conclusion of the episode, for it made me the happiest man in our regiment and has ever been one of the proudest moments of my life. When Colonel McCook saw his would-be assassin fall, he took me in his arms and with tears in his eyes kissed me as a father would his son.[23]

Surles served the remainder of the war uninjured, but at Atlanta in 1864 his older brother was killed instantly at his side.

Of all youngsters receiving the Medal of Honor,

Julian A. Scott became the most renowned. Known in his home state as "the Drummer Boy Hero," Julian was born February 14, 1846, outside Johnson, Vermont. When war erupted 15 years later he and two brothers left to fight for their country, a Scott family tradition.[24]

Three days after President Lincoln's initial call for troops 18-year-old Lucian Scott enlisted and joined Battery F, 4th U.S. Artillery. His military adventures were shared through letters mailed home and published in the local paper. Six months after enlistment his escapades almost were cut short when a cannon's re-

coil knocked him senseless during the October 1861 battle of Ball's Bluff, Virginia. Left for dead on the field, his pockets were rifled by victorious Confederates who had driven the small Union force back to the other side of the Potomac River. Late in the evening Lucian awoke to the possibility of becoming a prisoner, and instead crept past gray-clad pickets near the river and swam for safety. The current carried him to a small island where he concealed himself in a cornfield. He was found the next morning by a Union patrol that helped sweep Confederate pickets off the island with small arms

Deeds of Valor

'Don't shoot the damned little Yank!'

A runaway at 13, William H. Horsfall enlisted the last day of 1861 as a drummer in Company G, 1st Kentucky Infantry. He was exceptionally small, standing just four foot three, and proved quite difficult to clothe in a proper fitting uniform. Because government-issue brogans were too large for his feet, he preferred going barefoot to wearing shoes. Likewise, his drum was so large he habitually stumbled over it while marching. Eventually he "traded" the instrument for a musket.

During the 1862 siege of Corinth, Mississippi, the 1st Kentucky participated in a sharp skirmish on May 21. According to Horsfall: "The regiment had just made a desperate charge across [a] ravine. Captain [James T.] Williamson [of Company H] was wounded in the charge and ... left between the lines. Lieutenant [Louis H.] Hocke, approaching me, said, 'Horsfall, Captain Williamson is in a serious predicament; rescue him if possible.' So I placed my gun against a tree, and, in a stooping run, gained his side and dragged him to the stretcher bearers, who took

him to the rear."

Seven months later in the confusion of battle at Stones River, Tennessee, the diminutive drummer boy-turned-rifleman, now 14, was separated from his company and nearly "gobbled" by an advancing Confederate line. Realizing the lone soldier in blue was just a boy, and a very small one at that, one of the Rebels shouted, "Don't shoot the damned little Yank! I want him for a cage." Defiantly, Horsfall turned his back on the Southerners and "ran for his life," finding his regiment and safety.

In 1895, Horsfall received the Medal of Honor for gallantry in rescuing the wounded captain at Corinth. Interestingly, his recommendation came from Kentucky congressman Albert S. Berry — a former Confederate soldier. Horsfall afterward wrote to Berry: "I value my record not as a victor over the vanquished but as a personal vindication of my fidelity to the cause under which I enrolled and would desire it just the same had I followed the leadership of the famous heroes Lee and Jackson."

and cannon fire.[25] Lucian completed his tour with the battery and later joined a Vermont cavalry outfit, with which he was captured in December 1864. Paroled a few weeks later he returned home a veritable skeleton of his former self.[26]

At the outset, Lucian's letters home inspired his two younger brothers, Julian and Charles, to enlist.[27] Six weeks after Lucian's departure Julian joined Company E, 3rd Vermont. Standing barely five foot four with a fair complexion, brown hair and hazel eyes, he was unable to pass muster except as fifer for the company. As time passed he became enamored with the drum and acquired some competency with that instrument, even though he was not the official company drummer. Julian also was quite enthusiastic about drawing. In addition to his issued articles he always carried a sketchbook, which he used to draw every facet of military life surrounding him. The 3rd Vermont spent its first few months in the Washington defenses, so there was plenty of free time for him to sketch and expand his creativity. But when General McClellan put into motion his ill-fated Peninsular campaign, his regiment finally saw action.[28]

Julian's heroic exhibition took place soon afterward at an engagement near Lee's Mill, Virginia, on April 16, 1862. General William F. Smith's division was instructed to force the enemy to discontinue work strengthening his batteries, to silence their fire, and gain control of a dam existing at that point of the fortified Confederate line known as "the one gun battery." The first order issued to the advancing infantry was to open fire on any working parties. After progressing over marshy ground they encountered the Rebels, who answered with shrapnel and small-arms fire. But within an hour the Confederate guns fell silent.[29]

During the show of force it was noticed that a dummy wooden gun had been mounted in the fort, replacing the original, and that the parapets were thinly manned. Clues deciphered from the scene indicated a possible withdrawal, necessitating further reconnaissance. About 3 p.m., 18 Union guns were wheeled within 500 yards of the fort and began firing to cover a further advance. The Confederates replied, although their fire soon slackened again. Between the opposing antagonists was the Warwick River, 20 yards in front of the Rebel works. The flooded river at that point was described as being two to four feet deep, covering an area 100 yards wide. Roots, small trees and under-

brush disrupted the foamy current as the chilled water meandered by. Four companies of the 3rd Vermont were ordered to cross and capture rifle pits at the fort's base. If successful in carrying this first line they were to raise a white flag, notifying the cannoneers to cease firing and for reinforcements to follow.

Holding cartridge boxes above the water as best they could, the two leading companies moved forward and deployed without firing a shot as the other two followed in close order. The defenders commenced shooting at the oncoming Federals as soon as they entered the creek. The Vermonters returned fire upon emerging from the water, and the rifle pits hurriedly were abandoned to the onrushing soldiers in blue. At first, success seemed assured. Even one of the fort's earthworks was occupied by the swarming attackers. Suddenly, two masked Rebel infantry regiments rose up from behind another section of works and delivered a deadly volley. Undaunted, the four Vermont companies held their ground and with spirit tried to reply shot for shot, but increasingly lost their advantage in the exchange. They discovered that, despite care in crossing the river, many cartridges and percussion caps were fouled by water. And for some reason, instead of waving a white flag as ordered, a runner was sent to summon reinforcements, but none arrived. General Smith never heard from the runner. Finally, three gray-clad regiments moving by the flanks showered the Vermont companies with lead. After 45 minutes they were ordered to retire. The command was passed along but some men, fearful of leaving the protective works or because the order was not heard, did not move. It was repeated, the wounded were gathered, and all started back toward the swollen river. By some means the Confederates had further flooded the Warwick, raising the level two more feet, which nearly covered the retreating soldiers' heads. Many were badly wounded before entering the fast-moving water. Others were struck as they swam or slowly waded across.[30]

Standing on the far bank in the relative safety of pine trees, Julian, then 16, was deeply moved by the scene of his bloodied and desperate comrades struggling in the water. Ignoring intense fire from the opposite shore, he ventured out in the deep pool to retrieve wounded companions. Twice he crossed the stream and carried or helped at least nine men from its murky depths. On one attempt he and Ephraim Brown went

"The Rear Guard at White Oak Swamp" —
an engraved version of a Julian Scott drawing based
on his 1869 oil painting of the same title and subject.
At Scott's insistence the engraving appeared in
Volume 2 of The Century Company's *Battles and
Leaders of the Civil War.* The fifer-artist was severely
wounded June 30, 1862, in fighting at White Oak
Swamp near Richmond.

to the assistance of John C. Backum, who after being
shot through the chest, was struggling to survive. As
they pushed on Brown, too, was shot. Julian alone
labored to shore with Backum and then retrieved the
stricken Brown. Corporal James Fletcher of Company
E later told the teenager, "I can trace you out as being
foremost in all duties assigned to you, and running
yourself into unnecessary danger for the love of danger."

Julian was not the only soldier to rescue others
that day. In his report of the action, General Smith
concluded, "I will only add that among the four com-

panies of skirmishers of the Third Vermont Volunteers
who crossed the creek there were more individual acts
of heroism performed than I ever before read of in a
great battle." The fact that 82 of the 192 who crossed
the stream became casualties bore witness to Smith's
words.[31]

Under the general's directive to honor those
whose courageous deeds were performed at Lee's
Mill, he asked Lieutenant Colonel Wheelock G. Veazey of the 3rd to pick the most deserving for the Medal of Honor. Veazey's selection included the following
citation:

Julian Scott, Fifer. Gallant conduct at Lee's Mills, April
16, 1862, displayed in crossing the creek under a terrific
fire of musketry several times to assist in bringing off the
wounded.[32]

During the June 30 battle of White Oak Swamp,
Julian was wounded in the thigh as the Vermonters
rallied to allow time for the Army to fall back to Malvern Hill. From the battlefield he was transported to
several hospitals, and by August was listed as a patient
at the general hospital on David's Island in New York

harbor. He resumed passing his leisure time with pencil and paper, sketching scenes for his wardmates or for fun. One day a wealthy, well-connected New Yorker named Henry E. Clark visited the hospital and noticed Julian's exceptional talent displayed in his drawings. Impressed with the artwork, Clark supplied paper and utensils for the boy's use on subsequent visits. Friendship evolved between the two, and Clark offered Julian assistance in gaining admission to the National Academy of Design, the country's premier art school. Through his new patron he received an early discharge from his military obligation in April 1863 with the remark "by way of favor." Inside of a month Julian, with Clark's help, was trying to get back to the front lines as an illustrator. He eventually succeeded, and specialized in sketching soldiers in everyday camp settings or producing portraits. His work that summer started Julian in a professional art career that spanned the next four decades.[33]

Characterized by his realistic style and attention to historical accuracy, he freelanced as a military illustrator for leading magazines and also received numerous commissioned assignments. One of his best known works was the 1874 oil painting "The Battle of Cedar Creek." The canvas commissioned for the Vermont statehouse covered nearly 200 square feet.[34]

In addition to painting Civil War scenes and portraits, Scott became one of the best artists of native-American subjects after receiving the job of Indian agent for the 1890 census. The position moved him west to Oklahoma Territory, where he was directed to take the first Indian census of the region. Before arriving he purchased a camera that he used in combination with his artistic eye to record the Indians as they lived. At first Julian was not impressed with the natives, but as he learned more he grew to admire them. Not only did he photograph Indians, he sketched and conversed with them, and collected artifacts of their culture. His record greatly contrasted with the work of other contemporary artists, who depicted only warriors and buffalo hunts. Like his sketches of comrades in camp during the war, he chose to showcase the day-to-day life of average people. His work was not duplicated in its reality of their lifestyle.[35] By the time of his death on July 4, 1901, Julian Scott — a genuine war hero at age 16 — had become one of the leading American artists of the second half of the 19th century.[36]

Earning the respect of peers elevated a number of

Reminiscences of the War of the Rebellion

First Lieutenant Elbridge J. Copp, 3rd New Hampshire.

worthy youngsters to the non-commissioned ranks, or won them the right to wear shoulder straps. Understandably, however, some soldiers were not easily persuaded to place their trust in young officers. Older recruits attached to a regiment often displayed misgivings. Adjutant Elbridge Copp recalled dissatisfaction from a squad of replacements when it first encountered him in the camp of the 3rd New Hampshire in October 1864. "The next morning after the arrival of the recruits they were lined up in front of my tent, to be assigned to the different companies of the regiment in proportion to the strength of the companies. As I threw the flap of my tent back and stepped out, a smile went along the line, and quite a little nudging of el-

Pictorial History Thirteenth Regiment Vermont Volunteers

**Second Lieutenant Charles W. Randall
Company G, 13th Vermont.**

bows and uncalled for remarks. One within my hearing was "Look at the boy." I also remember that I had my own convictions as to the situation, mentally making note that a few weeks of discipline would teach them respect for the shoulder straps, if not for the individual."[37]

It is not surprising that Copp initially was treated with some disrespect. At age 18 he was commissioned a second lieutenant, and on July 20, 1863, was appointed first lieutenant and adjutant of his regiment. He originally mustered as a private in August 1861 when 16. By February 1, 1862, his soldierly deportment had gained him the position of sergeant major, and though young, he was well liked by subordinates as well as those in command.

Just who was the youngest Union officer? The question has been asked for decades. In the introduction of his published reminiscences, Copp concluded that he should be given the honor. "Some years ago," he wrote, "the question as to who was the youngest officer of the War was raised and discussed through the newspapers. In a communication to the *Boston Journal* William O. Clough, editor of the *Nashua Telegraph,* claimed that I was the youngest commissioned officer in the service who was commissioned from the ranks, having enlisted as a private and receiving my commission as Lieutenant at the age of eighteen. This statement was met by Gardner C. Hawkins of the 3rd Vermont Regiment, who said he was commissioned as a 2nd Lieutenant Oct. 18, 1864, that he was eighteen years old on the 11th day of February previous, and it was also claimed by Albert Clarke, secretary of the Home Market Club, who [belonged to] the 13th Vermont regiment, that a young officer of his regiment was commissioned as Lieutenant at the age of sixteen. This young [officer], Charles W. Randall, was the son of Colonel Francis V. Randall of the 13th Vermont ... and who commissioned his son from civil life to a lieutenancy in his own regiment.

"I was commissioned on January 1, 1863, five months and eight days after my eighteenth birthday. Hawkins received his commission something over nine months after his eighteenth birthday. Therefore the claim that I was the youngest commissioned officer so far as known who rose from the ranks is substantiated."[38]

According to military records Copp indeed was younger than Hawkins, and it is true Charles Randall's appointment was issued by his father when the former was only 16. Like Copp, young Lieutenant Randall at first was looked upon with misgivings, as pointed out by the 13th Vermont's historian. "When the Colonel promoted his son, a stripling of only 16, to the second lieutenancy of Company G there was some quiet grumbling, but the youth made a good officer."[39]

At Gettysburg Charles manfully fulfilled his duty as well as anyone in the regiment. On July 2, 1863, the 13th, a nine-month organization, was on Cemetery Hill until ordered forward to support a battery. A vicious fight engulfing the Third and much of the Second corps was underway in its front, and soon a rider approached bearing orders for Colonel Randall to report to General Winfield S. Hancock. The general in-

U.S. Army Military History Institute

Colonel Francis V. Randall Sr., 13th Vermont.

"At this time my horse was killed, and I fell to the ground with him. While on the ground, I discovered a rebel line debouching from the woods on our left, and forming substantially across our track about 40 rods in our front. We received one volley from them, which did us very little injury, when my men sprang forward with the bayonet with so much precipitancy that they appeared to be taken wholly by surprise, and threw themselves in the grass, surrendering, and we passed over them...."[40]

The guns were recaptured, as General Hancock desired.

During the action late that afternoon Charles approached First Lieutenant Clarke, commanding his company, and pleaded, "I want to go to the Colonel, he is shot." Clarke assented. In a few minutes he returned, almost breathless, saying, "He's all right; it was his horse." The next day the 13th Vermont was engaged again, doing great execution firing into the right flank of what became known as "Pickett's Charge."[41]

Francis V. Randall Jr. also accompanied the colonel and his brother that day. "Jimmy," as he was called, had followed his father, uninvited, to Washington shortly after the elder Randall offered his services to the government in 1861. Francis Sr. was made captain of Company F, 2nd Vermont, and when the 13th was being recruited in the fall of 1862 was appointed colonel. Jimmy finally was allowed at age 12 to enlist as a drummer in the 13th's Company F on January 1, 1863. More than once he barely escaped capture carrying dispatches as an orderly, and following the battle of Gettysburg General George J. Stannard, his brigade commander, personally thanked him for staying on the field with his command.[42]

When the 13th Vermont mustered out a few weeks after Gettysburg all three family members returned home, but only for a brief time. Colonel Randall was asked to retain his rank with the newly forming 17th Vermont. Charles and Jimmy also reenlisted and served the remainder of the war together in their father's regiment. Charles became extremely ill with smallpox, which he believed was contracted from used underwear he had purchased in Washington. On March 9, 1865, he was discharged and died in 1868 from the effects of his military illness.[43]

That Elbridge Copp was not impressed with Charles Randall's family-connected rank is a moot point.

formed Randall that one of his batteries had been captured and asked if his men could retake it. "I told him I thought I could," the colonel wrote a week later, "and that I was willing to try. He said it would be a hazardous job, and he would not order it, but, if I thought I could do it, I might try. By this time my regiment had come up, and I moved them to the front far enough so that when I deployed them in line of battle they would leave Hancock's men in their rear. They were now in column by divisions, and I gave the order to deploy in line, instructing each captain as to what we were to do as they came on to the line, and, taking my position to lead them, gave the order to advance.

There were numerous examples of underage officers in the Army if he had inquired further. James J. Chase, for one, attempted to enter the service on several occasions, but was denied each time because of his age, being born February 9, 1847. At age 16 in 1863, he was accepted as a substitute and reported to the drafted forces, where he remained until formation of the 32nd Maine the following spring. On April 5, 1864, Chase received a second lieutenant's commission when 17 years and three months old. That July he was one of 102 regimental casualties suffered in the battle of the Crater at Petersburg. Wounded in the head, he was first thought to be mortally injured. A bullet entered his left temple and exited through the right eye, ripping it from the socket. While still in the hospital he was promoted to first lieutenant before being discharged in December 1864. Still desiring to serve he reenlisted in the Maine Coast Guard, aiding the Union until after the war closed. A few years later he lost his

The Thirty-Second Maine Regiment of Infantry Volunteers

Second Lieutenant James J. Chase
Company D, 32nd Maine.

remaining vision and was plagued with other complications from the facial wound. But for the rest of his life he maintained a cheerful attitude, and became one of the best known members of the 32nd Maine's veteran association.[44]

Another young officer rising from the ranks was Joseph Benson Foraker. On January 4, 1863, "Ben" was appointed second lieutenant of Company A, 89th Ohio, when 16 years and six months old. In February 1864 he was made first lieutenant, and captain by brevet near the end of the war. Foraker first enlisted as a private, and if his promotions caused any hard feelings they were few. Reasons for the boy's support were provided by comrades George W. Doughty of Company F, and Henry Bieber of Company H. Bieber stated, "He was the same in manners from first to last. A good many of those fellows when they got shoulder straps on, wouldn't associate with the poor devils who hadn't the intelligence, or the influence, or the opportunity to get promoted. We couldn't all be officers, and Ben seemed to understand that, and think just as much of us anyhow." [45]

Doughty agreed, believing that "Nobody was more popular. He was so generous and unassuming that he was universally liked. When he was promoted he put on no airs. Neither did our Colonel Glenn [Lieutenant Colonel William H. Glenn] of Chillicothe. Yet it was unusual for men promoted from the ranks to behave so. 'Ben,' as we always called him, engaged in our sports, and was as much a boy with us as ever, though he could be dignified when it was necessary and proper." [46]

Not only was it important to be "dignified," as an officer one also needed to show leadership. Foraker fulfilled both requirements well. A good example of the latter was displayed during the Union assault of Missionary Ridge. The morning of November 25, 1863, Foraker returned from Ohio where he had been recruiting for the 89th's depleted ranks. Hearing of the proposed advance and learning of the extreme shortage of regimental officers (all but a handful had been captured two months earlier at Chickamauga), the young lieutenant hurried to his post, as he recorded in his journal:

Arrived just in time to engage in the fight. I found the regiment under arms. The army charged Missionary Ridge. Our brigade charged on [the] double quick over two miles and up an awfully steep mountain. I commanded two com-

U.S. Army Military History Institute

A knight-errant's 'legitimate successor'

Brevet Captain Joseph B. Foraker, standing fourth from right, was General Henry W. Slocum's youngest staff officer when the above photograph was taken in June 1865. With arms folded, Slocum sits at center. Standing at far left is Brevet Major William G. Tracy, who received the Medal of Honor in 1895 for meritorious action at Chancellorsville, where his right arm was broken.

Acting as Slocum's aide-de-camp the morning of March 19, 1865, at Bentonville, North Carolina, Foraker with Tracy and several mounted orderlies rode forward to investigate increasing musketry fire. They proved an easy mark as Tracy soon was hit in an ankle. Rebel prisoners divulged that General J.E. Johnston was ahead in force, information that Foraker hurried back to Slocum. The general scribbled a note requesting immediate reinforcements, entrusting his young aide to deliver it to General Sherman. "Ride well to the right," he advised Foraker, "to keep clear of the enemy's left flank, and don't spare horseflesh."

Foraker reached Sherman near sundown, recalling: "He was on the left side of the road on a sloping hillside, where, as I understood, he had just halted only a few minutes before for the night. Sherman saw me approaching and walked briskly towards me, took [the] message, tore it open, read it, and called out" for General John A. Logan, the Fifteenth Corps' commander. One of his divisions was ordered to succor Slocum, and Foraker had to ride back with news that help was coming. It was past midnight when he reached Slocum's headquarters.

At an 1889 reunion Sherman told Foraker, then Ohio's governor: "Well I remember ... as you came through the pine woods that day on your horse, covered with lather, and came up like a soldier-knight and reported to me. My friends, there is nothing more beautiful in life than a soldier. A knight-errant, with steel cuirass, his lance in hand, was a beautiful thing, and you are his legitimate successor."

panies, A and B, brave boys. I threw myself in front and told them to follow. They kept as pretty a line as I ever saw them make on drill. The rebs had two cross fires and a front one. They knocked us around. I reached the top of the hill without a scratch, but just as I leaped over their breastworks a large shell burst before me. A small fragment of it put a hole in my cap knocking it off my head.... As soon as I got into the breastworks and the rebs began to fall back I commenced rallying my men. I had the compan[ies] about formed when Capt. [William B.] Curtis, Gen. Turchin's adjutant general, galloped up to me and complimented me.... I never wish to see another fight. It is an awful sight to see men shot down all around you as you would shoot a beef.

On December 11 he wrote, "I have about 30 men left out of the one hundred and one we started with over a year ago. The regiment does not look the same.... Come what will, I shall stick to the company if I die with it."

Through the Atlanta campaign the following summer Foraker commanded Company A. Near Kingston, Georgia, on May 20, 1864, he confided, "I write this letter within gunshot of the skirmish line. The sun is just rising above the treetops. If the rebels make a stand a bloody day's work will soon commence.... My company stands up to the work like men. I wish no more honorable position than I now have."[47]

However happy he may have been commanding a company, Foraker was detailed to the Signal Corps in September. After passing required examinations and pledging secrecy, he was selected as one of the top five subalterns under Captain Samuel Bachtell, General Sherman's chief signal officer. During the celebrated march to the sea he served as signal officer and aide-de-camp on General Henry Slocum's staff. When Sherman's troops reached Savannah, the Union fleet anchored 18 miles below the city at the mouth of the Savannah River was without knowledge of their arrival. The important task of informing the fleet that Sherman had reached the coast was given to the lieutenant. The river was mined when Foraker shoved off in a small skiff manned by two black oarsmen and an orderly. Completing the perilous trip, he delivered

Sherman's famous note destined for President Lincoln: "I beg to present you as a Christmas gift the city of Savannah, with one hundred and fifty heavy guns and plenty of ammunition, and also about twenty-five thousand bales of cotton."[48]

Foraker's civilian life after the war was as outstanding and accomplished as his military record. Upon returning to Ohio he completed his education and by 1869 was an accredited lawyer in Cincinnati. From 1879 to 1882 he sat on the bench of the Superior Court, and from 1886-1890 served as governor of the Buckeye State. His political achievements were in large part tied to his Civil War service. He was particularly attuned to most Ohioans' propensity to remember its soldiers' deeds in the late war, and ran his campaigns with "Bloody Shirt" tactics. Combining his stellar Army service with polished oratory skill made him a favorite speaker at veterans' reunions and other public gatherings. When President Grover Cleveland in the late 1880s requested captured Confederate battle flags be returned to the South, Foraker forcibly announced, "No rebel flags will be surrendered while I am governor."

In 1896 Foraker was elected to the U.S. Senate. He was one of President William McKinley's close friends, but openly opposed McKinley's successor Theodore Roosevelt, with whom he greatly differed on various issues. After a political career spanning nearly 30 years, he retired in 1908. The former boy officer died May 10, 1917, ending a remarkable and distinguished life.[49]

Thousands of young soldiers contributed in numerous ways after the conflict. Some like John Kountz, Julian Scott and Joseph "Ben" Foraker became quite well known in different arenas. Two boys, however, stand out above all others as the war's most celebrated — John Lincoln Clem and Robert H. Hendershot. Strangely, their stories have much in common. Each served in Michigan regiments after running away from home, both were eminently successful self-promoters, and despite their widespread popularity mysteries still surround their service in the field.

CHAPTER 12

'Fancy a handful of a Hero'

Broken glass encased in splintered window frames reflected Confederate soldiers pouring a deadly fire on Union engineers attempting to lay a pontoon bridge over the Rappahannock River at Fredericksburg, Virginia, the morning of December 11, 1862. For more than a month the Army of the Potomac had waited on Stafford Heights for the pontoon boats to arrive. Through miscommunication they had not been delivered when promised, causing the Army to lose its advantage in taking the lightly garrisoned town. The delays provided critical time for Lee's Army of Northern Virginia to fortify the Rappahannock's west bank and concentrate its forces on the heights overlooking Fredericksburg's seemingly deserted streets.

At 6:30 a.m. on December 11 a thick haze shrouded the water as General Oliver O. Howard's 2nd Division of the Second Corps marched to the river in anticipation of the bridge being laid for its use in crossing. At 8 o'clock Colonel Norman J. Hall's 3rd Brigade was sent forward to aid the pontoniers, who were badly harassed by Confederate sharpshooters dug in and hidden along the riverbank. The 7th Michigan and 19th Massachusetts were deployed on the opposite shore and began countering the fire. Work on the bridge, however, remained at a standstill through the morning. By 3 p.m. Colonel Hall formulated the idea of crossing his men in pontoon boats. Lieutenant Colonel Henry Baxter, commanding the 7th Michigan,

volunteered to make the passage. Captain Harrison Weymouth also volunteered to support the 7th with his 19th Massachusetts. The hastily conceived plan called for a heavy cannonading of the town and Confederate-held west bank, while pontoons were carried to the water's edge and launched by engineer oarsmen who would ferry the infantry across. The Massachusetts men were to cover the advance as the Michiganders rushed to the boats, but after a half-hour bombardment the pontoons failed to reach the bank on account of the engineers running off as soon as the Rebels fired on their position.[1]

"No prospect appearing of better conduct," reported Colonel Hall, "I stated to Colonel Baxter that I saw no hopes of effecting the crossing, unless he could man the oars, place the boats, and push across unassisted. I confess I felt apprehensions of disaster in this attempt, as, without experience in the management of boats, the shore might not be reached promptly, if at all, and the party lost. Colonel Baxter promptly accepted the new conditions, and proceeded immediately to arrange the boats, some of which had to be carried to the water."

Before the boats on hand were loaded, the artillery was signaled to cease firing. Hall decided to launch those ready, rather than wait until all were filled. "The boats pushed gallantly across under a sharp fire," the colonel continued. "While in the boats, 1 man was killed and Lieutenant Colonel Baxter and several men were wounded. The party, which numbered from 60 to

70 men, formed under the bank and rushed upon the first street, attacked the enemy, and, in the space of a few minutes, 31 prisoners were captured and a secure lodgment effected. Several men were here also wounded, and Lieutenant [Franklin] Emery and 1 man killed. The remainder of the regiment meanwhile crossed, and I directed the 19th Massachusetts to follow and gain ground to the right, while the 7th was ordered to push to the left...."[2]

As the regiments advanced cautiously into the narrow streets the 20th Massachusetts followed in more boats while the engineers finally completed the bridge. The moment it was ready the balance of Hall's brigade crossed. Fighting in Fredericksburg became desperate as daylight dissipated, but through extreme effort the 20th Massachusetts forged ahead to secure the road leading from the bridge, sustaining a loss of 97 officers and men. Other regiments following also were engaged and within two hours, marked by two bayonet charges, roughly two city blocks were in Union control. After darkness smothered the fighting the Confederates retired to the heights beyond, leaving their blue-clad opponents in possession of the town.[3]

When the 7th Michigan first boarded the boats and rowed across the Rappahannock through the deluge of hostile fire, a young boy, without orders, ran into the midst of his comrades and crossed with them, his drum on his shoulder. At midstream he was noticed by his commanding officer, who promised him a thrashing when they returned to camp. Once ashore the lone musician beat his drum, inspiring his fellow Wolverines as they pushed back the Rebels stubbornly resisting their advance. The brave lad was heralded throughout the Army. His actions sparked a controversy that spanned the lives of two young soldiers, both of whom claimed the honor of beating his drum in Fredericksburg that day.[4]

The Drummer Boy of the Rappahannock

Robert Henry Hendershot was born fatherless on February 27, 1850, in Cambridge, Michigan.[5] His mother, Deborah, cared for the boy the best she could, but without a husband's financial help her family was very poor. Robert was a high-strung, fiercely independent child who lacked regard for authority. He frequently absented himself from school and was known to disappear from home for days at a time. Once, as the family cat walked across a room where Robert was loafing, he grasped the animal by its tail and swung it in the air until his mother intervened. While being scolded Robert brandished a broom and began chasing her in retaliation. During the dispute his brother-in-law grabbed him, and with Deborah's assistance tied him to a bedpost, gave him a good whipping and left the room. Instead of accepting his punishment Robert became more incensed. He loosened himself and picked up a shotgun leaning in the corner, determined to kill his brother-in-law for the beating. He entered an adjacent room where the man sat, aimed the weapon at his chest and pulled the trigger. The percussion cap failed. Alarmed, he dropped the gun, jumped through a window and ran to Cambridge's depot where he hopped the next train. For six months he remained on the road with the Dan Rice Circus, performing tumbling acts for food and board. After an accidental fall he summoned the courage to return home, where he reentered school and tried to behave. The effort was short-lived, for he soon scuffled with a classmate and, when reprimanded by the instructor, ran off again and lived on the streets and tracks. He earned enough to subsist with the help of eating leftover table scraps of train passengers.[6]

At last a break came his way when John D. Campbell, superintendent of the Lake Shore & Michigan Railroad, noticed the forlorn boy and offered him a messenger's job. He so impressed Campbell that Robert was allowed to sell popcorn and treats to passengers on the trains. He proved quite successful in his new endeavor, and was well received by customers and rail employees alike. By 1860 his family had moved to Jackson, Michigan. Robert reestablished relations and contributed to family finances with his popcorn income. His mother even persuaded him to come home and resume school.

The 10-year-old was just making progress when, like many others his age, he was sidetracked by news of the war. Robert immediately joined a boys' company in Jackson. Volunteering as a drummer, he procured an old instrument which he beat night and day until neighbors tired of the incessant banging and took it away. The company's captain, also irritated by the noise, persuaded Robert to become his fifer. It seemed a good idea, except he needed a fife. The boy overcame the problem by asking a music store owner if he

In this image by a Poughkeepsie, New York, photographer, Robert H. Hendershot posed with the drum he received from *New York Tribune* editor Horace Greeley in 1863. The William A. Pond & Co. instrument was manufactured with a German-silver shell and rosewood hoops. It was engraved with the sentiment "Presented by the *Tribune* Association, to Robert Henry Hendershot, of the Eighth Michigan Infantry, for his gallantry at the Attack on Fredericksburg, 11th Dec., 1862."

Author's Collection

could borrow one for an evening, but the night turned to weeks and still the fife was not returned. The store's proprietor finally visited his mother, who soundly expressed disgust at her son's actions but maintained she had not seen him for several weeks. With information obtained by the merchant and assistance from the company and a few policemen, Robert was located and once more severely disciplined. In spite of everything his was an independent soul that could not be conquered. He came home one last time before attaching himself to an encamped company of the 9th Michigan under Captain Charles V. Deland. Robert pleaded to be enlisted as a soldier but Deland countered that he was too young. When the company boarded a train for debarkation he concealed himself in a car with equipment. At its destination he popped out, talked the captain into accepting him as his helper and was permitted to remain, though not mustered. The delighted

youngster thought this was grand, but the captain knew his presence was only temporary because the men soon would pass back through Jackson, where he intended to excuse the boy. Within a few weeks, as the train neared Jackson's station, the mischievous youth hid in the coal bin while his mother and sister waited on the platform. The whistle blew, signaling the train's departure. He climbed out from his hiding place, ran to the rear of the train and waved at the crowd in achievement. The captain quickly learned of his subterfuge and paid for a ticket at the next stop, sending Robert home. Even before reaching Jackson the youngster hatched a new scheme, and in less than a week was back with the regiment. Realizing he was not in good standing with Deland, he offered his services to Company B, which was in need of a drummer. Captain Oliver Rounds, unaware of the boy's previous problems, accepted him wholeheartedly. After serving three months, while camped at Elizabethtown, Kentucky, the wayward boy finally was mustered at age 12 on March 1, 1862.[7]

Hendershot's behavior continued unabated. His first trouble arose when he found a loose pig and used "five bullets in transforming it from hog to pork." The incident landed him in the guardhouse for stealing. On another occasion soon afterward a frightened sentry fired a shot in the night. The regiment was called out and brave "Rob," overcome with fear, clung to a lieutenant's coattails, refusing to let go. The next day his antics were cause for laughter in the company. He then was arrested after leaving camp without orders, and was suspected of foraging freely from nearby residents by means highly questionable.

Near Murfreesboro, Tennessee, on July 13, 1862, almost the entire 9th Michigan was captured, including the young drummer. While marching away a prisoner, Robert declared he was sick and demanded to ride in a wagon. His bluff worked. He was taken to the wagon train and told to drive one loaded with wounded Confederate soldiers. In passing a bridge Robert deliberately ran the wagon over the side, dumping the injured Rebels in the water. He feigned disbelief and blamed the mules. The malicious act was not perceived as such by his captors, but most of the guards looked hard at him following the "accident." [8]

Two days after its capture the regiment was paroled and sent to Camp Chase in Ohio to await exchange. Robert, perhaps tiring of Army authority, pleaded for a discharge, claiming he suffered from epilepsy since the age of five. On July 31 the post surgeon heard his appeal and recommended his release, stating the condition "entirely incapacitates him from military service." [9]

Back in Michigan the boy decided to become a soldier again after two idle weeks at home. Traveling by train to Detroit, he enlisted there August 14 in the 8th Michigan under the fictitious name of Robert Harry Henderson. The regiment already belonged to the Army of the Potomac, so he was detailed to the recruitment party as its drummer. When his mother tracked him to Detroit he fled to Canada until she returned to Jackson, but he was charged with desertion for his absence. Forgiven, he resumed drumming for the recruitment party, all the while wanting to go to the front. Denied the opportunity on several occasions and bored with his detail, he left camp, was charged with desertion again and discharged. Surprisingly, he soon obtained permission to travel with a squad of recruits headed for the regiment in October, and was enlisted a third time on November 1. After transportation delays in Washington the small group reached the 8th Michigan's camp a few weeks afterward as the Army concentrated near Fredericksburg. [10]

According to Hendershot, he now was in place to become "the Drummer Boy of the Rappahannock." On December 11 the 8th Michigan was serving in the 2nd Brigade, 1st Division of the Ninth Corps. That day most of the brigade waited patiently as a third bridge was being built across the river. The 8th Michigan, which Robert had just joined, did not march over

the Rappahannock until the next morning. If he crossed with the 7th Michigan as he declared, it would have been without authority while his own regiment was held far back from the bridgehead on the 11th. [11]

Robert's story of crossing the river was included in the 1867 book *The Drummer Boy of the Rappahannock* by William S. Dodge. He obtained the information direct from Hendershot (who could not write) for the biography. It is the earliest published account as the boy told it. During early daylight of the 11th Robert supposedly left his regiment's camp with his drum on his back and ventured down to watch the engineers work on the bridges as the supporting infantry covered their work with musketry fire. Posing the question "And where was our Drummer-Boy during all this fiery ordeal?" Dodge alleged:

When the call was made for volunteers, and the Seventh so gallantly responded, he was the first to shout "I will," and the foremost one in the boats. The Captain in charge of the Company in this boat, seeing the boy with his drum slung to his back, ordered him out, telling him he was too small for such business, and that he would surely be killed. The reply of the brave lad was noble — Spartan in expression, and a truthful echo of the heartthrobs of the chivalrous crew that surrounded him. Standing up in the further end of the boat, swelling to his fullest height, he exclaimed, "I do not care if I am killed; I am willing to die for my country." Despite his cry the captain sent him out of the boat but the quick thinking boy then asked if he might at least help push the boat off and permission was granted. So when all was ready he pushed the boat off and let it drag him into the river, he clinging with his hands to the edge, and in this way he crossed the river. More than half the men in this boat were killed before touching shore, and so it was with those who came after. [This statement greatly differs with Colonel Hall's report of casualties].

As Robert climbed up the river's bank, his drum was struck by a piece of a broken shell and torn to pieces. This enraged him, and he seized a musket belonging to one of his comrades who had been shot close beside him, and went into a house nearby, where he encountered a tall, gaunt looking rebel just loading his gun. Robert brought his gun to the ready, and ordered him to surrender. The gray coat threw down his gun and cried out: "Don't shoot, I surrender." He then marched him back to the river, and found the first pontoon just completed. The Seventh Michigan seeing the boy and his prize, grew wild with excitement, and gave three rousing cheers for the "Drummer Boy of the Rappahannock." The hero then tramped his captive across the just completed bridge and started him to the rear. While en-route General Burnside noticed him and his prize. He then seemed known everywhere and men cheered as he marched along.[12]

In another version written under the auspices of Hendershot by H.E. Gerry in the 1890s, the story varied wildly:

On that morning the bands and drum corps had orders to remain in camp. Having no drum to use on this particular occasion Robert succeeded in going to the river. He hung around the pontoons until they were placed in the water and planked.

After helping to push the first boat from the shore he attempted to jump in himself but slipped and fell into the river. He caught hold of the left side of the boat and held on until the boat reached the opposite shore. When about half way over someone gave the order to "push that boy off and make him swim back." The order was not obeyed....

Robert immediately on reaching the shore followed the soldiers into the city, and following example given him, went into a house and set it on fire, stole a clock, two blankets, and some other small articles. With his arms full of plunder he started for the river to the point where the bridge was being completed.

He was compelled to wade out to the first boat, or rather the last boat that had been placed in position. He threw his plunder on the boat, re-loaded and went back to camp. Resting a few moments in camp he returned to the river again. During his trip to the camp the pontoon bridge had been completed. Seeing a stack of guns near the river Robert took one, strapped on a cartridge box and re-crossed the river. He went into different houses and assisted in destroying mirrors, pianos and other valuable property. He went into one very nice mansion, applied the match and passed out at the rear of the house. As he was leaving the building he saw a man with a double-barreled shotgun standing behind the yard gate waiting for an opportunity to shoot. Robert brought his gun to a ready and ordered him to surrender. The surprised rebel threw down his gun and cried out, "Don't shoot, I surrender." He then marched him to the river. Two soldiers who saw Robert capture his prize advised him to take his prisoner to General Burnside. They accompanied him and told the story to General Burnside.

The general said, "Well boy, if you keep on in this way many years you will soon be in my place." He then questioned the boy as to his regiment and told him he had better go back to camp.

Robert, flushed with success, and the generous compliment paid him by the commanding general, replied that he "preferred to go and capture another Johnny Reb.[13]

At that point in Gerry's version it is avowed the general's staff gave three cheers for Hendershot. It also was related that he did not return to the 8th Michigan, but went with "miscellaneous regiments" into the city again and was wounded in the leg during the next day's doomed assault of Marye's Heights, "breaking the bone." (In Dodge's earlier version it was only a flesh wound). He was carried from the field and taken

C. Gullmann,   Artist Po' Keepsie, N.Y.

An engraving styled after this Hendershot portrait illustrated the frontispiece of William S. Dodge's 1867 biography of the drummer.

Author's Collection

Hendershot's savvy promotion skills already were evident in the late 1860s when he donned an ornate military costume for this photograph. Without guilt he proclaimed himself to be "the most wonderful Drummer in the World."

U.S. Army Military History Institute

to Burnside's headquarters, where he quickly recuperated by December 15.[14]

The battle of Fredericksburg was a disaster for the North. Newspaper correspondents searching for anything positive to write about the struggle were enlightened to the "true" tale of a boy hero crossing the Rappahannock. Editors across the country picked up the story, and the unidentified lad was named "the Drummer Boy of the Rappahannock."

Later in December "Robert Harry Henderson's" real identity was exposed as well as his past military escapades. On the 27th he was discharged from the service a third time by order of General Orlando B. Willcox, the Ninth Corps' commander. The reasons again given were Robert's apparent epileptic condition and the fact he twice before had been discharged. Because of this he was denied pay for the entire time he spent with the 8th Michigan, but was allowed transportation home.[15]

After leaving the Army the adventuresome boy journeyed to New York City instead of heading back to Michigan. At the Astor House he registered for a room under the name "Robert Henry Hendershot, the Drummer Boy of the Rappahannock." The clerk, having read about the Fredericksburg episode, announced the youth's presence to other guests and a crowd soon gathered, lavishing him with praise. Thereafter, to his delight, the hero was introduced around the city, the object of admiration from a public badly in need of war-effort rejuvenation. Poets and writers penned glowing tributes, and the *New York Tribune* Association promised him a drum to replace the one shot from his hands on the banks of the river in Virginia. After a trip to England, where he was showered with additional accolades, he returned to Michigan to visit his family before proceeding to New York to receive his drum. Afterward he performed at P.T. Barnum's muse-

um, as did other drummers to promote patriotism as the war progressed.[16]

Robert next was invited by Professor Harvey G. Eastman to his college at Poughkeepsie, New York. The kindly man treated him like a son. By 1864, however, he was back in Washington and once more was enticed to enlist, on this occasion as a first class boy aboard the *Fort Jackson*. His naval service lasted less than three months. While the steamer was taking on coal June 26 at Norfolk, he simply left without receiving a proper discharge.[17]

Hendershot claimed befriending President Lincoln and other dignitaries, serving as a spy for General Grant, and obtaining an appointment to the U.S. Military Academy at the close of the war. With fame it is likely he met many influential people, but to what degree he was received by them is unknown. Whenever possible he used his celebrity to his advantage. Photographs of the uniformed boy posing with his gift drum were sold during and long after the war.[18]

At some point in 1863 or 1864, Hendershot met and became infatuated with Alice Blanchard, the daughter of a wealthy Rhode Island merchant. Without her parents' knowledge the two corresponded for three years — until 17-year-old Robert, in 1867, returned from temporary residence in Chicago to steal her away. The teenager knew he was disliked in the Blanchard household, so he planned an elaborate elopement.[19] Although the marriage began clouded by uncertainty, the couple was together for more than 50 years.

Over the years Robert, in company with his son, entertained for a fee at veterans' meetings, social clubs or anywhere he could gather a crowd. He distributed handbills across the country promoting himself as the "Drummer Boy of the Rappahannock," and was very successful as a performer. In some veterans' circles he readily was accepted as a bonafide hero, but by 1890 questions and doubt raised by others began dogging him about his actual experiences at Fredericksburg.

John T. Spillane was born in Killarney, Ireland, on August 8, 1844. In August 1861 the teenaged carpenter mustered at Detroit as a drummer for Company K, 7th Michigan. He served with the regiment until he was mustered out July 25, 1865, being present for duty four years except for a one-month hospital stay when he suffered an arm wound at Petersburg in October 1864. After the war John reenlisted for two years in the Regular Army before returning to Detroit, where he resided until his death December 31, 1932. The father of nine children, he was active in his church and several social groups, including the city's Fairbanks G.A.R. post, for which he served as a commander. He retired as a captain from the Detroit Police Department after more than 29 years on the force, a majority of that time spent commanding mounted patrols.[20]

Spillane was an esteemed member of the 7th Michigan and its post-war regimental association. After hearing Hendershot's claims and self-promotion for a quarter century, members of the association and citizens of Detroit finally reached the limits of tolerance. The whole affair probably would not have been publicized at the national level, but Hendershot started "puffing around," demanding to lead the parade of the G.A.R.'s 1891 national encampment in Detroit. On the heels of his request a flood of contentious articles and letters appeared in numerous Michigan newspapers and elsewhere. Almost all of them averred that Robert Hendershot never crossed the Rappahannock River in or behind any of the boats that ferried the 7th Michigan over it in December 1862. Like a swelling chorus veterans stepped forward and pronounced him a fraud, pointing out that many details in his story did not fit the historical record.[21]

Andrew P. Glaspin, a former member of the 7th's Company H, told readers of a Detroit newspaper: "We most emphatically declare that no such boy as he describes himself to have been, crossed the Rappahannock in or near the original five boats which first left the shore. Such a circumstance as a boy holding onto a boat in that bloody and chilly tide, with ice formed on the Fredericksburg side of the river, could not have possibly occurred without him having been seen and rescued by some of us at a time when we were all so anxiously solicitous for each other's well-being. [I] was in the third boat of the line and had just responded to Colonel Baxter's call for someone to aid in paddling the boat, when that officer was wounded and fell back into [my] arms. [I] asked the Colonel if we should convey him to the rear, but he said he only wanted to see his regiment across the river. This having delayed the boats a few moments, we were now the last boat and could see the sterns of the other four boats close in front of us, and I am willing to take the most solemn affidavit possible that neither boy nor man was clinging to any of the boats."

As for Hendershot's tale of capturing a Confederate soldier, William A. Herring, formerly of Company C and the 7th Michigan's principal musician, wrote to the same paper. "The drummers present were [Thomas M.] Robinson, Spillane and myself, none of us small boys.... The prisoners taken were brought across by our own men. No boy participated in this. I saw the file of prisoners, which was nearly as large as our regiment. They were all in one body. Several of the 19th Massachusetts, who followed us across the river, were present at Detroit [during the national G.A.R. encampment] and they are of the same opinion as myself to a man."

Hendershot's own regimental drum major also weighed in. He stated that on December 11, 1862, the boy was reported sick. Instead of passing the day with the 7th Michigan "he spent it in the hospital far from the minie ball's music." The hospital stewards, he

Drummer John T. Spillane's service with the 7th Michigan included the battles of Fair Oaks, Seven Days, Antietam, Fredericksburg, Gettysburg, the Wilderness, Spotsylvania and Petersburg.

Author's Collection

wrote, could prove his assertion. Although Hendershot was a member of the 8th Michigan's band, "he never had a drum of his own. The drum used by him and claimed to have been shattered by a shell belonged to [me], and is now in existence, which perforates one hole in Hendershot's story."[22]

Captain Henry A. Ford, who had served in the 19th Michigan, investigated Hendershot's story as G.A.R. editor of the *Detroit Evening Journal.* Interviews he conducted with former soldiers painted a bleak image of Robert's war record. Eighth Michigan chaplain George Taylor, for example, remembered the boy "could never take his place on dress parade without falling into a fit, and he was otherwise worse than useless." Ford concluded that Hendershot *did* cross

the Rappahannock on the pontoon bridge December 12, "but not under fire, unless from distant cannon. He was absent without leave and without his drum, and on a mission of plunder, which he began at once. He may have set fire to a building, as [alleged], though that is a new point to me; but if so, it will hardly increase his claims to honor. His much exploited capture of a Confederate soldier was merely compliance with the request of a wounded man, unable to get away, to be helped inside our lines. He captured some property, however, and with a stolen clock on his head was returning, when an exploding shell made him drop and break it. This was represented by correspondents with the army as the smash of his drum while slung to his shoulder, which prompted the presentation of the silver drum.... My conclusions, after exhaustive examination of the subject, were and remain as follows:

"**1.** Hendershot is undoubtedly the personage for nearly 30 years assuming to be and generally recognized as the 'Drummer Boy of the Rappahannock.'

"**2.** He never did any drumming, fighting, capturing, or anything else at the Rappahannock or anywhere else that gives him the least title to a place in history, the gratitude and honors of the country, or honorable engagements at the hands of the Grand Army or other bodies of Union veterans.

"**3.** What he did do at the historic river does entitle him to the name of the 'Forager of the Rappahannock.' In common life we should use a harsher term."[23]

With compelling evidence produced at the Detroit encampment and invitations to Hendershot to procure a witness on his behalf turned down, the 7th Michigan veterans' association issued a resolution in June 1892:

Resolved, That we, the surviving members of the 7th Michigan, do hereby emphatically protest against and deny the claim made by one Robert H. Hendershot to be the orig-

Author's Collection

John T. Spillane Robert H. Hendershot

The rivals

After Detroit's 1891 National G.A.R. Encampment spotlighted the Hendershot-Spillane controversy, opposing factions issued medals to the rival contenders. At a private Detroit business luncheon in February 1892, John Spillane was given a three-ounce gold medal designed and struck by F.G. Smith, Sons & Co. The circular drop featured a raised likeness of Spillane taken from a wartime photograph, encircled by the words, "The Drummer Boy of the Rappahannock Dec. 11, 1862." The reverse was inscribed, "Presented by the Citizens of Detroit to John T. Spillane, drummer of Co. K, Seventh Michigan Infantry, who crossed the Rappahannock with the regiment under Confederate fire Dec. 11, 1862."

Not to be outdone, Hendershot's followers decided to award their man as well. At the 1893

Indianapolis national encampment Hendershot was called to the stage in front of some 5,000 attendees, and presented a badge by former President Benjamin Harrison. The striking, diamond-studded G.A.R. badge was made of solid gold, and featured a small drum suspended from a top bar with the Women's Relief Corps emblem. Engraved on the reverse was the inscription, "Robert H. Hendershot, Drummer Boy of the Rappahannock, from the G.A.R. and W.R.C. comrades, Indianapolis, September 1893. Honor to whom honor is due."

Above, both men proudly displayed their awards. Hendershot, photographed about 1900, was attired in his Chicago G.A.R. Columbia Post 706 uniform.

inal and only drummer-boy of the Rappahannock River at Fredericksburg, Dec. 11, 1862, with said 7th, and challenge him to bring one witness who can testify that he saw the said Hendershot cross in one of the pontoon boats with the members of the 7th, as he claims. Failing in this, we feel ourselves justified in declaring in a public manner our belief that his claim is a fraud and an attempt to gain notoriety at the expense of those who voluntarily offered their lives, if necessary, in an undertaking almost unparalleled in the annals of human bravery, and declare our belief that the honor of such title belongs to comrade John Spillane, of Detroit; and we also emphatically protest against the alleged action of the managers of the National Encampment at Washington to be held in September, to place the said Hendershot at the head of the parade as a representative of our Association, as he has no part or connection with it.[24]

After the resolution passed Spillane was asked by a representative of the *Detroit Free Press* why it took him 25 years to come forward. "I have known all these years that Robert H. Hendershot was a fraud," he replied. "Why didn't I expose him long ago? Simply because it couldn't be done. A controversy through the press would only have given Hendershot an opportunity to show the letters which he claims were written by leading men and to still further boost himself.[25] A controversy in the press is nuts for him. He has all to gain and nothing to lose. Why, look at the man's nerve! Even now, after a whole regiment of 188 veterans — the regiment he claims to have crossed the Rappahannock with — has denounced him as a fraud, he still finds dupes to advocate his claims.... I haven't said a word for twenty-five years; but now I propose to make it warm for Mr. Hendershot at every attempt he makes to lay our boys in a lie."

William D. Longyear, who had been a drummer in Company C, 8th Michigan, also was pleased with the resolution. "I have always said and told people that his claims were false, and that he was not entitled to the honor, and I always said that if any drummer was entitled to the name, it was the drummer of the 7th Michigan. When I saw [Spillane's] statement in the *Free Press* about the matter, I was glad that someone of [the 7th Michigan] would say something to vindicate what W[ilbur] F. Dickerson said about Hendershot. Dickerson and myself were drummers in the Eighth, and bunkmates at the time of the battle of Fredericksburg, and we knew that Hendershot had no

drum; that he did not cross with [the 7th] and that he left the regiment right after the battle and was marked a deserter. He was only with our regiment a few [weeks] and through the influence of the old chaplain of our regiment his discharge was given him for disability, as he had fits, or pretended fits."[26]

Three decades after his regiment crossed the icy river, John Spillane officially was named the "Drummer Boy of the Rappahannock." The citizens of Detroit had a gold medal struck in his honor that he proudly wore at public events. On the other hand, Robert Hendershot continued claiming the title for the rest of his life. When he first became eligible for a pension he was denied because of the 1864 Navy desertion charge. He fought the pension board for years over his claim. The files show a bitter man trying to battle a bureaucracy while still heralding himself as Fredericksburg's heroic drummer boy. After several setbacks he resorted to threatening Army veterans who wrote the board opposing his claim. In frustration he bypassed the board entirely by appealing directly to Congress, which eventually approved a $50 monthly pension for him in December 1924. One year later the long-standing debate came to a close when Hendershot died of pneumonia at the age of 75. Although his reputation was irrevocably tarnished, he remains one of the most recognizable young boys to have worn the Union's blue uniform between 1861 and 1865.[27]

The Drummer Boy of Chickamauga

FT SAM HOUSTON TEX 1038AM MAY 15 1937

THE ADJUTANT GENERAL WAR DEPT WASHN DC
    SUPERINTENDENT ARLINGTON MAY FOURTEENTH
FUNERAL PARTY WILL ARRIVE VIA BALTIMORE AND OHIO AT SEVEN FIFTY FIVE AM TUESDAY EIGHTEENTH STOP REQUEST TRANSPORTATION FOR MRS CLEM AND SISTER TO MAYFLOWER HOTEL UPON ARRIVAL AND FOR SUBSEQUENT SERVICES STOP MRS CLEM HAS ENGAGED GAWLER TO MEET REMAINS AT STATION AND PERFORM SUBSEQUENT DUTIES STOP MRS CLEM HAS ARRANGED FOR CONDUCT OF SERVICES AT CHURCH STOP SHE DESIRES FULL MILITARY HONORS STOP SERVICES OF ARMY CATHOLIC CHAPLAIN AT CEMETERY NOT DESIRED STOP REQUEST YOU SELECT HONORARY PALLBEARERS

With the above radiogram's notification Captain David Barr of the Army's Provisional Brigade was detailed to prepare for the funeral of Major General John Lincoln Clem, U.S.A., Retired. He informed the Adjutant General the obsequies would take place in the eastern section of Arlington National Cemetery on Tuesday, May 18, 1937, at 11:30 a.m. Five days earlier in his San Antonio home, the 85-year-old former drummer boy joined his comrades "on the other side." He undoubtedly was the best known young celebrity to emerge from the Civil War.[28]

On August 13, 1851, Roman Klem patiently awaited the arrival of his first child in the family home just outside Newark in Licking County, Ohio. His wife Magdalene gave birth to a splendid boy who was named John Joseph Klem. When John was nine his mother was struck by a train while crossing a railyard and mortally injured. After her tragic death his family consisted of father Roman, sister Mary Elizabeth (Lizzie), brother Louis and eventually a stepmother, Elizabeth.[29] John's early years were spent like those of most youngsters growing up in small Ohio towns — attending school and church, playing with friends and doing household chores. Since his father was a railroader the boy was not straddled with farm work. It was a simple childhood.[30]

When news of war came to Newark and recruitment of its citizens began, John decided at once to be a part of the adventure. At nine years of age and standing roughly four feet tall, he was not an ideal recruit. Still, he envisioned himself a soldier and formulated plans to attain his goal.[31]

With the attack on Fort Sumter a Licking County Mexican War veteran, Leonidas McDougal, opened a recruiting stand April 19, 1861, in Newark's public square.[32] Almost immediately 42 young men composing Fire Company No. 2, the "Conquerors," offered themselves as volunteers. Before the day ended McDougal's company was filled to capacity. By April 22 the eager recruits arrived at Camp Jackson near Columbus, where they were designated Company H, 3rd Ohio Infantry. On the 27th they were mustered for three months and sent to Camp Dennison to help transform muddy cornfields into a usable rendezvous and training installation. While encamped there notice was received that the Federal government soon would be enlisting regiments for three years, and a majority of the 3rd reenlisted en masse.[33]

On June 13, 1861, the reorganized 3rd Ohio was mustered and on the 20th broke camp for the eastern seat of war. Conveyed by train via the Columbus & Xenia and Central Ohio railroads, it passed through Newark and other towns, receiving wild fanfare at every stop before reaching Bellaire on the 22nd. After a short stay in the Ohio River town it left the Buckeye State for Grafton, Virginia, which was being threatened by Rebel forces. The regiment campaigned in western Virginia until November, then was transferred to Kentucky, camping at Louisville and Elizabethtown before heading south to Nashville in late February 1862.[34]

For decades John Klem has been associated with and pictured attempting to enlist in Captain McDougal's company of the 3rd Ohio. If true, he only would have had a two-day window of opportunity to approach the 38-year-old officer and ask permission.[35] Understandably the captain, enjoying his company's rapid enlistment, was not at all interested in the small boy. Unfazed by rejection, John became more determined in his quest. Learning his young son had tried to enlist, Roman Klem emphatically insisted he would not grant consent. John, deprived of parental support as accepted stories contend, without permission stowed away on the train when the 3rd left for camp. The date of his escape in many accounts has been given as May 24, 1861.[36] This cannot be correct as the regiment already was at Camp Dennison at that time. It is more likely that if he attempted to hitch a ride, it was while the 3rd passed through Newark in June on its way to Bellaire.[37] One version of his departure appeared in an error-filled 1914 autobiographical sketch entitled "From Nursery to Battlefield," published in *Outlook* magazine:

"I climbed aboard the train with the men of the Third Ohio, got passage in that way as far as Cincinnati, and there I offered myself to the Twenty-second Michigan Regiment. Again I was rejected, by reason of my age; but this time I was not to be kept from joining by any mere legal obstacle. I went along with the regiment just the same as a drummer boy, and although not on the muster roll, drew a soldier's pay of thirteen dollars a month. The pay was not drawn from Government funds, however. It came out of the personal pockets of officers of the regiment, who 'chipped in' to make up the amount."[38]

Deep suspicion is cast on John's contention because the 22nd Michigan was not even mustered until August 29, 1862, and did not depart its home state until September 4, well over a year after the 3rd Ohio left Camp Dennison.[39]

John indeed ran away from home and was mustered May 1, 1863, in the 22nd Michigan. It also is a fact he left long before his official muster and for some time served as a regimental marker. In August 1864 Lieutenant Colonel Henry S. Dean of the 22nd apprised the Army's Adjutant General: "Said John Klem enlisted as a musician in Company C, 22nd Regiment Michigan Volunteer Infantry at Nashville, Tennessee on the 1st day of May 1863. He served as a Marker from about the 1st of January 1863, to the battle of Chickamauga, at which time he acted very gallantly...." Dean's disclosure indicates the boy joined the 22nd Michigan at a date earlier than January 1, 1863, even though he was not on the rolls. It is highly unlikely a young, inexperienced boy would have been given the important position of regimental marker any sooner than he was, lending credence to his probable connection with the regiment during the fall of 1862 when the 22nd first headed south. In addition, Dean mentioned John's presence at Chickamauga, where he soon found fame and a lasting place in the hearts and minds of Northern people.[40]

The morning of September 19, 1863, was bright and beautiful. Crisp, white frost glistened on the ground as the opposing armies of the Cumberland and Tennessee awoke to a day of destruction 10 miles south of Chattanooga. Skirmishing had erupted the previous day from Pea Vine Creek to Reed's and Alexander's bridges spanning West Chickamauga Creek. By 4 p.m. five Confederate brigades were across the creek, but due to Federal resistance and a number of unforseen setbacks the Rebels were unable to capitalize on what started as a well conceived battle plan. As the frost melted on the 19th the contest escalated with fervor. Despite desperate fighting neither side gained a decided advantage and the slaughter boiled over to September 20.

Early that Sunday morning thick fog obscured the battlefield. Confederate commander Braxton Bragg was on his horse before daylight expectantly waiting for his army's wings to attack, but for various reasons they were delayed until almost 9 a.m. The intervening hours were well spent by Union General William S. Rosecrans and his men, many of

The cardboard mount of this spring 1864 image bears Clem's properly spelled surname and hometown of Newark, Ohio. Before war's end the youngster changed his name to John Lincoln Clem in honor of the president.

Author's Collection

whom felled trees and constructed light fieldworks. By mid-morning the battle was renewed with tremendous fury. Divisions were thrust here and there, some driven back, others countering. During the fight's progress an ill-timed troop movement occurred that near-

Author's Collection

Seated on a blanket covering a camp stool, Clem held a spur in his left hand for the above field portrait taken prior to mid-February 1864. That spring he posed at Nashville's Morse & Peaslee Gallery of the Cumberland, right and preceding page, wearing on his blouse the "Roll of Honor" cloth badge given to him by General Rosecrans.

ly devastated Federal forces. Union General George H. Thomas' Fourteenth Corps was being pressed hard and he called for more reinforcements. As the blue-clad troops were being realigned to meet the surging Rebel tide a gap was created near the Union center, allowing General James Longstreet's Confederate command to split the National Army in half. The Union right and center began dissolving, their fragments soon sent

227

reeling in flight toward Rossville, Georgia, and Chattanooga. Swept up in the rout, reminding many of First Bull Run, were General Rosecrans and a host of other high-ranking Federal officers.[41]

Thomas, however, remained immovable in his position, which had taken a crescent formation. He stubbornly held his ground, earning him the sobriquet "The Rock of Chickamauga." Meanwhile, General Gordon Granger, commanding the Army of the Cumberland's Reserve Corps several miles north of Thomas, could not stand sitting idle any longer. Without orders he advanced one of his divisions in the direction where dust rising above the trees indicated the battle was at its pitch.

"At about 1 p.m. I reported to General Thomas," wrote Granger. "His forces were at that time stationed upon the brow of and holding a 'horseshoe ridge.' The enemy were pressing him hard in front and endeavoring to turn both his flanks. To the right of this position was a ridge running east and west, and nearly at right angles therewith. Upon this the enemy were just forming. They also had position of a gorge in the same, through which they were rapidly moving in large masses, with the design of falling upon the right flank and rear of the forces upon the Horseshoe Ridge. General Thomas had not the troops to oppose this movement of the enemy, and in fifteen minutes from the time when we appeared on the field, had it not been for our fortunate arrival, his forces would have been terribly cut up and captured. As rapidly as possible I formed General Whitaker's and Colonel Mitchell's brigades, to hurl them against this threatening force of the enemy....

"The gallant [General James B.] Steedman, seizing the colors of a regiment, led his men to the attack. With loud cheers they rushed upon the enemy, and after a terrific conflict lasting but twenty minutes, drove them from their ground and occupied the ridge and gorge. The slaughter of both friend and foe was frightful."[42]

One of the regiments attached to General Walter C. Whitaker's 1st Brigade under Steedman that day was the 22nd Michigan, containing musician John Klem. Whitaker formed his command in two lines with the 22nd on the left. "Both lines advanced at a double quick pace against the enemy," Whitaker reported. "The conflict was terrible. The enemy was driven near half a mile. Rallying, they drove my command a short distance, when they in turn were driven again with great loss. Both lines had been thrown into the conflict on the second charge, and the whole line kept up a deadly and well directed fire upon the enemy, who fought with great determination and vigor.... The Twenty-second Michigan [commanded by Colonel Heber LeFavour], after fighting for near three hours, having exhausted their ammunition, boldly charged into the midst of overwhelming numbers with the bayonet, driving them until overcome by superior strength."[43]

First Lieutenant William B. Hamilton of Company F, 22nd Michigan, afterward wrote that "We had advanced perhaps sixty or eighty rods when we were halted and faced to the left in line of battle. Then the order to advance was given, and as we began the ascent Lieutenant Colonel [William] Sanborn shouted, 'Fix bayonets!' With the rattle of the steel the men began to yell, and in the next two minutes they were over the ridge and chasing the Confederates down the south slope. But here we met a sudden check. A terrific fire was poured into us from front and flank, and in the few minutes we stood there endeavoring to return the fire about one-third of our brave fellows went down, killed or wounded. Our Lieutenant Colonel was shot through the foot and ankle. Captain William A. Smith, Company H, was mortally wounded. The whole color guard was shot down; four or five of them killed. All this during the ten or fifteen minutes we tried to hold the position."

Seeing the gravity of the situation, Colonel LeFavour called the regiment back to the ridge and there ordered his men to lie down and shelter themselves as much as possible. To their left lay the 21st Ohio and on their right the 89th Ohio. About sunset it became apparent to the three regiments' commanders that the rest of Steedman's division had withdrawn. LeFavour began pulling back from the ridge's crest when an officer rode up with orders to maintain the section of the ridge at all hazards. The Michigan and Ohio soldiers returned to their previous position near the summit. Within 20 minutes the sun slipped away and most of the three regiments, depleted of ammunition, were surrounded and captured. Even the surrender was frightening. Voices shouted "Don't shoot!" while the Confederates collected prisoners in the darkness. During the confusion another Rebel force at the bottom of the hill, unaware of the situation, fired a volley into

> **The rebels stole about all [Johnny] had, including his pocket book, which contained only twenty-five cents. 'But I would not have cared for the rest if they hadn't stolen my hat, which had three bullet holes in it, received at Chickamauga.'**

friend and foe alike. Pandemonium reigned for a few minutes as both blue and gray scrambled for cover, not knowing what to expect next. Fortunately for all only one volley was loosed, but the mixup afforded a chance for some Federals just captured to escape. The rest were rounded up and sent to the rear.[44]

When the 22nd Michigan first advanced and charged into battle on September 20, Klem's duty as marker was with the regiment and he, too, was surrounded with his comrades. The small boy's actions that day as described in varying contemporary accounts forever shaped his life as his deeds were publicized and elevated to boundless proportions. One of the first renditions of what transpired at Chickamauga, which also contained an overview of John's early service, was published December 16, 1863, in the *Columbus* (Ohio) *Daily Express*:

Last night at the Caledonian supper [in Cincinnati], General Rosecrans exhibited the photograph of a boy who he said was the youngest boy in the Army of the Cumberland. His name is John Clem, 12 years of age, a member of Company C, 22nd Michigan Infantry. His home is at Newark, Ohio. He first attracted Rosecrans' attention during a review at Nashville, where he was acting as marker for his regiment. His extreme youth (he is quite small for his age) and intelligent appearance interested the General, and, call-

ing him out, he questioned him as to his name, age, regiment, etc. General Rosecrans spoke encouragingly to the young soldier, and told him to come and see him whenever he came where he was.

He saw no more of Clem until Saturday last, when he went to his place of residence – The Burnet House – and found Johnny Clem sitting on his sofa, waiting to see him. Johnny had experienced some of the vicissitudes of war since last they met. He had been captured by Wheeler's cavalry near Bridgeport. His captors took him to Wheeler who saluted with: "What are you doing here, you d—n little Yankee scoundrel?" Said Johnny Clem, stoutly: "General Wheeler, I am no more a d—n scoundrel than you are, sir."

Johnny said the rebels stole about all that he had, including his pocket book, which contained only twenty-five cents. "But I would not have cared for the rest," he added, "if they hadn't stolen my hat, which had three bullet holes in it, received at Chickamauga."

He was finally paroled and sent North. On Saturday he was on his way [from] Camp Chase to join his regiment, having been exchanged. General Rosecrans observed that the young soldier had chevrons on his arm, and asked the meaning of it. He said he was promoted a [sergeant] for shooting a rebel colonel at Chickamauga.

The colonel was mounted, and stopped Johnny at some point on the field, crying, "Stop you little Yankee Devil." Johnny halted, bringing his Austrian rifle to an "order," thus throwing the colonel off his guard, cocked his piece (which he could do, being so short), and suddenly bringing it to his shoulder, fired, the colonel falling dead with a bullet through his breast.

The little fellow told his story simply and modestly, and the General determined to honor his bravery. He gave him the badge of the "Roll of honor," which Mrs. Saunders, wife of the host of the Burnet House, sewed upon Johnny's coat. His eyes glistened with pride as he looked upon the badge, and little Johnny seemed to have grown an inch or two taller, he stood so erect. He left his photograph with General Rosecrans, who exhibits it with pride. We may hear again from Johnny Clem, the youngest soldier in the Army of the Cumberland.[45]

Having already achieved a measure of celebrity, John was interviewed early in February 1864 for information to be printed on the reverse of a photograph then being marketed by an unknown photographer. "You see," he was quoted as saying, "at the battle of Chickamauga, our lines had been broken, and our men were retreating, and I was trying to rally them, when we were surrounded, and a rebel colonel rode up and said, 'Surrender, you son of a Yankee.' Now I had

Within six months of Chickamauga Clem's celebrity escalated at a fast pace. Photographers hoping to capitalize on the boy's popularity frequently ushered him before their cameras. Reputed to have shot a Rebel colonel from his horse at the close of the battle, John posed with a musket for one photographer in a "reenactment" of the incident.

Author's Collection

picked up a gun, and as I could not hold it up, I brought it to a charge and fired, when down came Mr. Rebel from his horse.[46] Then they took me prisoner, and sent me with others to the rear, where I rolled myself up in a blanket, and they went away and left me, so I found my way into our lines again."[47]

Chicago Journal correspondent Benjamin F. Taylor added to the boy's hero status with a colorful story reprinted in the *Belmont* (Ohio) *Chronicle* on April 28, 1864: "At Chickamauga, he filled the office of a 'marker,' carrying the guidon whereby they formed the lines. On the Sunday of the battle, the little fellow's occupation gone, he picked up a gun that had slipped from some dying hand, provided himself with ammunition, and began putting in the period quite on his own account, blazing away close to the ground like a firefly in the grass. Late in the waning day, the waif left almost alone in the whirl of the battle, a rebel Colonel dashed up and looked down at him, ordered him to surrender: 'Surrender!' he shouted, 'you little d—n son of a ——!' The words were hardly out of the rebel's mouth, when Johnny brought his piece to 'order arms,' and as his hand slipped down to the hammer, he crossed it back, swung up the gun to the position of 'charge bayonet,' and as the officer raised his saber to strike the piece aside, the glancing barrel lifted into range, and the proud Colonel tumbled dead from his horse, his lips fresh stained with the syllable of vile reproach he had flung upon a mother's grave in the hearing of her child."[48]

Unlike Clem's version of playing possum by hiding in a rolled blanket, Taylor credited his escape to a Union charge. "A few swift moments ticked off by musket shots, and the tiny gunner was swept up at a rebel swoop and borne away a prisoner. Soldiers bigger but not better were taken with him, only to be washed back again by a surge of Federal troopers, and the prisoner of thirty minutes was again John Clem of ours."[49]

Within a year Clem's Chickamauga exploits were being spread with marked inconsistencies. If the boy was freed by a Federal charge as Taylor told the story, it would place the shooting of the Confederate earlier in the evening and before the bayonet charge over the ridge as described by Lieutenant Hamilton. If he rolled himself in a blanket in the Rebel rear while playing dead, speculation as to when John was captured is fruitless. Did he even kill an enemy colonel? E.D. Pope, editor of *Confederate Veteran,* challenged that part of the story in a September 1926 article "Who was the Confederate Colonel?" After recapping the shooting in a synopsis, Pope wrote: "A very pretty story indeed, but the indefiniteness of the performance and the identity of the officer killed rather demand the proofs in the case. If any reader of the *Veteran* can recall the incident — for surely the 'surrounding rebels' would have been a witness of the brilliant deed — it would be interesting to hear about it; and the officer killed in this way should be identified by the records."

Inquiry as to any mention of the young warrior in the *Official Records* brought an answer from John C. Stiles of Brunswick, Georgia, whose work for years, according to Pope, had been a study of the records. Stiles responded:

John L. Clem is now [1926] on the retired list of the United States army as a major general, so that part of the narrative is correct.

General Clem's name does not appear on the list recommended by Rosecrans for Chickamauga honor, as published in the *Official Records,* nor does his name show in the *Official Records* at any time.

The colonel, lieutenant colonel, State and regimental flags, and most of the 22nd Michigan were captured at Chickamauga by [Robert C.] Trigg's and [John H.] Kelly's

Brigades, of [William] Preston's Division, and neither of the three last named officers mention any field officer being killed at this stage of the battle. However, Colonel Kelly's horse was shot from under him about this time, and Clem, who was undoubtedly a gallant little soldier, probably did it, and thought he had done what [was] reported.[50]

In Clem's 1914 *Outlook* account of his Chickamauga experience details changed, including his already having a gun before he entered the field and that, perhaps, he did not kill a colonel, as others at that time suggested.

At Chickamauga I carried a musket, the barrel of which had been sawed off to a length suitable to my size. I went into the battle seated on a caisson alongside of an artilleryman. If I may judge from historical accounts, it was quite a considerable scrimmage; but my own recollection of it is to some extent confused.

At the close of the day the Union forces were retiring toward Chattanooga, and my brigade was sore beset by the enemy. In fact, we were in a tight place. A Confederate colonel rode up and yelled at me, "Surrender, you damned little Yankee!"

Raising my musket without aiming, I pulled the trigger, and he fell off his horse, badly wounded.... I am glad to be able to add that, according to advice afterwards received, the Confederate colonel recovered from his wound.[51]

As I have said, however, it was a tight place. Three musket balls (as I subsequently ascertained) went through my cap. I decided that the best policy was to fall dead for the moment, and so did. I lay dead until after dark, when I "came alive" again and managed to find my way to Chattanooga.[52]

Of the 22nd Michigan's engaged strength of 455 at Chickamauga, 389 were killed, wounded or captured.[53] As the remaining 66 Wolverines began reuniting during the night retreat to Chattanooga, disbelief and pride must have filled their hearts with John's arrival. Someone impressed by the 12-year-old's actions that day brought them to General Thomas' attention, who soon afterward appointed him a sergeant, his rank to date from September 20, 1863.[54]

As previously mentioned in the December 1863 *Columbus Daily Express* article, Clem was captured 16 days following the battle of Chickamauga. The incident occurred while he rode with a wagon train hauling provisions from Bridgeport, Alabama, to Chattanooga. His captors belonged to General Joseph Whee-

FEBRUARY 6, 1864.]

SERGEANT JOHN CLEM.

OUR YOUNGEST SOLDIER.

SERGEANT JOHN CLEM, Twenty-second Michigan Volunteer Infantry, is the youngest soldier in our army. He is 12 years old, and small even for his age. His home is Newark, Ohio. He first attracted the notice of General Rosecrans at a review at Nashville, where he was acting as marker of his regiment. The General, attracted by his youth and intelligence, invited him to call upon him whenever they were in the same place. Rosecrans saw no more of Clem until his return to Cincinnati, when one day coming to his rooms at the Burnet House, he found the boy awaiting him. He had seen service in the mean while. He had gone through the battle of Chicamauga, where he had three bullets through his hat. Here he killed a rebel Colonel. The officer, mounted on horseback, encountered the young hero, and called out, "Stop, you little Yankee devil!" By way of answer the boy halted, brought his piece to "order," thus throwing the Colonel off his guard. In another moment the piece was cocked, brought to aim, fired, and the officer fell dead from his horse. For this achievement Clem was promoted to the rank of Sergeant, and Rosecrans bestowed upon him the Roll of Honor. He is now on duty at the head-quarters of the Army of the Cumberland.

SALTPETER CAVE NEAR

Based on a photograph, this _Harper's Weekly_ woodcut showed Clem wearing gauntlets and holding a blanket representative of the one in which he played dead in order to escape captivity at Chickamauga.

Author's Collection

ler's cavalry command, most of which had crossed the Tennessee River and was raiding behind Union lines.[55] After his October 6 capture John was held less than three days by the Rebels, then paroled and sent north, eventually reaching Camp Chase in Ohio near the end of the month, where he awaited exchange.[56]

In the meantime the little sergeant's reputation grew everywhere he went. Exchanged in December, it was during his return to his regiment when he stopped to visit General Rosecrans in Cincinnati. Relieved of Army of the Cumberland command in Chickamauga's aftermath, Rosecrans, perhaps, needed something positive to talk about, and thus quickly accepted and related the boy's tale to the newspapers by displaying Clem's picture at the Caledonian banquet. The next day John's adventures were grist for the press, and over the following six months the story circulated throughout the North to the enjoyment of everyone who read or heard of his feats.[57] Kate Chase, daughter of U.S. Treasury Secretary Salmon P. Chase, even asked her father to send a small medal to John to honor him.[58]

From Cincinnati he traveled to Chattanooga and on January 4, 1864, was attached to General Thomas' headquarters as an orderly along with his former 22nd Michigan tentmate, musician George Lutz.[59] That winter John served with Thomas, who had replaced Rosecrans, and was applauded by the many officers and enlisted men he met. His story inspired hundreds of boys at home longing to join the Army. Union General Richard W. Johnson touted Clem's exploits in a January 1864 motivational letter written to his own son:

For Harry my dear son,
    In my letter to your Ma yesterday I told her that I would write to you to day and I have commenced to make my promise good. What shall I write to you about? I will tell you a story of a little boy who once lived in Michigan.

His name is John Clem. Johnny's Father and Mother died leaving him a poor boy without friends and without money and when this war broke out he was enlisted by some officers as a drummer boy. He was only ten years old. He came to Kentucky with his Regt., marched when his Company marched and always rose early in order to beat his drum to awake all the men for reveille. He was a good boy – always obeyed his Captain and always tried to do his duty like a man. Being a good boy everyone liked him, because good boys always have a great many friends – he had many. Last summer his drum was broken by some accident and poor Johnny often cried because he had no drum to beat, but he always kept up with his Company in either hot or cold weather and often he had to sleep on the cold damp ground without a blanket. He has no good bed like Genl. Johnson's boys...."

The general summarized John's alleged deeds at Chickamauga and concluded his letter: "I saw him yesterday stepping around giving orders as big as if he

In this 1864 carte de visite image Clem sported the tailored uniform presented to him by Chaplain Lewis Raymond on behalf of a Chicago organization. The rear of the photograph was inscribed "Sergt. John Clem, The Hero Boy, of 22d Mich. Vol. aged 12 years last August, & weighs 63 lbs. Presented to George Henry Raymond by his Uncle Chaplain Lewis Raymond 51st Ill. Vol. Chattanooga, April 23, 1864."

Author's Collection

were grown. He wears the sergeant's chevron, but he looks like a very small soldier. He is studying to qualify himself for West Point and Genl. Thomas says he will send him there as soon as he is old enough. Johnny will make a great man some of these days and so will any boy who is obedient and faithful in the performance of his duty." [60]

Like other period narratives of John's background and war experiences, Johnson's was flawed in many respects. But for his small boy at home those errors made no difference, and Harry most likely was highly entertained by Clem's romantic adventures. Sadly, such uninformed stories passed verbally at the time have been an obstacle in pursuing Clem's history over the years.

As John's reputation spread, admirers wanted to help the boy in any way possible. In April 1864 Chaplain Lewis Raymond of the 51st Illinois delivered a new uniform for him tailored by A.D. Titsworth & Company of Chicago. Newspaperman B.F. Taylor was on hand shortly after the presentation. "This morning I happened [to be] at headquarters just as the belted and armed Sergeant was booted and ready to ride. Resplendent in his elegant uniform, rigged cap-a-pie, modest, frank, with a clear eye and manly face, he looks more like a fancy picture than a living thing. Said he to the Chaplain, 'you captured me by surprise, yesterday.' Now he is 'going on' thirteen, as our grandmothers used to say, but he would be no monster if we called him only nine. Think of a sixty-three pound Sergeant — fancy a handful of a Hero, and then read the 'Arabian Nights' and believe them." [61]

In early May the Federal drive to Atlanta commenced, keeping John busy carrying dispatches and

Clem proudly displayed the Kate Chase medal pinned to his "Chicago uniform" jacket during a late-war visit to the studio of Reeve & Watts in Columbus, Ohio.

Gary Delscamp Collection

running errands for General Thomas and his staff. For these endeavors he was presented with a pony. Meanwhile, the 22nd Michigan was assigned as provost guard for Army of the Cumberland headquarters. Although detached from his regiment he remained in daily contact with his former officers and many enlisted comrades.[62]

The Georgia campaign was a struggle from first to last, and the dutiful orderly was not immune to its dangers. While delivering a message for Thomas near Atlanta, John suffered a slight ear wound and was nicked by a piece of shell in the hip on a second occasion.[63] By late July some of those closest to the youngster began thinking of procuring a discharge for him with the intent of helping him receive an education. A contributing factor could have been his wounding. Another possible reason was that the War Department issued General Order 224 on July 6, prescribing the discharge of all personnel under age 16 and imposing stiff penalties on non-conforming officers.[64]

On August 9, 1864, four days before Clem became a teenager, Lieutenant Colonel Dean of the 22nd Michigan wrote at length about his experiences, requesting approval of a discharge. "Said John Klem is thirteen years of age, of very light, small stature, and would in time be of more service to the government in another capacity than as an enlisted man. That he may have a better opportunity for educating himself, I ask for his discharge." Within five days the paper was in the hands of John's friend, General Thomas, who en-

dorsed the document, "Approved with a view to enabling Musician Klem to obtain an education and ultimately an appointment in the Naval Academy."[65]

On the same day Dean composed his request, Clem was on his way north with General John M. Palmer, who was headed there after a squabble over rank relieved him from Fourteenth Corps' command.[66] Chaplain John J. Hight of the 58th Indiana took the same train and observed the boy. "I rode to the depot, in company with General Palmer and Johnny Clem.... [He] is a pleasant child of some twelve summers. He is a noted person in the army, and a crowd is nearly always about him wherever he goes...."[67]

Clem's destination was Carlinville, Illinois, Palmer's place of residence, where he entered school on extended furlough while awaiting his discharge. "I am going to school here and am very much pleased with the institution and my schoolmates," John confided September 16, 1864, in a letter to Captain Sanford C. Kellogg, one of General Thomas' aides. "Please tell my Colonel to write to me as soon as he can and send my 'Descriptive list.' How is Georgie Lutz getting along? Who has my little pony now? Give my respects to General Thomas and General Whipple [chief of staff]. If any of the officers are willing to write to me I would be very much pleased to hear from them. I would write to General Thomas but I am afraid he would not answer me. I did write to Col. LeFavour but have not heard from him yet. Give my regards to Major [Southard] Hoffman [another staff officer]. Truly yours (signed) Jno. Clem Sergt Co. C 22nd Mich. Infantry."[68]

Three days later he officially was discharged from the Army, but John and his instructors were unaware of the fact. As late as January 1865 the document still had not been delivered to him.

Curiously, Clem stated years afterward that his pony was killed under him at Atlanta the day he received his ear wound. Yet, in his September 1864 letter it is divulged the animal was very much alive.[69]

Although discharged, John Clem's military career was only beginning. After the war he attended various schools, graduating from Newark's high school in 1870. He then was accepted at the U.S. Military Academy, but was unable to make the grade. Unflustered, he moved to Washington and successfully appealed to President Grant for an Army appointment. John had many influential friends, coupled with his war record, to gain the honor. Grant appointed him a second lieu-

tenant in the 24th U.S. Infantry (Colored) on December 18, 1871. Five weeks later he took the oath of office and finally was an officer in the Army he loved. When asked to name his residence for his official records, Lieutenant Clem, true throughout his life to his hometown, replied, "When appointed I was a resident of Washington, D.C., but my bona fide residence is *Newark, Ohio.*"[70]

For the next 43 years Clem served his country as an officer, enjoying numerous promotions, until he was retired August 13, 1915.[71]

The Drummer Boy of Shiloh

Shortly before Clem received his lieutenancy an article by W.W. Carter of Baltimore detailing John's life appeared in a number of newspapers.[72] In late May 1872 Carter sent a copy of his story to President Grant, along with a letter asking that it be per-

In this circa-1870 photograph Clem wore a Type III Grand Army of the Republic membership badge. The 1869-patented emblem often was confused with the Medal of Honor due to its eagle's uplifted wings. Attached to the ribbon is the small, circular medal presented to him by Kate Chase in 1864. Also displayed is his signature, which invariably was written as Jno. L. Clem.

U.S. Army Military History Institute

manently attached to Lieutenant Clem's military file as a fitting tribute to his heroic actions during the war. The request was granted, and on June 11 he wrote to Adjutant General Edward D. Townsend: "I have much pleasure in acknowledging receipt of your favor of the 6th instant, informing me that the Sketch of the military record of *Little Johnny Clem, The Drummer Boy of Chickamauga,* which I enclosed to his Excellency the President on the 31st ulto, accompanied by a letter begging that the sketch might be placed upon the Military Records of the country, as a prodigy without his peer in the military annals of the Old World or the New, had been referred to your Department and filed accordingly."[73]

The privately written history was duly added to Clem's official personal records without anyone in the military establishing its accuracy. Unfortunately, Carter's sketch was flawed when comparing it to any amount of war-dated evidence. The article was circulated for years as a pamphlet, from which many historians and writers have gleaned their information. Carter quoted earlier secondary sources, and in fact copied some without credit. One of those excerpted

was Benson Lossing's *Pictorial History of the Civil War,* published in 1866. Lossing related Clem's Chickamauga story of escape and supposed killing of the Confederate colonel. Carter also included his capture by Wheeler's men, his appointment to sergeant and other factual points of interest. But mixed through the presentation was a host of errors, starting with the boy's enlistment. Early in his account Carter declared:

The regiment [3rd Ohio] was on its way to the front, and having taken passage on the cars for Cincinnati, our little hero went down upon the same train, where he offered himself to the Twenty-second Michigan Regiment, who also declined to muster him in on account of his size and years, but owing to the persevering spirit with which he maintained his determination to follow the fortunes of his country upon the field he was allowed to accompany the regiment in all its subsequent movements until at length he was beating the "long roll" in front of Shiloh in April, 1862, where his soldierly spirit so won the confidence and admiration of the officers of the regiment that, in June or July, 1862, he was enlisted at Covington, Kentucky, as a drummer, but serving afterwards also as a "marker."

At Shiloh (known as Pittsburg Landing) his drum was

Drummer William A. Steele of Company I, 53rd Ohio, was one of a number of musicians who later called himself the "Drummer Boy of Shiloh." His case was presented in the 53rd's history, published in 1900. Author John K. Duke, who served a year as a private in Company F, expounded: "W.A. Steele claims the distinction of having beat the first long roll at the battle of Shiloh, April 6th, 1862, and that his instructions were received personally from Colonel [Jesse J.] Appler. He also insists that he is the drummer boy who has been so effectively poetized. This distinction, however, is claimed by others and resembles somewhat the mooted question as to 'who struck Billy Patterson?' During the first day's fight at Shiloh he was struck a glancing shot upon the left side of [his] head and ear, which rendered him unconscious. He was subsequently discharged. After regaining his health he donned the blue as a drum major and served three years. He was perhaps the most youthful drummer boy of the 15th Corps."

History of the Fifty-third Regiment Ohio Volunteer Infantry

smashed by a shell, which occurrence won for him the appellation of "Johnny Shiloh," as a title of distinction for the fearless manner in which he discharged his duty at that bloody battle....[74]

Carter's statement of John's participation at Shiloh was a first. Because of the 1871 account newspaper writers and well-meaning historians, who apparently did not compare it to his military files, have continued to place the young boy on the west bank of the Tennessee River as the "Drummer Boy of Shiloh" for the past 13 decades.[75]

Following Carter's first mention of his presence at Shiloh with the 22nd Michigan — which was not even mustered until five months after the battle — Clem's adventures on that field have become more grand and convoluted with time. Jay S. Hoar's 1999 book *Callow Brave & True* allots 14 pages to Clem's story, the author concluding John served with the 24th Ohio during the battle. According to Hoar, "The colonel of the 24th Ohio was ordered to have a drummer ready to 'beat the long roll.' Johnny, at 4:15 a.m. [April 7, 1862, the battle's second day] was roused abruptly from sleeping and told to report to Gen. Grant's tent and to remain there. Moments later, equipped, and having dashed cold water several times over his face, the ten-year-old stood at attention before the general and saluted. Grant, taken aback by the diminutive musician, questioned him. Could he stand up to it? Beat the long roll (call to battle), sustain it amid distractions without losing his concentration? Still at attention, Johnny vowed he could."

Hoar stated John played near Shiloh Church as columns of blue marched past into battle until, at last, his wearied hands were set free by a shell fragment smashing his drum.[76]

Grant's own depiction of the early morning hours of April 7 flatly contradicts such assumptions, starting with the tent. The general recalled: "During the night rain fell in torrents, and our troops were exposed to the storm without shelter. I made my headquarters under a tree a few hundred yards back from the riverbank. My ankle was so much swollen from the fall of my horse the Friday night preceding, and the bruise was so painful, that I could get no rest. The drenching rain would have precluded the possibility of sleep, without this additional cause. Some time after midnight, growing restive under the storm and the continuous pain, I

moved back to the log house on the bank. This had been taken as a hospital, and all night wounded men were being brought in, their wounds dressed, a leg or an arm amputated, as the case might require, and everything being done to save life or alleviate suffering. The sight was more unendurable than encountering the enemy's fire and I returned to my tree in the rain."[77]

Grant's bivouac under the tree and not in a tent was far removed from Shiloh Church, where later in the day a drummer boy (whose duty in battle was to assist the wounded) would not have been needed to sound a charge. Also, it is unlikely cold water would have been necessary to dash "several times" over the face of a sleeping boy to wake him in the midst of a rainstorm. Furthermore, the 24th Ohio at Shiloh was not commanded by a colonel, but by Lieutenant Colonel Frederick C. Jones. And, nowhere in Clem's military files is mention made of his having served *at any time* with this regiment.

On Sunday, April 6, 1862, General Albert Sidney Johnston's Confederates had attacked Grant's largely unsuspecting troops encamped near the Tennessee River. The raging battle lasted two days, claiming roughly 3,500 lives and maiming another 16,000.[78] By controlling the field the Federals proclaimed victory, but for families on both sides that lost loved ones it was a time for grief.

Drummer boys had become established symbols of patriotism as early recruitment in the opposing armies progressed. After the terrible April battle Will S. Hays combined the two in poetic verse that he set to music and called *The Drummer Boy of Shiloh*. When first published in the summer of 1862 the cover illustrated a Confederate drummer boy, but the words mentioned neither cause. Its melancholy stanzas became an instant favorite both North and South.

> On Shi-loh's dark and bloody ground
> The dead and wounded lay;
> Amongst them was a drummer boy
> Who beat the drum that day.
> A wounded soldier held him up
> His drum was by his side;
> He clasp'd his hands, then rais'd his eyes,
> And prayed before he died....[79]

Favorable public response to *The Drummer Boy of Shiloh* led to similar poems and songs about other fic-

Different productions of Samuel Muscroft's play *The Drummer Boy* continued into the 20th century. John Zimmer, left, portrayed the lead character in a scene called "On the Battlefield." Six photographic views of the play's five acts were published by Haines of Albany, New York. Eight-year-old Laura McKinney, right, played the drummer boy in 1899 at Lebanon, Pennsylvania's opera house.

titious boy soldiers, including "Mother Kissed Me in my Dream" about a wounded lad at Antietam, and "Kiss My Mother Dear for Me" relating a young soldier's death at Gettysburg.[80] Both were touching ballads but never achieved the popularity of Hays' Shiloh composition. From its 1862 debut onward, drummer boys were associated with the song no matter where they served. Its title became a representative phrase describing all youthful drummers.

Shortly after the war Samuel J. Muscroft, who had served with the 102nd Ohio, wrote a five-act play entitled *The Drummer Boy; or the Battle-Field of Shiloh.* The popular drama, introduced in 1868, portrayed

the actions of a fictitious drummer named "Johnny Howard" through the battle of Shiloh and ultimately to his death in Andersonville prison at the hands of a Confederate guard. It was performed for the next 40 years, especially as a fundraiser for schools and veterans' groups. During its lengthy run it contributed greatly to the creation of the name "Johnny Shiloh." The play eventually was retitled *The Drummer Boy of Shiloh* to match the wartime song.[81]

Was John Joseph Klem, who was moved to change his name to John Lincoln Clem, present at Shiloh? Or was he called "The Drummer Boy of Shiloh" because of the coined, catch-all phrase? There are no known wartime references to Clem being at Shiloh, and none apparently exist written shortly after the war. He realized soon after Chickamauga that his celebrity could be beneficial to him for the rest of the conflict, and later in his military career. From using connections to secure appointment as a second lieutenant, to receiving leaves of absence or special assignments, numerous letters in Clem's military files show he was apt to capitalize on his drummer-boy past for his own advantage.

On October 10, 1873, Lieutenant Clem appealed to the Army's Adjutant General to be detailed to the Artillery School at Fort Monroe. He mentioned that "I entered the service during the late war at the age of nine years and nine months and served upwards of three years as a 'Drummer Boy' and sergeant. I was assigned to duty at General Geo. H. Thomas' Head Quarters January 4, 1864 and was honorably discharged [from] the service in order to prepare myself for the Naval Academy at Annapolis Maryland." [82] In a letter to President Grant seven months earlier he wrote, "I entered the volunteer service in May 1861, at the age of nine years as a 'Drummer Boy'" According to his birthdate, both statements placed his affiliation with the Army prior to the battle of Shiloh, but did not answer where and with whom he served.[83]

Five years later while filling out a government form summarizing his service in the volunteer Army as an enlisted man, Clem wrote that he was a drummer in Company C, 22nd Michigan, and was appointed a sergeant on September 20, 1863. He also endorsed the document with regard to his "earlier" service. "I went out with the 3rd Ohio in June 1861 as a drummer boy but on account of my youth (nine years old) I was not enlisted. I was with the 22nd Michigan some time before I was enlisted. I do not know the exact dates of my enlistment or discharge but they can be found in the Adjutant General's Office. I was detailed per special Field orders No. 4, Part IV, Jan. 4, 1864, on duty at Major General George H. Thomas' Headquarters as orderly." [84]

This _official_ form outlining Clem's Civil War service is the only one among hundreds of documents and correspondence in his military files. It clearly does not state he served with any regiment other than the 3rd, which rejected him from the start, and the 22nd Michigan. It is reasonable to assume that if he wrote of his brief attempt to join the 3rd Ohio, he also would have mentioned a regiment that he supposedly served with at Shiloh. Throughout his career, in every letter but one written by Clem in which he refers to his Civil War escapades, he stated he was the "Drummer Boy of Chickamauga," which corresponds with war-dated accounts. The only Clem letter mentioning Shiloh was written while he was stationed at Fort Whipple, Virginia, between August 1876 and February 1877. In the

Following Clem's death in 1937 the press quickly replaced him with Lewis H. Easterly, the "baby" of the Grand Army of the Republic. This news service photo of Easterly, captioned "Drummer Boy of Shiloh," was taken at the August 1941 National G.A.R. Encampment in Columbus, Ohio. As an eight-year-old musician he had served with the 9th Illinois Infantry, and truly was at Shiloh.

Author's Collection

undated missive to President Grant asking to be appointed a captain in the Signal Corps, Clem asserted: "I entered the volunteer service before I was ten years old and was made a sergeant when twelve years of age, at the battle of Chickamauga, for killing a rebel Colonel. My senior officers and comrades bestowed upon me the title of the 'Drummer Boy of Shiloh & Chickamauga.'[85] Even in this lone reference to Shiloh he simply stated that others gave him the appellation, and never intimated or mentioned participating in the battle. Clem's insistence upon introducing himself to Grant on every occasion he wrote the president asking for promotion negates the assumption the two were well acquainted at any time. If the former drummer and general really crossed paths at Shiloh, it is curious Clem never brought up the incident in his correspondence.

By the turn of the century Clem's military career had advanced rapidly, but still not to his liking. In 1903 his efficiency report showed an aging soldier who was, as General Frederick Dent Grant wrote, "a kind hearted generous man, immensely popular with the community but more apt to act from feelings — which are always generous — than from careful thought."[86]

In the 1914 *Outlook* article, Clem wrote, "At Shiloh my drum was smashed by a fragment of shell. They called me 'Johnny Shiloh' for a while after that. But I ought to explain that in May, 1862, I became a full-fledged soldier, being regularly enlisted at Covington, Kentucky, as a drummer."[87]

Since the article's publication a majority of historians believed Clem was at Shiloh because he was credited with saying he was. When comparing the text of W.W. Carter's 1871 sketch to the 1914 autobiography, so many parallel errors arise it becomes plain that Clem either employed the earlier account as an outline, or someone ghost-wrote the article for *Outlook* using Carter's sketch with authorship credited to

National Archives

General John L. Clem, circa 1915.

Clem. Both give his enlistment at Covington in 1862; both state he enlisted in the 22nd Michigan, having first gone south with the 3rd Ohio on the same train to Cincinnati; both have him riding on to the battlefield at Shiloh on a caisson; both say he carried a cut-down musket at Chickamauga, which contradicts Clem's wartime statements that he picked up a weapon on the field; both erroneously claim his pony was killed at Atlanta; and both conclude with the same quoted story that he exchanged his drum for the gun because "I did not like to stand and be shot at without shooting back."[88]

General Leonard Wood's report in 1916 of Clem's Army record provided the concluding chapter to a valiant life of service to the country. "It was necessary to relieve him as Chief Quartermaster of the Central Department for the best interest of the service," Wood declared. "This was done with as little publicity as possible. He was told he would be relieved at Chicago and it would be advisable for him to ask for retirement. Colonel Clem requested that he be authorized to remain on duty until he became the last of the Civil War Veterans on the active list. This was agreed to by the Secretary [of War] and he was assigned to Washington and given charge of the division of national cemeteries. He filed an application in writing to be retired when he became the last surviving veteran of the Civil War on the active list."[89]

Clem achieved the rank of Major General, U.S.A., Retired, through an act of Congress August 29, 1916.[90] His rise from drummer boy to general earned him a lofty place in the nation's military history. At Chickamauga he definitely entered the thick of battle, and on a dimly lit, smoke-shrouded hillside probably wounded or killed a Confederate soldier demanding his surrender. Was Clem at Shiloh? One need only visit Arlington National Cemetery and view his grave's massive marker inscribed "The Drummer Boy of Chickamauga." The word "Shiloh" is nowhere to be found.

CHAPTER 13

'Willing hands to help us poor tired kids'

October 4, 1862, was a date drummer David Auld never forgot. That day the battle of Corinth was fought in northeast Mississippi, and his regiment, the 43rd Ohio, suffered the loss of its colonel, adjutant and 94 other officers and enlisted men. One of the casualties was his oldest brother Archibald Bradford Auld, a Company B private who was grievously wounded in the left shoulder by a large shell fragment while the 43rd lay waiting for the first Rebel assault on Battery Robinett. Lying next to him was James Conger, David's future lifelong business partner, whose uniform was stained with Bradford's blood. David and younger brother Demas, Company B's fifer, lifted their sibling to a stretcher just as Colonel J.L. Kirby Smith and Adjutant Charles Heyl were shot from their horses a few yards away. The two teenagers carried Bradford to a shallow ditch alongside the Memphis & Charleston Railroad tracks, where a temporary brigade field hospital was located. The depression offered some protection from the hail of whining bullets crisscrossing overhead, and quickly was filled with wounded men. They deposited their brother on the ground, reluctantly leaving him to the surgeons. Sprinting back to the regiment with their stretcher, they little knew Bradford soon would be dead. [1]

Years later David Auld prepared a manuscript narrative of Corinth's ferocious fight. "The scene at this time no pen can describe," he wrote. "But I cannot resist the temptation of making a feeble effort to record some of the scenes that passed before my vision and the thoughts that filled my brain...."

At 10 a.m. Oct. 4th 1862 the Regiment [43rd Ohio] lay on the ground in line of battle[,] the right resting directly in rear of [the right embankment of] Battery Robinett and about 20 yards from the ditch. The regiment faced directly west, the left lay near the M&C RR cut almost in line with the west face of Battery Williams, and had laid in this position 12 hours without fires or blankets. Just before daylight the Confederates opened a destructive fire on our position from three batteries (of fourteen guns) which they had planted during the night within 200 or 300 yards and directly on our regimental right flank[,] enfilading our line with shrapnel and canister until silenced by Batteries Robinett, Williams and others about daylight. From this time until about 11 a.m. a very searching flank fire was poured into our lines by sharpshooters concealed in brush, fallen timber, and trees at the edge of the woods.

Soon after 10 a.m. great columns of Confederates poured from the woods north of us with arms at right shoulder, their tattered banners unfurled, and spread out in vast lines of battle over the plain north of the town of Corinth[,] sweeping all before them into the town. No battle scene in modern times, not even Pickett's at Gettysburg, surpassed the picture that unfolded to our vision. Looking almost directly to the rear of our regimental line we could see every man engaged in both armies at that time. The 30-lb. Parrott guns and others in and near Battery Williams were sending great numbers of shells screaming closely over our heads into the flanks of the distant charging columns.

Archibald Bradford Auld was the oldest of four brothers who fought for the Union. This ninth-plate tintype was taken April 16, 1861, the day he enlisted in the 20th Ohio. As a private in the 43rd Ohio he was mortally wounded at Corinth.

When not pressed with duties David Auld whiled away his free hours sketching. The talented artist illustrated the fight at Battery Robinett, below, shortly after the October 1862 battle of Corinth. As a business venture, David and Private James Conger of the 43rd Ohio soon had the drawing lithographed in Cincinnati to sell to the troops.

Author's Collection

At about 11 a.m. above the sounds of the more distant battle there came nearer sounds from the northwest that reminded us of the big raindrops that used to fall on the roof of our boyhood homes preceding the storm. It was the opening sounds of our battle. Our time had come, our single line of farmer boys and school boys, many of them mere children, were to be tried in the fire of battle and given the most severe manhood test of their lives, "massed American Infantry at close quarters." There can be no test more severe. My thoughts were, "Can they stand it, will they stand

it?" The Confederate columns [were] pouring from the northwest [and] the whole space between the Rail Road and the woods seemed filled with them. Kirby Smith mounted his horse[,] drew his sword and in the same loud clear voice we had so often heard[,] commanded, "Attention Battalion, fix bayonets, charge front forward on the first company, by company right half wheel!" The command was never finished. A ball passed through his head and his voice was stilled forever. Lieutenant Colonel [Wager] Swayne assumed command, his head bleeding from a wound by a

David Auld enlisted with his brothers Bradford and Demas in the three-month 20th Ohio, and again September 14, 1861, in Company B, 43rd Ohio. Demas, 15, and David, 17, served as the company's fifer and drummer, respectively, until they mustered out in July 1865.

Courtesy
of James Featherston

sharpshooter and was again wounded in the leg. About this time Adjutant Heyl was killed from his horse, Major [Walter F.] Herrick was wounded slightly in the leg, also Sergeant Major [Cornelius] McCaffrey.

The officers were doing their utmost to prevent firing until the change of front was complete. The line swinging to the right on the run was quickly brought close to the flanks of the Confederate columns converging toward the Chewalla Road which now ran nearly parallel to our line. Our men were falling in great numbers along the whole line but had not yet opened fire. My thoughts were, "Why don't they fire, will they never fire? Another minute will be too late, they will all be down." The same thoughts must have passed through the brains of those farmer boys in the ranks (who almost to a man were expert with a rifle), for the whole line brought their guns to their shoulders and without command fired into the flank of the massed columns almost within reach of their bayonets near the Battery. In an instant the whole scene to the left of Robinett had changed. Heaps of dead and wounded lay on the ground, in the ditch of Robinett, and across our whole front. The Confederate columns already much disordered from their rushing charge over fallen timber and brush, and [with] the crossfire from the 63d [Ohio] and left of the 27th [Ohio] and the guns of Robinett, now lost all formation and suffering terrible losses, crowded forward in great masses toward and up the em-

bankment of Robinett with the desperate resolve of breaking over that work and through our shattered lines.

The enemy, although broken in formation, was still desperately dangerous and aggressive. The front ranks of the whole mass continued their deadly fire nearly all at the range of only a few yards. As many as could line up on top of the earthwork of Robinett poured a deadly fire into that work, killing or wounding Lieutenant [Henry C.] Robinett and half his artillery men and driving the balance out to the rear. The changing front of the 43d, having brought companies A and G into Battery Robinett, the duty of defending it quickly fell to them, which duty they nobly performed, losing more than half their number in the few minutes following.

The rear of the Confederate columns [was] still crowding forward (not knowing the fate of their comrades at the front) who[,] having been stopped by our battle line at Robinett, each moment growing more helpless from losses and crowding, were attempting to deploy in battle line to the right and left of Robinett and were shot to pieces on the right of that work by the 63d and the 27th and on the left by the 43d, and their remnants [were] quickly driven in utter rout from the field and back to the woods.

But these remnants, still dangerous, lost no time in re-forming, and were joined by a still larger force, and immediately these great outnumbering columns moved upon our

243

depleted lines for the second assault, more desperate if possible than the first....

The second assault was almost a repetition of the first except that the enemy was in greater numbers and their losses much heavier, as our boys were less nervous and more determined after their first success, and poured their deadly fire into the flanks of the enemies [*sic*] columns with greater rapidity and accuracy, throwing them into confusion, causing a repetition of the overcrowding and terrible slaughter on a larger scale. The second assault made no more headway than the first after reaching the battery and our line of regiments, the 63d and 27th, was closed up toward Robinett on the right and the 43d on the left to close the gaps in the ranks caused by losses. The men on both sides were melting away fast. This dreadful carnage could not endure long. Several Confederate color-bearers had fallen from the parapet of Robinett, when Colonel [William P.] Rogers, leading the assault, seized the colors of the 2d Texas and rushed to the top of the earthwork shouting to his men to follow, and was instantly shot dead by a soldier of Company A, 43d. Seeing their leader fall amid heaps of their dead and wounded, the men could no longer breast the storm of lead being poured into their crowded and disordered ranks, and broke and fled in complete rout. The battle was over and the victory won except the shouting which was long and loud....

When the firing ceased there [were] many willing hands to help us poor tired kids in finishing the most trying day's work of our lives. In a few minutes the last of our wounded were in the hands of the surgeons for first aid. Then we gathered up the ghastly dead and placed them in long rows for burial, and in all the regiments that fought that day our row of dead was the longest.[2]

Lying among the 43rd Ohio's "farmer boys and school boys" gathered for burial were Private John Curren of Company F, who enlisted at age 16, and Perry County native James Dew. The blue-eyed Dew, 15 years old at the time he was recruited by Wager Swayne the previous November, belonged to Company H. The regiment had been formed during the fall of 1861 when recruiting bogged down almost to a standstill. To compensate for the manpower shortage Swayne turned to boys like James Dew. Of Company H's original members 28 were 18 years old or younger. David Auld's description of "children" fighting at Corinth was not an exaggeration. The 43rd's official roster contained 257 soldiers listed as being 18, 51 as 17 and 23 as 16 or below. Company H musician John McClay, 13, was one of those categorized as being 18,

1862

Recollections of the Civil War

On November 4, 1862, eight-year-old Maud E. Morrow arrived at Corinth to help care for her sick father, Assistant Surgeon Corridon Morrow of the 43rd Ohio. Morrow, who had set up the temporary field hospital in the railroad ditch where Bradford Auld was carried, contracted a severe fever after the battle and summoned his wife from Ohio. She brought Maud and her five-month-old sister, Mary. Upon arriving, Maud was overwhelmed by the stench of dead horses and mules being burned on the battlefield. The Morrows lived for six months in Corinth as Maud's mother administered to her husband and other officers. The girl freely roamed the hospital grounds, becoming well known for her cheerful conversation and supplying patients with water. Twice she and her little sister fell deathly ill themselves. In the spring of 1863 they started for home, but were almost killed in an Indiana train wreck caused by suspected Southern sympathizers. Maud was just one of an unknown number of young girls who helped Union soldiers in hospitals during the war.

At age 15, musician William S. Meek enlisted in Company A, 43rd Ohio, on October 1, 1861. This photograph was taken in Louisville in 1865.

Author's Collection

raising the question of how many more also were younger.[3]

The 43rd, 27th, 39th and 63rd Ohio constituted Fuller's Ohio Brigade. It was named for its first commander, Colonel John W. Fuller of the 27th, who was born in England and resided in Toledo at war's outbreak. In Missouri at the end of February 1862 the brigade commenced a 50-mile march over swampy ground toward New Madrid. As the greenhorn boys of the 43rd tramped along they quickly learned that many treasures recently sent from home were not worth hauling. All along the way discarded items littered the column's trail. On March 3 the enemy's outposts were confronted, and for the next four days the Ohioans were exposed to Confederate cannon and rifle fire. Few of the youngsters looked for or claimed fame. Most had enlisted innocently. Commitment to comrades as they lay in or double-quicked through cornfields near New Madrid induced them to stay the course as much as any general's order or article of war. For everyone in the ranks the realities of battle had begun. At Iuka, Mississippi, that September the regiment was warmly engaged, but it was at Corinth two weeks later near Battery Robinett where Fuller's brigade practically turned the tide in favor of Union forces. The valiant stand by the 43rd and its fellow Ohio regiments gained a worthy place in the history of the rebellion.[4]

Of more than 330 teenagers in the 43rd's ranks, 39 died during their service. Among them were James B. Bowen, a prisoner of war; Nathan Thornburg, at Resaca, Georgia; William Gamble, at Pocataligo Station, South Carolina; Justice Paxton and John Werner, at Dallas, Georgia; John Curren, John Tipton, David Wallace and James Dew, at Corinth; Levi Kelly, at New Madrid; Mathias Kelly, near Kennesaw Mountain; and James H. Deury, at Bentonville, North Carolina.[5]

The 43rd can be called one of the Union Army's

boy regiments with such a high number of youthful members. The drum corps possessed a full complement of beardless boys whose friendships and camaraderie were built on a foundation of shared adventures. The original musicians included Milton A. Wells, John Couch, Stewart Roberts, John Schick, Edwin Stein, Francis Logsdon, William S. Meek, David and Demas L. Auld, Lewis Schramm, Jeremiah Stull and Hamden Heatherington. Schramm and Heatherington, who were older, acted as principal musicians and tried to keep the boys in line.[6]

The regiment's youngest musician was 13-year-old John McClay. While on his way to Sunday school near Galena, Ohio, he ran away and enlisted in October 1863. Although not with the regiment during its early service, he was present for Sherman's drive to Atlanta and in all subsequent campaigns leading to the Grand Review in Washington in 1865. In a series of post-war newspaper interviews with McClay recorded by George M. Ziegler, numerous anecdotes about the 43rd's drummer boys were preserved.[7]

The first engagement the 43rd participated in af-

ter McClay's arrival was the storming of Decatur, Alabama, on December 8, 1863. In the early morning boats were lowered into the Tennessee River for the purpose of crossing to the Decatur side for the assault. Colonel Swayne, previous to the launching, emphatically ordered the musicians to stay behind, but McClay, with innocent eagerness to meet the foe, persuaded a sergeant in Company H to let him go along. After short but stubborn resistance the town was taken. The following morning Swayne chanced to see McClay sitting in the post office and inquired, "Little boy, did I not issue an order for the drummers of the regiment to remain behind?" He replied, "I could not see you going off and leaving me behind." Instead of receiving a dose of discipline the plucky drummer was detailed as the colonel's orderly for the next two months.[8]

The 43rd's drummers spent their fair share of time close to the front and even on the skirmish line during the Atlanta campaign. On May 13, 1864, in the opening phase of the battle of Resaca, Company A's drummer William Meek noted in his diary: "Left our drums and knapsacks in camp this morning and went out about two miles and took our place in line of battle. Commenced our advance about three o'clock and drove the rebels about three miles. Loss of the 43d one killed and 4 wounded." His May 15 entry stated,

Another lithographed drawing by David Auld depicted an incident of the battle of Resaca. Fellow musician and friend John McClay described the scene: "General John A. Logan (right center) and staff of the 15th Corps appeared upon the battlefield while the engagement was going on. David Auld, who was an expert artist, was sketching the battle. A Rebel battery had been giving us considerable trouble. At this moment one of General Logan's staff was pointing out some object, when a piece of shell carried away the extended arm. Auld saw the occurrence and sketched it at the moment it happened." Auld included himself in the scene, seated on a tree stump at lower left. The one-legged officer on crutches observing the action at left center was General Daniel E. Sickles.

Author's Collection

"Pretty heavy skirmishing all day. Nobody hurt severely. Bullets flew uncomfortably close though." As the regiment approached the hamlet of Dallas on the 25th, Meek found reason to celebrate although rain poured down in a deluge. "This day is the eighteenth anniversary of my birth, marched all night nearly." On

the 27th he recorded that their drum major was injured. "Had a good nights rest. Were formed in line this morning, and moved out of the woods. Skirmishing progressing briskly. Lewis Schramm got a slight wound in the hip by a spent ball which had went through [Henry T.] Fultz's leg." Despite the obvious danger Meek wrote two days later, "Laid in line of battle all day. Went out to the skirmish line and tried a few shots myself. The rebels made a charge on our lines this evening but we sent them back considerably whipped." Again on June 14 he mentioned, "After dinner I went out to the line and tried a few shots." [9]

McClay also related being at the front with weapons. On one occasion while the drummers were watching an attack, a Confederate sharpshooter began warming their place of concealment. David Auld used a pair of field glasses to search the hillside for the antagonist. Before long he was discovered and as Mc-

The haversack was an indispensable item of a soldier's equipment. David Auld carried the commercially-sold leather one above, shown with his drum sling buckle and watch chain inscribed with battles he participated in on one side and corps badges of Sherman's forces on the other. The leather-bound portfolio and silver cup were found while foraging in the war's waning weeks. Auld wrote in the portfolio: "Cheraw, South Carolina March 6th 1865. Taken from the Confederate Quartermasters office after town was captured by assault with 36 Confederate Cannon by 1st Division 17th A.C. Major General Joseph Mower Division Commander. While marching through with Sherman's Army." All of the 43rd Ohio musicians obtained a silver cup, according to William Meek's diary entry for April 9, 1865.

Author's Collection

247

Clay observed their marks, David and brother Demas caught the sharpshooter in a crossfire. David's second shot was fatal for the Rebel, to the boys' relief. [10]

Outside Atlanta the Signal Corps had erected a signaling platform in a large oak tree behind the 43rd's position near a battery. Metal cleats were driven into the trunk's backside for ease of climbing. McClay, his curiosity whetted, loitered at the tree's base in anticipation of a chance to climb up when no one was looking and sneak a view of the city. The battery commander, noticing his peculiar behavior, shooed him away from the tree. Not dismayed, a day or two later he found an opportunity and quickly ascended to the platform. The stunt and his sightseeing did not last long. Within moments of reaching the top a Rebel shell struck the bottom of the tree, exploded and shattered the trunk. Scared out of his wits, the boy scampered down much faster than his ascent and headed back to the line, wiser if not braver. [11]

He was not the only one who made a hasty retreat at the front. During the Federal attack at Resaca a new surgeon arriving in camp was eager to see a battle. "Billy" Meek and McClay agreed to escort him to a nearby vantage point where they could observe the assault. As they approached the spot the boys explained to their guest that he soon would hear a volley as their regiment was just then advancing. At that moment the main line opened fire and so did the enemy. Meek turned to tell the doctor that it was a volley, but the newcomer's inquisitiveness was well satisfied and he went running back to camp. [12]

Although at times it seemed the youngsters took many unnecessary risks, they all learned survival skills and knew when to lay low and stay out of danger. One incident related by McClay to George Ziegler concerned self-justified insubordination near Atlanta. "The drummers were busily engaged in carrying off the wounded from the battlefield while the engagement was at the highest pitch. Johnny McClay, Frank Logsdon, Billy Meek and Sam Poke, who were on the firing line, were commanded by a captain of the 43d, who had taken refuge behind a tree, to remove a dead Rebel who had been killed the day before, and was lying near the tree, giving out quite a stench. Johnny replied that they would look after their own wounded first and then the Rebels. Johnny told the captain that if that tree was not large enough he could hunt a bigger one. This dignified brave captain, as soon as he

could get away from his tree, reported Johnny to Colonel Swayne, who, on seeing Johnny, called him and asked what the trouble was between him and the captain. He told his story as above related, also adding that the tree was not large enough for him and that was the cause of all the trouble. With a broad smile on his face, Swayne wheeled his horse and rode away, and thus ended the episode." [13]

This was not the only occasion McClay temporarily rode the hot seat. While marching with Sherman toward Savannah he and a group of 43rd and 63rd Ohio foragers arrived at a large plantation. Above the grand house flew the Stars and Stripes, indicating the inhabitants were loyal Unionists. A sergeant of the 63rd coaxed the elderly man living there into a conversation about the war and how badly the Rebels had been whipped in recent battles. Growing visibly agitated, the old man lost control of his tongue and vehemently chastised the assembled Yankees, extolling his two sons who were then fighting for the Confederacy. He further remarked that if he was a younger man he, too, would be in the service. Hearing this, McClay spoke up, "How about that American flag flying over a Rebel house." The sergeant told him, "Little one, go up and take it down, and I will stand by you." McClay climbed to the roof, lowered the flag and folded it neatly. No sooner had the soldiers left than the aged Rebel hastened to the Union camp and complained of the flag's theft. When McClay strolled in a little later two guards took him to General John W. Sprague, who asked if he was "the chap that tore down the American flag from this old gentleman's house." The boy retorted, "I did not tear it down; I took it down and folded it up." The general then remonstrated that the Georgian was a strong Union sympathizer. At that McClay asked permission to find the 63rd Ohio sergeant who had questioned the old man at his house. The affair was soon settled in Johnny's favor and the plantation owner was escorted outside Union lines. [14]

Southern hospitality was as unpredictable as the old man's story. On a different foraging excursion McClay and Sergeant Frederick Schneider of Company H were prowling around another plantation when they spied a locked smokehouse. McClay exclaimed that all of Sherman's bummers had a set of keys. He pulled out a revolver and blew the lock off. Just as they opened the door a noise was heard from behind. The pair turned in time to see a young woman level a

Cigars did little to disguise the youth of John McClay, center, drummer William Brown, right, of Company G, 43rd Ohio, and an unidentified comrade. For years McClay retained many of his prized possessions from the war, including this battered bugle.

Author's Collection

double-barreled shotgun at them. "My husband is out killing Yankees," she said, "and I will do the same." She then pulled the trigger but the blast missed its targets. After wresting away the gun and smashing it against the ground, Schneider detained the distraught lady while McClay explored the smokehouse. He was rewarded with a fine haul of seasoned sausage and hams.[15]

Foraging also was a subject mentioned in William Meek's diary. On February 4, 1865, in South Carolina,

he penned, "Went out foraging this morning and returned after dinner heavily laden with spoils. A chicken, half bushel of meal, lots of pork, and a large bag full of potatoes." On the 14th he "Roamed all over the country and was lucky enough to get lost. Forage scarce." Its absence continued, as noted the next day. "Left camp at 7 this morning. Went off the road about 8 miles foraging but didn't get anything." On February 16 his luck was worse. "I went out foraging out to the Saluda Mills. While there my horse was shot right

249

"My Last Canteen John McClay Co. H 43 O.V.V.I." was lettered on a now worn label affixed to a relic of the musician's service. McClay donated other war memorabilia to the Ohio Historical Society — including his drum that was used by the 43rd Ohio as a ballot box in the 1864 presidential election, and a plow made of gun barrels and bayonets found after the battle of Corinth.

Author's Collection

the colored man taking the lead. They had gone no great distance when Johnny discovered a cloud of dust ahead, and rode into the timber at the side of the road to take observation; he discovered that it was the enemy and started through the woods on his horse. The enemy soon discovered him and gave chase through the woods. The underbrush was in his favor, but the horse made a splendid object to follow whenever there was an opening in the timber. The chase continued for nearly two hours. Seeing that the enemy was gaining on him, he dismounted in a thicket and tied his horse to a sapling, and started on foot. He had been losing too much valuable time in letting down fences. The enemy were so close upon him he could recognize them. This little piece of strategy threw them off the track. Getting his bearings, he started in the direction of the troops....

As darkness was coming on, he discovered and reached our troops, when he found that he was with the Third Division of the 17th Corps. In the course of one hour he reached his own command, tired and hungry. But during the evening before taps was sounded, he had given the boys an account of his wonderful escape from the enemy during the day.[17]

On a previous occasion, Ziegler recounted, McClay encountered some Confederates alone, and bested them in an entirely different manner:

The morning following the battle of Jonesboro [Georgia, August 31-September 1, 1864], while on the march, Johnny and Sergeant Hugh Daugherty of Co. I were skirmishing around for water, and upon going down in a deep ravine they discovered a nice clear stream. Filling their canteens, they started back for the regiment when Johnny discovered smoke on the opposite side of a ridge.

The sergeant continued on up the hill where they had left the troops, but Johnny's curiosity led him to see what the smoke was. Getting close to it, he discovered a Confederate soldier sitting down beside a tree fast asleep, and up-

through the fore leg." Daily expeditions hunting for food could be hazardous, as described in Meek's February 28 entry: "Went out foraging this morning. Went to Wilkes Mills got dinner there. As we were leaving a squad of rebels dashed up and demanded our surrender. We went into the house and commenced skirmishing with them and finally drove them off. We were just leaving when a larger party came up and there we abandoned the field and left for camp. A few of the 1st Division were captured. Related the affair to General Blair [commanding the Seventeenth Corps], when he sent me to guide a regiment out. Went out with them and returned to camp at 9. Very wet, skirmishing in front of the cavalry."[16]

Close calls were becoming common for McClay, too, as Ziegler wrote:

On this day's foraging Johnny was accompanied by a colored refugee, who had been with the regiment for some time. As he was older than Johnny he began giving him some advice, as they rode along, saying if they were caught together it would mean sure death to both of them; and he proposed to ride some distance in the front. They had been quite successful in gathering up a nice bunch of eatables,

on looking around he saw three others lying on the ground asleep, their guns being stacked.

Slipping around quietly he captured their guns. Laying them down in the tall sage grass which hid them from sight, he slipped back to the sleeping sentinel, and with revolver in hand, he jerked the gun away from the sentinel. As he awoke he thrust his revolver into his face, saying, "You are my prisoner." The man replied, "the hell I am."

Keeping his prisoner in front of him, he proceeded to wake up the other soldiers who were not more than 10 paces away. A corporal, upon being awakened, commenced upbraiding the soldier for sleeping on post, when Johnny ordered them to fall in front of him and started for the regiment at the top of the hill.

Carrying the four captured guns on his shoulder, with his revolver in his hand, he came upon the colonel of the 39th Ohio Regt., who said, "Little one, where did you get those fellows?" Johnny replied, "I surrounded them."

He marched them to his own regiment and turned them over to Col. Swayne, who said, "You acted very foolish in running this great risk. What would you have done had the sentinel wakened up and resisted?" Johnny replied, "I would have put him to sleep with my revolver."

Johnny's great feat became noised about the camp that

Twenty-five years after the war surviving members of the 43rd Ohio's drum corps reunited for a group portrait. Standing from left: Alexander Roberts, Edwin Stein, Hugh Mosher, Francis Logsdon and Stewart Roberts. Seated from left: John McClay, Demas L. Auld, Lewis Schramm, David Auld, William S. Meek and William Stull.

Author's Collection

evening and he became the hero of the occasion. The boys declared that he had drowned them with the water from his canteen before capturing them. The prisoners proved to be pickets holding an outpost which the enemy had failed to notify in their eagerness to get away from Jonesboro.[18]

The boys regularly had tales to share around the campfire at night. During yet another foraging excursion a few of the drummers searched the grounds of a mansion for buried treasure, having learned it was not unusual for Southerners to bury their valuables upon

251

the Yankees' approach. McClay noticed freshly turned soil in the garden and began probing with a ramrod. Everyone joined in and before long McClay's ramrod struck something solid. With a shovel brought to the scene the boys started digging in earnest. Two feet down they uncovered a Dutch oven stuffed with two white bags stenciled "50,000." The drummers excitedly envisioned untold riches as they continued to dislodge their newfound fortune. Finally the oven was carried to a secluded thicket where the bags were opened. Instead of money they discovered 100,000 army percussion caps, which they angrily scattered over the yard. Later the disheartened boys learned another group of soldiers unearthed a kettle in the same garden containing two gold watches and a set of fine silverware.[19]

Pranks constantly were played within the boys' circle of friends. One day McClay found a three-foot stuffed snake in an old house, which he draped over his shoulders as if it were alive. Wearing a Confederate captain's coat acquired at the same place he returned to camp a comical sight. He grasped the reptile by the head and approached Stewart Roberts of Company C, who grabbed his rifle and called out, "If you come near me with that snake I will shoot you." The prankish game was tried on all the regiment's drummers until they tore the creature away and beat it to pieces. The Rebel coat was ripped and shredded in like manner.[20]

McClay the snake charmer was not always in a playful mood. Ziegler related that the boy, though very popular, sometimes displayed childish behavior:

Having been the pet of the regiment and humored by everyone, he soon came to the conclusion that he was just as important as if he had full command of the regiment, that what he said was law and that no one would dare to dispute him. Lew Schramm, who had been promoted to drum major, was one of his warmest friends, and on many occasions on the march had carried his knapsack. Being almost a giant in stature, he took pity on the little boy and tried to make life more pleasant for him.

Lew, who had been wounded [near Dallas, Georgia] and sent home, returned to the regiment at Pocataligo. During the evening something came up which caused quite an argument, and during the discussion Johnny called the drum major a liar, when he told him if he did that again he would slap his mouth. Daredevil like, out came the word again, and true to his promise Lew slapped his mouth and gave him a good spanking besides.

Johnny, in his wrath, crying all the time, told him if they lived to get home and he became a man, he would whip him the first time they met. Johnny and the drum major slept together, and at the sounding of taps, Johnny crawled in alongside of Lew and cried himself to sleep. Lew felt so badly about it that the next morning he told some of the boys that he would never slap the little one again, no matter what he did. The matter was soon forgotten and they became fast friends again.

Some fifteen years later they met at Mt. Vernon, Ohio, at their first regimental reunion. The boys were gathered in groups fighting the war over again. The old drum major remarked to Johnny, "You are as much of a man as you ever will be," and Johnny replied, "Yes, I suppose I am."

Then in a laughing way the drum major began pulling off his coat. Johnny asked, "What is the matter, Lew?" and he replied, "Don't you remember at Pocataligo, South Carolina, you said if we lived through the war and got home, you would whip me the first time we met. I am ready to take that whipping." Johnny replied, "Lew, put on that coat. I have changed my mind. I remember when we lay down like the lion and the lamb and ate rice like the ox," which caused a round of applause from the old comrades who were standing about.[21]

The boys of the 43rd who shared so much during the war had become friends for life.

CHAPTER 14

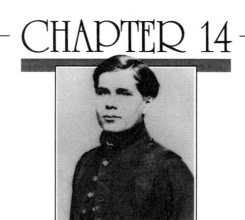

'I thanked God for peace and home'

On April 8, 1865, General George Armstrong Custer's 3rd Division of the Army of the Potomac's Cavalry Corps pushed toward Appomattox Court House, Virginia. Six days earlier the Confederates evacuated Petersburg and Richmond, their battered army under Robert E. Lee marching in haste to the west. Custer learned the enemy was moving a large supply train and ordered a full advance across his front with hopes of overtaking it. During the movement his 1st Brigade arrived at Appomattox Station, capturing three trains of cars loaded with provisions intended for the hungry Rebels. After spoils of the capture were secured the brigade moved on the road to the Court House and camped for the night facing a Confederate force in its front. The main bodies of both armies settled down with only a few hundred yards separating them. As twilight descended over the surrounding fields, a sense of victory permeated the line of Federal troopers.[1]

The 1st Brigade band, buoyed by the day's success, was ordered forward between the lines and struck up "Yankee Doodle." Astride his mount in the group of musicians sat Edward F. "Jerry" Smith of the 2nd Ohio Cavalry, playing a keyed bugle. Jerry, an Ashland County, Ohio, native, had joined the 7th Ohio Infantry in 1861 at age 15, and served briefly with the 42nd Ohio's band before enlisting in the cavalry. Being an accomplished musician he quickly was promoted chief bugler of the 2nd Ohio. His abilities, in fact, were recognized far beyond his command, and in December 1864 he was detailed to the 1st Brigade band.[2]

By the time the teen bugler reached Appomattox he had served the Union for four years and participated in dozens of engagements. He was now a young man who had garnered considerable respect for his merit. On the last full day of hostilities for the Army of the Potomac, Jerry Smith not only won the esteem of his comrades, he earned vocal plaudits from the enemy as well.[3] In his 1907 obituary the *Shelby* (Ohio) *Daily Globe* reported:

"Both armies watched in silence this band, mounted on horseback, march to the middle ground between them; but when the band pealed forth 'Yankee Doodle' it was too much for rebel endurance and they sent a storm of bullets into the boys that sent them flying to the rear. Their retreat was the signal for terrific cheering along the rebel line, but judge the astonishment of these same rebels a moment later as they heard loud, clear and distinct, a single key bugle send forth 'Yankee Doodle' in defiance of shot and shell, and as the smoke of their guns and dust of the retreating band cleared away, Mr. Smith could be seen sitting upon his horse playing with the assurance and nerve of a centaur; and when the last strain, with every note round and full, had fallen on the rebels' ears, he deliberately turned and walked him back to our lines, receiving from his comrades an ovation seldom accorded by the army to its commanders.

For this intrepidity and nerve, Mr. Smith received from General Custer a silver medal — a medal of honor he never was ashamed of."[4]

On April 9 General Lee accepted terms of capitulation offered by General U.S. Grant. "When the surrender was announced the Union soldiers shouted, hurrahed, danced and manifested their joy in all sorts of boyish pranks," wrote Delavan Miller of the 2nd New York Heavy Artillery. "But it soon passed off, and as they beheld the ragged, starved, wearied and sad-eyed veterans who had followed Lee into the last ditch their joy was turned to pity and sorrow and the blue divided with the gray their rations and they drank coffee from the same tin cups and water from the same canteens."[5]

After Lee's surrender at Appomattox most of the Army of the Potomac began heading north to Washington. For its soldiers it was a time of happiness and reflection, as Miller recalled: "The armies of Grant and Sherman [in North Carolina] turned their backs on the South and took up their lines of march for Washington, where they had been ordered to report for a general review and muster out. We passed through Richmond and retraced our steps over much of the same ground that had been fought over the previous year, and all along the route were reminders of the terrible struggles between the two great armies. Earthworks that had swarmed with soldiers were now deserted. Everywhere there were bleaching bones of horses and men; grinning skulls, disabled artillery caissons, rusty sabers, bayonets, gun-barrels, canteens, haversacks, weather-stained clothing and mounds of earth that marked the resting places of many whose army records were closed with the single word 'missing.' We were a jolly lot, however, realizing that our battles, hardships and marches were about over."[6]

Elation in the North after Grant's victory was transformed to dismay and sorrow following the assassination of President Lincoln on April 14. For two weeks his remains toured leading Northern cities by train until they reached their final resting place at Springfield, Illinois. Along the way at least one boy soldier participated in the funeral ceremonies.

Henry M. Brown was a farmer's son in Guernsey County, Ohio, when the war broke out. Only 15, he was forced by his parents to wait more than two years before they allowed him to enlist. In July 1863 he was mustered into the 88th Ohio, which spent most of its

term of service guarding Confederate prisoners at Camp Chase in Columbus. When Lincoln's body was exhibited in the rotunda of the Ohio statehouse, Henry was detailed to stand guard beside the catafalque during the two-day viewing.[7]

Brown was one of the war's fortunate young soldiers, as was Adelbert Batchelder of Trempealeau County, Wisconsin. A month after his 15th birthday Adelbert enlisted February 15, 1864, with 28 others in Company I of the newly formed 36th Wisconsin. As the Army of the Potomac prepared for its spring campaign, he fell sick with measles and did not return to the company until the following winter at Petersburg. Of the 28 recruits who enlisted with him, only nine were present to greet him. Three had been discharged for disability; five were prisoners (four of whom died in captivity); five had been wounded; four killed; and three had succumbed to disease. Batchelder served

Private Henry M. Brown, Company E, 88th Ohio.

Drummer George L. Miller mustered at age 15 with Company F, 1st Massachusetts Heavy Artillery, on July 1, 1861. In August 1864 he was afflicted with sunstroke and spent four months recuperating — his only absence from the regiment. Just before the fall of Richmond he was honored with appointment to principal musician.

Author's Collection

through to Appomattox and was discharged with the regiment on July 12, 1865.[8]

On May 10, 1865, President Andrew Johnson proclaimed armed resistance was at an end. Two days later the last land battle of the war took place in Texas at Palmito Ranch on the banks of the Rio Grande River. Ironically, the small affair concluded in the Confederates' favor.[9]

For hundreds of boys who entered the ranks and survived to see victory, a rewarding sense of accomplishment was felt like none most ever would experience again in their lifetimes. The government planned an enormous celebratory parade in Washington for the two main Federal armies. The Army of the Potomac participated on May 23, followed by Sherman's troops on the 24th. Both days drew thousands of spectators to the capital to witness the last grand review of the Union's citizen-soldiers before they returned to civilian life. The event was a tremendous success.[10]

Elbridge Copp, although discharged for wounds received in 1864, journeyed to Washington and by way of favor obtained a seat May 23 near the reviewing stand erected in front of the White House. From his position he clearly could see the assembled dignitaries as well as observe the parade. Near the end of the reviewing stand sat General Grant, accompanied by his three boys, Jesse, Ulysses and Fred. At 9 a.m. a signal gun sounded and General Meade's troops stepped off smartly. Bands played patriotic airs as each corps and division marched down Pennsylvania Avenue with flags unfurled to the breeze. Copp admired "the sight of one's life — this magnificent army — the Army of the Potomac." It took six full hours for the massed blue columns to pass by the reviewing stand.[11]

The next day showcased Sherman's lean, stalwart veterans. Prior to their march John McClay of the 43rd Ohio was chosen to act as regimental marker and placed directly in front of the main grandstand, almost directly across from the Ohio stand. He received strict orders to keep eyes front and not converse with anyone. As the troops strode by, spectators in the stands questioned McClay as to who was this general or that. With obedience to orders he remained mute, ignoring their entreaties. Someone finally blurted out, "That fellow must be deaf." The boy continued carrying out his duty while watching the remainder of the impressive parade.[12]

With the spectacle's conclusion most of the soldiers were dispersed to their homes over the following weeks and months. Harry Kieffer of the 150th Pennsylvania wrote:

But before we could go home we must be mustered out. And then we must return to our State capital to be paid off and finally discharged, and say a last good-bye to our com-

Eleven-year-old Nathan M. Gove joined the 3rd New Hampshire in 1861 as a drummer. After being discharged in 1862 he reenlisted with the 2nd Brigade Band, Tenth Corps, in January 1863 and soldiered to the close of the war. The band and 3rd New Hampshire served many months on Hilton Head Island, South Carolina, where Nathan appeared in at least three camp photographs taken by Henry P. Moore. In 1867 Gove enlisted in the Navy, serving aboard the U.S.S. *Franklin*. The post-war military contained no shortage of boys who earlier served the Union.

Author's Collection

rades in arms, the great majority of whom we should never, in all probability, see again. And a more hearty, rough and ready, affectionate good-bye there never was in all this wide world. In the rooms of one of the hotels at the State capital we were gathered, waiting for our representative trains. Knapsacks slung, Sharps rifles at a "right shoulder shift" or a "carry," songs were sung, hands were shaken, or rather wrung; loud, hearty "God bless you, old fellow!" resounded, and many were the toasts and the healths that were drunk before the men parted for good and all.

It was past midnight when the last campfire of the 150th broke up. "Good-bye, boys! Good-bye! God bless you, old fellow!" was shouted again and again, as by companies, or in little squads, we were off for our several trains, some of us bound north, some east, some west — all bound for home!

Of the thirteen men who had gone out from our little village (whither my father's family had meanwhile removed), but three had lived to return home together. One had already gone home the day before. Some had been discharged because of sickness or wounds, and four had been killed. As we rode along over the dusty turnpike ... in the rattling old stage coach that evening in June, we could not help thinking how painful it would be for the friends of Joe

Gutelius and Jimmy Lucas and Joe Ruhl and John Diehl to see us return without their brave boys, whom we had left on the field.

Reaching the village at dusk, we found gathered at the hotel where the stage stopped, a great crowd of our schoolfellows and friends, who had come to meet us. We almost feared to step down among them, lest they should quite tear us to pieces with shaking of hands. The stage had scarcely stopped when I heard a well-known voice calling —

"Harry! Are you there?"

"Yes father! Here I am!"

"God bless you, my boy!"

And, pushing his way through the crowd, my father plunges into the stage, not able to wait until it has driven around to the house; and if his voice is husky with emotion, as he often repeats, "God bless you, my boy!" and gets his arm around my neck, is it any wonder?

But my dog, Rollo, can't get into the stage, and so he runs barking after it, and is the first to greet me at the gate, and jumps up at me with his great paws on my shoulders. Does he know me? I rather think he does.

Then Mother and sisters come around, and they call for a lamp and hold it close to my face, and look me all over from head to foot, while father is saying to himself, again and again, "God bless you, my boy!"

Although I knew my name was never forgotten in the evening prayer all the while I was away, yet not once, perhaps, in all that time was father's voice so choked in utterance as when now, his heart overflowing, he came to give thanks for my safe return. And when I lay down that night in a clean white bed, for the first time in three long years, I thanked God for peace and home.[13]

John W. Brooks' pride in his service as an
11-year-old soldier in Company H, 122nd Illinois,
lasted long after the war. In the mid-1890s
a Wichita, Kansas, photographer combined "past
and present" images of Brooks for the former
drummer's family members.

Author's Collection

Many boys returning from the war quickly cast off their uniforms and enrolled in school to finish their education. Charles Bardeen of the 1st Massachusetts Infantry spent two years at the Lawrence Academy in Groton, Massachusetts, before entering Yale University, where he graduated in 1869. Private colleges and academies flourished in the post-war years. Other ex-soldiers unwilling to resume lessons in the classroom used Army acquaintances to procure jobs. With so many men — and boys — being discharged at once there was keen competition for good positions.[14]

The country seemed a lot smaller now. For countless boy-veterans who most likely would have remained near their hometowns or farmsteads, the desire for adventure and travel did not dissipate. Scores of them moved west, and with manhood acquired in the Army they helped tame the wild prairies, hills and mountains that reached to California.

James K. Brady, who survived service with the 64th Ohio and the explosion of the *Sultana,* remembered: "I came home and went around to see my friends and neighbors, but when I went around it seemed as though everybody was gone or dead. Being in so much company for three years I became restless, packed my kit and went to Missouri. It was a little more lively there, as every man I met had a large navy revolver strapped to him. It made no difference whether he was a banker, dry goods man or a farmer; it was all the same, the revolver was there. I remained there eighteen months and was never treated better by any people anywhere, and I never carried a weapon of any kind." [15]

C. Perry Byam, however, lived unsettled for years, moving from Iowa to New York, California and a dozen other places. The wayward son of a colonel jumped from job to job, was constantly in trouble with the law and owned what is known as a "bad reputation." Yet, despite his problems he was always welcome among veterans, who generally were willing to help soldiers of the late war. [16]

On the other hand, the vast majority learned discipline, work ethics, the desire to succeed and self-reliability in the Army that sustained them in successful post-war careers. Seldon Kingsbury, who had enlisted at 15 in the 7th Ohio Infantry, served in the state supreme courts of Michigan, Idaho, Hawaii and Utah before appointment to the U.S. Supreme Court. [17]

A host of boy soldiers followed the path of John Lincoln Clem, staying in the Army or various state and local military organizations. At 13, Henry Gimpel served in the famed Irish Brigade with Company E, 69th New York, and afterward rose to lieutenant colonel of the 5th New York National Guard, retiring in 1880. Charles Smith, after soldiering through the war with the 49th Pennsylvania and Hancock's Veteran Corps, reenlisted for two more terms, finally leaving the military in 1871. [18]

Quite a number of late 19th-century business entrepreneurs were mere boys during the war. The nation's industrial, manufacturing and commercial enterprises expanded steadily under such capitalists as Franklin G. Rockefeller who, with older brothers John D. and William Rockefeller, gained fame and wealth by refining petroleum. Franklin served more than 20 years as vice president of the Standard Oil Company. Later, he raised pure-bred cattle on a 10,000-acre ranch in Kansas. Back in 1861 Rockefeller had joined the 7th Ohio Infantry at 16 as a private in Company A. He was severely wounded the following August at Cedar Mountain, Virginia, one day after his 17th birthday. [19]

Fifer Demas L. Auld of the 43rd Ohio founded a die and enameling company in Columbus, Ohio, bearing his name. It is still operated today by his descendants. When the first Ford automobiles were produced, Auld received an order from Henry Ford to manufacture the oval blue Ford emblem that graced his driving machines. He also secured patents and early-car emblem orders for Chevrolet, Buick and others. Interestingly, years after his death his company manufactured World War II victory medals and other decorations for soldiers of another generation. [20]

Whether they succeeded or failed in civilian pursuits, all shared the bond of experience in war throughout their lives. The Grand Army of the Republic, the country's largest veterans' organization, was filled with former boy soldiers. John McClay, 43rd Ohio drummer, first joined in 1868 and was a charter member in 1886 of the John A. Miller Post in Gahanna, Ohio. For more than 30 years he was post commander, furnishing a small building at his home for the "boys" to meet. In 1927 he was elected G.A.R. department commander of Ohio. [21]

Gaylord M. Saltzgaber, who mustered into the 3rd Ohio Cavalry at 15, served as mayor of Van Wert, Ohio, and among other accomplishments was appointed commissioner of pensions by President Woodrow Wilson. As a member of the G.A.R. he was appointed Ohio department commander in 1922, and the following year national commander at the Milwaukee encampment. [22] Many youthful veterans rose to such honorable and responsible positions with the passing of older comrades. Over time they became the last guardians and voices of the once powerful organization.

Even before the Civil War the perception of a drummer boy was one emblematic of patriotism. Between 1861 and 1865 poetry and accounts about the Army's youthful soldiers, both factual and exaggerated, filled Northern newspapers and periodicals. Through prose and publicity their deeds and sacrifices were brought to the forefront of public notice. At an 1864 U.S. Sanitary Commission benefit for Brooklyn and Long Island soldiers in New York, a newspaper called *The Drum Beat* published the touching verses of Alfred B. Sweet's poem "The Drummer Boy" —

> Dear Mother, I wish you were with me:
> I'm lying here all alone!
> I see but the dead around me,
> I hear but the dying groan;
> I'm very, very faint, mother,
> my wound is throbbing so bad;
> Could I see you for even a moment,
> I should feel to my heart right glad!

My blood is staining the hollow,
it reddens the drum I dropped
When the quick, hot ball shot through me,
and within me stopped;
My drum, my delight and glory,
that I carried all through the day
Rolling and beating and tapping,
as to and fro went the fray;
I wish I could beat it again,
it was ever my glory and joy,
But I cannot – ah! Ah! This spasm – oh, mother!
Come, come to your boy![23]

Today, a yellowed or scratched image of a young soldier from the war still can stir patriotic feelings and arouse the imagination. On November 14, 1999, a bronze statue of John Lincoln Clem was dedicated at Veterans Park in Newark, Ohio. The event drew more than 1,000 spectators, including reenactors, students from the John L. Clem Elementary School, veterans, politicians and a number of other dignitaries.[24] Over the years several towns across the country have similarly honored their drummer boy heroes.

Unfortunately, the stories and memories of so many other boys who served the Union well have all but faded away. Minnesotan Charles Goddard was one of them. He was twice wounded by bullets at Gettysburg, in the shoulder and the thigh. On December 9, 1868, he died at 22 of complications from his war injuries.[25] Seven and a half years after leaving family and home for the Army, Goddard's life and perhaps a promising future, like scores of those before him, were cut far too short.

SOURCES & NOTES

Introduction

1. Howard Aston, *History and Roster of the Fourth and Fifth Independent Battalions and Thirteenth Regiment Ohio Cavalry Volunteers* (Columbus: Press of Fred J. Heer, 1902), p. 19.

2. *Ibid.,* p. 96.

3. *Ibid.,* p. 97. The injured trooper was Private Isaac C. Hoard of Company H. His wound was slight, the bullet passing through his doubled-up gum blanket.

4. *Ibid.,* p. 97.

5. Nathaniel M. Gwynne compiled military service records, National Archives, Washington, D.C.

6. W.F. Beyer and O.F. Keydel, *Deeds of Valor: How American Heroes Won the Medal of Honor* (Detroit: The Perrien-Keydel Company, 1907), p. 394.

7. George Lang, Raymond L. Collins and Gerald F. White, compilers, *Medal of Honor Recipients 1863-1994,* vol. I (New York: Facts on File, Inc.), p. 518.

8. Nathaniel M. Gwynne pension records, National Archives.

9. Nathaniel M. Gwynne compiled military service records.

10. *Deeds of Valor,* p. 394.

11. Aston, p. 98.

12. Nathaniel M. Gwynne pension records.

13. Aston, p. 99.

OPPOSITE: A young, unidentified artilleryman posed holding his M1858 Army hat replete with black ostrich feather, red worsted cord and regimental numerals above brass crossed-cannons insignia.

Author's Collection

14. George A. Otis, *The Medical and Surgical History of the War of the Rebellion,* part II, vol. II (Washington: Government Printing Office, 1876), p. 725; *History and Roster of Maryland Volunteers, War of 1861-5,* vol. I (Baltimore: Guggenheimer, Weil & Co., 1898), p. 307.

15. Nathaniel M. Gwynne compiled military service records.

16. Ibid.

17. Lang, et.al., *Medal of Honor Recipients 1863-1994,* vol. I, p. 518.

18. Nathaniel M. Gwynne compiled military service records.

19. Nathaniel M. Gwynne pension records.

Chapter 1

1. David B. Guralnik, editor in chief, *Webster's New World Dictionary of the American Language* (New York: Simon and Schuster, 1982), p. 169.

2. Eleanor C. Bishop, *Ponies, Patriots and Powder Monkeys: A History of Children in America's Armed Forces 1776-1916* (Del Mar, Calif.: The Bishop Press, 1982), p. 4-5.

3. *General Regulations for the Army* (Washington, 1821), p. 312.

4. *General Regulations for the Army; or, Military Institutes* (Washington: Davis & Force, 1825), p. 354.

5. Asbury Dickins and John W. Forney, editors, *American State Papers. Documents, Legislative and Executive, of the Congress of the United States, from the First Session of the Twenty-Second to the First Session of the Twenty-Fourth Congress, Inclusive: Commencing March 15, 1832, and Ending January 5, 1836,* vol. V (Washington: Gales & Seaton, 1860), p. 121, 122, 123.

6. *General Regulations for the Army* (Washington: Francis P. Blair, 1834), p. 84, 85.

7. *General Regulations for the Army of the United States 1841* (Washington: J. and G.S. Gideon, 1841), p. 119, 121, 128.

8. *General Regulations for the Army of the United States 1847* (Washington: J. and G.S. Gideon, 1847), p. 133, 134.

Herb Peck Jr. Collection

Unidentified cavalry trooper armed with revolver and saber.

1861, p. 130.

19. Tripler, p. 11.

20. Jeremiah C. Allen, *Subject Index of the General Orders of the War Department, from January 1, 1861, to December 31, 1880* (Washington: Government Printing Office, 1882), p. 293.

21. Adjutant General's Office, *General Orders Affecting the Volunteer Force, 1861* (Washington: Government Printing Office, 1862), p. 18, 19.

22. *Ibid.,* p. 29.

23. *Ibid.,* p. 33.

24. *Ibid.,* p. 53.

25. Adjutant General's Office, *General Orders Affecting the Volunteer Force, 1863* (Washington: Government Printing Office, 1864), p. 128.

26. Thomas L. Livermore, *Numbers and Losses in the Civil War in America 1861-65* (Carlisle, Pa.: John Kallmann Publishers, 1996), p. 79-104.

27. Record Group 153, Records of the Judge Advocate General's Office (Army), court-martial file LL3030, National Archives.

28. Adjutant General's Office, *General Orders Affecting the Volunteer Force, 1864* (Washington: Government Printing Office, 1865), p. 34, 35.

29. *Ibid.,* p. 107.

30. Benjamin A. Gould, *Investigations in the Military and Anthropological Statistics of American Soldiers* (New York: Hurd and Haughton, 1869), p. 30-49.

31. *Ibid.,* p. 30-49.

32. George L. Kilmer, "Boys in the Union Army," *The Century* (June 1905), p. 269-274.

33. Ibid., p. 269.

34. Gould, p. 30-49; Kilmer, p. 269-274.

35. Ovid P. Webster pension records, National Archives.

36. Ovid P. Webster compiled military service records.

37. Allen D. Albert, *History of the Forty-Fifth Regiment Pennsylvania Veteran Volunteer Infantry 1861-1865* (Williamsport, Pa.: Grit Publishing Company, 1912), p. 381.

38. Henry A. Bull compiled military service records, National Archives; 1860 census records for Huron, N.Y., microfilm, National·Archives.

39. Frederick H. Dyer, *A Compendium of the War of the Rebellion,* vol. I (New York: Thomas Yoseloff, 1959), p. 11.

40. Ohio Roster Commission, *Official Roster of the Soldiers of the State of Ohio in the War of the Rebellion, 1861-1866,* 12 vols. (Akron, Cincinnati, Norwalk, 1886-1895).

41. Whitelaw Reid, *Ohio in the War: Her Statesmen, Generals and Soldiers,* vol. II (Cincinnati: Robert Clarke, 1895), p. 3.

42. Albert C. White compiled military service records, National Archives; Ebenezer Z. Hays, *History of the Thirty-second Regiment Ohio Veteran Volunteer Infantry* (Columbus: Cott & Evans, Printers, 1896), p. 197, 152.

43. Henry C. Houston, *The Thirty-second Maine Regiment of*

9. *Regulations for the Army of the United States 1857* (New York: Harper & Brothers, 1857), p. 423, 429.

10. Nathaniel M. Gwynne compiled military service records.

11. *Regulations for the Army of the United States 1857,* p. 423, 424.

12. *Ibid.,* p. 424.

13. *Revised Regulations for the Army of the United States 1861* (Philadelphia: J.B. Lippincott & Co., 1861), p. 502, 511.

14. *Ibid.,* p. 130.

15. Charles S. Tripler, M.D., *Manual of the Medical Officer of the Army of the United States* (Cincinnati: Wrightson & Co., 1858), p. 114, 115, 116.

16. Delavan S. Miller, *Drum Taps in Dixie: Memories of a Drummer Boy 1861-1865* (Watertown, N.Y., 1905), p. 16.

17. Harry M. Kieffer, *The Recollections of a Drummer Boy by Harry M. Kieffer late of the One Hundred and Fiftieth Regiment Pennsylvania Volunteers* (New York: Houghton Mifflin Company, 1888), p. 36.

18. *Revised Regulations for the Army of the United States*

Sixteen-year-old Henry Roof served as a musician in Companies H and E, 54th Ohio. Although the Hardin County native missed the battle of Shiloh while sick aboard a Tennessee River hospital ship, he participated in all his regiment's engagements of the Vicksburg and Atlanta campaigns.

Logan County, Ohio, Historical Society

Infantry Volunteers (Portland: Southworth Brothers, 1903), p. 45-47, 456.

44. Wilbur F. Hinman, *The Story of the Sherman Brigade* (Alliance, Ohio: Press of Daily Review, 1897), p. 55-56.

45. Ezra J. Warner, *Generals in Blue: Lives of the Union Commanders* (Baton Rouge: Louisiana State University Press, 1977), p. 235-236.

46. John C. Arbuckle, *Civil War Experiences of a Foot-Soldier Who Marched with Sherman* (Columbus, 1930), p. 45-47.

Chapter 2

1. E.B. Long, *The Civil War Day by Day: An Almanac 1861-1865* (New York: Doubleday & Company, 1971), p. 56, 69.

2. Elbridge J. Copp, *Reminiscences of the War of the Rebellion 1861-1865* (Nashua, N.H.: Telegraph Publishing Company, 1911), p. 11, 12.

3. George T. Ulmer, *Adventures and Reminiscences of a Volunteer, or a Drummer Boy from Maine* (1892), p. 5.

4. Charles W. Bardeen, *A Little Fifer's War Diary* (Syracuse, N.Y.: C.W. Bardeen Publisher, 1910), p. 17-19.

5. Commodore Perry Byam pension records, National Archives.

6. William Bircher, *A Drummer-Boy's Diary: Comprising Four Years of Service with the Second Regiment Minnesota Veteran Volunteers, 1861-1865* (St. Paul: St. Paul Book and Stationery Co., 1889), p. 11-13.

7. "The Youngest Soldier," *The National Tribune,* May 1881.

8. Kilmer, op. cit., p. 270.

9. Ibid., p. 270, 271; Abraham J. Palmer, *The History of the Forty-Eighth Regiment New York State Volunteers, in the War for the Union, 1861-1865* (Brooklyn, 1885), p. 2-3; William J. Carlton, *Company D ("The Die-No-Mores") of the Forty-Eighth Regiment, New York State Volunteers, 1861-5* (privately printed, 1892), p. 13-18.

10. Oscar L. Jackson, *The Colonel's Diary* (Sharon, Pa., 1922), p. 36-41.

11. Adjutant General's Office, *Regulations for the Recruiting Service of the Army of the United States, Both Regular and Volunteer* (Washington: Government Printing Office, 1862), p. 1-31.

12. William H. Albee compiled military service and pension records, National Archives.

13. Arbuckle, p. 43.

14. *Regulations for the Recruiting Service ...,* p. 48, 49.

15. George H. Washburn, *A Complete Military History and Record of the 108th Regiment N.Y. Vols. from 1862 to 1894* (Rochester: E.R. Andrews, 1894), p. 337.

16. Cyrus Ellwood was recruiting for the 48th Ohio at the time.

17. J.F. Orr, "The Story of 'Little Gib,' Youngest Union Civil War Soldier," *The Gazette,* Xenia, Ohio, February 28-March 8, 1938.

18. Stanton P. Allen, *A Boy Trooper with Sheridan* (Boston: Lothrop Publishing Company, 1899), unpaginated.

19. Alfred S. Roe, *The Tenth Regiment Massachusetts Volunteer Infantry 1861-1864, a Western Massachusetts Regiment* (Springfield, Mass.: F.A. Bassette Co., 1909), p. 307-309.

20. William W. Belknap, *History of the Fifteenth Regiment Iowa Veteran Volunteer Infantry from August 1861, to August 1865* (Keokuk: R.B. Ogden & Son, 1887), p. 202-203. Loren S. Tyler of Company H actually was the author of most of this regimental history.

21. *Ibid.,* p. 193.

22. J.F. Orr, "The Story of 'Little Gib'...." Various spellings of Gilbert's surname have been recorded. Upon enlistment his father and Gilbert both signed their last name as Vanzant.

23. Copp, p. 12, 13.

24. Matthias Kelly compiled military service records, National Archives.

25. Eugene W. Leach, *Racine County Militant: An Illustrated Narrative of War Times, and a Soldiers' Roster* (Racine, Wis.:

E.W. Leach, 1915), p. 150, 151; John D. Walker compiled military service records, National Archives.

26. Frances and Dorothy Wood, _I Hauled These Mountains In Here_ (Caldwell, Idaho: The Caxton Printers Ltd., 1977), p. 14.

27. Albert, p. 381, 382.

28. Delavan S. Miller, p. 12-16; Frederick Phisterer, _New York in the War of the Rebellion 1861 to 1865,_ vol. II (Albany: J.B. Lyon Company, 1912), p. 1235, 1240.

29. George Ulmer's service records state he enlisted March 23, 1864, and was mustered April 2, 1864, at Belfast, Maine. His narrative of events reaching the 8th Maine in the field meshes with correct dates, but it is unknown why he used September 15, 1863, as his date of muster.

30. Ulmer, p. 9-22.

31. Hinman, p. 796-800.

32. Ibid., p. 800-803.

33. James A. Dickinson diary, Manuscript Collections, Rutherford B. Hayes Presidential Center, Fremont, Ohio.

34. Asa W. Bartlett, _History of the Twelfth Regiment New Hampshire Volunteers in the War of the Rebellion_ (Concord, N.H.: Ira C. Evans, 1897), p. 718.

35. Washburn, p. 243, 244.

36. Luther S. Dickey, _History of the 103d Regiment Pennsylvania Veteran Volunteer Infantry 1861-1865_ (Chicago: L.S. Dickey, 1910), p. 131.

37. Lucious Harris pension records, National Archives.

38. Dickey, p. 103, 104.

39. Ibid., p. 102.

40. Joseph C.G. Kennedy, _Preliminary Report on the Eighth Census, 1860_ (Washington, 1862), p. 29.

41. Charles H. Smith, _The History of Fuller's Ohio Brigade 1861-1865: Its Great March, with Roster, Portraits, Battle Maps and Biographies_ (Cleveland: J. Watt, 1909), p. 389, 390.

42. Lonnie Speer, "When Orphan Trains Rolled West," _Wild West_ (February 1995), p. 53.

43. Ibid., p. 53.

44. Ibid., p. 53.

45. Ibid., p. 56-57.

46. RG 153, court-martial file NN3250, National Archives; Joseph Revelle compiled military service records.

47. James Barrington compiled military service records, National Archives.

Chapter 3

1. _Regulations for the Recruitng Service ...,_ p. 9.

2. Not all regiments were able to stay in camp and learn their instruction. Most raised early in the war occupied such rendezvous camps until they reached full regimental strength, when they quickly were rushed to the front.

3. Kieffer, p. 36-40.

4. Ulmer, p. 25, 26.

5. C. Perry Byam pension records, National Archives.

6. Charles A. Willison, _Reminiscences of a Boy's Service with the 76th Ohio_ (Menasha, Wis.: The George Banta Publishing Co., 1908), p. 66-67. Reprinted in 1995 by Blue Acorn Press.

7. George M. Ziegler, "War Sketches of John McClay," published as a serial in unidentified newspaper, unknown dates, John McClay papers, Author's Collection.

8. The Army had a standing rule that soldiers could receive credit from appointed sutlers, with the understanding that paymasters would deduct amounts owed to sutlers on pay day.

9. H.L. Scott, _Military Dictionary: Comprising Technical Definitions on Raising and Keeping Troops; including Makeshift and Improved Material; and Law, Government, Regulations, and Administration Relating to Land Forces_ (New York: D. Van Nostrand, 1861), p. 487.

10. Bircher, p. 122-129.

11. Bardeen, p. 74.

12. Willison, p. 20.

13. Tripler, p. 10.

14. Washburn, p. 215, 216. George H. Washburn of Company D, 108th New York, was 17 when he enlisted, but was small for his age. He wrote the regiment's history and acted as secretary of the 108th New York Association for many years.

15. Ibid., p. 157, 158.

16. Willison, p. 21.

17. James A. Dickinson diary, Manuscript Collections, R.B. Hayes Presidential Center, Fremont, Ohio.

18. Bircher, p. 23.

19. C. Perry Byam pension records.

20. Allen, _A Boy Trooper with Sheridan,_ unpaginated.

21. Hinman, p. 52.

22. Allen, _A Boy Trooper with Sheridan,_ unpaginated.

23. Scott, _Military Dictionary,_ p. 238.

24. Joseph B. Foraker, _Notes of a Busy Life,_ vol. I (Cincinnati: Stewart & Kidd Company, 1917), p. 22-24.

25. Belknap, p. 147, 320.

26. Kieffer, p. 71.

27. Ibid., 69, 70.

28. Officers were allowed two servants to accompany them, receiving rations' pay from the Army. By entering his son as such, an officer could obtain Army subsistence for him, yet the boy could be sent home at any time.

29. Dickey, p. 92-93.

30. Gilbert Vanzant to the editor, August 1, 1863, published in _The Clinton Republican,_ Wilmington, Ohio, August 14, 1863.

Chapter 4

1. Gallipolis, Ohio, stonecarver's memorandum book, private collection.

2. Alonzo D. Roush compiled military service records, National Archives.

3. Tripler, p. 9, 10.

4. Hartwell Osborn, _Trials and Triumphs: The Record of the Fifty-fifth Ohio Volunteer Infantry_ (Chicago: A.C. McClurg & Co., 1904), p. 251.

5. _Ohio Rosters,_ vol. II, p. 255-257.

6. Franklin Sawyer, _A Military History of the 8th Regiment Ohio Vol. Inf'y, its Battles, Marches and Army Movements_ (Cleveland: Fairbanks & Co., 1881), p. 15-16. Reprinted in 1994 by Blue Acorn Press.

7. Ibid., p. 17-20.

8. Ibid., p. 20-22.

9. _Ohio Rosters,_ vol. II, p. 257.

10. Ibid., p. 16; vol. IV, p. 233; vol. V, p. 400.

11. Letter written July 28, 1861, by a member of the 2nd New

York State Militia believed to be Norman Farrar, Stephen Altic Collection, Columbus, Ohio.

12. Letter of July 30, 1861, by John B. Wilson, 2nd New York State Militia, Stephen Altic Collection.

13. John Boulton Young compiled military service records, National Archives; Gary Leister, " 'Our Pet Boltie' Drummer Boy, 47th Pa.," *North South Trader's Civil War* (Christmas 1993), p. 20-23.

14. Ibid., p. 20-23.

15. Ibid., p. 22.

16. Ibid., p. 22.

17. Ibid., p. 22.

18. Ibid., p. 22.

19. Richard Eddy, *History of the Sixtieth Regiment New York State Volunteers* (Philadelphia: Crissey & Markley, 1864), p. 53.

20. Miller, *Drum Taps in Dixie,* p. 28-29.

21. William F. Fox, *Regimental Losses in the American Civil War 1861-1865* (Albany: Albany Publishing Company, 1898), p. 48-49.

22. Lorenzo A. Barker, *Military History (Michigan Boys) Company "D" 66th Illinois Birge's Western Sharpshooters in the Civil War 1861-1865* (Reed City, Mich., 1905), p. 58. Reprinted in 1994 by Blue Acorn Press.

23. Thomas Parkinson compiled military service records, National Archives.

24. Bartlett, p. 12, 697.

25. Thomas C. Strong, *The Little Drummer Boy, Clarence D. McKenzie, the Child of the Thirteenth Regiment, N.Y.S.M., and the Child of the Mission Sunday School* (New York: Reformed Protestant Dutch Church, 1861), p. 29-32.

26. The 13th New York State Militia became the 13th New York Infantry when federalized April 23, 1861, for the term of three months. Dyer's *Compendium* shows the regiment left for Annapolis on April 21, where it stayed through June 1861. The next month it was at Baltimore. Perhaps the company Clarence belonged to left on April 30, or the date given was wrong.

27. Strong, *The Little Drummer Boy,* p. 29-50.

28. *Ibid.,* p. 51-53.

29. If the weapon was in good working order and the hammer placed in a half-cocked position, it could not be forced down.

30. Strong, *The Little Drummer Boy,* p. 65-69.

31. *Ibid.,* p. 70-71.

32. *Ibid.,* p. 71-77.

33. *Ibid.,* p. 118.

34. *Ibid.,* p. 75, 76.

35. *Ibid.,* p. 94-95.

36. *Ibid.,* 96-99.

37. *Ibid.,* p. 101-110.

38. *Ibid.,* p. 105-110.

39. *Ibid.,* p. 123-134.

40. *Ibid.,* p. 84-89.

41. *Ibid.,* p. 99-100.

42. *Ibid.,* p. 131-133.

43. Andrew J. Smith compiled military service records, National Archives; Andrew J. Smith, *The Light of Other Days; or, Passing under the Rod* (Dayton, Ohio: United Brethren Publishing House, 1878), p. 95-99.

44. *Ibid.,* p. 114-116.

45. Within a few months of the battle Smith fell ill and was discharged. After the war he became a minister in the United Brethren Church and lived in Pleasant Hill, Ohio.

46. Ezra H. Smith compiled military service records, National Archives; H. Warren Phelps, "Record of the 95th Ohio Infantry," in William P.

An unidentified mother and soldier son photographed at Bishop & Caufman's gallery in Harrisburg, Pennsylvania.

Author's Collection

For the lad at right, posing with a comrade at Benton Barracks, Missouri, gave his family at home little hint of real warfare to come.

Brian Boeve Collection

Gault, *Ohio at Vicksburg. Report of the Ohio Vicksburg Battlefield Commission* (1906), p. 210-211.

47. *Ibid.,* p. 211.

48. *Ibid.,* p. 211-212.

49. Dean W. Lambert, *When the Ripe Pears Fell: The Battle of Richmond, Kentucky* (Richmond, Ky.: Madison County Historical Society, 1995), p. 84-87.

50. *Ibid.,* p. 86-88.

51. *Ibid.,* p. 87-90; Phelps in Gault, *Ohio at Vicksburg,* p. 213.

52. *Ibid.,* p. 213; Ezra H. Smith compiled military service records.

53. Ibid.; Ezra H. Smith diary and personal papers, Author's Collection.

54. John Baker compiled military service records, National Archives.

55. Robert S. Westbrook, *History of the 49th Pennsylvania Volunteers* (Altoona, Pa., 1898), p. 124, 125; Samuel P. Bates, *History of Pennsylvania Volunteers, 1861-1865,* vol. I (Harrisburg: B. Singerly, State Printer, 1869), p. 1238; William A. Frassanito, *Antietam: The Photographic Legacy of America's Bloodiest Day* (New York: Charles Scribner's Sons, 1978), p. 192-195.

56. Sawyer, p. 42, 43; *Ohio Rosters,* vol. II, p. 249.

57. Charles C. Greene, *Sparks from the Campfire* (Philadelphia, 1889), p. 142-145. No Edward Lee appears in Volume I of *Roster and Record of Iowa Soldiers in the War of the Rebellion* (Des Moines: Emory H. English, State Printer, 1908). Like many boys he probably served unmustered.

58. A. Marsh letter of March 17 [year unknown], Author's Collection.

59. Samuel Galloway letter of September 16, 1863, Mark Reese Collection.

60. Copp, p. 19.

61. John Dirst compiled military service records, National Archives.

62. Ralph O. Sturtevant, *Pictorial History Thirteenth Regiment Vermont Volunteers, War of 1861-1865* (1910), p. 530.

63. Allen, *A Boy Trooper with Sheridan,* unpaginated.

64. George Meyer compiled military service records, National Archives.

65. Avery Brown compiled military service records, National Archives.

66. *Ohio Rosters,* vol. V, p. 385, 386.

67. Letter of May 1, 1861, author unknown, Mark Reese Collection.

68. Albert C. White compiled military service records; *Ohio Rosters,* vol. V, p. 446; Hinman, *The Story of the Sherman Brigade,* p. 81.

69. *Ibid.,* p. 103-105.

70. *Ibid.,* p. 138-147.

71. Albert C. White compiled military service records.

72, Edmund H. Dodge compiled military service records, National Archives; "Talking of Drummer Boys," *The National Tribune,* June 26, 1884; "A Drummer Boy at Eight," *The National Tribune,* June 19, 1884.

Chapter 5

1. William R. Kiefer, *History of the One Hundred and Fifty-third Regiment Pennsylvania Volunteer Infantry, 1862-1863* (Easton, Pa.: The Chemical Publishing Company, 1909), p. 174.

2. Henry F. Anners, *Hoyle's Games, Containing the Established Rules and Practice* (Philadelphia, 1845), p. 1-4.

3. Bartlett, p. 354-355.

4. Bardeen used the fictitious name "Nick Dranger" because

the person he represented was still living in 1910, and he thought it best the man's family did not learn these facts. The other soldiers named all served in Company D, 1st Massachusetts Infantry.

5. Bardeen, p. 176-181.

6. Andrew J. Smith compiled military service records.

7. Smith, *The Light of Other Days,* p. 106-109.

8. Eddy, p. 95-96.

9. Elderkin Rose pension records, National Archives.

10. Sutlers issued metal tokens or paper scrip as change because government money always was in short supply. "Sutler money" was widely used among soldiers as legal tender despite the fact it was only redeemable with the sutler issuing it.

11. Miller, *Drum Taps in Dixie,* p. 31-36.

12. Bardeen, p. 44-45.

13. Copp, p. 79-83.

14. Dickey, p. 131-132.

15. Ibid., p. 134.

16. James M. Wilson was mustered as corporal of Dickey's company in 1862. During his service he rose to the rank of first lieutenant.

17. Dickey, p. 134-135.

18. Ibid., p. 136-137.

19. Ulmer, p. 56-68.

20. Bardeen, p. 64-67.

21. Copp, p. 310-313.

22. Kieffer, *The Recollections of a Drummer Boy,* p. 145-153.

23. *Ibid.,* p. 129-131.

24. *Ibid.,* p. 132.

25. Bircher, p. 146-151.

26. James Shanklin, "Another Young Soldier," *The National Tribune,* February 14, 1889.

27. Bircher, p. 88-89.

28. Sturtevant, p. 679.

29. Miller, *Drum Taps in Dixie,* p. 215-219.

30. Bircher, p. 97.

31. Thomas P. Lowry, *The Story the Soldiers Wouldn't Tell: Sex in the Civil War* (Mechanicsburg, Pa.: Stackpole Books, 1994), p. 78.

32. Edwin M. Haynes, *A History of the Tenth Regiment, Vermont Volunteers, with Biographical Sketches* (Rutland, Vt.: The Tuttle Company, Printers, 1894), p. 177-179.

33. Bardeen, p. 163.

34. Byron Fairbanks 1864 pocket diary, Author's Collection.

35. Melvin Grigsby, *The Smoked Yank* (Sioux Falls, Dakota Terr.: Bell Publishing Company, 1888), p. 34-35.

36. James A. Dickinson diary, Manuscript Collections, R.B. Hayes Presidential Center, Fremont, Ohio.

37. Smith, *The Light of Other Days,* p. 109.

38. Bartlett, p. 356-357.

39. Palmer, p. 56-59.

40. Copp, p. 129.

Chapter 6

1. Thomas P. Lowry, *Don't Shoot that Boy! Abraham Lincoln and Military Justice* (Mason City, Iowa: Savas Publishing Company, 1999), p. 9-11.

2. The deserter shot was Private Henry Holt. His execution by firing squad took place April 15, 1864. Officially, Holt's death was marked as taking place two days after the offense, but it is not known if that is when the paperwork was finished and if he already was dead by that time. Either way, his shooting was one of the four shortest spans between offense and execution recorded during the war.

3. Copp, p. 212-217.

4. *Revised Regulations for the Army of the United States 1861,* p. 502; Robert I. Alotta, *Civil War Justice: Union Army Executions under Lincoln* (Shippensburg, Pa.: White Mane Publishing Company, 1989), p. 202-210.

5. Lowry, *Don't Shoot that Boy!* p. 86.

6. RG 153, court-martial file NN1345, National Archives.

7. RG 153, court-martial file LL1106.

8. The date of August 1862 for George Held's desertion does not match his father's September 8, 1863, enlistment date when considering his defense stated he left to be with his father. It is possible the father's enlistment date is in error in the Pennsylvania rosters.

9. RG 153, court-martial file NN2699.

10. RG 153, court-martial file LL584.

11. RG 153, court-martial file LL746.

12. RG 153, court-martial file OO388.

13. RG 153, court-martial file LL1611.

14. RG 153, court-martial file KK716. In late 1861 the 14th Massachusetts was reorganized as the 1st Massachusetts Heavy Artillery, but the designation was not changed officially until September 19, 1863.

15. *Revised Regulations for the Army of the United States 1861,* p. 507.

16. RG 153, court-martial file LL1296.

17. RG 153, court-martial file LL1503.

18. RG 153, court-martial file NN131; James Lebarre compiled military service records, National Archives.

19. RG 153, court-martial file LL2910.

20. RG 153, court-martial file LL284.

21. Grigsby, p. 41-43.

22. RG 153, court-martial file MM1591.

23. General Orders No. 3, Headquarters, Department of the Missouri, copy in the Author's Collection; Alotta, p. 153-155.

Chapter 7

1. Fox, p. 449.

2. Gregory Jaynes, *The Killing Ground: Wilderness to Cold Harbor* (Alexandria, Va.: Time Life Books Inc., 1986), p. 164-165.

3. Bartlett, p. 574.

4. Ibid., p. 586.

5. Ibid., p. 697.

6. Ibid., p. 592.

7. Ibid., p. 608.

8. Charles B. Fairchild, *History of the 27th Regiment N.Y. Vols.* (Binghamton, N.Y.: Carl & Matthews, Printers, 1888), p. 48-49.

9. Willison, p. 35-39.

10. Ulmer, p. 38-39.

11. Bardeen, p. 105-111.

12. C. Perry Byam pension records.

13. Miller believed the officer was major of the 1st Massachusetts Infantry. But the only major of that regiment killed in action was Charles P. Chandler — at Glendale, Virginia, June 30, 1862.

14. Miller, *Drum Taps in Dixie,* p. 82-92.

15. Copp, p. 131-141.

16. Washburn, p. 298-299.

17. Account of Captain Harvey J. Dutton in Isaac H. Elliott, *History of the Thirty-third Regiment Illinois Veteran Volunteer Infantry in the Civil War, 22nd August, 1861 to 7th December, 1865* (Gibson City, Ill.: Press of Gibson Courier, 1902), p. 83, 84.

18. Washburn, p. 286.

19. John C. Roosa compiled military service records, National Archives; Albert, p. 132-137, 381-384.

20. Ibid., p. 132-137.

21. Ibid., p. 132-137, 269-271, 381-384; Ira Odell compiled military service and pension records, National Archives.

22. Albert, p. 376-377.

23. Palmer, p. 159-160; George Richman was 17 when he enlisted in the 48th New York in 1861.

24. Washburn, p. 245-246; Hugh Craig compiled military service records, National Archives.

25. Hinman, p. 337-341. Later in the war Snider became a captain in the 13th U.S. Colored Troops, and 25 years afterward a congressman from Minnesota.

26. John F.W. Mains compiled military service and pension records, National Archives; Dyer, *Compendium,* p. 1122.

27. Washburn, p. 263; Otho Gash compiled military service records, National Archives.

28. Barker, p. 157.

29. Washburn, p. 292-294.

30. Samuel P. Snider pension records, National Archives.

31. Albert C. Matthias family papers, courtesy of James M. Merkel, Columbus, Ohio.

32. Hinman, p. 519-524.

33. David H. Moore recommendation letter for A.C. Matthias, May 11, 1864, courtesy of James M. Merkel.

34. Albert C. Matthias compiled military service records, National Archives.

35. John C. Matthias letter of May 20, 1864, courtesy of James M. Merkel.

36. Albert C. Matthias letter of July 9, 1864, courtesy of James M. Merkel.

37. Albert C. Matthias family papers.

38. Miller, *Drum Taps in Dixie,* p. 109; William Whitney compiled military service records, National Archives.

39. *The War of the Rebellion: A Compilation of the Official Records of the Union and Confederate Armies,* series I, vol. XXV, pt. 1, p. 1123. Hereafter referred to as *Official Records* and assumed to be series I. Edmonds enlisted at age 15 on January 23, 1862, with his father Stephen. After his leg was amputated he remained in the hospital until discharged for disability February 11, 1864.

40. Osborn H. Oldroyd, *A Soldier's Story of the Siege of Vicksburg, from the Diary of Osborn H. Oldroyd* (Springfield, Ill., 1885), p. 56.

41. Haynes, p. 441.

42. Byron Fairbanks compiled military service records, National Archives; Byron Fairbanks 1864 pocket diary, Author's Collection.

43. Bardeen, p. 281-282.

44. Jaynes, *The Killing Ground,* p. 29-31.

45. Richard Moe, *The Last Full Measure: The Life and Death of the First Minnesota Volunteers* (New York: Henry Holt and Company, 1993), p. 6.

46. *Ibid.,* p. 67-68.

47. *Ibid.,* p. 205.

48. *Ibid.,* p. 142-145.

49. *Ibid.,* p. 142-145.

A tailored jacket adorned with black velvet collar and cuffs was well suited to this unidentified subject who sat for Alexandria, Virginia, photographer Peter McAdams. The young soldier belonged to the Second Corps, as indicated by the metal trefoil badge pinned at his left breast.

Author's Collection

Born February 18, 1848, in Canada, Willis A. Olmstead enlisted with his mother's consent nine days following his 16th birthday in Company E, 36th Illinois. Most of his first year's service was spent sick in Murfreesboro's general hospital. In February 1865 he was detailed to that town's post headquarters as an orderly, and from mid-summer until his October 1865 muster-out served as a Military Division of the Gulf headquarters' messenger in New Orleans. Of note here are the small brass regimental numerals affixed to Olmstead's cap, triangular Fourth Corps badge attached to his blouse, and M1851 eagle-wreath belt plate worn upside down.

Gil Barrett Collection

50. Undated letter of Albert C. Matthias, courtesy of James M. Merkel.

51. Andrew Routt compiled military service records, National Archives.

52. Bartlett, p. 222, 714.

53. Sturtevant, p. 697.

Chapter 8

1. *Ohio Rosters,* vol. VI, p. 128.

2. Fox, p. 50.

3. Lawrence Wilson, *Itinerary of the Seventh Ohio Volunteer Infantry 1861-1864* (New York: The Neale Publishing Company, 1907), p. 330-334, 438.

4. Washburn, p. 303, 304.

5. Abraham J. Palmer compiled military service records, National Archives.

6. Palmer, p. 112-115.

7. Ibid., p. 116-119.

8. Ibid., p. 223.

9. Abraham J. Palmer compiled military service records.

10. Otis Smith compiled military service records, National Archives; Albert, p. 376-377.

11. Ibid., p. 376-377.

12. Otis Smith compiled military service records.

13. Lucius Hull, "The Youngest Soldier," *The National Tribune,* November 29, 1888. In this article Hull stated he joined the 116th Ohio in 1861, which is incorrect as the regiment was not organized until September-October 1862. He also stated he was 12 years and six months old when joining the 18th Ohio. This does not match with his birth and enlistment dates. *Ohio Rosters,* vol. II, p. 576, 619.

14. William Jewell compiled military service records, National Archives; *Official Records,* vol. XX, part 1, p. 423.

15. Leach, *Racine County Militant,* p. 150, 151; John D. Walker compiled military service records.

16. James M. Aubery, *The Thirty-sixth Wisconsin Volunteer Infantry* (Milwaukee: Evening Wisconsin Co., 1900), p. 58-68, 371-373.

17. Grigsby, *The Smoked Yank,* p. 52-62.

18. *Ibid.,* p. 62, 63.

19. *Ibid.,* p. 90, 91.

20. *Ibid.,* p. 149-169.

21. *Ibid.,* p. 169-187.

22. *Ibid.,* p. 188-226.

23. Mary Ann Crane widow's Army pension application, January 17, 1864, National Archives.

24. Rashio Crane memorial, Jeffrey J. Kowalis Collection, Orland Park, Illinois.

25. Thomas M. Hale compiled military service records, National Archives.

26. Ronald H. Bailey, *Battles for Atlanta* (Alexandria, Va.: Time Life Books Inc., 1985), p. 138-139.

27. *Official Records,* vol. XXXVIII, pt. 2, p. 914.

28. Josephus Gephart compiled military service records, National Archives.

29. Jerry O. Potter, *The Sultana Tragedy: America's Greatest Maritime Disaster* (Gretna, La.: Pelican Publishing Company, 1992), p. 7-23.

30. *Ibid.,* p. 43-72, 131.

31. *Sultana* survivor William Block was a member of Company H, 9th Indiana Cavalry.

32. Chester D. Berry, *Loss of the Sultana and Reminiscences of Survivors* (Lansing, Mich.: Darius D. Thorp, Printer and Publisher, 1892), p. 149-152.

33. *Ibid.,* p. 62-66.

34. Charles Myers compiled military service records, National Archives.

35. John McElroy, *This Was Andersonville* (New York: The Fairfax Press, 1979), p. 118, 119, 351.

36. Harold L. Scott Sr., *The Civil War Memoirs of Little Red Cap, Drummer Boy at Andersonville Prison* (Cumberland, Md., 1997), p. 2-4; Ransom T. Powell, "Prison Life," *Frostburg Mining Journal,* March 13, 1875–January 15, 1876.

37. Ibid.

38. Ibid.

39. Ibid.

40. Ibid.

41. Ibid.

42. Ibid.

43. Harold L. Scott Sr., p. 61-63.

Chapter 9

1. American Civil War Research Database, Historical Data Systems, Kingston, Md.; *Official Records,* series III, vol. II, p. 325.

2. Fox, p. 437.

3. C. Perry Byam pension records, National Archives.

4. Ibid.

5. Ibid.

6. Ibid. Not only did Byam cause considerable trouble in camp as a boy, he spent many of his adult years living under assumed names and looking over his shoulder for the law or unpaid creditors. The pension commissioner who investigated his claims of having "severe diarrhea" noted that Byam had been charged with larceny and embezzlement, was considered a "common saloon bum and loafer," and was living in Detroit at the time so he easily could slip across the border to Canada when the law got too close. In a final analysis of his case it was stated, "Of course, any person using liquor to the extent claimant has is more or less affected with 'whiskey diarrhea' and stomach and bowel trouble generally at intervals."

7. American Civil War Research Database.

8. Joseph J. Sutton, *History of the Second Regiment West Virginia Cavalry Volunteers during the War of the Rebellion* (Portsmouth, Ohio, 1892), p. 132-135. Reprinted in 1992 by Blue Acorn Press.

9. Richard M. Crane, Rashio Crane and Stephen Crane compiled military service records, National Archives.

10. Richard M. Crane 1864 diary, Jeffrey J. Kowalis Collection.

11. Richard M. Crane letter of May 19, 1864, Jeffrey J. Kowalis Collection.

12. Richard M. Crane compiled military service records.

13. George W.M. and William T. Masury compiled military service records, National Archives.

14. Ibid.; John C. Masury compiled military service records and William T. Masury pension records, National Archives.

15. William T. Masury compiled military service records.

16. John C. Masury compiled military service records.

17. William T. Masury compiled military service records.

18. John C. Masury compiled military service records.

19. George Ulmer compiled military service records.

20. Ulmer, p. 9, 32-35.

21. Albert Roberts pension records and Edward Roberts compiled military service records, National Archives; Albert, p. 476, 517, 523.

22. Albert Roberts pension records. Thomas Welsh died of disease August 14, 1863, in Cincinnati.

23. Albert Roberts pension records.

24. Albert, p. 390.

25. Ibid., p. 395, 398.

26. Albert Roberts pension records.

27. Ibid.

28. Ibid.

29. Albert, p. 114-117.

30. Ibid., p. 117.

31. Albert Roberts pension records.

32. Albert, p. 476.

33. Fox, p. 3, 265.

34. *Ohio Rosters,* vol. I, p. 683-722; Edward Knox diary, Jeffrey S. Creamer Collection, Toledo, Ohio.

35. Benjamin Knox compiled military service records, National Archives.

36. Edmund E. Nutt, "Twentieth Ohio at Atlanta," *The Ohio Soldier,* July 28, 1894.

37. Larry M. Strayer and Richard A. Baumgartner, *Echoes of Battle: The Atlanta Campaign* (Huntington, W.Va.: Blue Acorn Press, 1991), p. 252, 253.

38. Benjamin Knox compiled military service records.

39. *Ohio Rosters,* vol. III, p. 418.

40. *Ohio Rosters,* vol. II, p. 693.

41. Joseph Fissell compiled military service records, National Archives; *Ohio Rosters,* vol. IV, p. 323-324.

42. *Ibid.;* Johnda T. Davis, "Joseph Fissell – Darbyville's Drummer Boy," *Pickaway Quarterly* (Spring 1981), p. 15-16; Reid, *Ohio in the War,* vol. II, p. 282.

43. *Ibid.,* p. 282-284; Silas J. Mann papers, Author's Collection.

44. Joseph Fissell compiled military service records; Johnda T. Davis, op. cit., p. 15-16.

45. Joseph Fissell compiled military service records.

46. David W. Wood, *History of the 20th Ohio Regiment V.V. Inft. and Proceedings of the First Reunion at Mt. Vernon, Ohio April 6, 1876* (Columbus: Paul & Thrall Book and Job Printers, 1876), p. 50; *Ohio Rosters,* vol. II, p. 693.

47. *Ohio Rosters,* vol. III, p. 418.

48. *Ibid.,* vol. IV, p. 182; vol. X, p. 52; James Shanklin, "Another Young Soldier," *The National Tribune,* February 14, 1889.

49. James L. Backus compiled military service records, National Archives; Luther Backus compiled military service and pension records; Dyer, *Compendium,* p. 1078.

Author's Collection

A sixth-plate tintype of two unidentified comrades.

50. Thomas Hubler compiled military service records, National Archives; Kieffer, p. 160-161.

51. *Ohio Rosters,* vol. VII, p. 158, 179; vol. VI, p. 292-295.

52. *Ibid.,* vol. VI, p. 494.

53. William H. Ambrose compiled military service records, National Archives.

54. *Report of the Adjutant General of the State of Illinois* (Springfield: Phillips Bros., State Printers, 1900), vol. I, p. 655, 674; vol. III, p. 687, 692, 693. Hereafter referred to as *Illinois Rosters;* Lyston D. and Orion P. Howe compiled military service records, National Archives.

55. *Illinois Rosters,* vol. III, p. 692, 713, 714.

56. Orion Howe was not mustered, though present, until nine months after the regiment left Camp Douglas.

57. *The Story of the Fifty-Fifth Regiment Illinois Volunteer Infantry in the Civil War 1861-1865* (Clinton, Mass.: W.J. Coulter, 1887), p. 237-240. Reprinted in 1993 by Blue Acorn Press.

58. *Ibid.,* p. 237-241.

59. *Ibid.,* p. 240, 241; Orion P. Howe compiled military service records.

60. Lang, et.al., *Medal of Honor Recipients 1863-1994,* vol. I, p. 107.

61. Richard A. Baumgartner and Larry M. Strayer, *Echoes of Battle: The Struggle for Chattanooga* (Huntington, W.Va.: Blue Acorn Press, 1996), p. 82-85; Reid, *Ohio in the War,* vol. II,

p. 150-151; *Ohio Rosters,* vol. III, p. 36, 37.

62. George S. Canfield compiled military service records, National Archives.

63. *The Military History of Ohio,* Franklin County edition (New York, Toledo and Chicago: H.H. Hardesty, Publisher, 1886), p. 311.

64. Bircher, p. 10, 11.

65. Bartlett, p. 47, 710.

66. Ibid., p. 30, 740.

67. Thomas Crofts, *History of the Service of the Third Ohio Veteran Volunteer Cavalry in the War for the Preservation of the Union from 1861-1865* (Toledo, 1910), p. 128-132, 250. Reprinted in 1997 by Blue Acorn Press; 3rd Ohio Cavalry reunion handbill, Monroeville, Ohio, August 17, 1910, Author's Collection; Charles O. Brown compiled military service records, National Archives.

68. George Lutz compiled military service records, National Archives; *Record of Service of Michigan Volunteers in the Civil War 1861-1865,* vol. 22 (Kalamazoo: Ihling Bros. & Everhard, 1905), p. 93; Dyer, *Compendium,* p. 1291.

69. George Lutz letter of December 8, 1863, James Frasca Collection, Croton, Ohio; *Official Records,* vol. XXX, pt. 1, p. 177.

70. George Lutz compiled military service records; *Record of Service of Michigan Volunteers,* vol. 22, p. 93.

71. John A. Cockerill, "A Boy at Shiloh," *Sketches of War History 1861-1865,* vol. VI (Cincinnati: Monfort & Company, 1908), p. 15-34.

72. William L. Curry, *History of Jerome Township, Union County, Ohio* (Columbus: The Edward T. Miller Co., 1913), p. 110-111.

73. *Ohio Rosters,* vol. VI, p. 138.

74. Samuel H. Hurst, *Journal-History of the Seventy-third Ohio Volunteer Infantry* (Chillicothe, Ohio, 1866), p. 40-43.

75. Asa Harper compiled military service records, National Archives.

76. Spillard F. Horrall, *History of the Forty-second Indiana Volunteer Infantry* (Chicago: Donohue & Henneberry, Printers, 1892), p. 189-195; John W. Messick compiled military service records, National Archives.

77. Sturtevant, p. 746, 747.

78. William M. Ferraro, "More Than a General's Wife: Ellen Ewing Sherman," *Timeline* (January-February 2000), p. 8-33.

79. "A Touching Episode of the War – Gen. Sherman on the Death of his Son," *Belmont* (Ohio) *Chronicle,* October 29, 1863.

80. Ibid.

81. William M. Ferraro, op. cit., p. 8-33.

82. Lawrence A. Frost, *U.S. Grant Album: A Pictorial Biography of Ulysses S. Grant from Leather Clerk to the White House* (Seattle: Superior Publishing Company, 1966), p. 37-51.

83. Frederick Dent Grant, "With Grant at Vicksburg," *The Ulysses S. Grant Association Newsletter* (October 1969), p. 4, 5, 7, 8.

84. Ibid., p. 10.

85. Jesse Root Grant, *In the Days of My Father General Grant* (New York: Harper & Brothers, 1925), p. 14-17.

86. *Ibid.,* p. 23-28.

87. Kieffer, p. 58-63.

88. *Annual Report of the Adjutant-General of the State of New York. For the Year 1900,* serial no. 23 (Albany: James B. Lyon, State Printer, 1901), p. 597, 600.

89. James M. Drake, *Historical Sketches of the Revolutionary and Civil Wars* (New York: Webster Press, 1908), p. 248-250.

90. Gustave A. Schurmann compiled military service records, National Archives.

91. According to Schurmann's obituary published July 20, 1905, in the *Washington Evening Star,* Tad Lincoln's horse was running away with him and Gus stopped its progress under the admiring eye of Mary Lincoln, who asked that Gus be transferred to the White House. The president agreed and then asked General Sickles for the favor.

92. Drake, p. 248-250.

93. Stewart Sifakis, *Who Was Who in the Union* (New York: Facts on File, Inc., 1988), p. 237.

Chapter 10

1. David B. Guralnik, editor in chief, *Webster's New World Dictionary of the American Language,* p. 966.

2. Albion W. Tourgée, *The Story of a Thousand* (Buffalo: S. McGerald & Son, 1896), p. 147, 148.

3. Miller, *Drum Taps in Dixie,* p. 101-102.

4. Belknap, p. 322.

5. Ziegler, "War Sketches of John McClay."

6. Washburn, p. 158.

7. Kieffer, p. 111-113.

8. Ziegler, "War Sketches of John McClay."

9. Walter Cheney pension records, National Archives.

10. Miller, *Drum Taps in Dixie,* p. 218-219.

11. Nathaniel C. Deane, *The Spirit of the American Red Cross: A Chapter from the Autobiography of Nathaniel Carter Deane* (1918), unpaginated.

12. Joseph G. Patterson letter of July 17, 1863, courtesy of R. Gary Ronk, Roanoke, Virginia.

13. Bardeen, p. 114-115.

14. Bartlett, p. 371.

15. Leander W. Cogswell, *A History of the Eleventh New Hampshire Regiment, Volunteer Infantry in the Rebellion War, 1861-1865* (Concord: Republican Press Association, 1891), p. 546-547.

16. *Revised Regulations for the Army of the United States 1861,* p. 71-75.

17. J.F. Orr, "The Story of 'Little Gib,' Youngest Union Civil War Soldier," *The Gazette,* Xenia, Ohio, February 28-March 8, 1938.

18. Allen, *A Boy Trooper with Sheridan,* unpaginated.

19. Richard R. Walsh compiled military service records, National Archives; Benjamin W. Crowninshield, *A History of the First Regiment of Massachusetts Cavalry Volunteers* (New York: Houghton, Mifflin & Company, 1891), unpaginated.

20. Henry Funk compiled military service records, National Archives; *Ohio Rosters,* vol. IV, p. 509-510.

21. Bruce Miller compiled military service records, National Archives.

22. Charles O. Brown compiled military service records.

23. Hendrick E. Paine compiled military service records, National Archives.

24. William M. Dunn Jr.'s age at enlistment was 17. He was

Musician Andrew Parsons played a drum painted with the Ohio state seal and scrolls designating his regiment. He served 34 months in Company H, 103rd Ohio.

L.M. Strayer Collection

born August 20, 1843.

25. William M. Dunn Jr. compiled military service records, National Archives; Jesse R. Grant, *In the Days of My Father General Grant,* p. 27-28.

26. *Official Records,* vol. XLIV, p. 726-728, 816.

Chapter 11

1. Address of John S. Kountz, "From Camp Brown to Mission Ridge" in *Ninth Reunion of the 37th Regiment O.V.V.I., St. Marys, Ohio, Tuesday and Wednesday, September 10 and 11, 1889* (Toledo: Montgomery & Vrooman, Printers, 1889), p. 28-29.

2. Ibid., p. 11.

3. Ibid., p. 18.

4. Ibid., p. 23.

5. Robert B. Beath, *History of the Grand Army of the Republic* (New York: Willis McDonald & Co., 1888), p. 290; Kate B. Sherwood, *Camp-Fire, Memorial Day, and Other Poems* (Chicago: Jansen, McClurg & Company, 1885); *American Decorations 1862-1926* (Washington: Government Printing Office, 1927), p. 60.

6. *Ohio Rosters,* vol. IV, p. 24; *American Decorations 1862-1926,* p. 94.

7. Willard A. Heaps, *The Bravest Teenage Yanks* (New York: Duell, Sloan and Pearce, 1963), p. 8, 9.

8. William Johnston compiled military service records, National Archives.

9. *Official Records,* vol. XI, pt. 2, p. 462-464.

10. George G. Benedict, *Vermont in the Civil War: A History of the Part Taken by the Vermont Soldiers and Sailors in the War for the Union 1861-5,* vol. I (Burlington, Vt.: The Free Press Association, 1886), p. 140-141; Lang, et.al., *Medal of Honor Recipients 1863-1994,* vol. I, p. 115.

11. William Johnston compiled military service records.

12. Benjamin B. Levy compiled military service records, National Archives; Heaps, p. 119-124.

13. Ibid., p. 123-124.

14. Ibid., p. 124; *Deeds of Valor,* vol. I, p. 56.

15. *Ibid.,* p. 56-57; *Official Records,* vol. XI, pt. 2, p. 186.

16. Heaps, p. 125.

17. *Deeds of Valor,* vol. I, p. 57.

18. Heaps, p. 126-129.

19. Ibid., p. 57-59.

20. *Deeds of Valor,* vol. I, p. 75-76; Lieutenant Stewart reported a loss of 40 officers and enlisted men.

21. Heaps, p. 63.

22. *Ohio Rosters,* vol. II, p. 51.

23. *Deeds of Valor,* vol. I, p. 94-96.

24. Robert J. Titterton, *Julian Scott: Artist of the Civil War and Native America* (Jefferson, N.C.: McFarland & Company, Inc., 1997), p. 6, 9, 11.

25. *Ibid.,* p. 15-19.

26. *Ibid.,* p. 45, 61.

27. Charles W. Scott was born October 31, 1849. At age 13 he enlisted with the 1st Vermont Artillery on July 11, 1863. After serving the remainder of that year he was discharged because of "tender age" and feeble constitution. The following spring he entered the 28th Massachusetts as Company I's bugler. He also gained attention for saving a drowning, escaped Union prisoner who was shot attempting to swim the Rapidan River. Charles swam out and brought the man to safety. Wounded in the head and knocked to the ground by a shell's concussion at Cold Harbor, he, too, spent considerable time at David's Island Hospital before being discharged near war's end. Julian Scott's 1889 painting "Flag of Truce," depicting a young bugler at Cold Harbor waving a white flag to gain permission to bury the dead, likely was inspired by brother Charles' duties on that field.

28. Titterton, p. 19-25.

29. *Official Records,* vol. XI, pt. 1, p. 363-364.

30. *Ibid.,* p. 365-376.

31. Titterton, p. 32-33; *Official Records,* vol. XI, pt. 1, p. 367, 376.

32. Titterton, p. 33.

33. Ibid., p. 35-57.

34. Ibid., p. 90-93.

35. Ibid., p. 185-206.

36. Ibid., p. 294.

37. Copp, p. 295.

38. Ibid., p. 7.

39. Sturtevant, p. 597.

40. *Official Records,* vol. XXVII, pt. 1, p. 351-354.

41. *Ibid.,* p. 353-354; Sturtevant, p. 597.

42. Sturtevant, p. 597.

43. Ibid., p. 597; Theodore S. Peck, *Revised Roster of Vermont Volunteers* (Montpelier: Press of the Watchman Publishing Co., 1892), p. 575, 581, 586.

44. Houston, p. 360-361, 420-421.

45. Foraker, *Notes of a Busy Life,* vol. I, p. 1; Joseph B. Foraker compiled military service records; *Sketch of Joseph Benson Foraker, 1883, with an Appendix* (Dayton: Press of U.B. Publishing House, 1885), p. 23.

46. *Ibid.,* p. 23.

47. *Ibid.,* p. 24-27.

48. *Ibid.,* p. 16-19.

49. Everett Walters, "Joseph B. Foraker 1886-1890," in *The Governors of Ohio* (Columbus: The Stoneman Press, 1954), p. 121-123.

Chapter 12

1. *Official Records,* vol. XXI, p. 262-285.

2. *Ibid.,* p. 282-285.

3. *Ibid.,* p. 284-285.

4. John T. Spillane scrapbook of newspaper articles, Author's Collection. Most of the undated clippings contained in the scrapbook are from Michigan newspapers and *The National Tribune,* circa 1880-1900.

5. Robert H. Hendershot's last name also is spelled Hendershott on many documents. He signed his name both ways. His death certificate is filled out "Hendershott."

6. Robert H. Hendershot compiled military service records, National Archives; H.E. Gerry, *Camp Fire Entertainment and True History of Robert Henry Hendershot, the Drummer Boy of the Rappahannock* (circa 1904), p. 11-13.

7. *Ibid.,* p. 13-21.

8. *Ibid.,* p. 21-29.

9. Robert H. Hendershot compiled military service records.

**"First Lessons on the Drum,"
a wartime illustration by Ed. Frere.**

Author's Collection

18. Ibid.

19. *Providence* (R.I.) *Daily Journal,* June 6, 1867.

20. John T. Spillane pension records, National Archives; Spillane scrapbook.

21. Spillane scrapbook.

22. Ibid.

23. *The National Tribune,* September 24, 1891.

24. When Hendershot's request to lead the 1891 G.A.R. parade in Detroit was denied, he sought permission to lead the Michigan delegation the following year at the Washington, D.C. national encampment.

25. Hendershot supposedly possessed letters from such luminaries as President Lincoln and General U.S. Grant. Years later when trying to procure a pension, he was asked to produce these letters but came up empty-handed.

26. Spillane scrapbook.

27. Ibid.; Robert H. Hendershot pension records, National Archives.

28. John L. Clem, Adjutant General's Office File 201, National Archives.

29. Supposedly, nine children were born but only three lived beyond infancy.

30. Mercedes Rodriguez, "The Drummer Boy John Lincoln Clem: The Civil War Years," master of arts degree thesis presented to Department of History faculty at San Jose State University (June 1974), p. 9-10.

31. Ibid., p. 12.

32. *The Military History of Ohio,* Licking County edition (New York: H.H. Hardesty, Publisher, 1886), p. 305.

33. *Ibid.,* p. 312.

34. Reid, *Ohio in the War,* vol. II, p. 28-29.

35. When reorganization of the three-year 3rd Ohio Infantry began, recruiting parties were sent out to fill vacancies created in the ranks by those who chose not to reenlist. In the list of new recruits for Company H none were from Licking County, thereby establishing that Captain McDougal did not go back to enlist more Newark residents.

36. Rodriguez, p. 12-16.

37. Reid, *Ohio in the War,* vol. II, p. 28-29.

38. John L. Clem, "From Nursery to Battlefield," *Outlook,* July 4, 1914, p. 546-548.

39. Dyer, *Compendium,* p. 1291.

40. Henry S. Dean to Lorenzo Thomas, August 9, 1864, in Clem File 201, AGO, National Archives.

41. John L. Wilson, *Battles of America by Sea and Land with Biographies of Naval and Military Commanders,* vol. III (New York: Patterson & Neilson, 1878), p. 547-556.

Hendershot's files state he was paroled with the rest of the captured 9th Michigan soldiers, but he claimed he and three others escaped the night of the wagon wreck when they feared retribution from Confederate guards. After stumbling through the night and part of the next day, the four found and joined their paroled comrades who were heading north. Hendershot also claimed he was discharged because of extreme youth.

10. Robert H. Hendershot compiled military service records; Gerry, p. 31-36.

11. *Official Records,* vol. XXI, p. 310-315.

12. William S. Dodge, *Robert Henry Hendershot; or, the Brave Drummer Boy of the Rappahannock* (Chicago: Church and Goodman, 1867), p. 141-145.

13. Gerry, p. 37-39.

14. Ibid., p. 39.

15. Robert H. Hendershot compiled military service records.

16. Dodge, p. 151-172.

17. Ibid., p. 173-180; Robert H. Hendershot compiled military service records.

A boy among men — musicians of the 15th U.S. Infantry band, photographed in Nashville or Chattanooga.

Author's Collection

federate colonel shouted at Clem. One has him saying, "Stop, you little Yankee devil!" But the predominating phrase found in early accounts is "Stop, you little son of a bitch."

49. Ibid.

50. E.D. Pope, "Who Was the Confederate Colonel?" *Confederate Veteran* (September 1926), p. 324.

51. While stationed in Texas years after the war, Clem, so the story goes, was introduced to a Confederate veteran who told him, "So it was you who shot me at Chickamauga." No name was provided for the supposed recipient of Clem's shot.

52. "From Nursey to Battlefield," p. 546-548.

53. *Official Records,* vol. XXX, pt. 1, p. 858.

54. John L. Clem compiled military service records.

55. *Official Records,* vol. XXX, pt. 2, p. 663-677; John L. Clem compiled military service records.

56. Ibid. Information on Clem's P.O.W. record sheet was obtained from Camp Chase, Ohio, paroled prisoner rolls, vol. 232, 238.

42. *Official Records,* vol. XXX, pt. 1, p. 855.

43. *Ibid.,* p. 863.

44. William B. Hamilton quoted in Archibald Gracie, *The Truth About Chickamauga* (Boston: Houghton Mifflin Co., 1911), p. 431-436; Baumgartner and Strayer, *Echoes of Battle: The Struggle for Chattanooga,* p. 88-95.

45. "The Youngest Soldier in the Army of the Cumberland," *Columbus Daily Express,* December 16, 1863.

46. It often has been surmised that Clem shot the mounted Confederate near the end of the battle about the time others of the 22nd Michigan were being rounded up as prisoners. This could not have happened, as the capitulation was made by regimental decision and everyone was hoping the Rebels would not shoot as they surrendered. It is highly unlikely Clem would have fired at, wounded or killed anyone during the last minutes of twilight and jeopardize the surrender.

47. John L. Clem quoted on rear of commercially produced carte-de-visite, imprinted with the date February 15, 1864.

48. "The Little Ohio Orderly," *Belmont* (Ohio) *Chronicle,* April 28, 1864. This article by Benjamin F. Taylor originated in the *Chicago Journal.* Several variations exist of what the alleged Con-

57. *Columbus Daily Express,* December 16, 1863.

58. *Belmont* (Ohio) *Chronicle,* April 28, 1864.

59. George Lutz letter collection, courtesy of James Frasca, Croton, Ohio; John L. Clem compiled military service records.

60. Richard W. Johnson to his son, January 27, 1864, private collection.

61. *Belmont* (Ohio) *Chronicle,* April 28, 1864.

62. Dyer, *Compendium,* p. 1291.

63. "From Nursery to Battlefield," p. 546-548.

64. Adjutant General's Office, *General Orders Affecting the Volunteer Force, 1864* (Washington: Government Printing Office, 1865), p. 107.

65. Henry S. Dean to Lorenzo Thomas, August 9, 1864. George H. Thomas endorsement on back of letter. Clem File 201, AGO, National Archives.

66. Warner, *Generals in Blue,* p. 358-359.

67. John J. Hight quoted in Gilbert R. Stormont, *History of the Fifty-eighth Regiment of Indiana Volunteer Infantry, its Organization, Campaigns and Battles, from 1861 to 1865* (Princeton, Ind.: Press of the Clarion, 1895), p. 352-353.

68. John L. Clem to Sanford C. Kellogg, September 16, 1864,

Clem File 201, AGO, National Archives.

69. "From Nursery to Battlefield," p. 546-548.

70. John L. Clem to William W. Belknap, January 23, 1872, Clem File 201, AGO, National Archives.

71. Clem File 201, AGO, National Archives.

72. Carter's article first was published in April 1871.

73. W.W. Carter to E.D. Townsend, June 11, 1872, Clem File 201, AGO, National Archives.

74. W.W. Carter, *Little Johnny Clem, The Drummer Boy of Chickamauga*, originally was published in April 1871 in various newspapers. A copy from one of these was clipped and inserted in Clem File 201, AGO. The article also was published in pamphlet form as late as 1916. The author is in possession of one of these pamphlets initialed by Clem.

75. The author has never encountered any war-dated Clem documents or material mentioning Shiloh.

76. Jay S. Hoar, *Callow Brave & True: A Gospel of Civil War Youth* (Gettysburg, Pa.: Thomas Publications, 1999), p. 119-120.

77. Ulysses S. Grant, "The Battle of Shiloh," *Battles and Leaders of the Civil War,* vol. I (New York: The DeVinne Press, by the Century Co., 1884), p. 477.

78. Long, p. 195-196.

79. Will S. Hays, *The Drummer Boy of Shiloh* (Louisville: D.P. Faulds, 1862).

80. J.R. Thomas, "Mother Kissed Me in my Dream" (New York: William A. Pond & Co., 1864); Linden L. Parr, "Kiss My Mother Dear for Me" (Brooklyn: E.D. & D.S. Holmes, 1863).

81. Samuel J. Muscroft, *The Drummer Boy: or the Battle-Field of Shiloh* (Mansfield, Ohio: L.D. Myers & Bro., 1872).

82. John L. Clem to E.D. Townsend, October 10, 1873, Clem File 201, AGO, National Archives.

83. John L. Clem to Ulysses S. Grant, March 7, 1873, Clem File 201, AGO, National Archives.

84. Clem File 201, AGO, National Archives. Writing August 5, 1878, at Fort McIntosh, Texas, Clem headed the official form: "Services rendered as an enlisted man in the Armies of the United States, regular or volunteer, by John L. Clem now 1st Lieut. 24th U.S. Infantry."

85. John L. Clem to Ulysses S. Grant, undated letter written from Fort Whipple, Virginia, Clem File 201, AGO, National Archives.

86. John L. Clem 1903 efficiency report, Clem File 201, AGO, National Archives.

87. "From Nursery to Battlefield," p. 546-548.

88. Ibid.; W.W. Carter, *Little Johnny Clem, The Drummer Boy of Chickamauga.*

89. John L. Clem 1916 efficiency report, Clem File 201, AGO, National Archives.

90. Ibid.

Chapter 13

1. David Auld, "What a Drummer Boy Saw During a Strenuous Day at Corinth, Miss., October 4th, 1862." Auld's first draft of this manuscript, possessed by the author, was written for the 1909 *History of Fuller's Ohio Brigade 1861-1865.* Though similar to the published version, the first draft contained enough significant differences to warrant inclusion here.

2. Ibid. According to statistician William F. Fox, the 43rd Ohio

lost 20 killed at Corinth, while the 7th Iowa Infantry and 63rd Ohio counted 21 and 24 dead, respectively. These figures were exclusive of soldiers mortally wounded.

3. Charles H. Smith, *History of Fuller's Ohio Brigade 1861-1865* (Cleveland: Press of A.J. Watt, 1909), p. 29; Reid, *Ohio in the War,* vol. II, p. 273; *Ohio Rosters,* vol. IV, p. 244-292; John Curren and James Dew compiled military service records, National Archives.

4. Smith, *History of Fuller's Ohio Brigade 1861-1865,* p. 47-91.

5. *Ohio Rosters,* vol. IV, p. 244-292.

6. Smith, *op. cit.,* p. 434.

7. Ziegler, "War Sketches of John McClay."

8. Ibid.

9. William S. Meek 1864 pocket diary, courtesy of Mike McClung, Columbus, Ohio.

10. Ziegler, "War Sketches of John McClay."

11. Ibid.

12. Ibid.

13. Ibid.

14. Ibid.

15. Ibid.

16. William S. Meek 1865 pocket diary, courtesy of Mike McClung.

17. Ziegler, "War Sketches of John McClay."

18. Ibid.

19. Ibid.

20. Ibid.

21. Ibid.

Chapter 14

1. *Official Records,* vol. XLVI, pt. 1, p. 1132, 1136-1137.

2. *Shelby* (Ohio) *Daily Globe,* July 11, 1907; Edward F. Smith compiled military service records, National Archives.

3. Ibid.

4. *Shelby* (Ohio) *Daily Globe,* July 11, 1907.

5. Miller, *Drum Taps in Dixie,* p. 177.

6. *Ibid.,* p. 179.

7. Henry M. Brown compiled military service records, National Archives.

8. Aubery, p. 377-388.

9. Long, p. 670-689.

10. Ibid., p. 681-690.

11. Copp, p. 515-521.

12. Ziegler, "War Sketches of John McClay."

13. Kieffer, p. 248-250.

14. Bardeen, p. 319.

15. Berry, p. 68-69.

16. C. Perry Byam pension records.

17. Wilson, *Itinerary of the Seventh Ohio Volunteer Infantry 1861-1864,* p. 437-438.

18. Henry Gimpel history of service, Author's Collection.

19. Wilson, p. 395-396; *The National Cyclopaedia of American Biography,* vol. XXI (New York: James T. White & Company, 1931), p. 67.

20. Information about Demas L. Auld's die and enameling company provided by Douglas L. Auld, New Albany, Ohio.

21. John McClay papers, Author's Collection.

22. *Roster and Proceedings of the 65th Annual Encampment of the Department of Ohio Grand Army of the Republic* (Columbus: The F.J. Heer Printing Company, 1931), p. 143.

23. R.S. Storrs Jr., editor, *The Drum Beat,* February 22, 1864.

24. Program, John L. Clem statue dedication, Newark, Ohio, November 14, 1999.

25. Charles E. Goddard, mother's pension applications, National Archives.

BIBLIOGRAPHY

Manuscript materials

Auld, David (43rd Ohio), manuscript, "What a Drummer Boy Saw During a Strenuous Day at Corinth, Miss., October 4th, 1862," and miscellaneous Auld papers and photographs, Author's Collection.

Clem, John L. (22nd Michigan), File 201, Adjutant General Office records, National Archives.

Crane, Rashio (7th Wisconsin), memorial, Jeffrey J. Kowalis Collection, Orland Park, Illinois.

Crane, Richard M. (7th Wisconsin), diary and letters, Jeffrey J. Kowalis Collection.

Dickinson, James A., diary, Manuscript Collections, Rutherford B. Hayes Presidential Center, Fremont, Ohio.

Fairbanks, Byron (12th Wisconsin), diary, Author's Collection.

Farrar, Norman (2nd New York State Militia), letter, Stephen Altic Collection, Columbus, Ohio.

Gallipolis, Ohio, stonecarver's memorandum book, private collection.

Galloway, Samuel, letter, Mark Reese Collection, Columbus, Ohio.

General Orders No. 3, January 9, 1865, Headquarters, Department of the Missouri, Author's Collection.

Johnson, Richard W., letter, private collection.

Knox, Edward (20th Ohio), diary, Jeffrey S. Creamer Collection, Monclova, Ohio.

Lutz, George (22nd Michigan), letters, courtesy of James C. Frasca, Croton, Ohio.

Mann, Silas J. (45th Ohio), letters and papers, Author's Collection.

Marsh, A., letter, Author's Collection.

Matthias, Albert C. (65th Ohio), letter and papers, courtesy of James M. Merkel, Columbus, Ohio.

Matthias, John C. (65th Ohio), letter, courtesy of James M. Merkel.

McClay, John (43rd Ohio), miscellaneous papers and photographs, Author's Collection.

Meek, William S. (43rd Ohio), diaries, courtesy of Mike McClung, Columbus, Ohio.

Moore, David H. (125th Ohio), letter, courtesy of James M. Merkel.

Patterson, Joseph G. (90th Pennsylvania), letter, private collection.

Smith, Ezra H. (95th Ohio), diary, papers and photographs, Author's Collection.

Spillane, John T. (7th Michigan Infantry), scrapbook, miscellaneous papers and photographs, Author's Collection.

Wilson, John B. (2nd New York State Militia), letter, Stephen Altic Collection.

Published diaries & correspondence

Bardeen, Charles W., *A Little Fifer's War Diary,* Syracuse, N.Y.: C.W. Bardeen Publisher, 1910.

Bircher, William, *A Drummer-Boy's Diary: Comprising Four Years of Service with the Second Regiment Minnesota Veteran Volunteers, 1861-1865,* St. Paul: St. Paul Book and Stationery Co., 1889.

Jackson, Oscar L., *The Colonel's Diary,* Sharon, Pa.: privately printed, 1922.

Oldroyd, Osborn H., *A Soldier's Story of the Siege of Vicksburg,*

OPPOSITE: Armed with an Enfield rifle musket, two knives and two revolvers thrust beneath his belt, an unidentified teenager embodied the indomitable spirit of early-war recruits — "I felt that I could have conquered the rebellious faction alone, so confident was I of my fighting ability."

Brian Boeve Collection

from the Diary of Osborn H. Oldroyd, Springfield, Ill.: H.W. Rokker, 1885.

Memoirs, reminiscences & recollections

Allen, Stanton P., *A Boy Trooper with Sheridan,* Boston: Lothrop Publishing Company, 1899.

Arbuckle, John C., *Civil War Experiences of a Foot-Soldier Who Marched with Sherman,* Columbus, Ohio: privately printed, 1930.

Beatty, John, *The Citizen-Soldier; or, Memoirs of a Volunteer,* Cincinnati: Wilstach, Baldwin & Co., 1879.

Cockerill, John A., "A Boy at Shiloh," *Sketches of War History 1861-1865,* vol. I, Cincinnati: Montfort & Company, 1908.

Copp, Elbridge J., *Reminiscences of the War of the Rebellion 1861-1865,* Nashua, N.H.: Telegraph Publishing Co., 1911.

Deane, Nathaniel C., *The Spirit of the American Red Cross: A Chapter from the Autobiography of Nathaniel Carter Deane,* 1918.

Grant, Jesse R., *In the Days of My Father General Grant,* New York: Harper & Brothers, 1925.

Greene, Charles C., *Sparks from the Campfire,* Philadelphia: 1889.

Grigsby, Melvin, *The Smoked Yank,* Sioux Falls: Bell Publishing Co., 1888.

Kieffer, Harry M., *The Recollections of a Drummer Boy,* Boston: Houghton Mifflin Company, 1888.

Kountz, John S., "From Camp Brown to Mission Ridge," *Ninth Reunion of the 37th Regiment O.V.V.I., St. Marys, Ohio, Tuesday and Wednesday, September 10 and 11, 1889,* Toledo: Montgomery & Vrooman, Printers, 1889.

Miller, Delavan S., *Drum Taps in Dixie: Memories of a Drummer Boy 1861-1865,* Watertown, N.Y.: Hungerford Holbrook Co., 1905.

Simon, John Y., editor, *The Personal Memoirs of Julia Dent Grant,* New York: G.P. Putnam's Sons, 1975.

Smith, Andrew J., *The Light of Other Days; or, Passing Under the Rod,* Dayton: United Brethren Publishing House, 1878.

Strong, Thomas C., *The Little Drummer Boy, Clarence D. McKenzie, the Child of the Thirteenth Regiment, N.Y.S.M., and the Child of the Mission Sunday School,* New York: Reformed Protestant Dutch Church, 1861.

Ulmer, George T., *Adventures and Reminiscences of a Volunteer, or a Drummer Boy from Maine,* 1892.

Willison, Charles A., *Reminiscences of a Boy's Service with the 76th Ohio,* Menasha, Wis.: The George Banta Publishing Co., 1908. Reprinted in 1995 by Blue Acorn Press.

Newspapers & periodicals

Belmont Chronicle, St. Clairsville, Ohio, October 29, 1863, April 28, 1864.

The Clinton Republican, Wilmington, Ohio, August 14, 1863.

Columbus Daily Express, Columbus, Ohio, December 16, 1863.

The Drum Beat, Brooklyn, N.Y., February 22, 1864.

Harper's Weekly, December 19, 1863, February 6, 1864.

Providence Daily Journal, Providence, R.I., June 6, 1867.

Shelby Daily Globe, Shelby, Ohio, July 11, 1907.

Washington Evening Star, July 20, 1905.

"A Drummer Boy at Eight," *The National Tribune,* June 19, 1884.

"Talking of Drummer Boys," *The National Tribune,* June 26, 1884.

"The Youngest Soldier," *The National Tribune,* May 1881.

Clem, John L., "From Nursery to Battlefield," *Outlook,* July 4, 1914.

Davis, Johnda T., "Joseph Fissell – Darbyville's Drummer Boy," *Pickaway Quarterly,* Spring 1981.

Ferraro, William M., "More than a General's Wife: Ellen Ewing Sherman," *Timeline,* Ohio Historical Society, January-February 2000.

Ford, Henry A., "Drummer Hendershott: Capt. Ford Insists that after much Research he is a Fraud," *The National Tribune,* September 24, 1891.

Grant, Frederick D., "With Grant at Vicksburg," *The Ulysses S. Grant Association Newsletter,* October 1969.

Hull, Lucius W., "The Youngest Soldier: The Drum-Major of the 18th Ohio Makes a Good Claim," *The National Tribune,* November 29, 1888.

Jeffrey, William H., "The Union's Youngest Defender," *Blue and Gray,* June 1893.

Kilmer, George L., "Boys in the Union Army," *The Century,* June 1905.

Leister, Gary, " 'Our Pet Boltie' Drummer Boy, 47th Pa.," *North South Trader's Civil War,* Christmas 1993.

Orr, J.F., "The Story of 'Little Gib' Youngest Union Civil War Soldier," *The Gazette,* Xenia, Ohio, February 28-March 8, 1938.

Pope, E.D., "Who Was the Confederate Colonel?" *Confederate Veteran,* September 1926.

Powell, Ransom T., "Prison Life," *Frostburg Mining Journal,* Frostburg, Md., March 13, 1875–January 15, 1876.

Shanklin, James, "Another Young Soldier," *The National Tribune,* February 14, 1889.

Speer, Lonnie, "When Orphan Trains Rolled West," *Wild West,* February 1995.

Stanchak, John E., editor, "The Children's Crusade," *Civil War Times Illustrated,* May 1982.

Ziegler, George M., "War Sketches of John McClay," serialization from unidentified newspaper, Author's Collection.

Government publications & records

Allen, Jeremiah C., *Subject Index of the General Orders of the War Department, from January 1, 1861, to December 31, 1880,* Washington: Government Printing Office, 1882.

Alphabetical General Index to Public Library Sets of 85,271 Names of Michigan Soldiers and Sailors Individual Records, Lansing: Wynkoop, Hallenbeck, Crawford Co., 1915.

Annual Report of the Adjutant General of the Commonwealth of Massachusetts, Boston: Wright & Potter, State Printers, 1864.

Annual Report of the Adjutant-General of the State of New York for the Year 1879, Albany: Weed, Parsons and Company, 1880.

Bates, Samuel P., *History of Pennsylvania Volunteers, 1861-1865,* Harrisburg: B. Singerly, State Printers, 1869.

Davis, George B., Perry, Leslie J. and Kirkley, Joseph W.; Cowles, Calvin D., compiler, *Atlas to Accompany the Official Records of the Union and Confederate Armies,* Washington: Government Printing Office, 1891-1895.

Dickins, Asbury and Forney, John W., *American State Papers. Documents, Legislative and Executive, of the Congress of the United States, from the First Session of the Twenty-Fourth Congress, Inclusive: Commencing March 15, 1832, and ending Janaury 5, 1836,* vol. V, Washington: Gales & Seaton, 1860.

Gault, William P., *Ohio at Vicksburg: Report of the Ohio Vicksburg Battlefield Commission,* 1906.

General Orders Affecting the Volunteer Force, 1861, Washington: Government Printing Office, 1862.

General Orders Affecting the Volunteer Force, 1863, Washington: Government Printing Office, 1864.

General Orders Affecting the Volunteer Force, 1864, Washington: Government Printing Office, 1865.

General Regulations for the Army, Washington, 1821.

General Regulations for the Army; or, Military Institutes, Washington: Davis & Force, 1825.

General Regulations for the Army, Washington, 1834.

General Regulations for the Army of the United States 1841, Washington: J. and G.S. Gideon, 1841.

General Regulations for the Army of the United States 1847, Washington: J. and G.S. Gideon, 1847.

Illinois, *Report of the Illinois Adjutant General Containing Reports for the Years 1861-1866,* 8 volumes, Springfield: Phillips Bros. State Printers, 1900-1902.

Indiana, *Report of the Adjutant General of the State of Indiana,* 8 volumes, Indianapolis: W.R. Holloway, State Printers, 1865-1868.

Iowa, *Roster and Record of Iowa Soldiers in the War of the Rebellion Together with Historical Sketches of Volunteer Organizations 1861-1865,* 6 volumes, Des Moines: Emory H. English, State Printer, 1908-1911.

Kennedy, Joseph C.G., *Preliminary Report on the Eighth Census, 1860,* Washington: Government Printing Office, 1862.

Kentucky, *Report of the Adjutant General of the State of Kentucky,* 2 volumes, Frankfort: John H. Harney, Public Printer, 1866-1867.

Maryland, *History and Roster of Maryland Volunteers, War of 1861-5,* vol. I, Baltimore: Guggenheimer, Weil & Co., 1898.

Massachusetts Adjutant General, *Massachusetts Soldiers, Sailors, and Marines in the Civil War,* 8 volumes and index, various publishers, 1931-1937.

Massachusetts Adjutant General, *Record of the Massachusetts Volunteers 1861-1865,* 2 volumes, Boston: Wright & Potter, 1868-1870.

New York, 1860 Census records, Microfilm Division, National Archives, Washington.

New York, *Annual Report of the Adjutant-General of the State of New York,* 43 volumes, various publishers, 1894-1905.

Ohio Roster Commission, *Official Roster of the Soldiers of the State of Ohio in the War of the Rebellion, 1861-1866,* 12 volumes, Akron, Cincinnati, Norwalk: 1886-1895.

Otis, George A., *The Medical and Surgical History of the War of the Rebellion,* vol. II, pt. II, Washington: Government Printing Office, 1876.

Record of Service of Connecticut Men in the Army and Navy of the United States during the War of the Rebellion, Hartford: Press of The Case, Lockwood & Brainard Company, 1889.

Records of the Judge Advocate General's Office (Army), Record Group 153, Court-Martial Case Files: NN3250, LL3030, NN1345, LL1106, NN2699, LL584, LL746, OO388, LL1611, KK716, LL1296, LL1503, NN131, LL2910, LL284, MM1591, National Archives.

Regulations for the Army of the United States 1857, New York: Harper & Brothers, 1857.

Regulations for the Recruiting Service of the United States, both Regular and Volunteer, Washington: Government Printing Office, 1862.

Report of the Adjutant & Inspector General of the State of Vermont, from Oct. 1, 1864, to Oct. 1, 1865, Montpelier: Walton's Steam Printing Establishment, 1865.

Report of the Adjutant General of the State of New Hampshire, for the Year Ending May 20, 1865, vol. I, Concord: Abraham G. Jones, 1865.

Report of the Adjutant General of the State of New Hampshire, for the Year Ending June 1, 1866, vol. II, Concord: George E. Jenks, State Printer, 1866.

Revised Regulations for the Army of the United States, 1861, Philadelphia: J.B. Lippincott & Co., 1861.

Tripler, Charles S., M.D., *Manual of the Medical Officer of the Army of the United States,* Cincinnati: Wrightson & Co., Printers, 1858.

U.S. Adjutant General's Office, *Official Army Register of the Volunteer Force of the United States Army for the Years 1861, '62, '63, '64, '65,* Gaithersburg, Md.: Olde Soldier Books Inc., 1987.

U.S. War Department, *War of the Rebellion: A Compilation of the Official Records of the Union and Confederate Armies,* 128 volumes, Washington: Government Printing Office, 1891-1902.

Vermont Adjutant General, *Revised Roster of Vermont Volunteers and Lists of Vermonters Who Served in the Army and Navy of the United States during the War of the Rebellion, 1861-66,* Montpelier: Press of the Watchman Publishing Co., 1892.

West Virginia, *Annual Report of the Adjutant General of the State of West Virginia, for the Year Ending December 31, 1864,* Wheeling: John F. McDermot, Public Printer, 1865.

Wisconsin, *Roster of Wisconsin Volunteers, War of the Rebellion, 1861-1865,* 2 volumes, Madison: Democrat Printing Company, 1886.

Unit histories

Albert, Allen D., *History of the Forty-fifth Regiment Pennsylvania Veteran Volunteer Infantry 1861-1865,* Williamsport, Pa.: Grit Publishing Co., 1913.

Aston, Howard, *History and Roster of the Fourth and Fifth Independent Battalions and Thirteenth Regiment Ohio Cavalry Volunteers,* Columbus: Press of Fred J. Heer, 1902.

Aubery, James M., *The Thirty-sixth Wisconsin Volunteer Infantry,* Milwaukee: Evening Wisconsin Co., 1900.

Barker, Lorenzo A., *Military History (Michigan Boys) Company "D" 66th Illinois Birge's Western Sharpshooters in the Civil War 1861-1865,* Reed City, Mich.: 1905. Reprinted in 1994 by Blue Acorn Press.

Bartlett, Asa W., *History of the Twelfth Regiment New Hampshire Volunteers in the War of the Rebellion,* Concord: Ira C. Evans, 1897.

Belknap, William W., *History of the Fifteenth Regiment Iowa Veteran Volunteer Infantry from August 1861, to August, 1865,*

Keokuk: R.B. Ogden & Son, 1897.

Cogswell, Leander W., *A History of the Eleventh New Hampshire Regiment, Volunteer Infantry in the Rebellion War, 1861-1865,* Concord: Republican Press Association, 1891.

Crofts, Thomas, *History of the Service of the Third Ohio Veteran Volunteer Cavalry in the War for the Preservation of the Union from 1861-1865,* Toledo: 1910. Reprinted in 1997 by Blue Acorn Press.

Crowninshield, Benjamin W., *A History of the First Regiment of Massachusetts Cavalry Volunteers,* Boston: Houghton, Mifflin and Company, 1891.

Dickey, Luther S., *History of the 103d Regiment Pennsylvania Veteran Volunteer Infantry 1861-1865,* Chicago: L.S. Dickey, 1910.

Eddy, Richard, *History of the Sixtieth Regiment New York State Volunteers,* Philadelphia: Crissey & Markley, Printers, 1864.

Elliott, Isaac H., *History of the Thirty-Third Regiment Illinois Veteran Volunteer Infantry in the Civil War, 22nd August, 1861 to December, 1865,* Gibson City, Ill.: Press of Gibson Courier, 1902.

Fairchild, Charles B., *History of the 27th Regiment N.Y. Vols.,* Binghamton, N.Y.: Carl & Matthews Printers, 1888.

Haynes, Edwin M., *A History of the Tenth Regiment, Vermont Volunteers, with Biographical Sketches,* Rutland, Vt.: The Tuttle Company, 1894.

Hays, Ebenezer Z., *History of the Thirty-second Regiment Ohio Veteran Volunteer Infantry,* Columbus: Cott & Evans, Printers, 1896.

Hinman, Wilbur F., *The Story of the Sherman Brigade,* Alliance, Ohio: Press of Daily Review, 1897.

Horrall, Spillard F., *History of the Forty-second Indiana Volunteer Infantry,* Chicago: Donohue & Henneberry, 1892.

Houston, Henry C., *The Thirty-second Maine Regiment of Infantry Volunteers,* Portland, Maine: Southworth Brothers, 1903.

Hurst, Samuel H., *Journal-History of the Seventy-third Ohio Volunteer Infantry,* Chillicothe, Ohio: 1866.

Kiefer, William R., *History of the One Hundred and Fifty-third Regiment Pennsylvania Volunteer Infantry,* Easton, Pa.: The Chemical Publishing Company, 1909.

Moe, Richard, *The Last Full Measure: The Life and Death of the First Minnesota Volunteers,* New York: Henry Holt and Company, 1993.

Nourse, Henry S., et.al., *The Story of the Fifty-fifth Regiment Illinois Volunteer Infantry in the Civil War 1861-1865,* Clinton, Mass.: W.J. Coulter, 1887. Reprinted in 1993 by Blue Acorn Press.

Osborn, Hartwell, *Trials and Triumphs: The Record of the Fifty-fifth Ohio Volunteer Infantry,* Chicago: A.C. McClurg & Co., 1904.

Palmer, Abraham J., *The History of the Forty-Eighth Regiment New York State Volunteers, in the War for the Union,* Brooklyn: 1885.

Roe, Alfred S. *The Tenth Regiment Massachusetts Volunteer Infantry 1861-1864, A Western Massachusetts Regiment,* Springfield, Mass.: F.A. Bassette Co., 1909.

Sawyer, Franklin, *A Military History of the 8th Regiment Ohio Vol. Inf'y: Its Battles, Marches and Army Movements,* Cleveland: Fairbanks & Co., 1881. Reprinted in 1994 by Blue Acorn Press.

Sherman, S.M., *History of the 133d Regiment, O.V.I.,* Columbus: Champlin Printing Co., 1896.

Smith, Charles H., *The History of Fuller's Ohio Brigade 1861-1865, Its Great March, with Roster, Portraits, Battle Maps and Biographies,* Cleveland: J. Watt, 1909.

Stormont, Gilbert R., *History of the Fifty-eighth Regiment of Indiana Volunteer Infantry, its Organization, Campaigns and Battles, from 1861-1865,* Princeton, Ind.: Press of the Clarion, 1895.

Sturtevant, Ralph O., *Pictorial History Thirteenth Regiment Vermont Volunteers War of 1861-1865,* privately printed, 1910.

Sutton, Joseph J., *History of the Second Regiment West Virginia Cavalry Volunteers during the War of the Rebellion,* Portsmouth, Ohio: 1892. Reprinted in 1992 by Blue Acorn Press.

Tourgée, Albion W., *The Story of a Thousand, being a History of the Service of the 105th Ohio Volunteer Infantry in the War for the Union,* Buffalo, N.Y.: McGerald & Son, 1896.

Washburn, George H., *A Complete Military History and Record of the 108th Regiment N.Y. Vols. from 1862 to 1894,* Rochester: E.R. Andrews, 1894.

Westbrook, Robert S., *History of the 49th Pennsylvania Volunteers,* Altoona, Pa.: 1898.

Wilson, Lawrence, *Itinerary of the Seventh Ohio Volunteer Infantry 1861-1864,* New York: The Neale Publishing Company, 1907.

Wood, David W., *History of the 20th Ohio Regiment V.V. Inft. and Proceedings of the First Reunion at Mt. Vernon, Ohio, April 6, 1876,* Columbus: Paul & Thrall Book and Job Printers, 1876.

Biographies & autobiographies

Carter, W.W., *Little Johnny Clem, The Drummer Boy of Chickamauga,* 1916.

Dodge, William S., *Robert Henry Hendershot; or, the Brave Drummer Boy of the Rappahannock,* Chicago: Church and Goodman, 1867.

Foraker, Joseph B., *Notes of a Busy Life,* 2 volumes, Cincinnati: Stewart & Kidd Company, 1917.

Frost, Lawrence A., *U.S. Grant Album: A Pictorial Biography of Ulysses S. Grant from Leather Clerk to the White House,* Seattle: Superior Publishing Company, 1966.

Gerry, H.E., *Camp Fire Entertainment and True History of Robert Henry Hendershot, the Drummer Boy of the Rappahannock,* circa 1904.

Ohio Historical Society, *The Governors of Ohio,* Columbus: The Stoneman Press, 1954.

Rodriguez, Mercedes, "The Drummer Boy John Lincoln Clem: The Civil War Years," master's thesis, San Jose State University, 1974.

Scott, Harold L. Sr., *The Civil War Memoirs of Little Red Cap, Drummer Boy at Andersonville Prison,* Cumberland, Md., 1997.

Sketch of Joseph Benson Foraker, 1883, with an Appendix, Dayton: Press of U.B. Publishing House, 1885.

Styple, William B., *The Little Bugler: The True Story of a Twelve-Year-Old Boy in the Civil War,* Kearny, N.J.: Belle Grove Publishing Company, 1998.

Titterton, Robert J., *Julian Scott: Artist of the Civil War and Native America,* Jefferson, N.C.: McFarland & Company, Inc., 1997.

Local histories

Curry, William L., *History of Jerome Township, Union County, Ohio,* Columbus: The Edward T. Miller Co., 1913.

Hill, N.N. Jr., *History of Knox County, Ohio: Its Past and Present,* Mt. Vernon, Ohio: A.A. Graham & Co. Publishers, 1881.

Leach, Eugene W., *Racine County Militant: An Illustrated Narrative of War Times, and a Soldiers' Roster,* Racine, Wis.: E.W. Leach, 1915.

Wood, Frances and Dorothy, *I Hauled These Mountains in Here,* Caldwell, Idaho: The Caxton Printers, Ltd., 1977.

Music, plays & poetry

Bruce, George B., *The Drummer's and Fifer's Guide: or Self-Instructor,* New York: Firth, Pond & Co., 1862.

Hays, Will Shakespeare, *The Drummer Boy of Shiloh,* Louisville: D.P. Faulds, 1862.

Muscroft, Samuel J., *The Drummer Boy: or the Battle-Field of Shiloh,* Mansfield, Ohio: L.D. Myers & Bro., 1872.

Parr, Linden L., "Kiss My Mother Dear for Me," Brooklyn: E.D. & D.S. Holmes, 1863.

Sherwood, Kate Brownlee, *Camp-fire, Memorial-day, and Other Poems,* Chicago: Jansen, McClurg & Co., 1885.

Thomas, J.R., "Mother Kissed Me in My Dream," New York: William A. Pond & Co., 1864.

General works

Alotta, Robert I., *Civil War Justice: Union Army Executions under Lincoln,* Shippensburg, Pa.: White Mane Publishing Co., 1989.

Anners, Henry F., *Hoyle's Games: Containing the Established Rules and Practice,* Philadelphia: 1845.

Battles and Leaders of the Civil War, 4 volumes, New York: The DeVinne Press, by the Century Co., 1884-1887.

Baumgartner, Richard A. and Strayer, Larry M., *Echoes of Battle: The Struggle for Chattanooga,* Huntington, W.Va.: Blue Acorn Press, 1996.

Beath, Robert H., *History of the Grand Army of the Republic,* New York: Willis McDonald & Co., 1889.

Benedict, George G., *Vermont in the Civil War, A History of the Part Taken by the Vermont Soldiers and Sailors in the War for the Union 1861-65,* Burlington, Vt.: The Free Press, 1886.

Berry, Chester D., *Loss of the Sultana and Reminiscences of Survivors,* Lansing, Mich.: Darius D. Thorp, Printer and Publisher, 1892.

Beyer, W.F. and Keydel, O.F., editors, *Deeds of Valor: How American Heroes won the Medal of Honor,* 2 volumes, Detroit: The Perrien-Keydel Company, 1907.

Bishop, Eleanor C., *Ponies, Patriots and Powder Monkeys: A History of Children in America's Armed Forces 1776-1916,* Del Mar, Calif.: The Bishop Press, 1982.

Boatner, Mark M., *The Civil War Dictionary,* New York: David McKay Co., 1959.

Casey, Silas, *Infantry Tactics, for the Instruction, Exercise, and Maneuvers of the Soldier, a Company, Line of Skirmishers, Battalion, Brigade, or Corps D'Armee,* 3 volumes, New York: D. Van Nostrand, 1862.

Dornbusch, C.E., *Military Bibliography of the Civil War,* vols. I, II, III, New York: The New York Public Library, 1975.

Drake, James M., *Historical Sketches of the Revolutionary and Civil Wars,* New York: Webster Press, 1908.

Dyer, Frederick H., *A Compendium of the War of the Rebellion,* 3 volumes, New York: Thomas Yoseloff, 1959.

Fox, William F., *Regimental Losses in the American Civil War 1861-1865,* Albany, N.Y.: Albany Publishing Company, 1898.

Frassanito, William A., *Antietam: The Photographic Legacy of America's Bloodiest Day,* New York: Charles Scribner's Sons, 1978.

Gould, Benjamin A., *Investigations in the Military and Anthropological Statistics of American Soldiers,* New York: Hurd and Haughton, 1869.

Gracie, Archibald, *The Truth About Chickamauga,* Boston: Houghton Mifflin Co., 1911.

Heaps, Willard A., *The Bravest Teenage Yanks,* New York: Duell, Sloan and Pearce, 1963.

Heitman, Francis B., *Historical Register and Dictionary of the United States Army, from its Organization, September 29, 1789, to March 2, 1903,* 2 volumes, Gaithersburg, Md.: Olde Soldier Books Inc., 1988.

Hinman, Wilbur F., *Corporal Si Klegg and his Pard,* Cleveland: The Williams Publishing Co., 1887.

Hoar, Jay S., *Callow Brave & True: A Gospel of Civil War Youth,* Gettysburg, Pa.: Thomas Publications, 1999.

Johnson, Kenneth R., and Floyd, Jeffrey B., *Membership and National Encampment Badges of the Grand Army of the Republic 1866-1949,* Duluth, Ga.: OMSA Publications, 1997.

Lambert, Dean W., *When the Ripe Pears Fell: The Battle of Richmond, Kentucky,* Richmond, Ky.: The Madison County Historical Society, 1995.

Lang, George, Collins, Raymond L. and White, Gerald, compilers, *Medal of Honor Recipients 1863-1994,* vol. I, New York: Facts on File, Inc.

Livermore, Thomas L., *Numbers and Losses in the Civil War in America 1861-1865,* Carlisle, Pa.: John Kallmann, 1996.

Long, E.B., *The Civil War Day by Day, An Almanac 1861-1865,* New York: Doubleday & Co., 1971.

Lossing, Benson J., *Pictorial History of the Civil War in the United States of America,* vol. I, Philadelphia: George W. Childs, Publisher, 1866.

Lowry, Thomas P., *Don't Shoot That Boy! Abraham Lincoln and Military Justice,* Mason City, Iowa: Savas Publishing Company, 1999.

Lowry, Thomas P., *The Story the Soldiers Wouldn't Tell: Sex in the Civil War,* Mechanicsburg, Pa.: Stackpole Books, 1994.

Marten, James, *The Children's Civil War,* Chapel Hill: The University of North Carolina Press, 1998.

McElroy, John, *This Was Andersonville,* New York: The Fairfax Press, 1979.

Miller, Francis T., editor, *The Photographic History of the Civil War,* 10 volumes, New York: The Review of Reviews Company, 1911.

Phisterer, Frederick, compiler, *New York in the War of the Rebellion 1861-1865,* 5 volumes and index, Albany: J.B. Lyon Company, 1912.

Potter, Jerry O., *The Sultana Tragedy: America's Greatest Maritime Disaster,* Gretna, La.: Pelican Publishing Company Inc., 1992.

Reid, Whitelaw, *Ohio in the War: Her Statesmen, Generals and Soldiers,* 2 volumes, Cincinnati: The Robert Clarke Company, 1895.

Roster and Proceedings of the 65th Annual Encampment of the Department of Ohio, Grand Army of the Republic, Columbus: The F.J. Heer Printing Company, 1931.

Scott, H.L., *Military Dictionary: Comprising Technical Definitions on Raising and Keeping Troops; Including Makeshift and Improved Material; and Law, Government, Regulations, and Administration Relating to Land Forces,* New York: D. Van Nostrand, 1861.

Sifakis, Stewart, *Who Was Who in the Union,* New York: Facts on File, Inc., 1988.

Strayer, Larry M. and Baumgartner, Richard A., *Echoes of Battle:* *The Atlanta Campaign,* Huntington, W.Va.: Blue Acorn Press, 1991.

The Civil War, 27 volumes and index, Alexandria, Va.: Time Life Books Inc., 1983-1987.

The Military History of Ohio, Franklin and Licking County editions, New York: H.H. Hardesty Publisher, 1886.

The National Cyclopaedia of American Biography, vol. XXI, New York: James T. White & Company, 1931.

U.S. War Department, *American Decorations 1862-1926,* Washington: Government Printing Office, 1927.

Waite, Otis F.R., *New Hampshire in the Great Rebellion,* Claremont, N.H.: Tracy, Chase & Company, 1870.

Warner, Ezra J., *Generals in Blue: Lives of the Union Commanders,* Baton Rouge: Louisiana State University Press, 1977.

Wilson, John L., *Battles of America by Sea and Land with Biographies of Naval and Military Commanders,* vol. III, New York: Patterson & Neilson, 1878.

Wise, Arthur and Lord, Francis A., *Bands and Drummer Boys of the Civil War,* New York: Thomas Yoseloff, 1966.

INDEX

Page numbers appearing in boldface indicate photographs or illustrations.

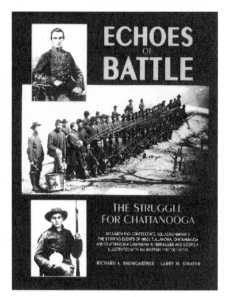
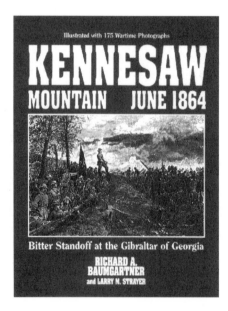